Animal ACADEMY

HAKOBUNE HAKUSHO

はこぶね白書

Volume 7

by

MOYAMU FUJINO

TOKYOPOP®

HAMBURG // LONDON // LOS ANGELES // TOKYO

Animal Academy: Hakobune Hakusho Volume 7
Created by Moyamu Fujino

Translation - Katherine Schilling
English Adaptation - Ysabet Reinhardt MacFarlane
Retouch and Lettering - Star Print Brokers
Production Artist - Star Print Brokers
Copy Edit - Jill Bentley
Cover Design - Rosa Marie

Editor - Lillian Diaz-Przybyl
Print Production Manager - Lucas Rivera
Managing Editor - Vy Nguyen
Senior Designer - Louis Csontos
Art Director - Al-Insan Lashley
Director of Sales and Manufacturing - Allyson De Simone
Senior Vice President - Mike Kiley
President and C.O.O. - John Parker
C.E.O. and Chief Creative Officer - Stu Levy

A **TOKYOPOP** Manga

TOKYOPOP Inc.
5900 Wilshire Blvd. Suite 2000
Los Angeles, CA 90036

E-mail: info@TOKYOPOP.com
Come visit us online at www.TOKYOPOP.com

ISBN: 978-1-4278-1633-7

First TOKYOPOP printing: March 2011
10 9 8 7 6 5 4 3 2 1
Printed in the USA

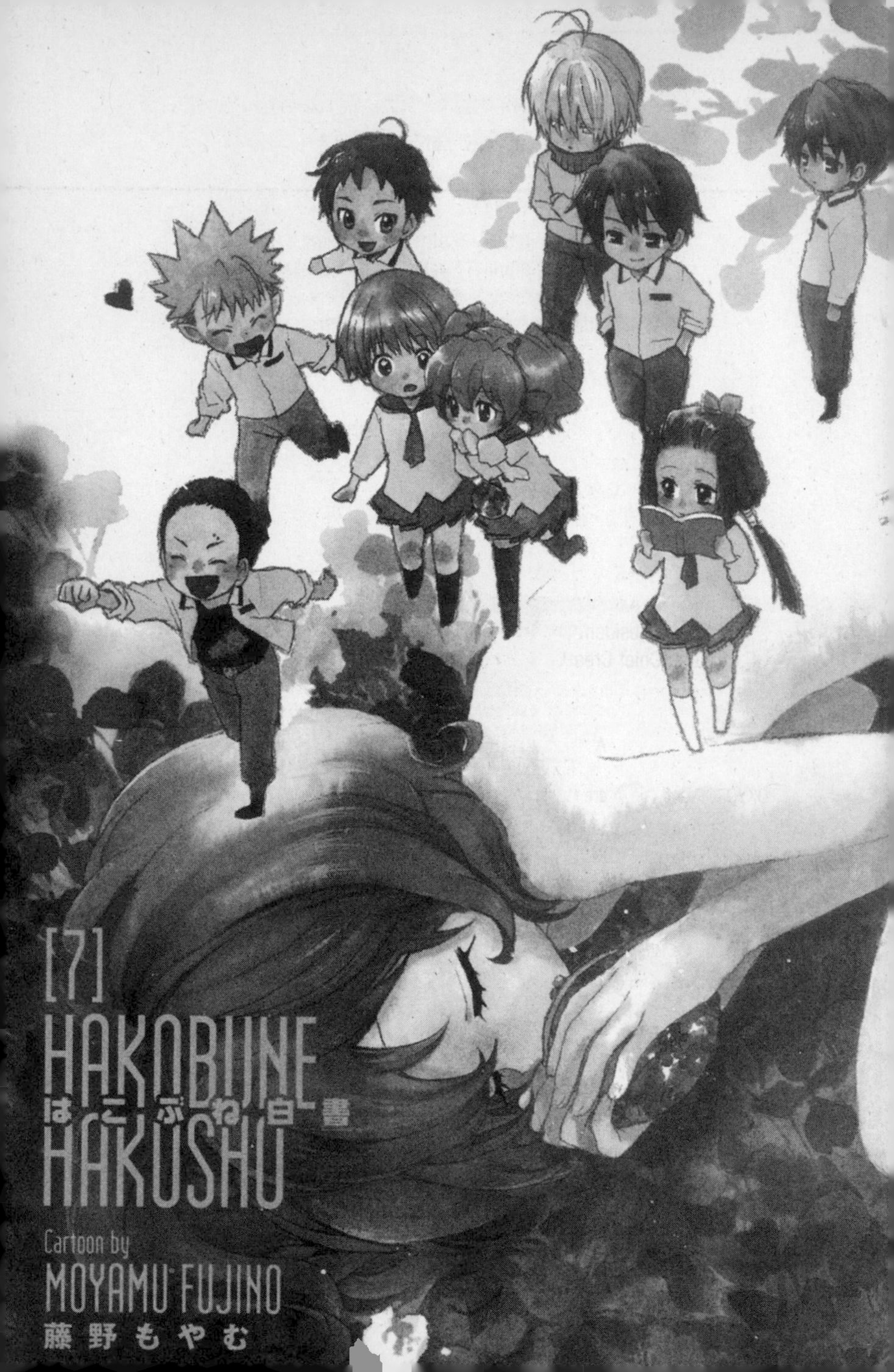
[7]
HAKOBUNE HAKUSHO
はこぶね白書
Cartoon by
MOYAMU FUJINO
藤野もやむ

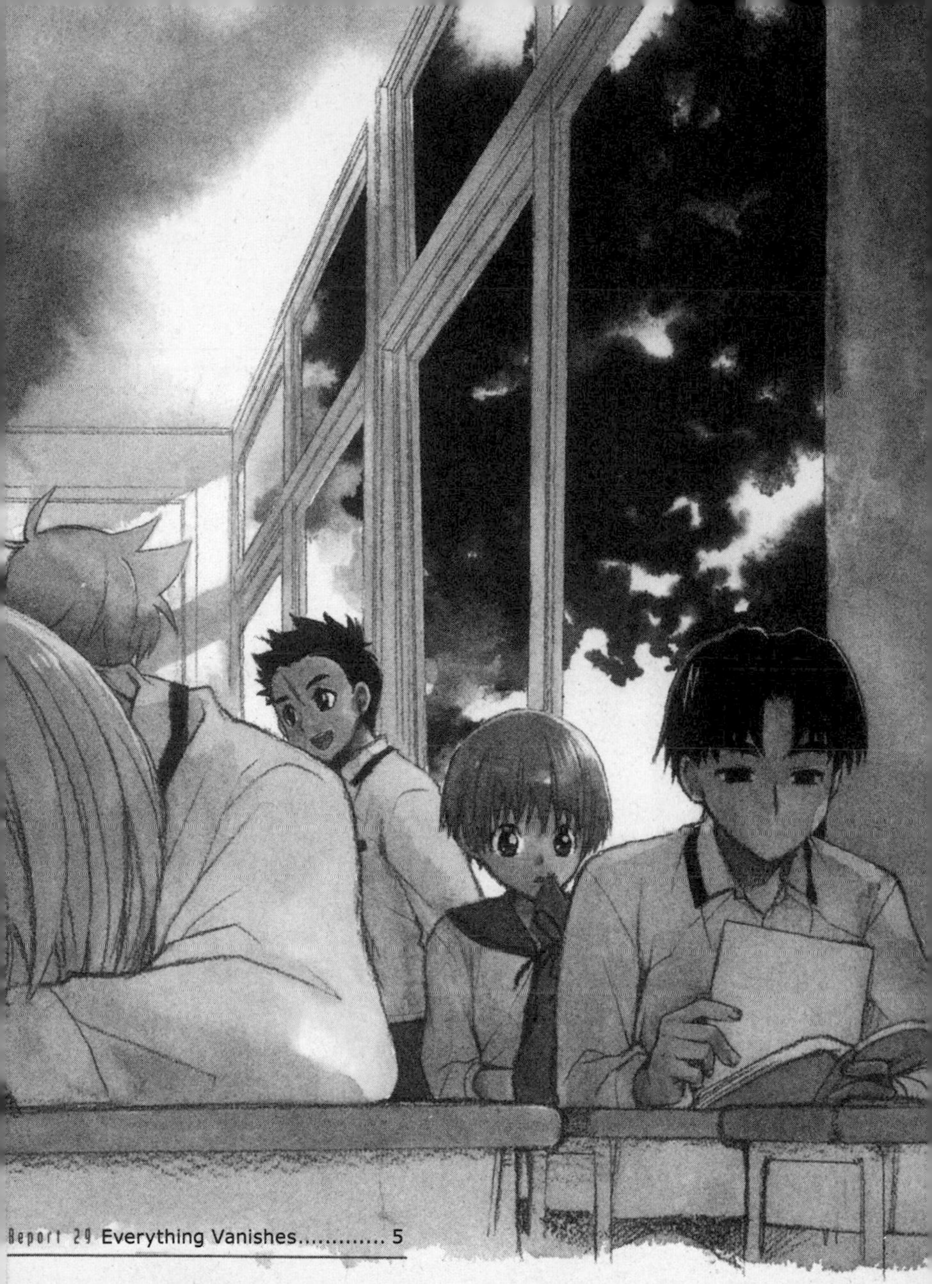

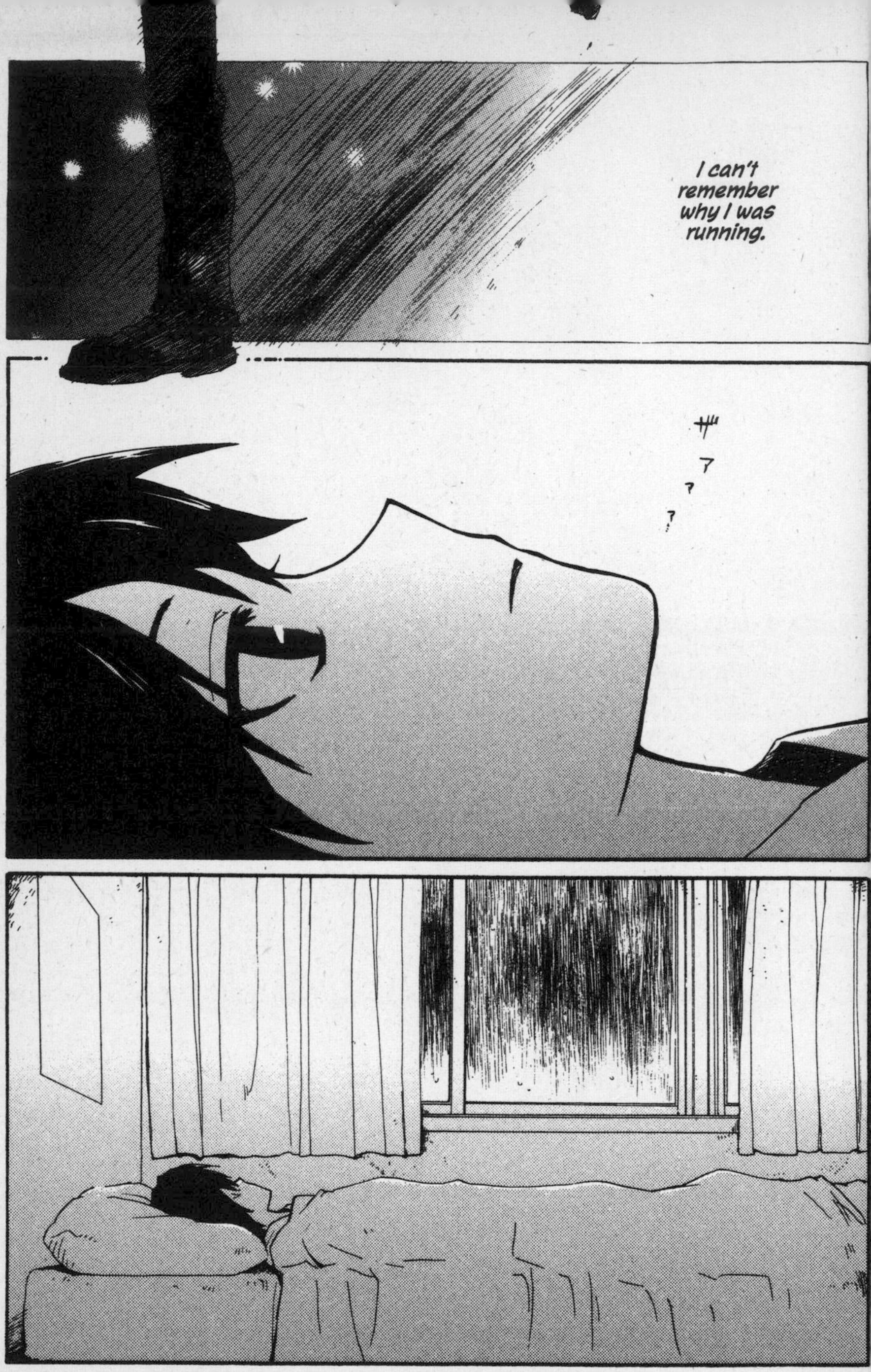
I can't remember why I was running.
ザァァァ

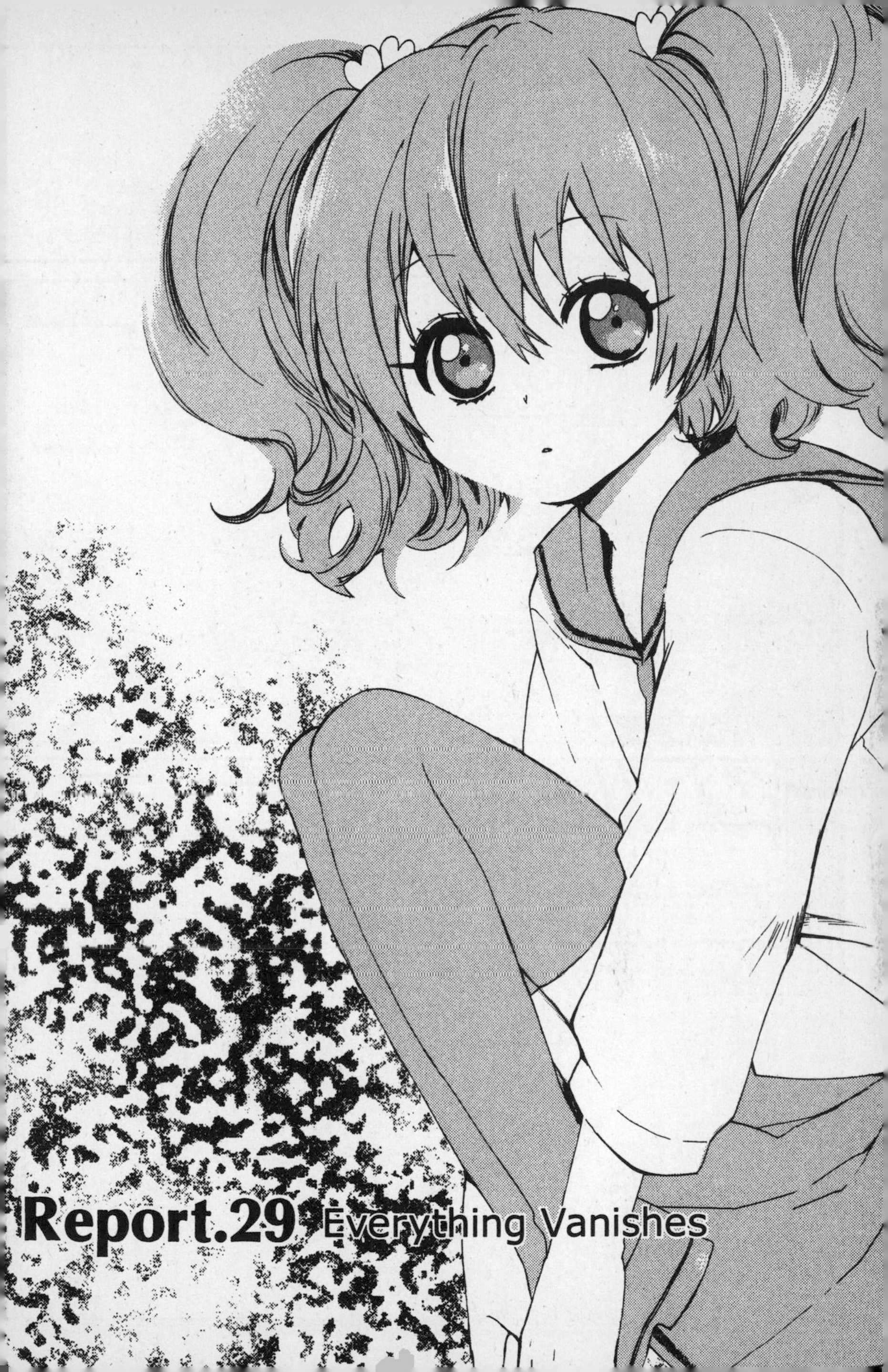
Report.29 Everything Vanishes

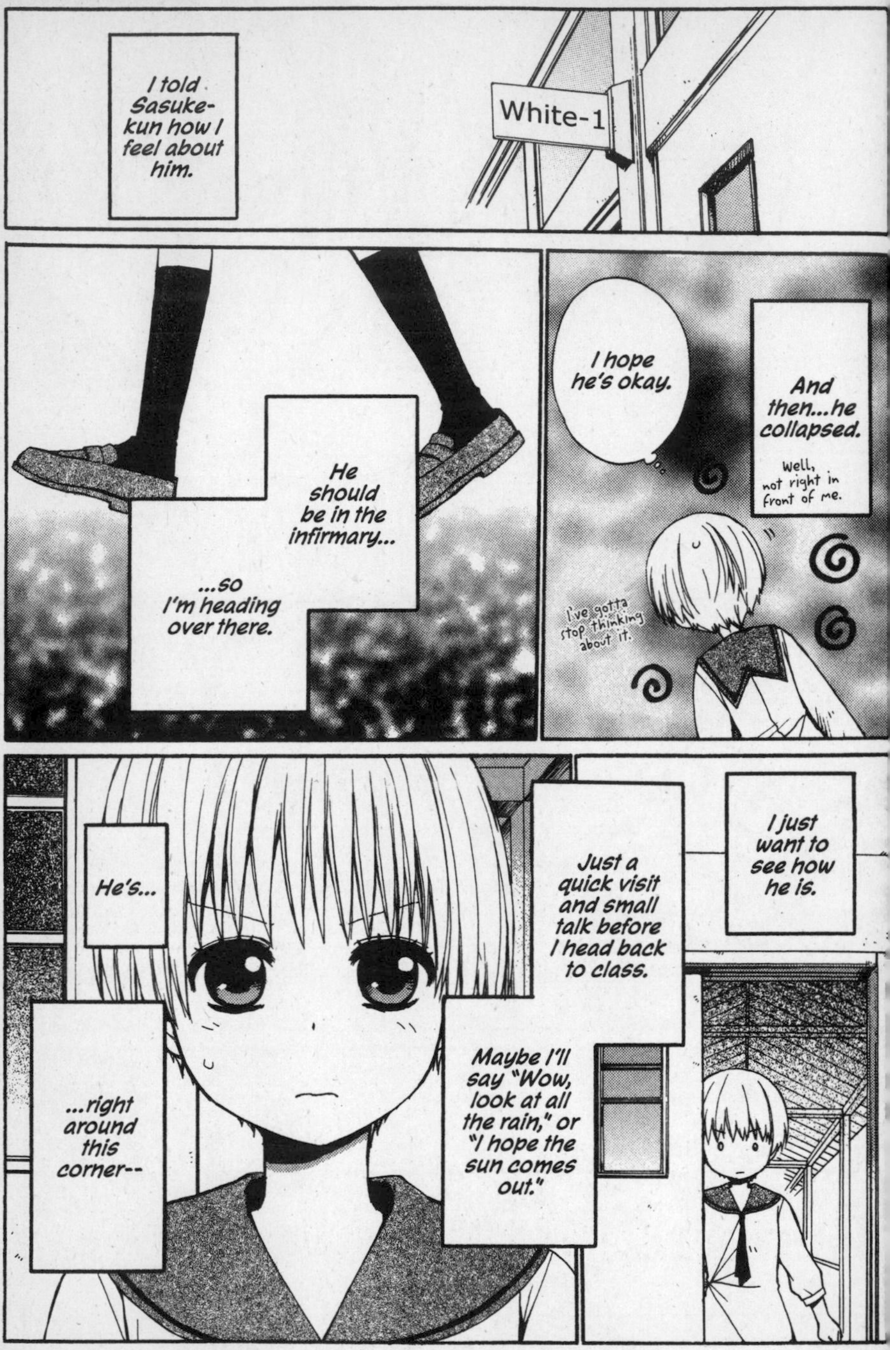
White-1
I told Sasuke-kun how I feel about him.
And then...he collapsed.
Well, not right in front of me.
I hope he's okay.
I've gotta stop thinking about it.
He should be in the infirmary...
...so I'm heading over there.
I just want to see how he is.
Just a quick visit and small talk before I head back to class.
Maybe I'll say "Wow, look at all the rain," or "I hope the sun comes out."
He's...
...right around this corner--

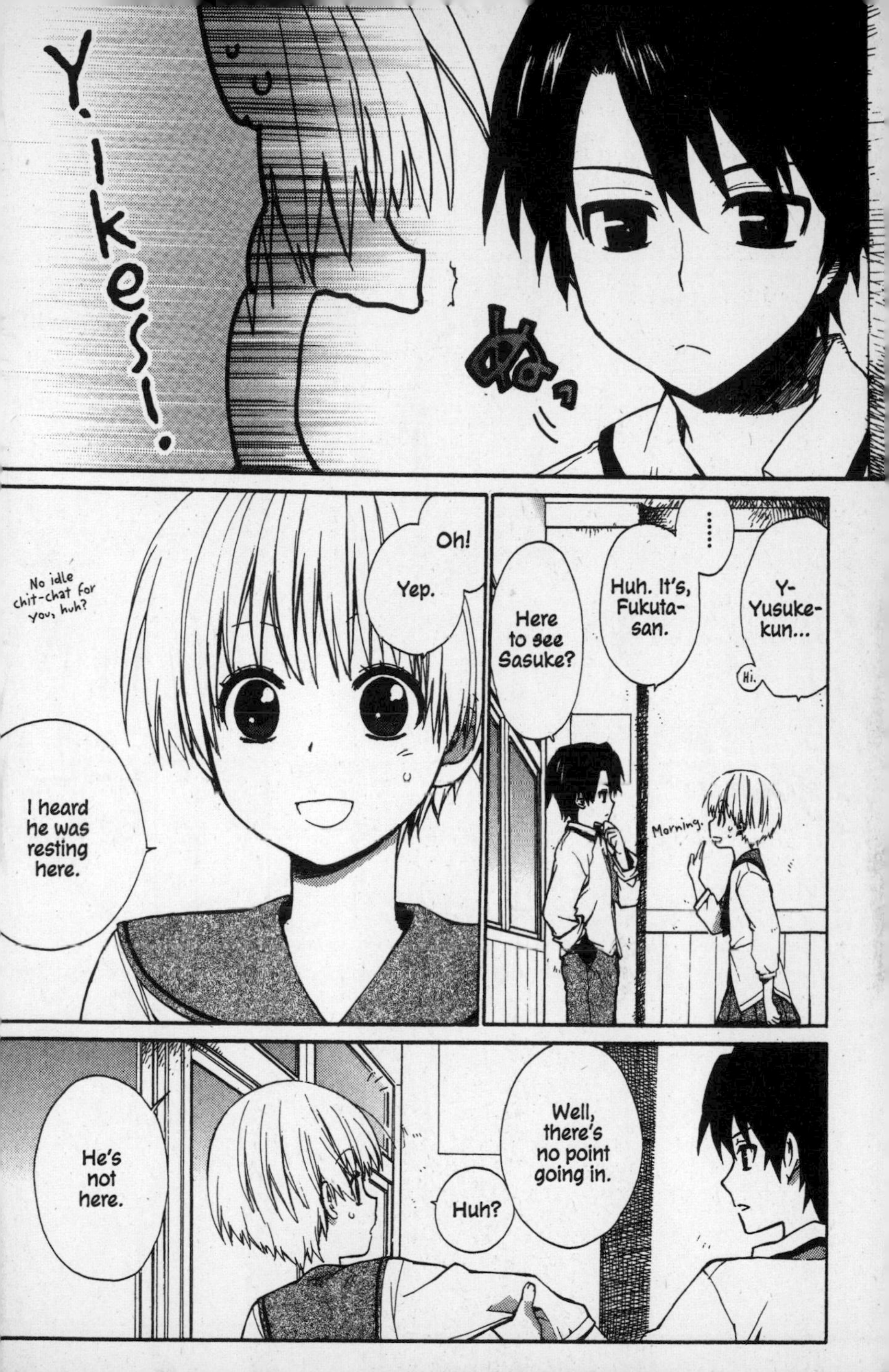
ぬっ
Y-ikes~.
Y-Yusuke-kun...
Hi.
......
Huh. It's, Fukuta-san.
Here to see Sasuke?
Morning.
Oh!
Yep.
No idle chit-chat for you, huh?
I heard he was resting here.
Well, there's no point going in.
Huh?
He's not here.

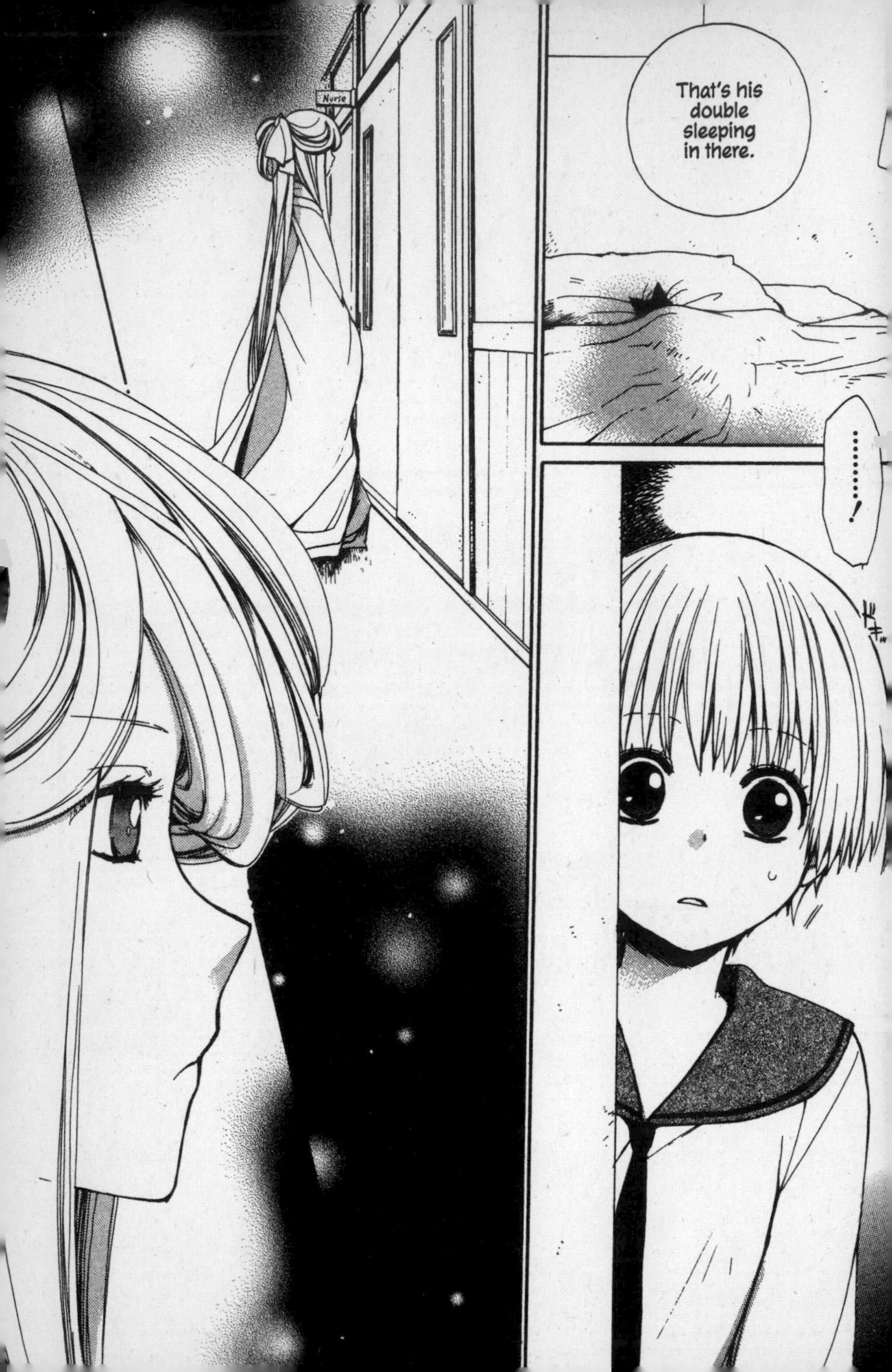

That's his double sleeping in there.
......!
Nurse

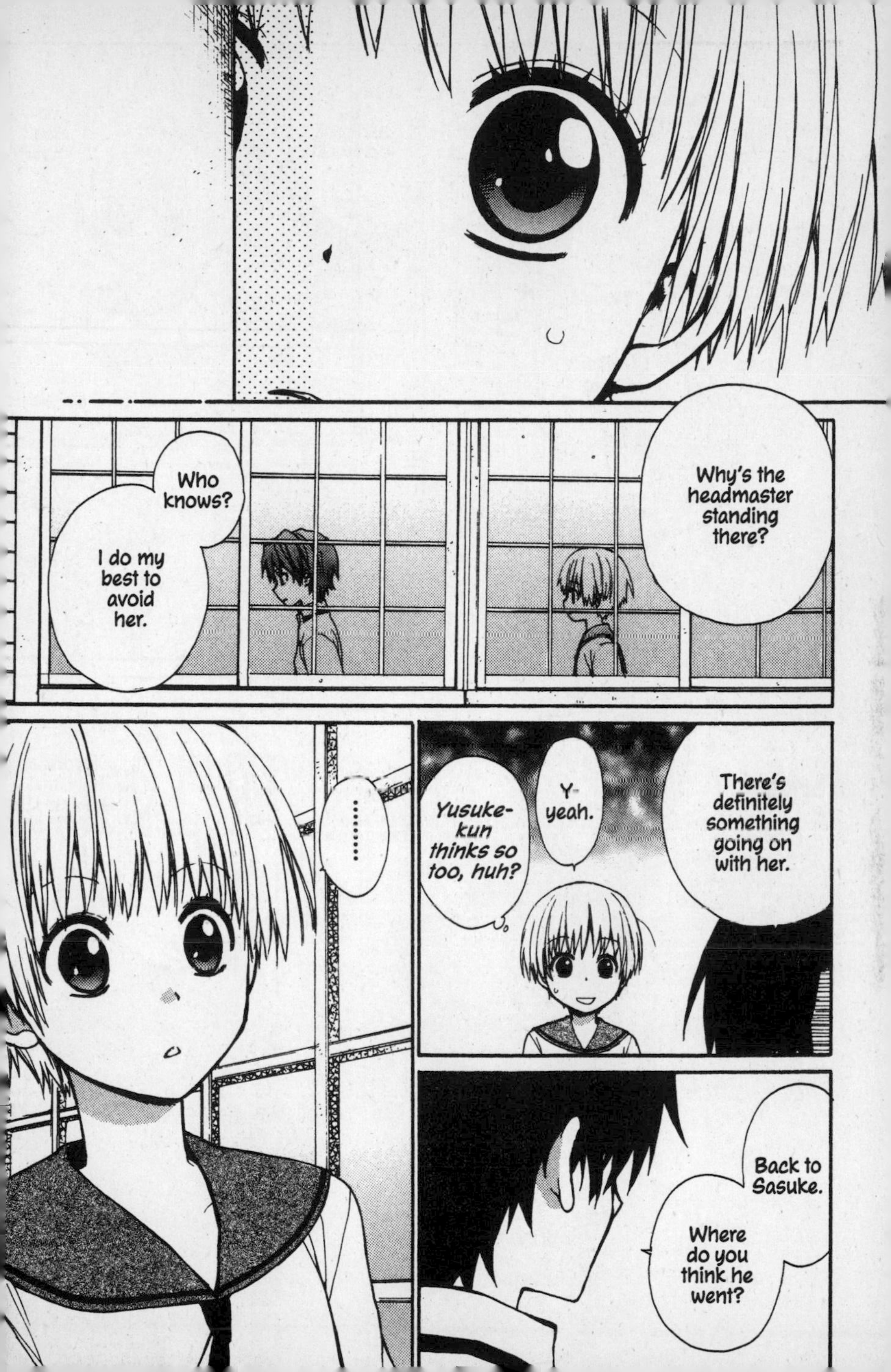
Why's the headmaster standing there?
Who knows?
I do my best to avoid her.
There's definitely something going on with her.
Y-yeah.
Yusuke-kun thinks so too, huh?
Back to Sasuke.
Where do you think he went?
....

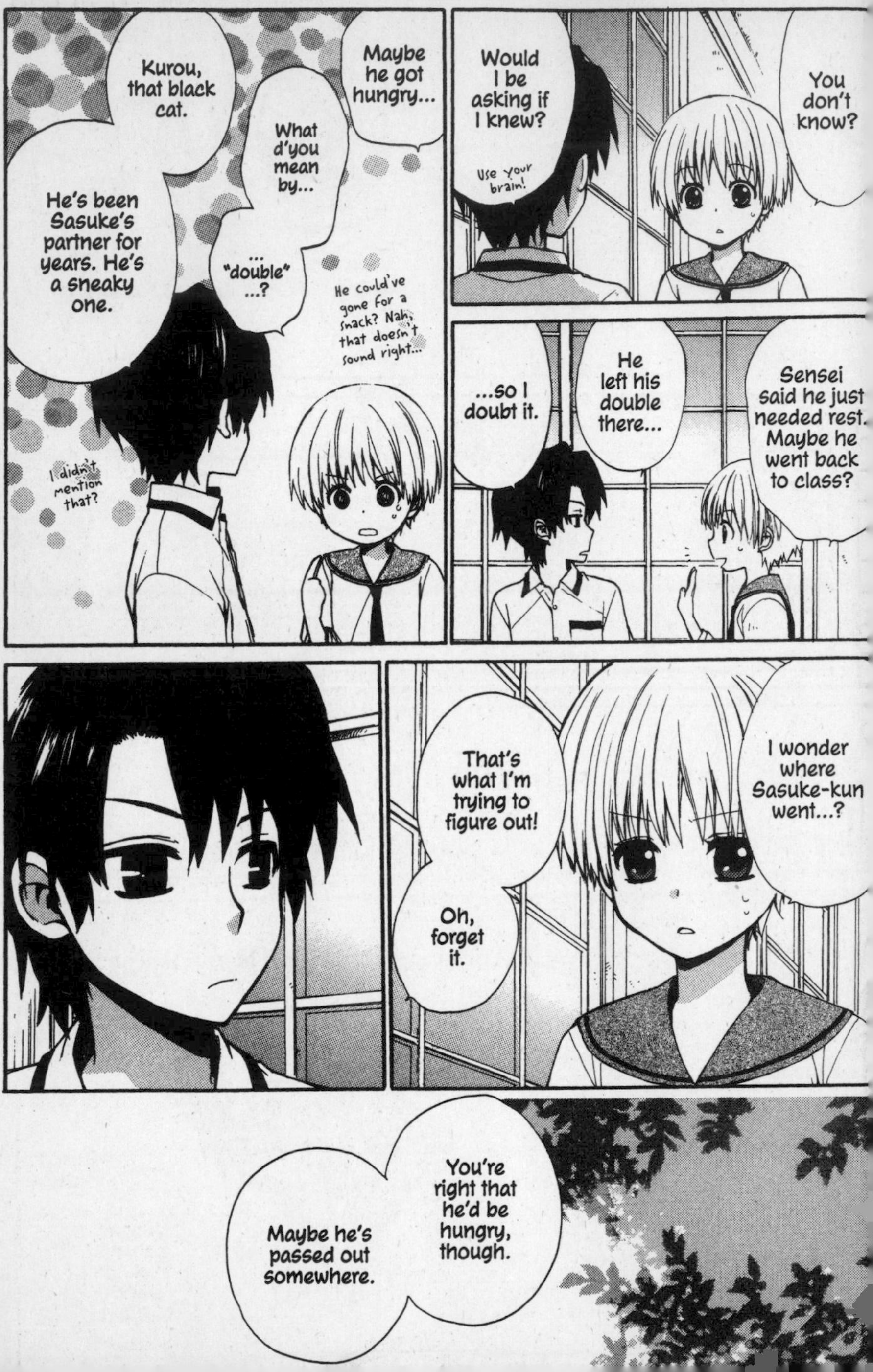

You don't know?
Would I be asking if I knew?
Use your brain!
Sensei said he just needed rest. Maybe he went back to class?
He left his double there...
...so I doubt it.
Maybe he got hungry...
He could've gone for a snack? Nah, that doesn't sound right...
What d'you mean by...
... "double" ...?
Kurou, that black cat.
He's been Sasuke's partner for years. He's a sneaky one.
I didn't mention that?
I wonder where Sasuke-kun went...?
That's what I'm trying to figure out!
Oh, forget it.
You're right that he'd be hungry, though.
Maybe he's passed out somewhere.

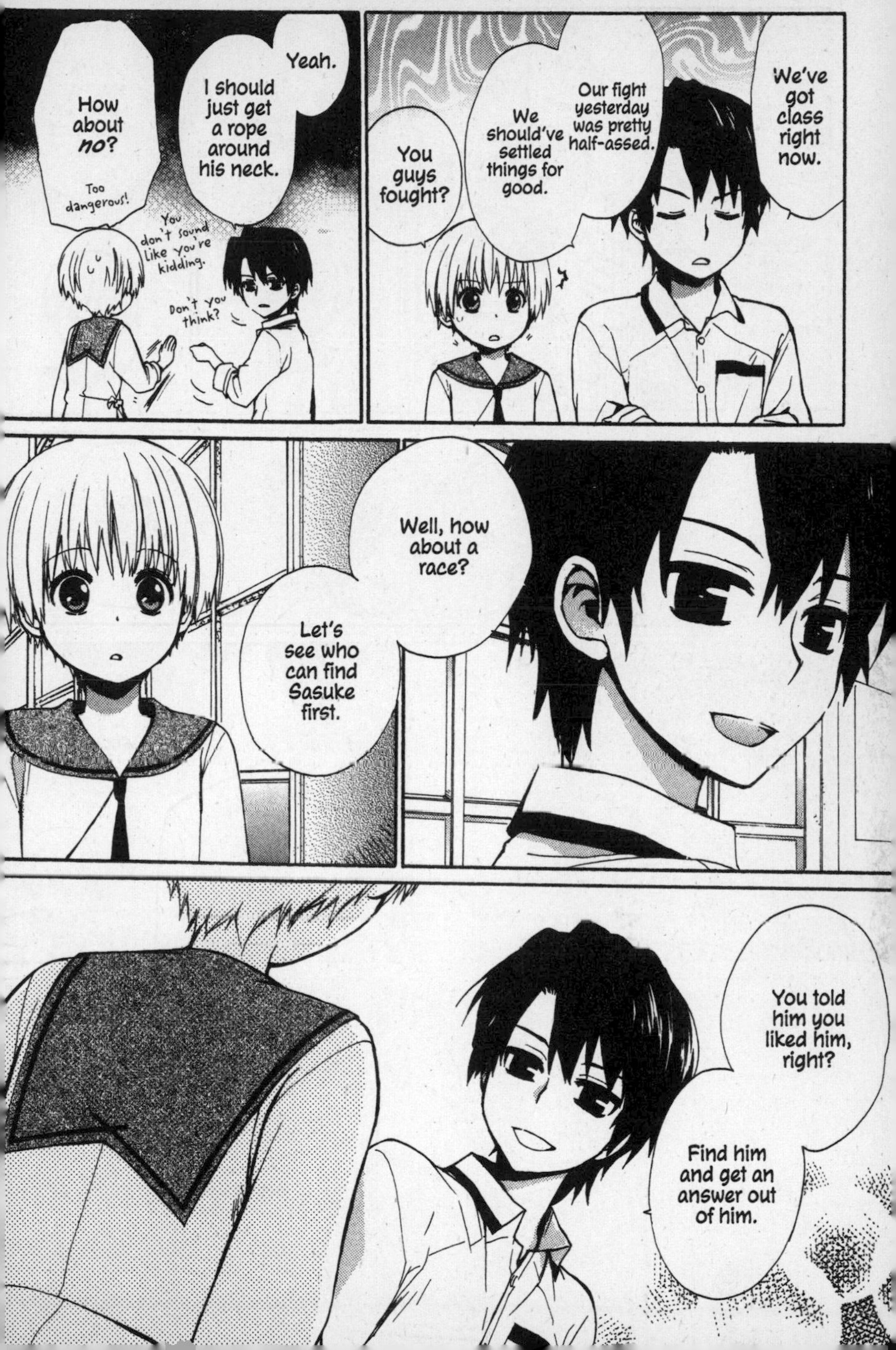
We've got class right now.
Our fight yesterday was pretty half-assed.
We should've settled things for good.
You guys fought?
Yeah.
I should just get a rope around his neck.
How about *no*?
Too dangerous!
You don't sound like you're kidding.
Don't you think?
Well, how about a race?
Let's see who can find Sasuke first.
You told him you liked him, right?
Find him and get an answer out of him.

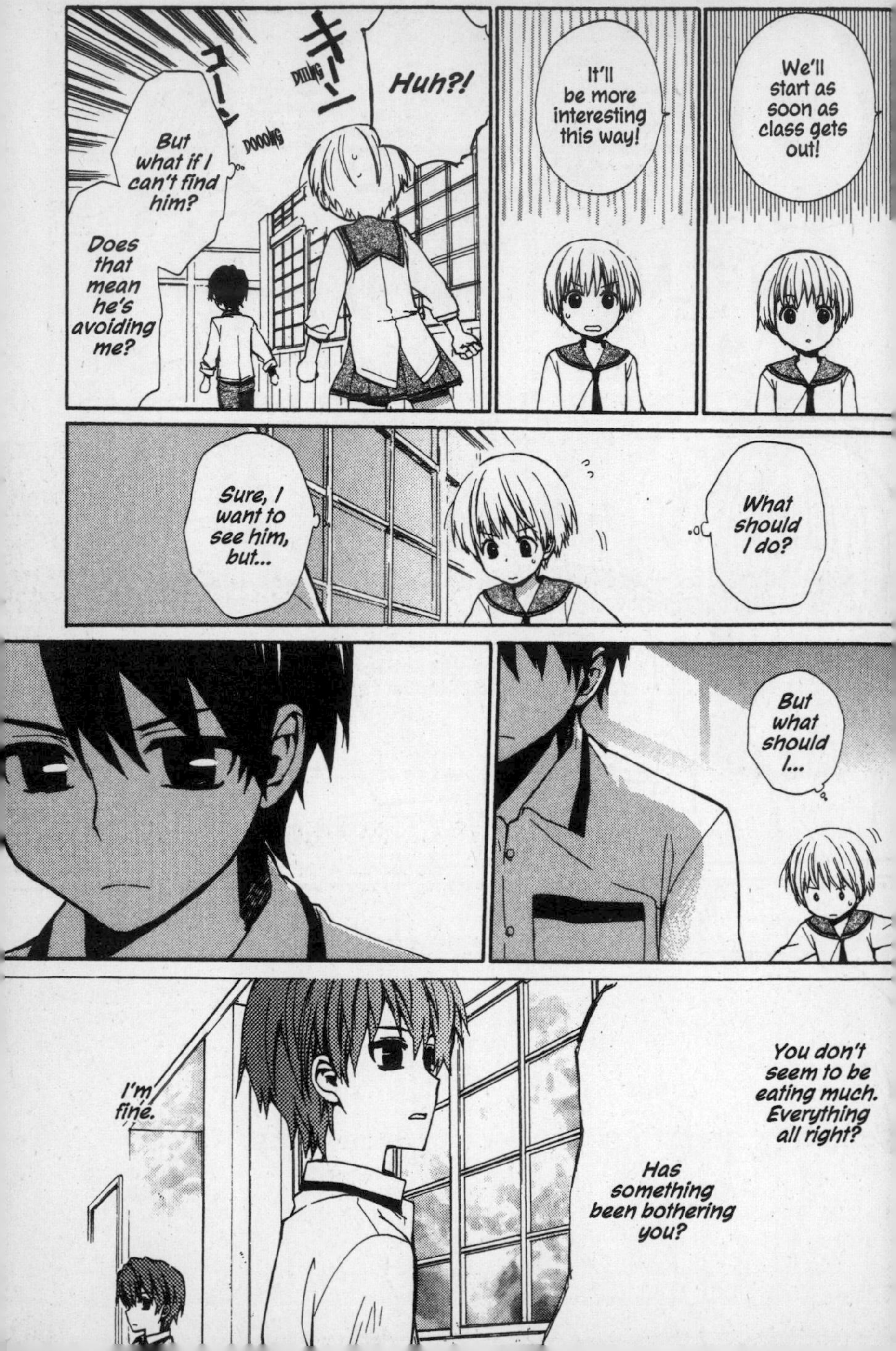
We'll start as soon as class gets out!
It'll be more interesting this way!
Huh?!
キーン
DIIING
コーン
DOOONG
But what if I can't find him?
Does that mean he's avoiding me?
What should I do?
Sure, I want to see him, but...
But what should I...
You don't seem to be eating much. Everything all right?
Has something been bothering you?
I'm fine.

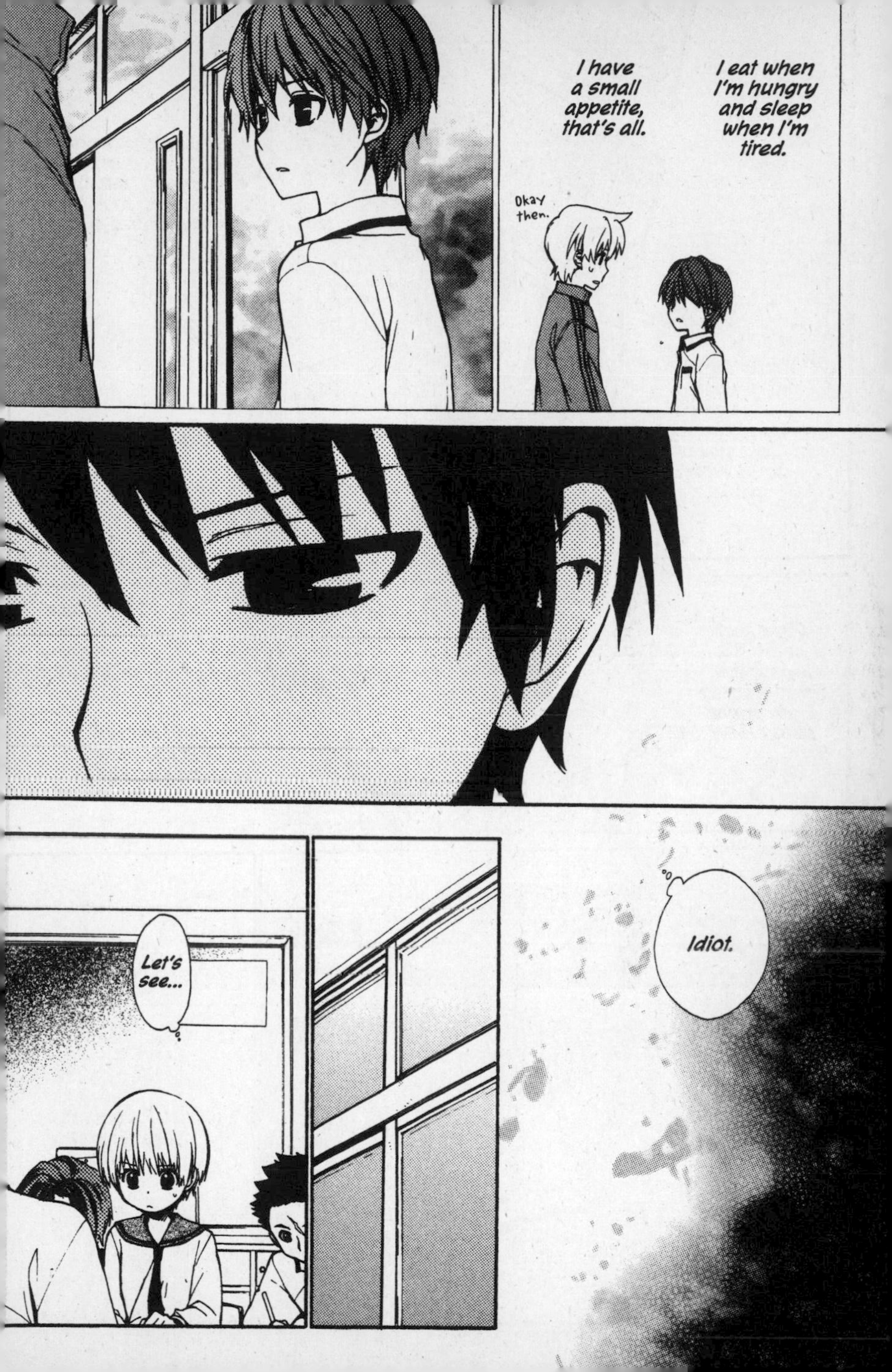
I eat when I'm hungry and sleep when I'm tired.
I have a small appetite, that's all.
Okay then.
Idiot.
Let's see...

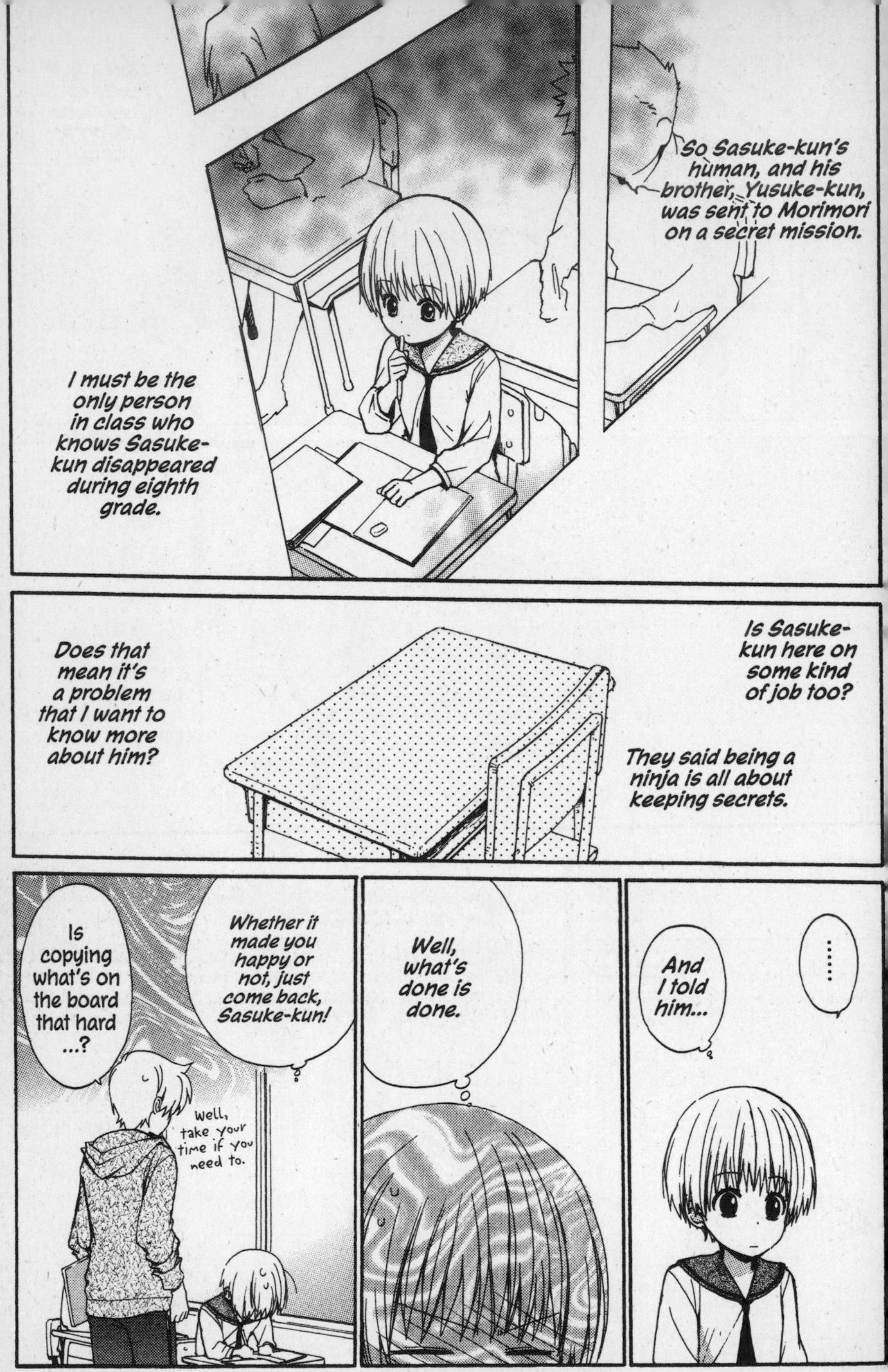
So Sasuke-kun's human, and his brother, Yusuke-kun, was sent to Morimori on a secret mission.
I must be the only person in class who knows Sasuke-kun disappeared during eighth grade.
Is Sasuke-kun here on some kind of job too?
They said being a ninja is all about keeping secrets.
Does that mean it's a problem that I want to know more about him?
......
And I told him...
Well, what's done is done.
Whether it made you happy or not, just come back, Sasuke-kun!
Is copying what's on the board that hard ...?
Well, take your time if you need to.

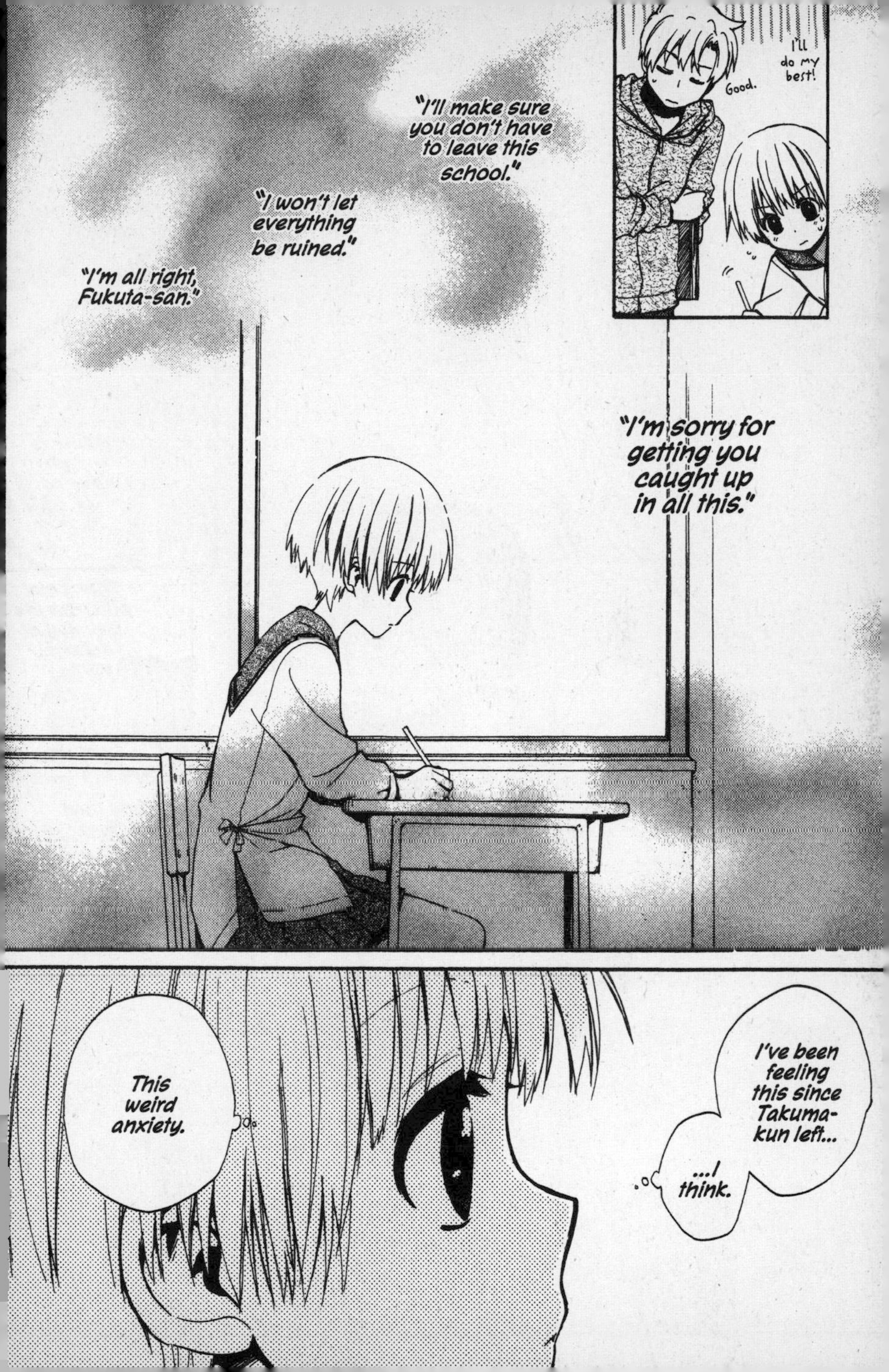
I'll do my best!
Good.
"I'll make sure you don't have to leave this school."
"I won't let everything be ruined."
"I'm all right, Fukuta-san."
"I'm sorry for getting you caught up in all this."
I've been feeling this since Takuma-kun left...
...I think.
This weird anxiety.

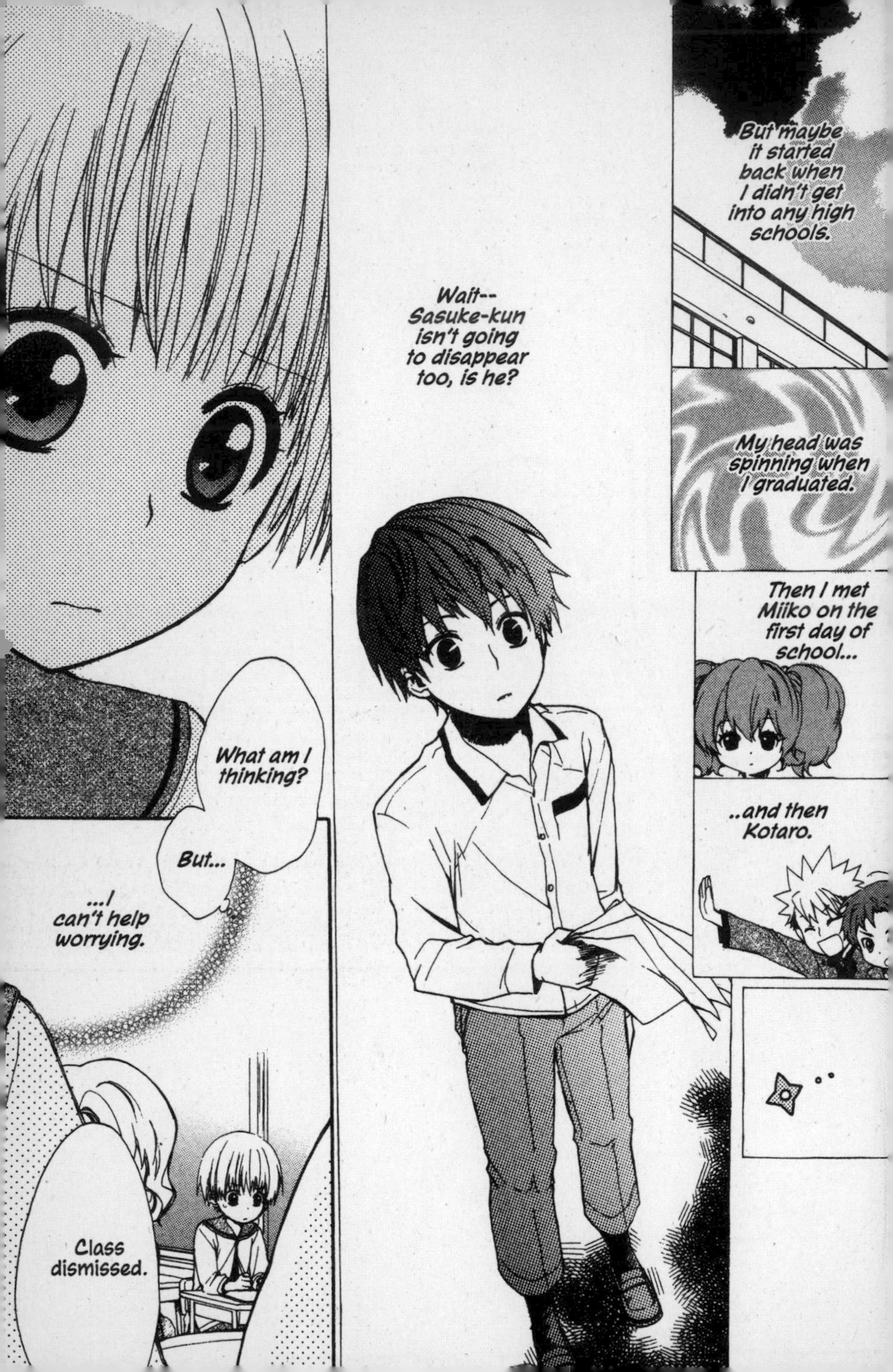
But maybe it started back when I didn't get into any high schools.
My head was spinning when I graduated.
Then I met Miiko on the first day of school...
..and then Kotaro.
Wait-- Sasuke-kun isn't going to disappear too, is he?
What am I thinking?
But...
...I can't help worrying.
Class dismissed.

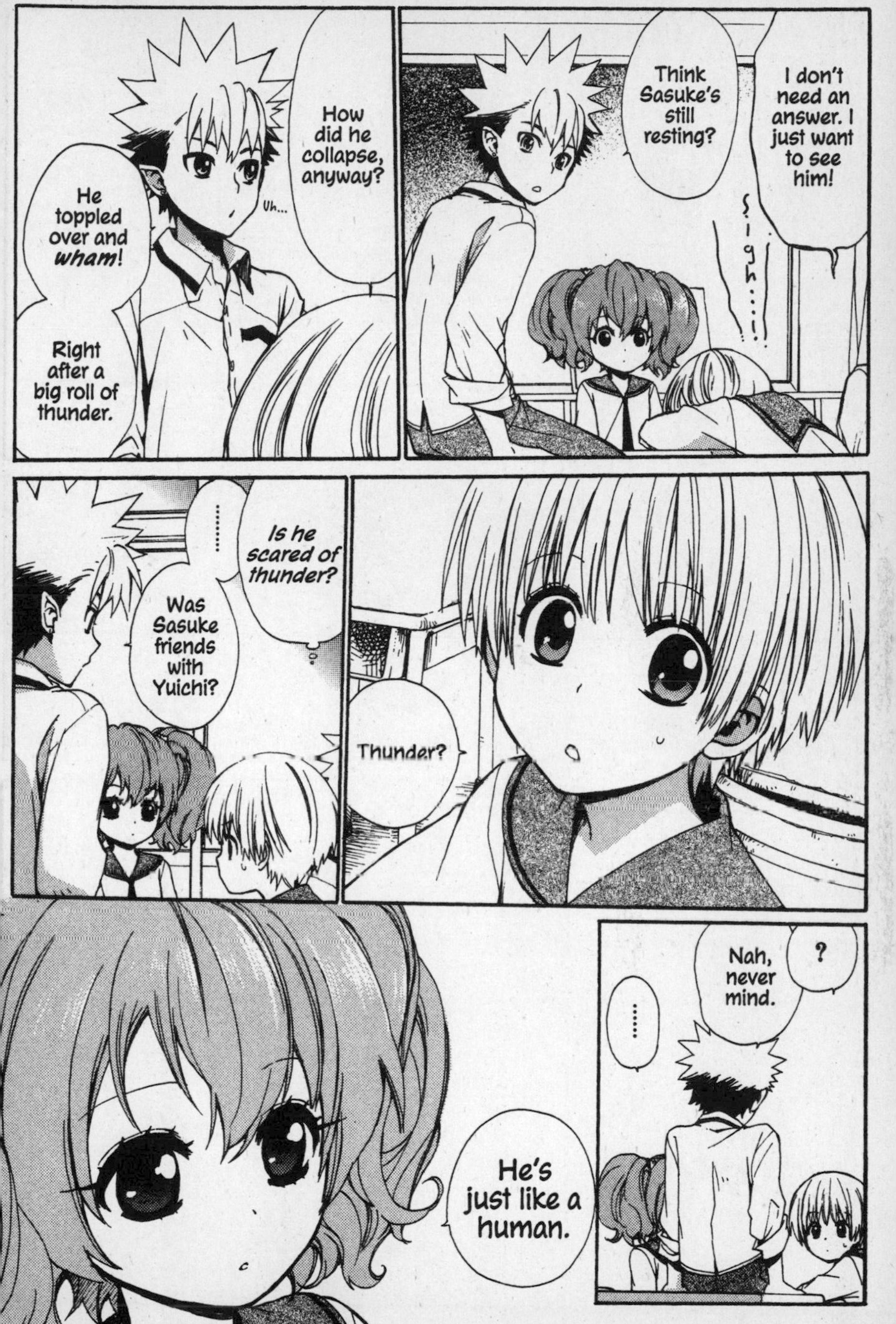

I don't need an answer. I just want to see him!
Think Sasuke's still resting?
Sigh...!
How did he collapse, anyway?
Uh...
He toppled over and *wham*!
Right after a big roll of thunder.
Thunder?
Is he scared of thunder?
......
Was Sasuke friends with Yuichi?
?
Nah, never mind.
......
He's just like a human.

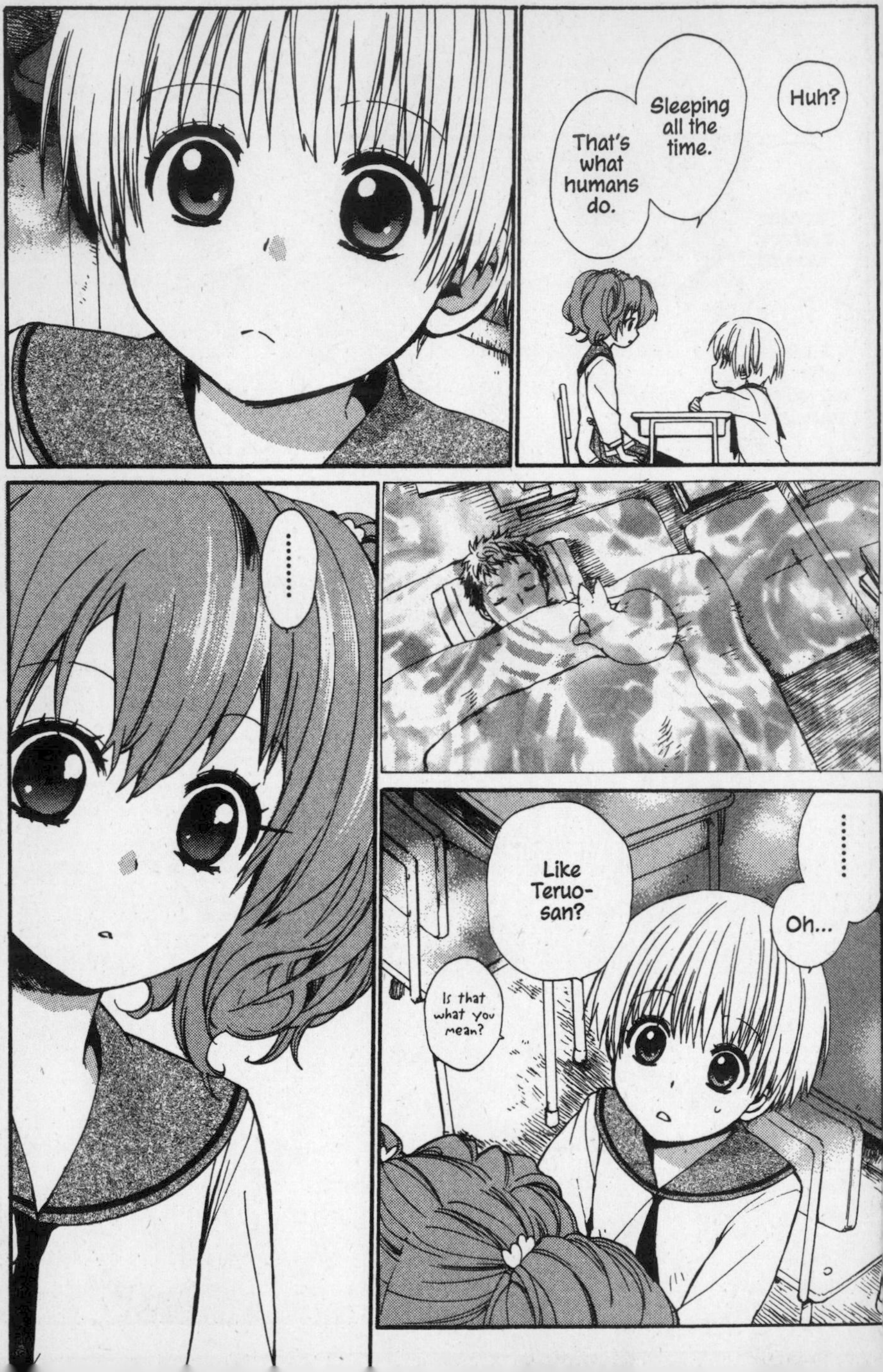
Huh?
Sleeping all the time.
That's what humans do.
....
Oh...
Like Teruo-san?
Is that what you mean?
....

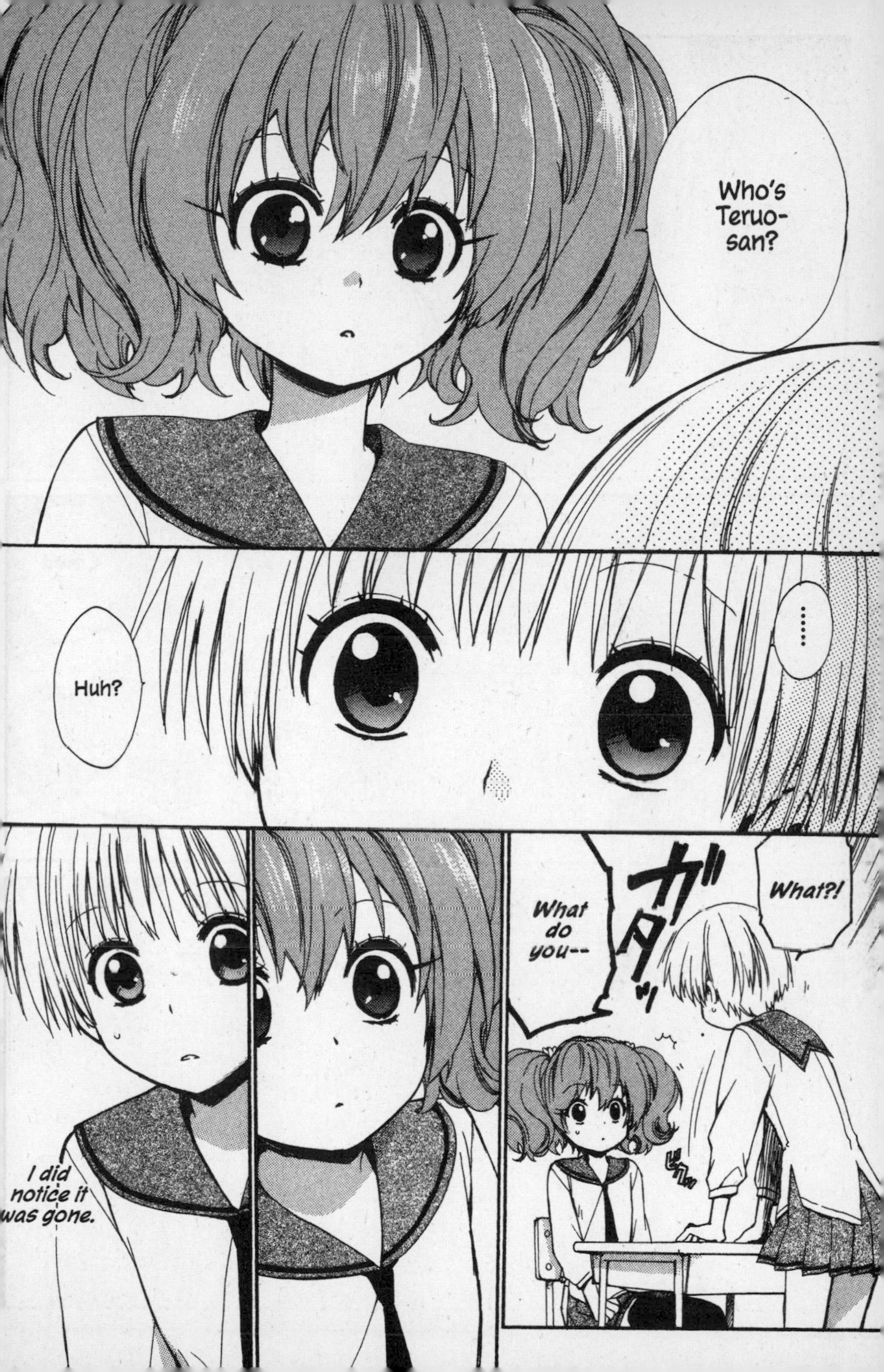
Who's Teruo-san?
......
Huh?
What?!
ガタッ
What do you--
I did notice it was gone.

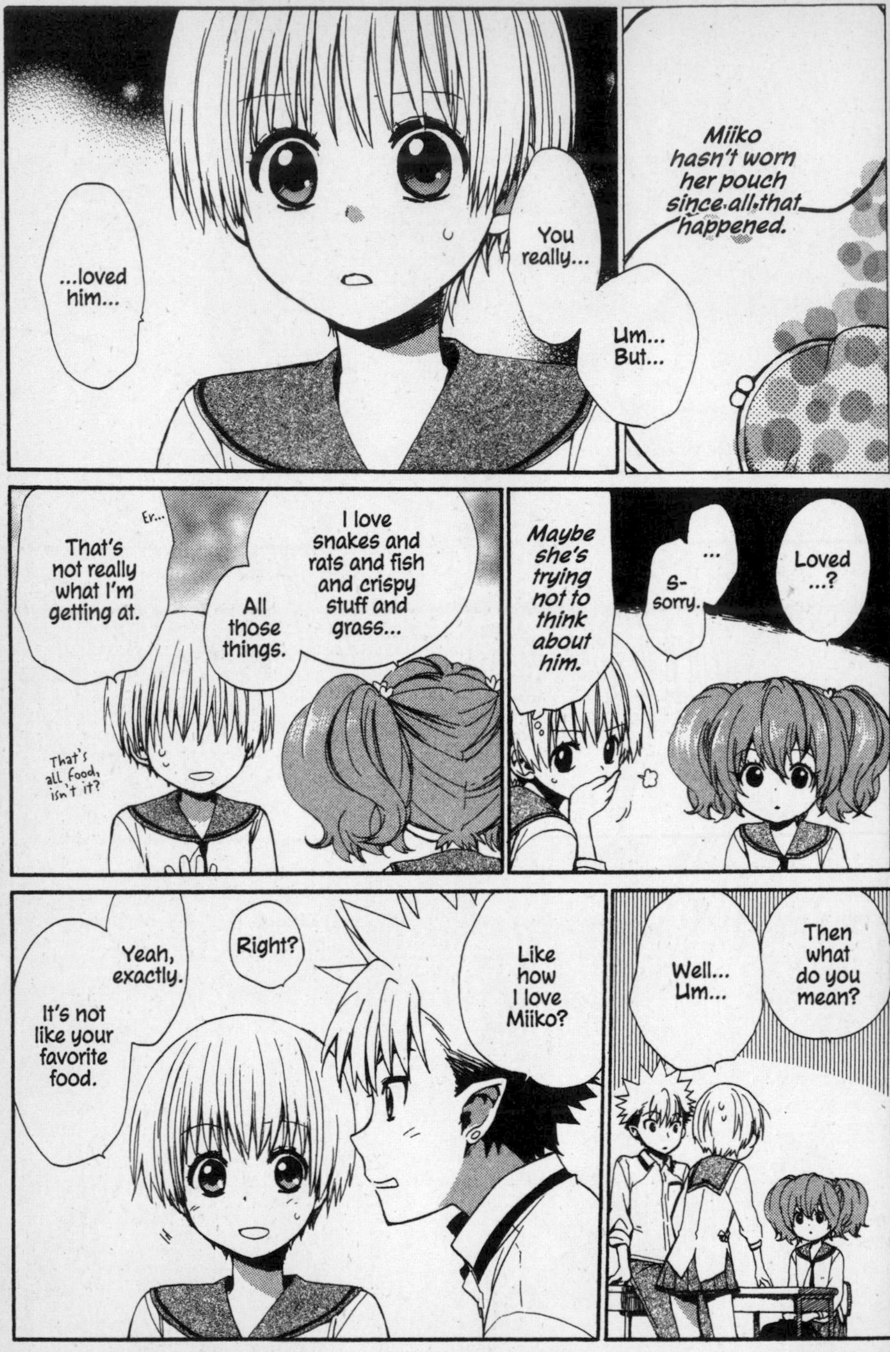
Miiko hasn't worn her pouch since all that happened.
Um... But...
You really...
...loved him...
Loved ...?
... S-sorry.
Maybe she's trying not to think about him.
I love snakes and rats and fish and crispy stuff and grass...
All those things.
Er...
That's not really what I'm getting at.
That's all food, isn't it?
Then what do you mean?
Well... Um...
Like how I love Miiko?
Right?
Yeah, exactly.
It's not like your favorite food.

But...
...you were so...
"I want to see him."
"I couldn't stand it if Miiko dropped out."
"I want to be with Teruo."
"A long, twisty snake."
"I wish it could wrap around all of Miiko's sad feelings..."
"...and pull them all away into the center of the earth."
"I want to tell him I love him!"

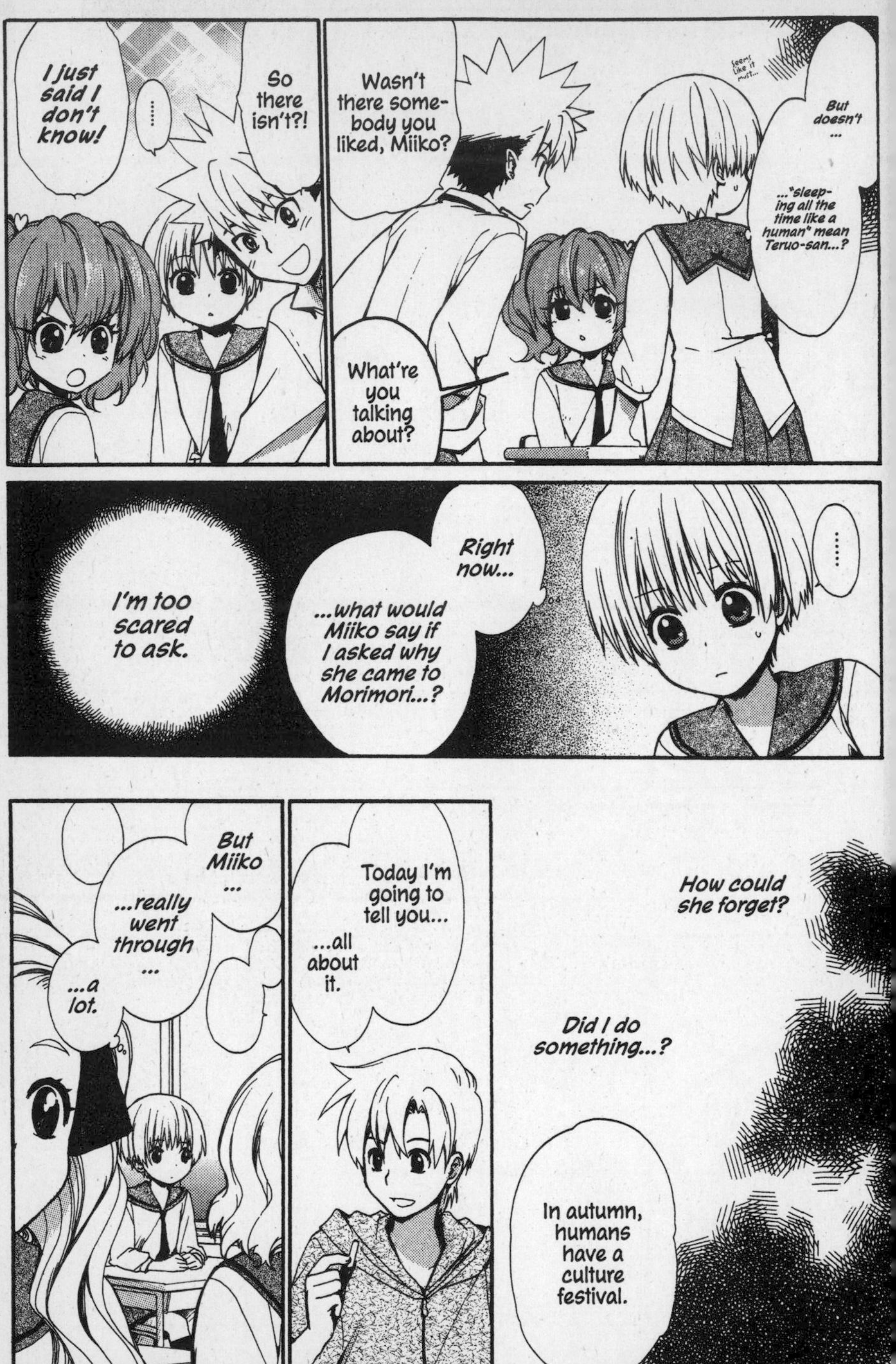

But doesn't ...
...“sleeping all the time like a human” mean Teruo-san...?
Seems like it must...
Wasn't there somebody you liked, Miiko?
What're you talking about?
So there isn't?!
......
I just said I don't know!
......
Right now...
...what would Miiko say if I asked why she came to Morimori...?
I'm too scared to ask.
How could she forget?
Did I do something...?
In autumn, humans have a culture festival.
Today I'm going to tell you...
...all about it.
But Miiko ...
...really went through ...
...a lot.

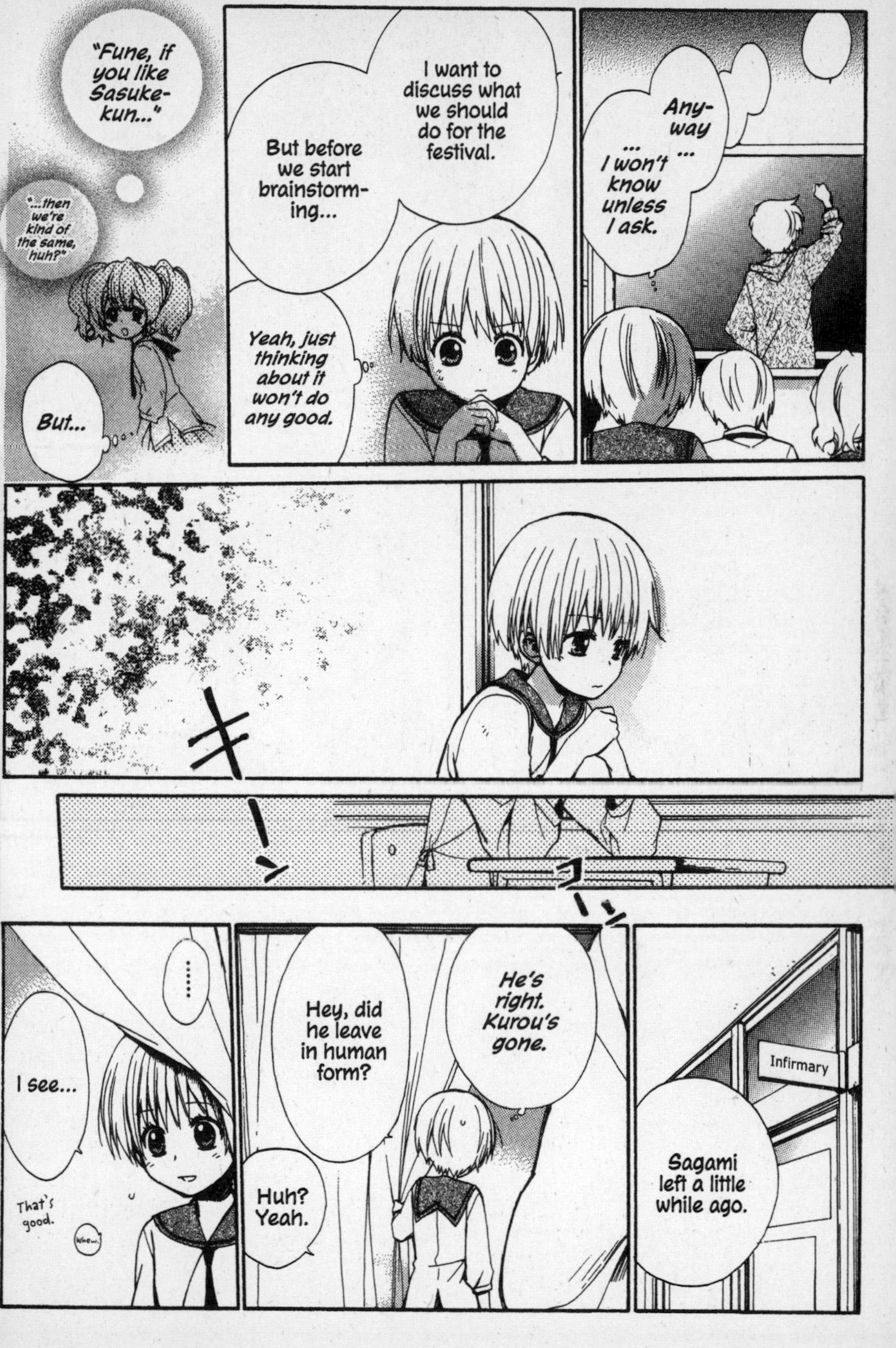
Any-way ... I won't know unless I ask.
I want to discuss what we should do for the festival.
But before we start brainstorming...
Yeah, just thinking about it won't do any good.
"Fune, if you like Sasuke-kun..."
"...then we're kind of the same, huh?"
But...
Infirmary
Sagami left a little while ago.
He's right. Kurou's gone.
Hey, did he leave in human form?
Huh? Yeah.
......
I see...
That's good.
Whew.

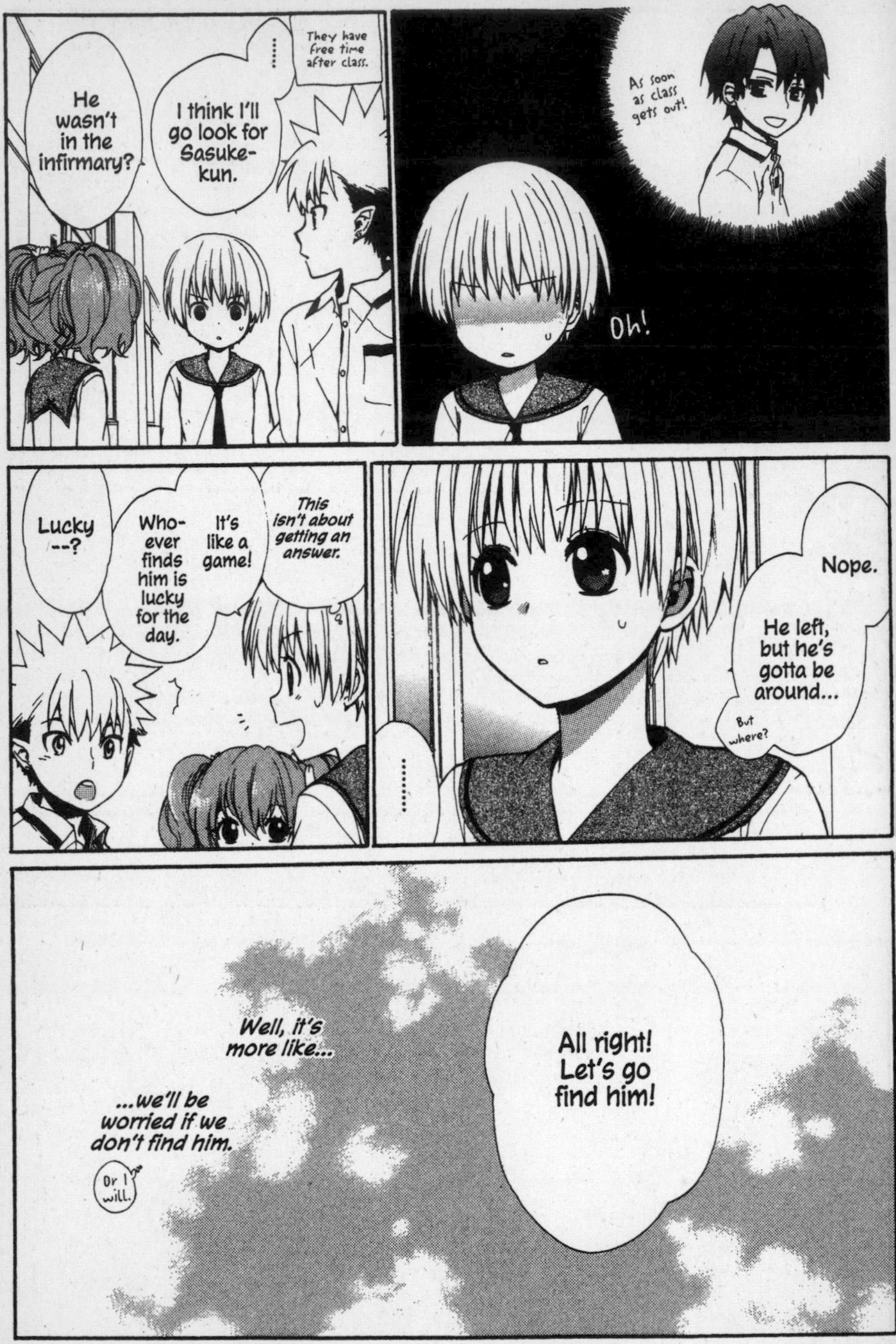
As soon as class gets out!
Oh!
They have free time after class.
......
I think I'll go look for Sasuke-kun.
He wasn't in the infirmary?
Nope.
He left, but he's gotta be around...
But where?
......
This isn't about getting an answer.
It's like a game!
Who-ever finds him is lucky for the day.
Lucky --?
All right! Let's go find him!
Well, it's more like...
...we'll be worried if we don't find him.
Or I will.

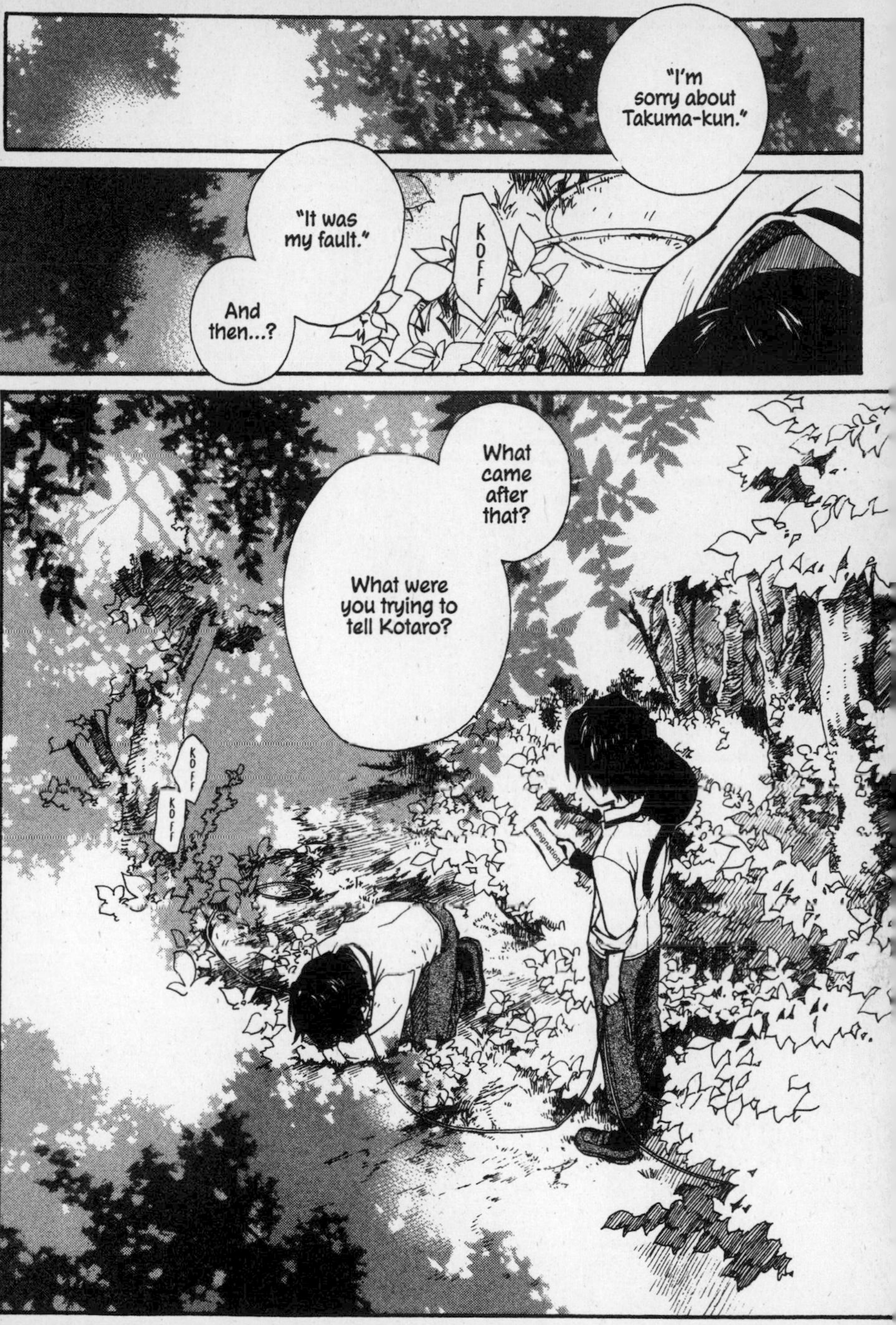
"I'm sorry about Takuma-kun."
KOFF
"It was my fault."
And then...?
What came after that?
What were you trying to tell Kotaro?
Resignation
KOFF
KOFF

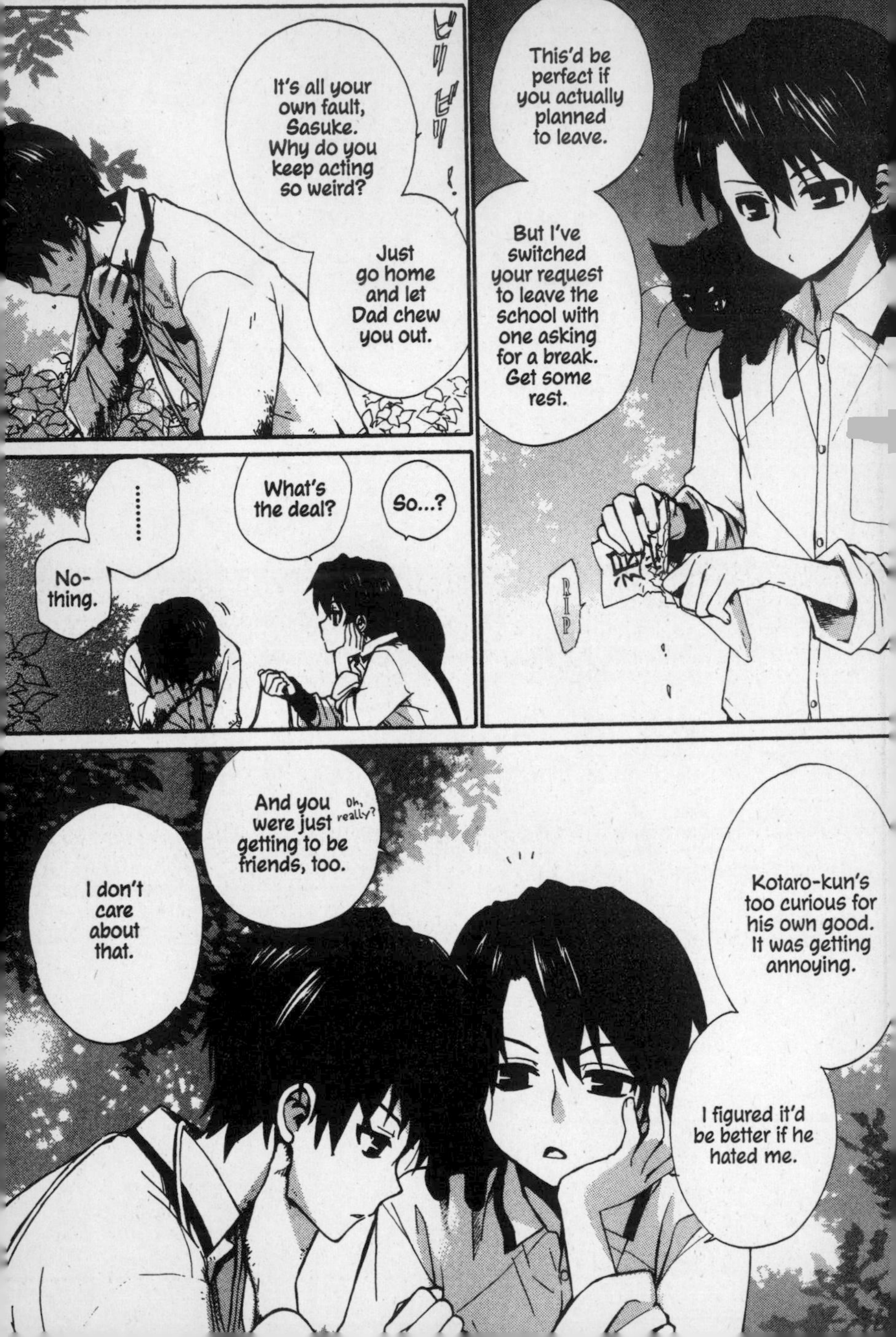
This'd be perfect if you actually planned to leave.
But I've switched your request to leave the school with one asking for a break. Get some rest.
RIP
ビリビリ!
It's all your own fault, Sasuke. Why do you keep acting so weird?
Just go home and let Dad chew you out.
So...?
What's the deal?
....
No-thing.
Kotaro-kun's too curious for his own good. It was getting annoying.
I figured it'd be better if he hated me.
And you were just getting to be friends, too.
Oh, really?
I don't care about that.

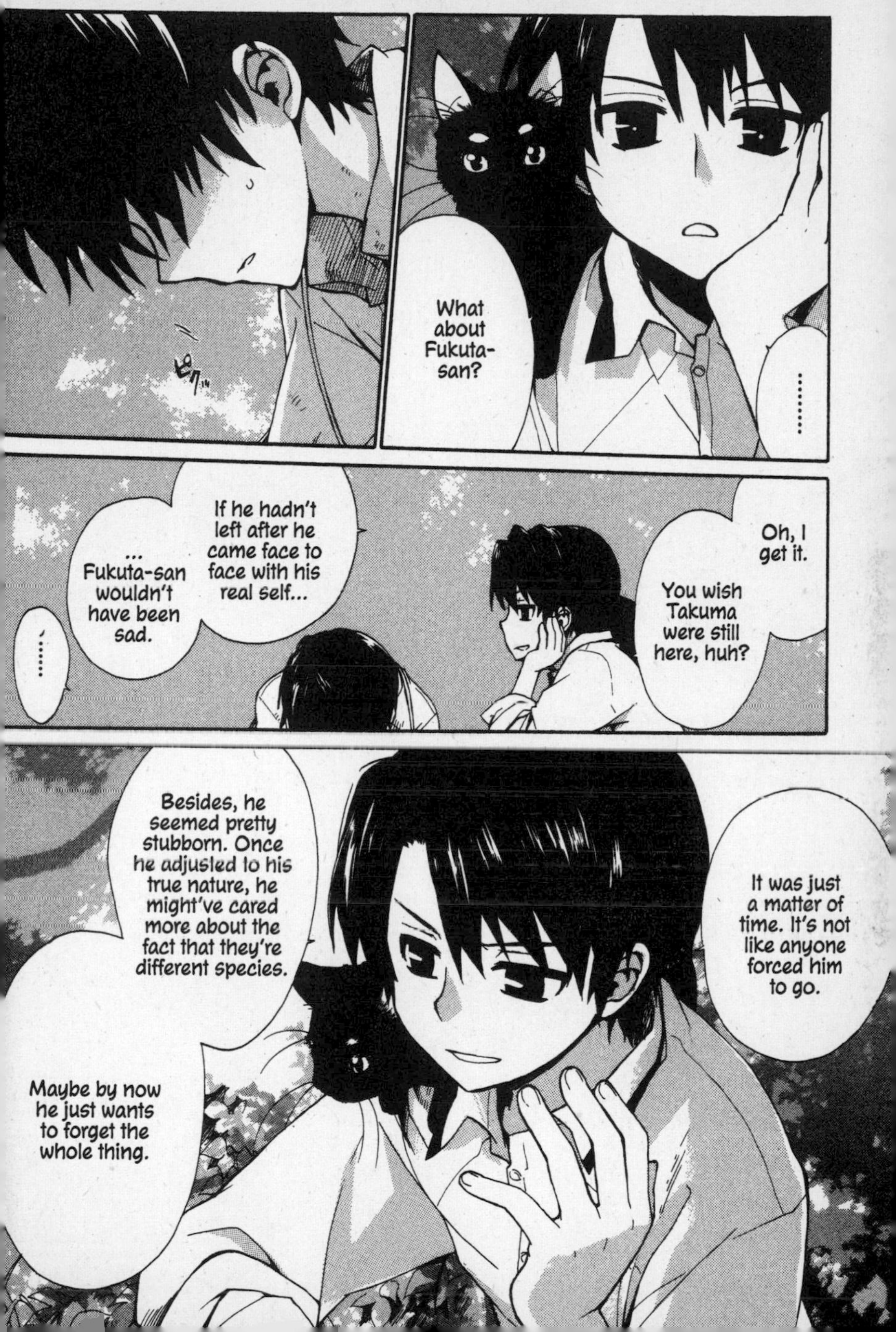

....
What about Fukuta-san?
Oh, I get it.
You wish Takuma were still here, huh?
If he hadn't left after he came face to face with his real self...
... Fukuta-san wouldn't have been sad.
......
It was just a matter of time. It's not like anyone forced him to go.
Besides, he seemed pretty stubborn. Once he adjusled to his true nature, he might've cared more about the fact that they're different species.
Maybe by now he just wants to forget the whole thing.

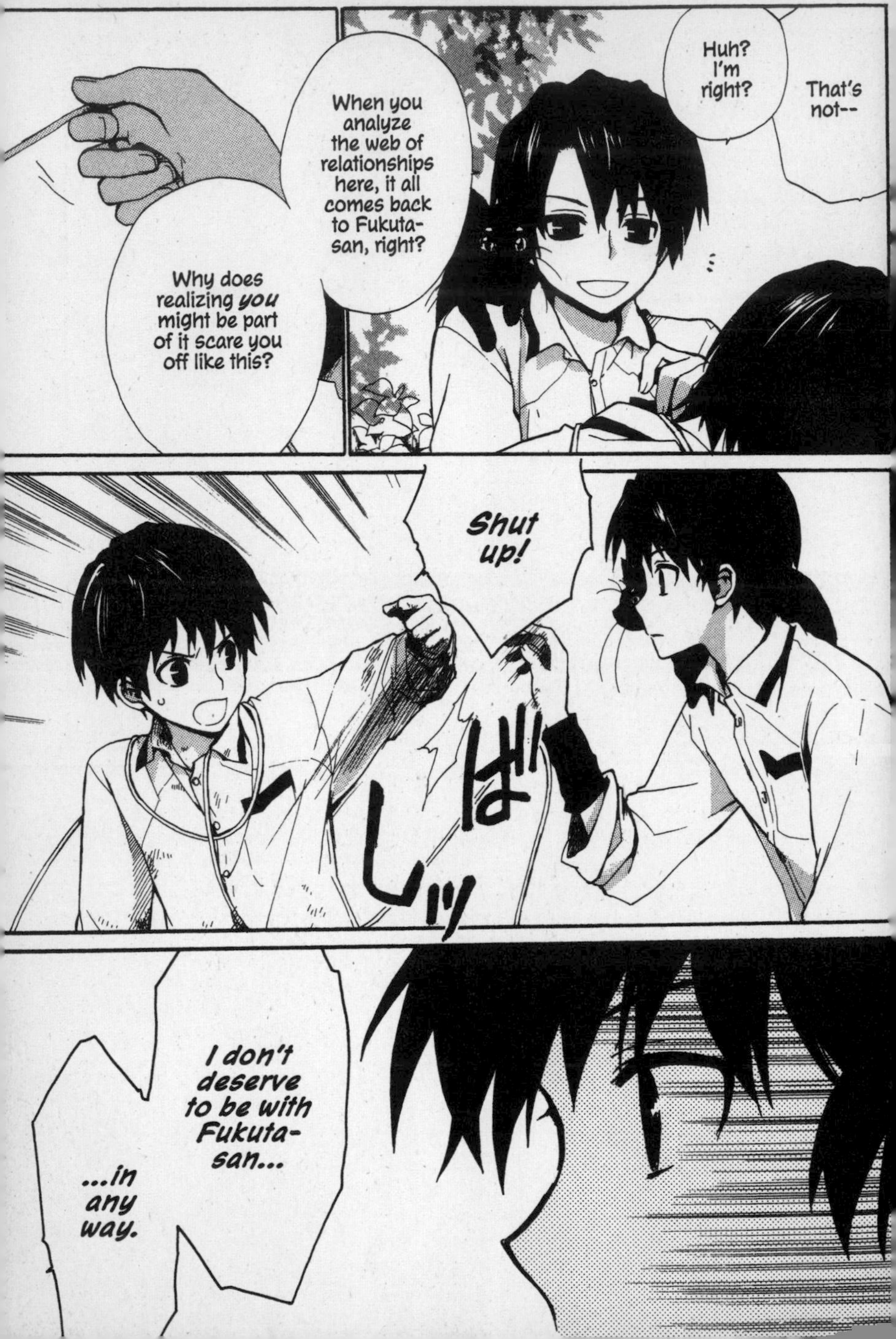

That's not--
Huh? I'm right?
When you analyze the web of relationships here, it all comes back to Fukuta-san, right?
Why does realizing *you* might be part of it scare you off like this?
Shut up!
ばしッ
I don't deserve to be with Fukuta-san...
...in any way.

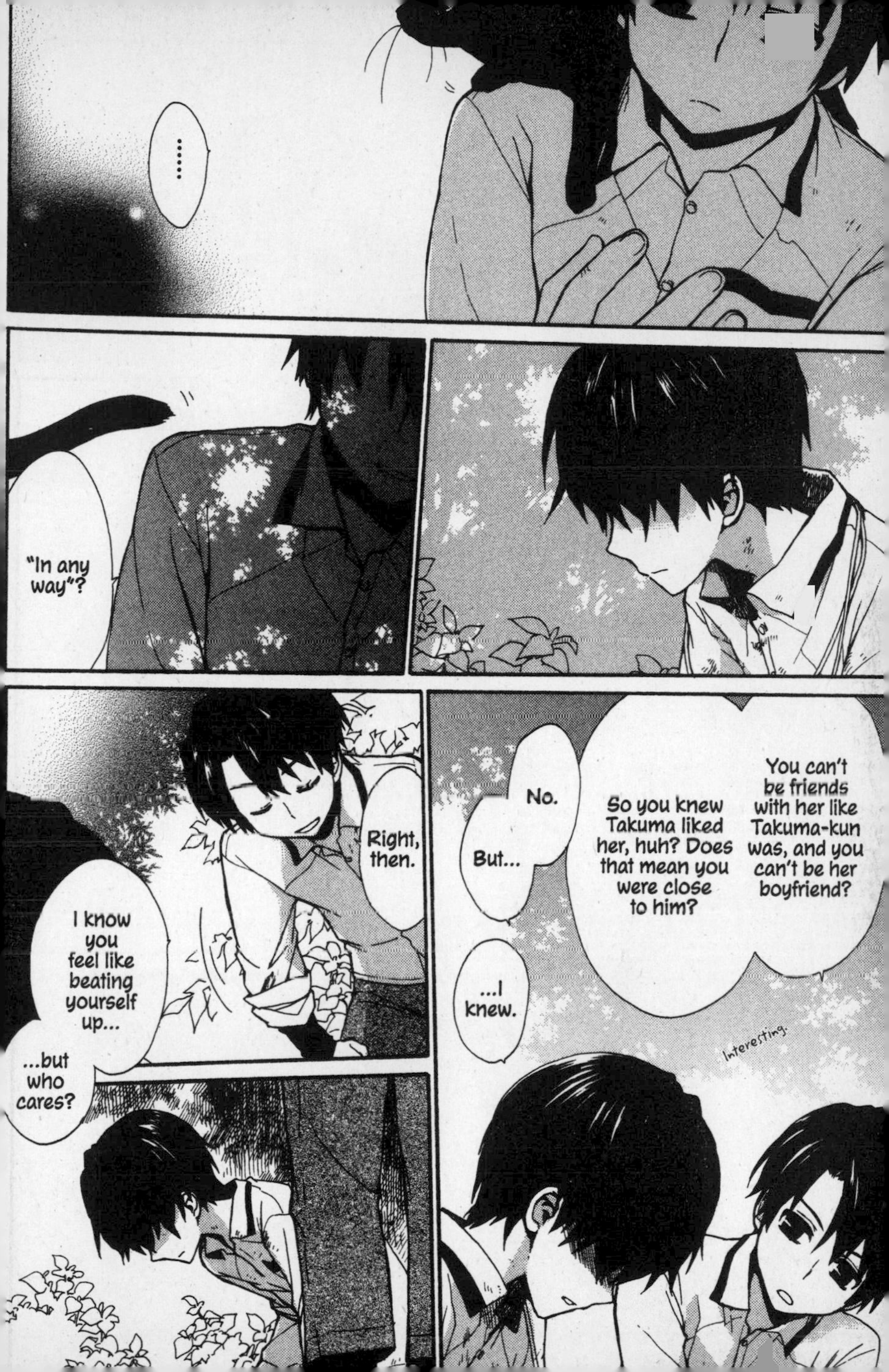
......
"In any way"?
You can't be friends with her like Takuma-kun was, and you can't be her boyfriend?
So you knew Takuma liked her, huh? Does that mean you were close to him?
No.
But...
...I knew.
Interesting.
Right, then.
I know you feel like beating yourself up...
...but who cares?

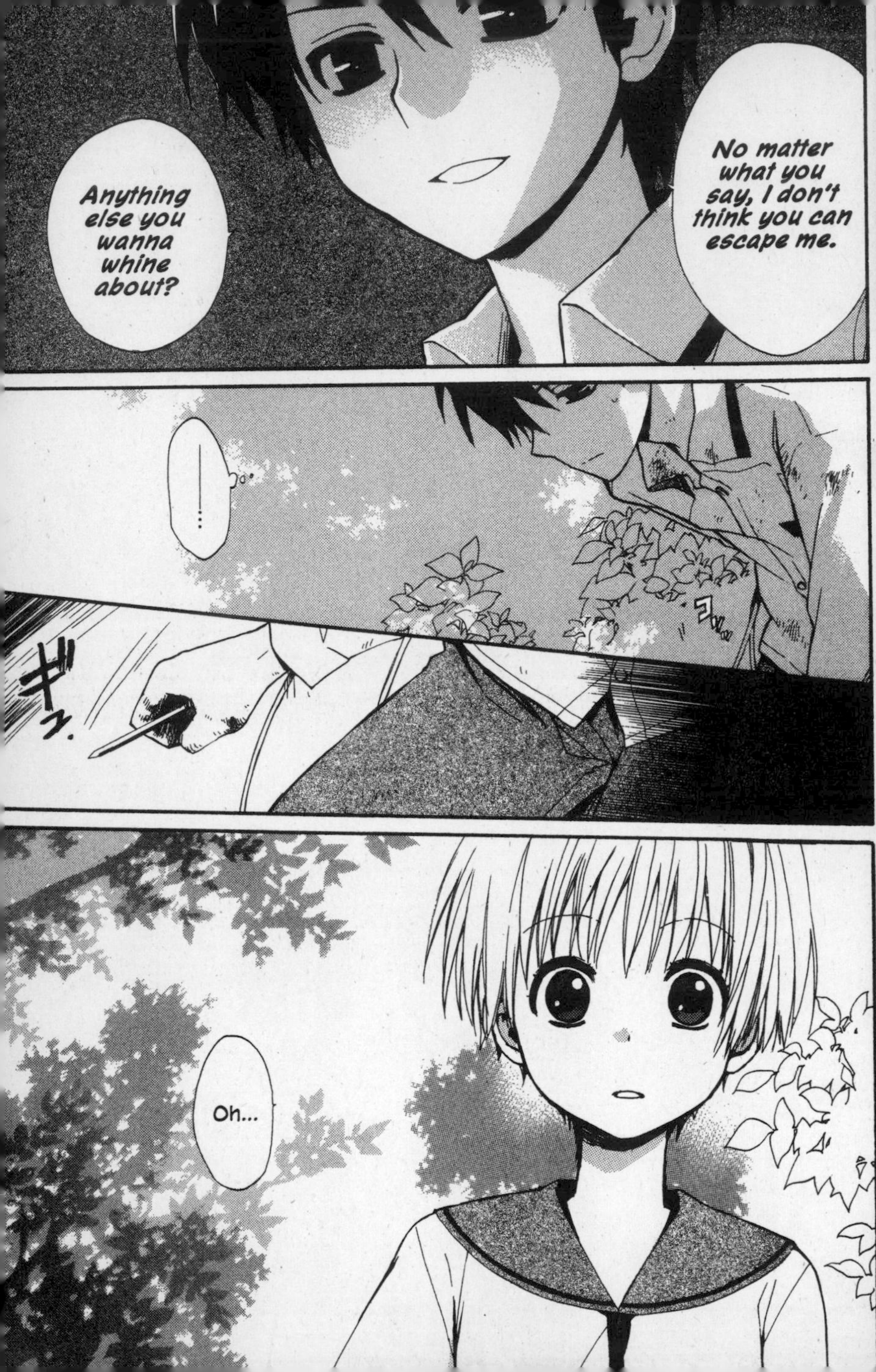
No matter what you say, I don't think you can escape me.
Anything else you wanna whine about?
......
ギュ.
Oh...

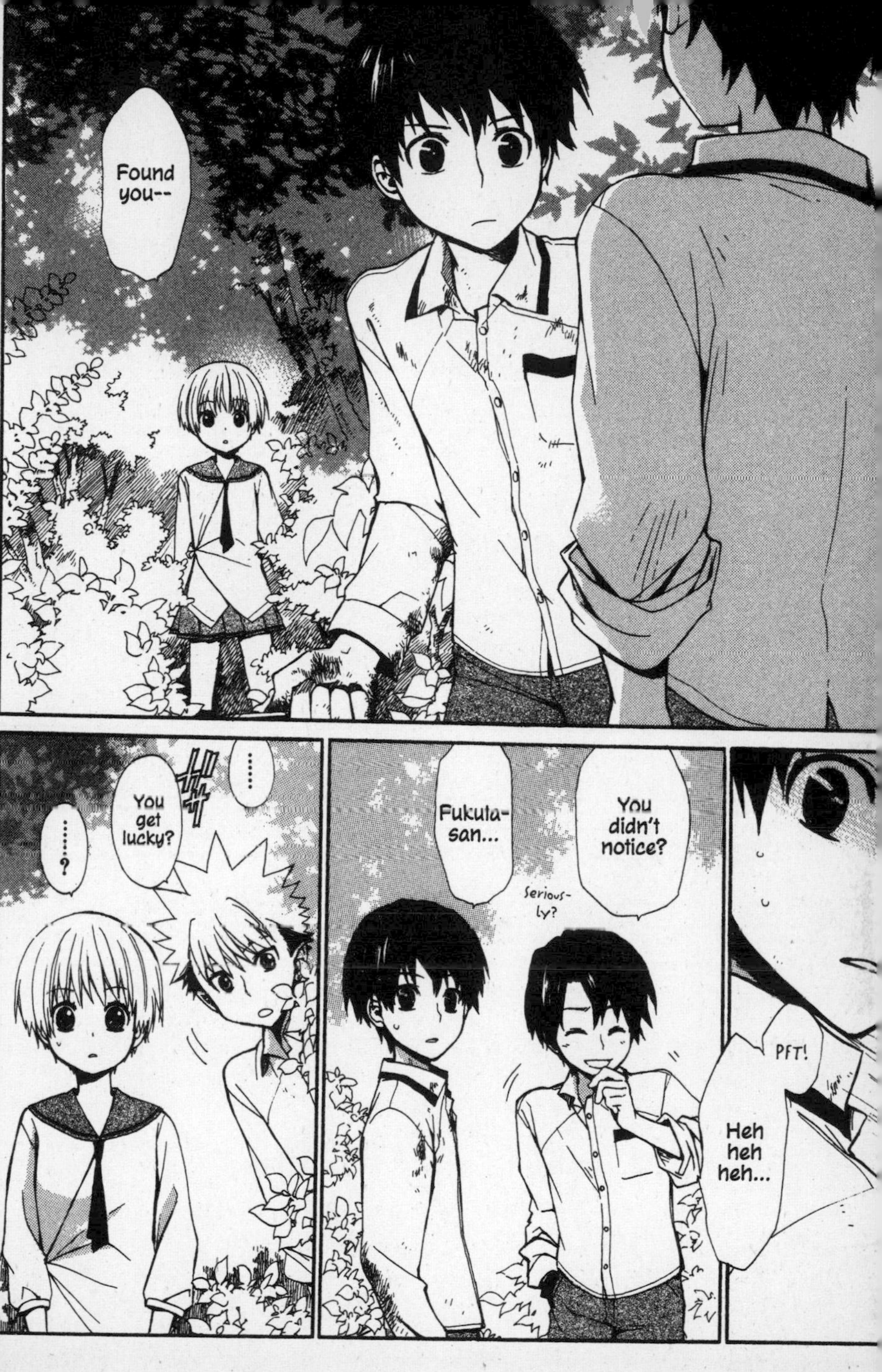
Found you--
PFT!
Heh heh heh...
You didn't notice?
Serious-ly?
Fukuta-san...
......
You get lucky?
......?

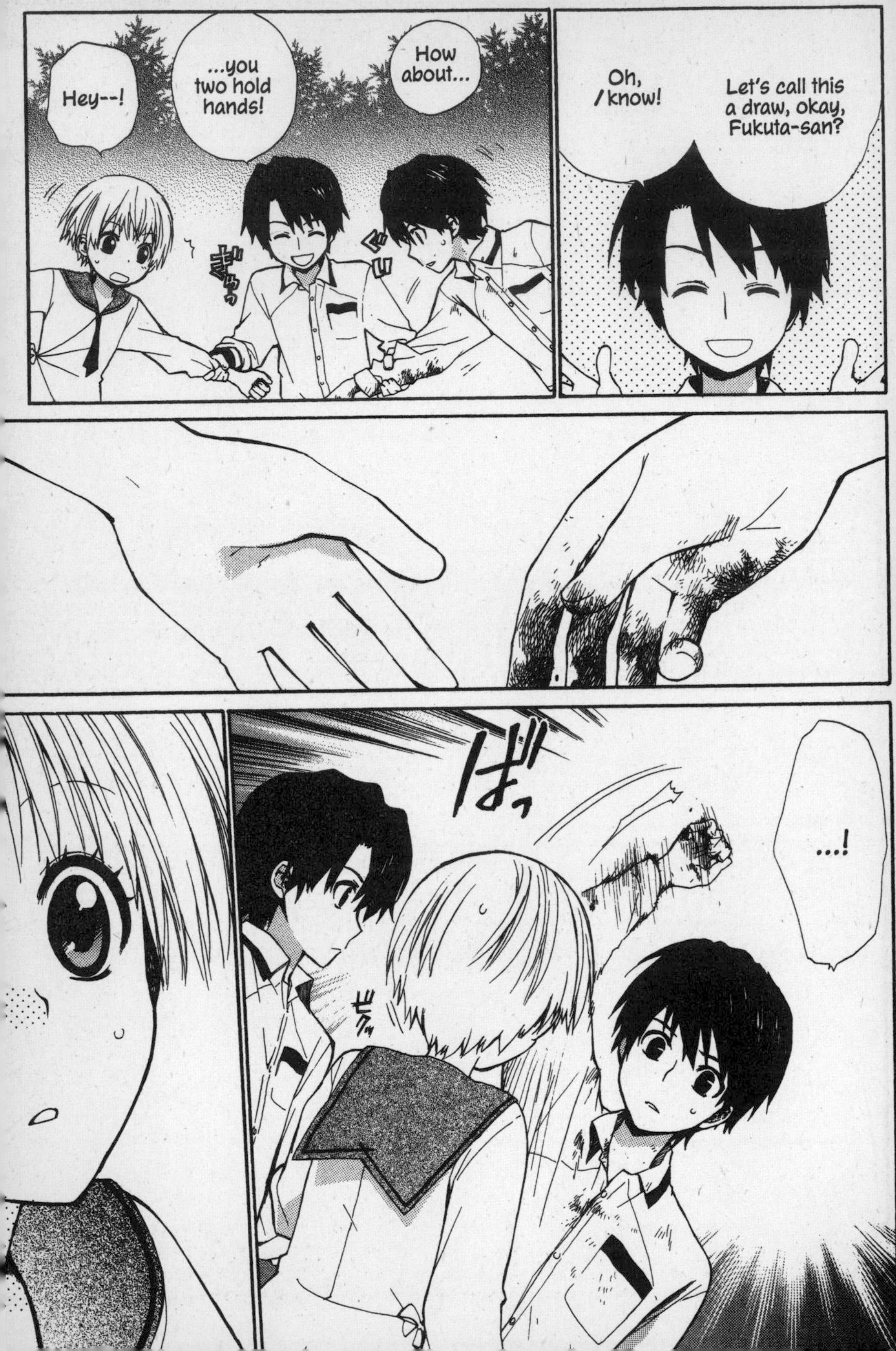

Let's call this a draw, okay, Fukuta-san?
Oh, I know!
How about...
...you two hold hands!
Hey--!
ぱっ
...!

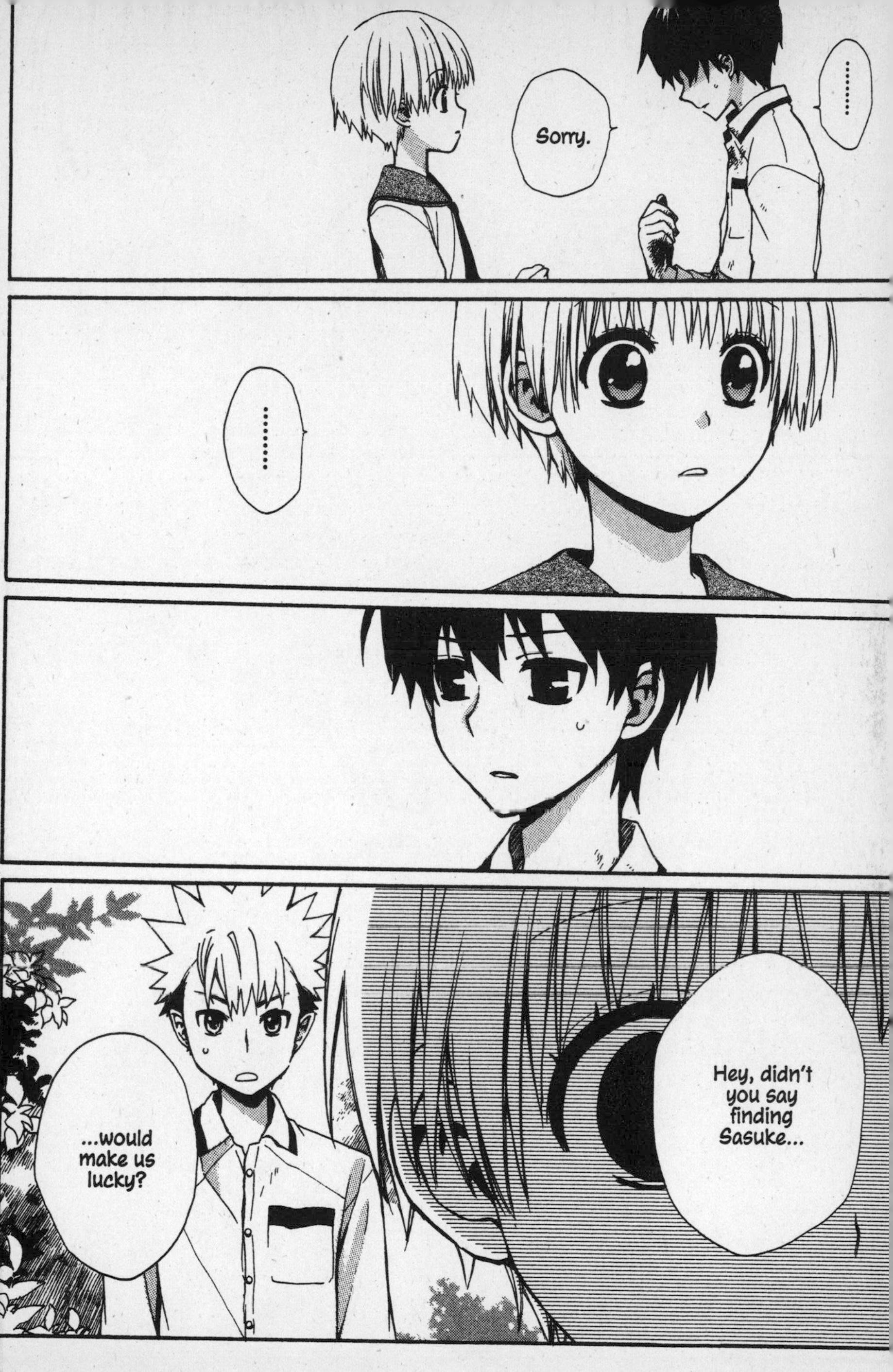
....
Sorry.
....
Hey, didn't you say finding Sasuke...
...would make us lucky?

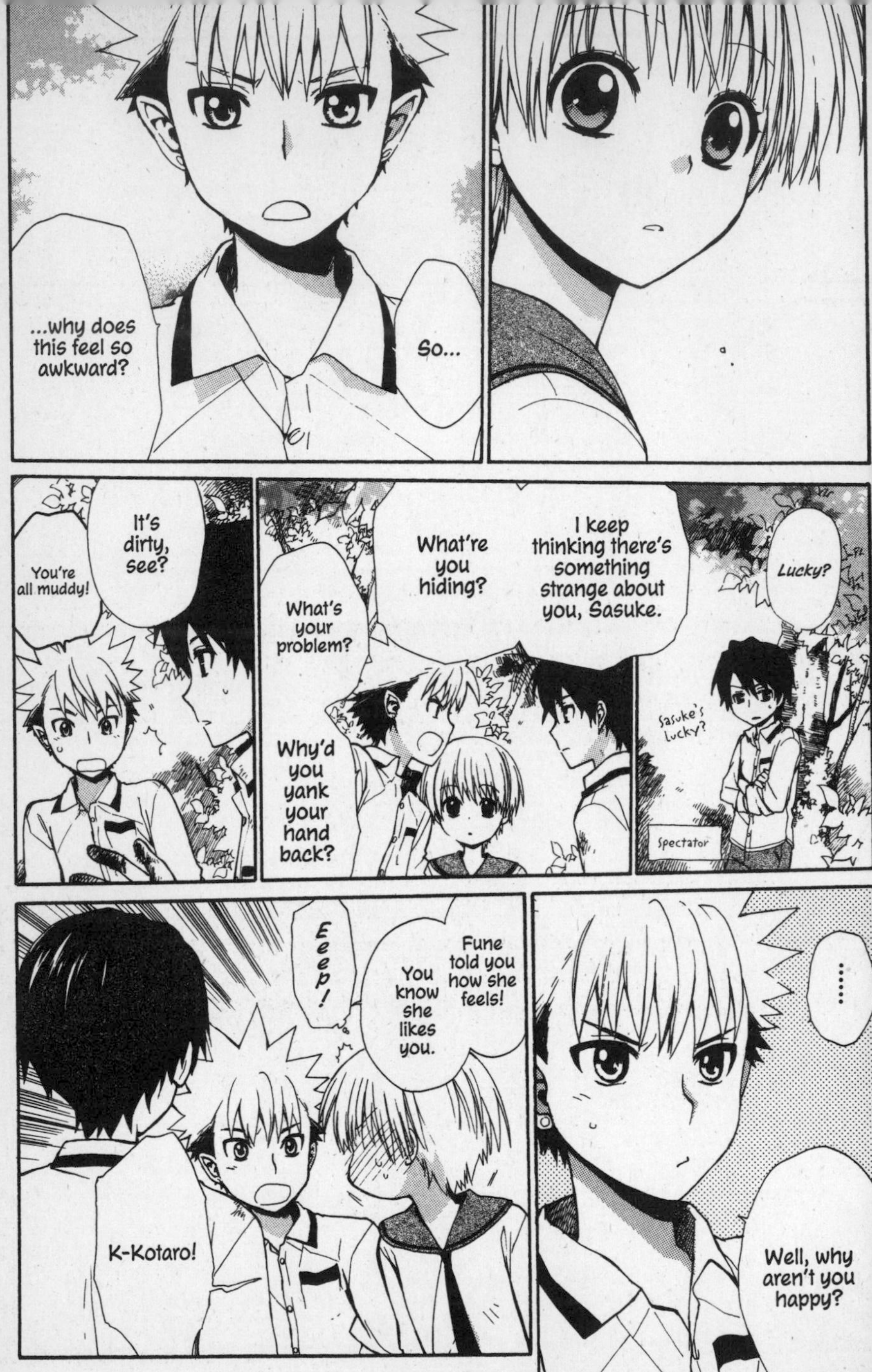
So...
...why does this feel so awkward?
Lucky?
Sasuke's Lucky?
Spectator
I keep thinking there's something strange about you, Sasuke.
What're you hiding?
What's your problem?
Why'd you yank your hand back?
It's dirty, see?
You're all muddy!
......
Well, why aren't you happy?
Fune told you how she feels!
You know she likes you.
Eeep!
K-Kotaro!

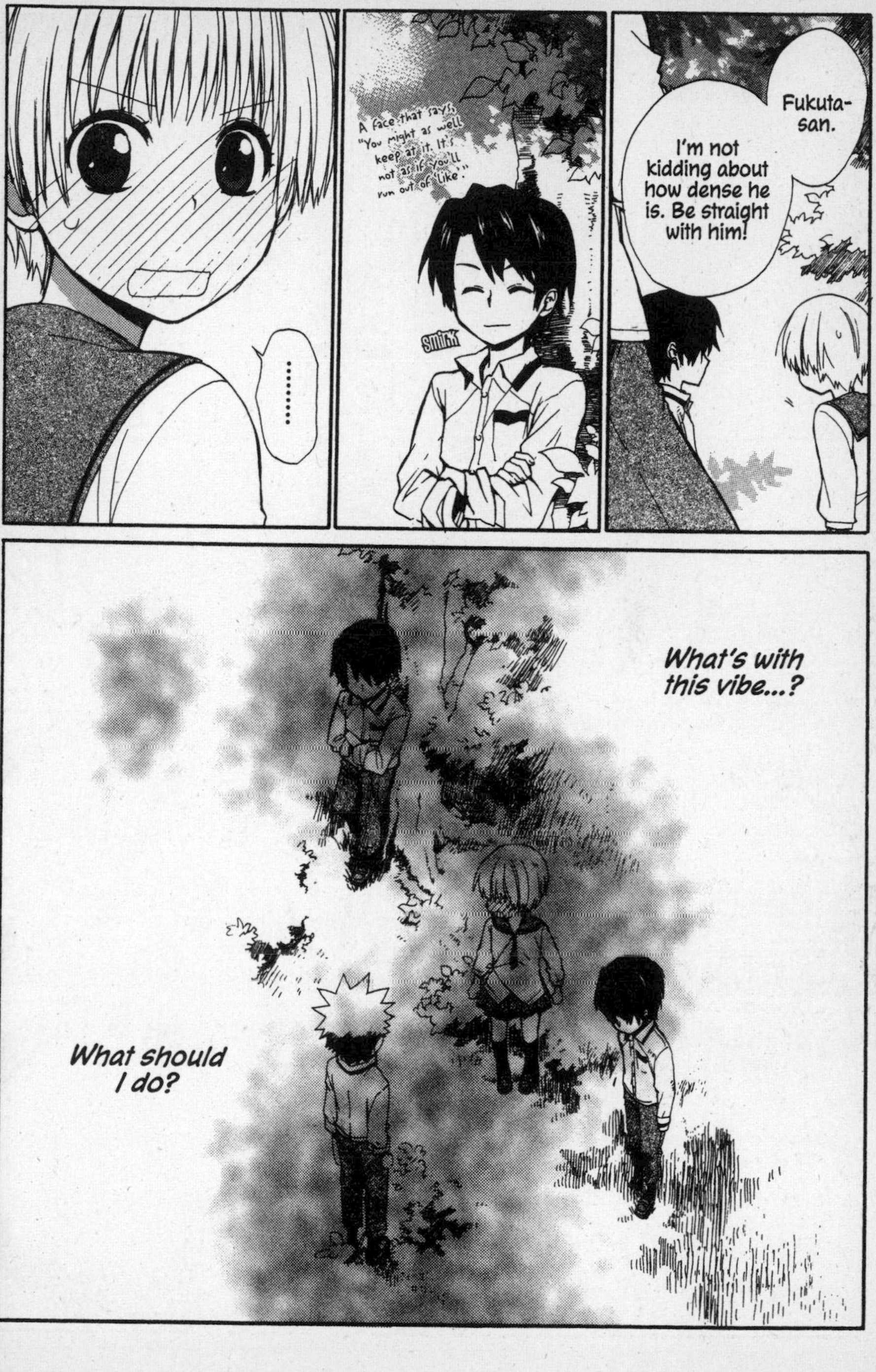
Fukuta-san.
I'm not kidding about how dense he is. Be straight with him!
A face that says, "You might as well keep at it. It's not as if you'll run out of 'like.'"
SMIRK
......
What's with this vibe...?
What should I do?

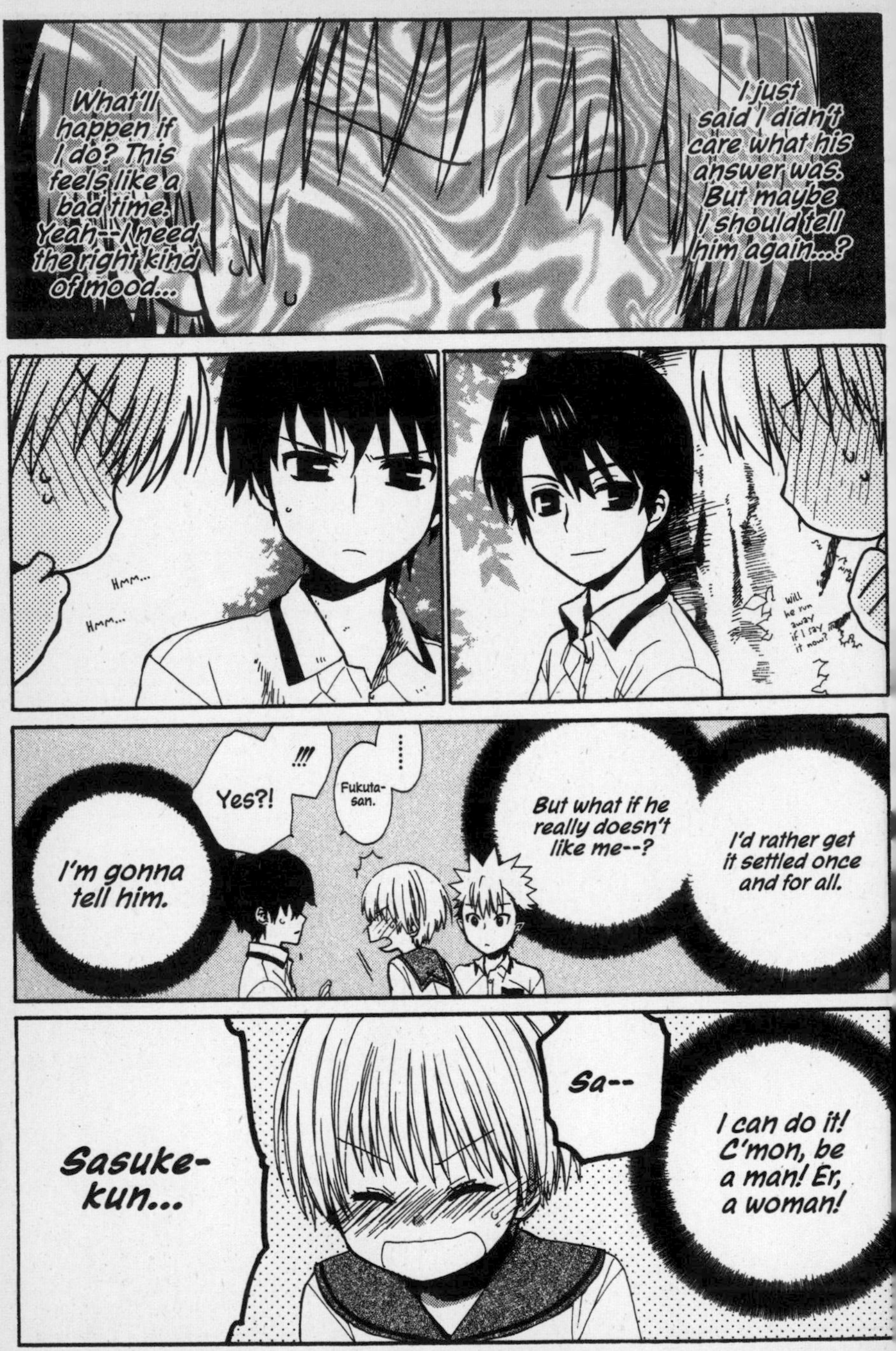
I just said I didn't care what his answer was. But maybe I should tell him again...?
What'll happen if I do? This feels like a bad time. Yeah--I need the right kind of mood...
Will he run away if I say it now?
Hmm...
Hmm...
I'd rather get it settled once and for all.
But what if he really doesn't like me--?
......
Fukuta-san.
!!!
Yes?!
I'm gonna tell him.
I can do it! C'mon, be a man! Er, a woman!
Sa--
Sasuke-kun...

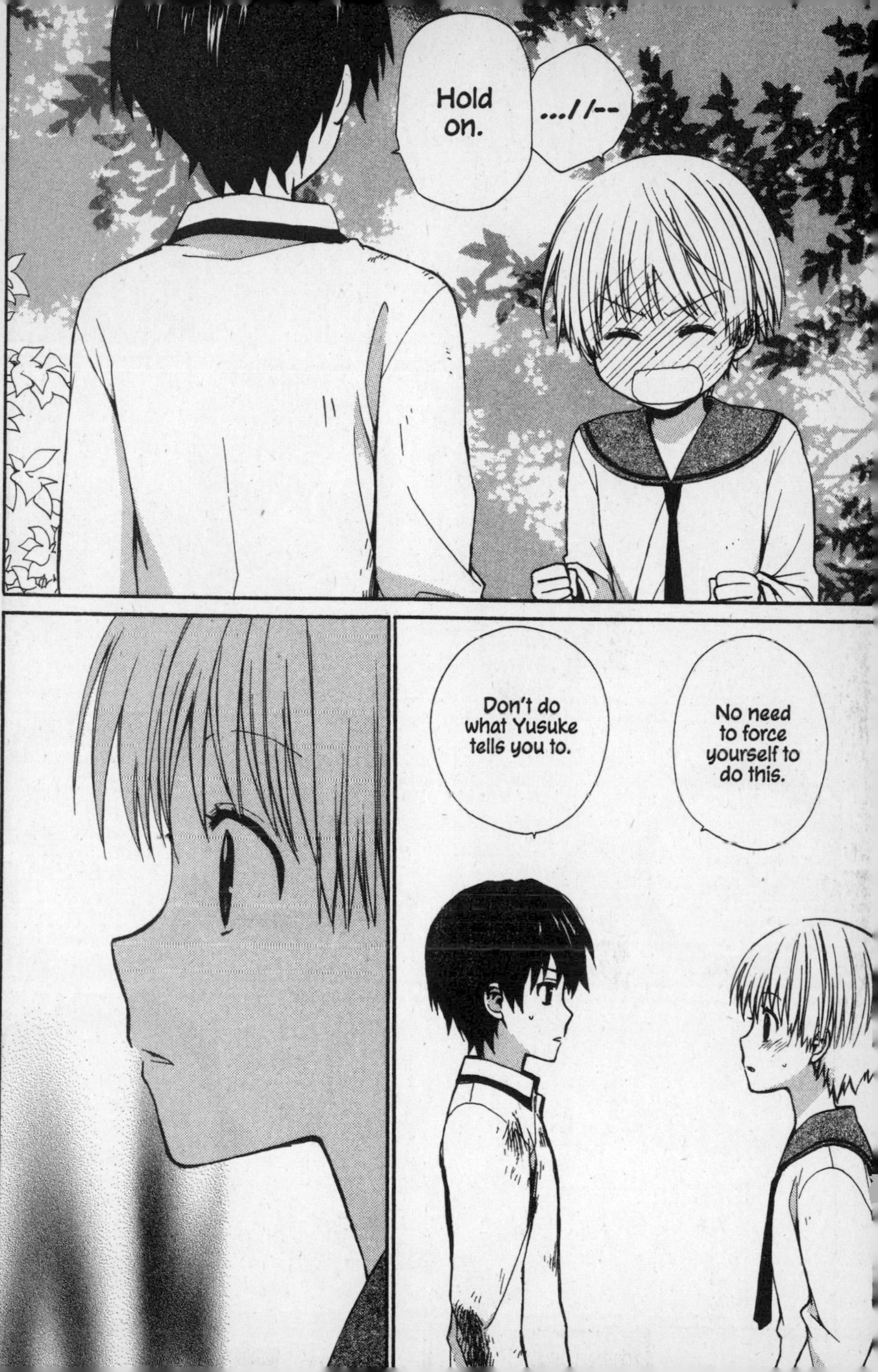
...//--
Hold on.
No need to force yourself to do this.
Don't do what Yusuke tells you to.

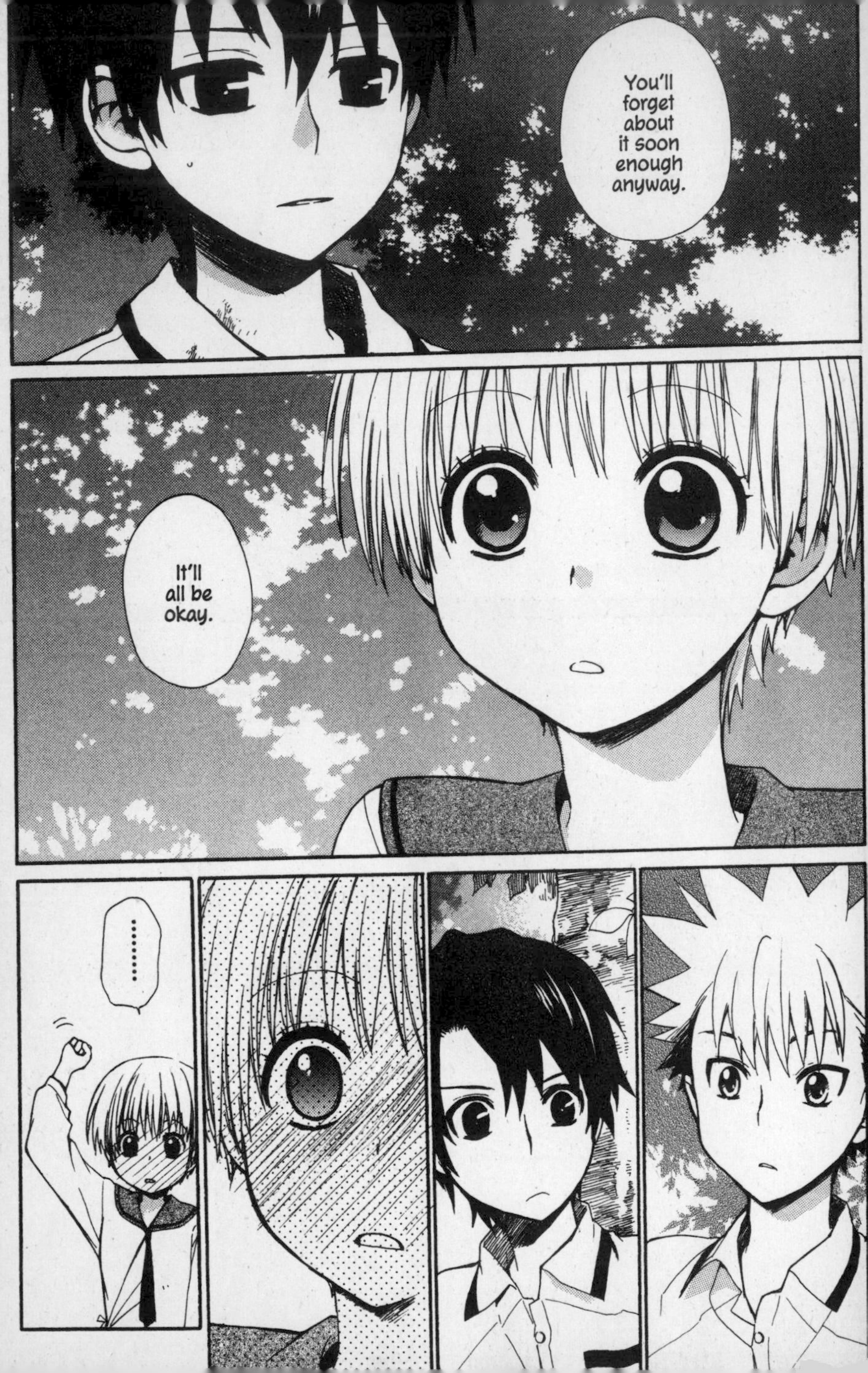
You'll forget about it soon enough anyway.
It'll all be okay.
......

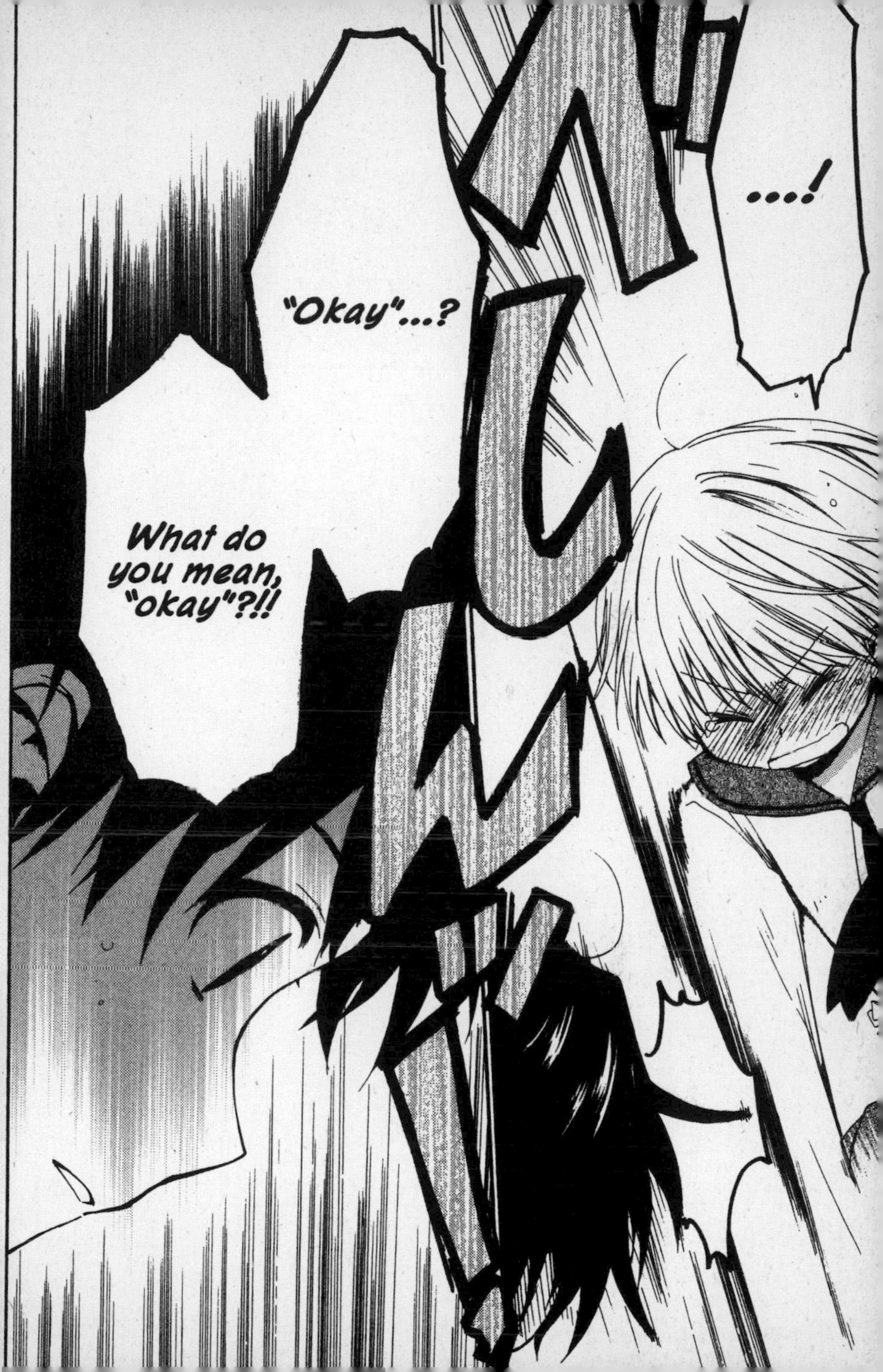
...!
"Okay"...?
What do you mean, "okay"?!!

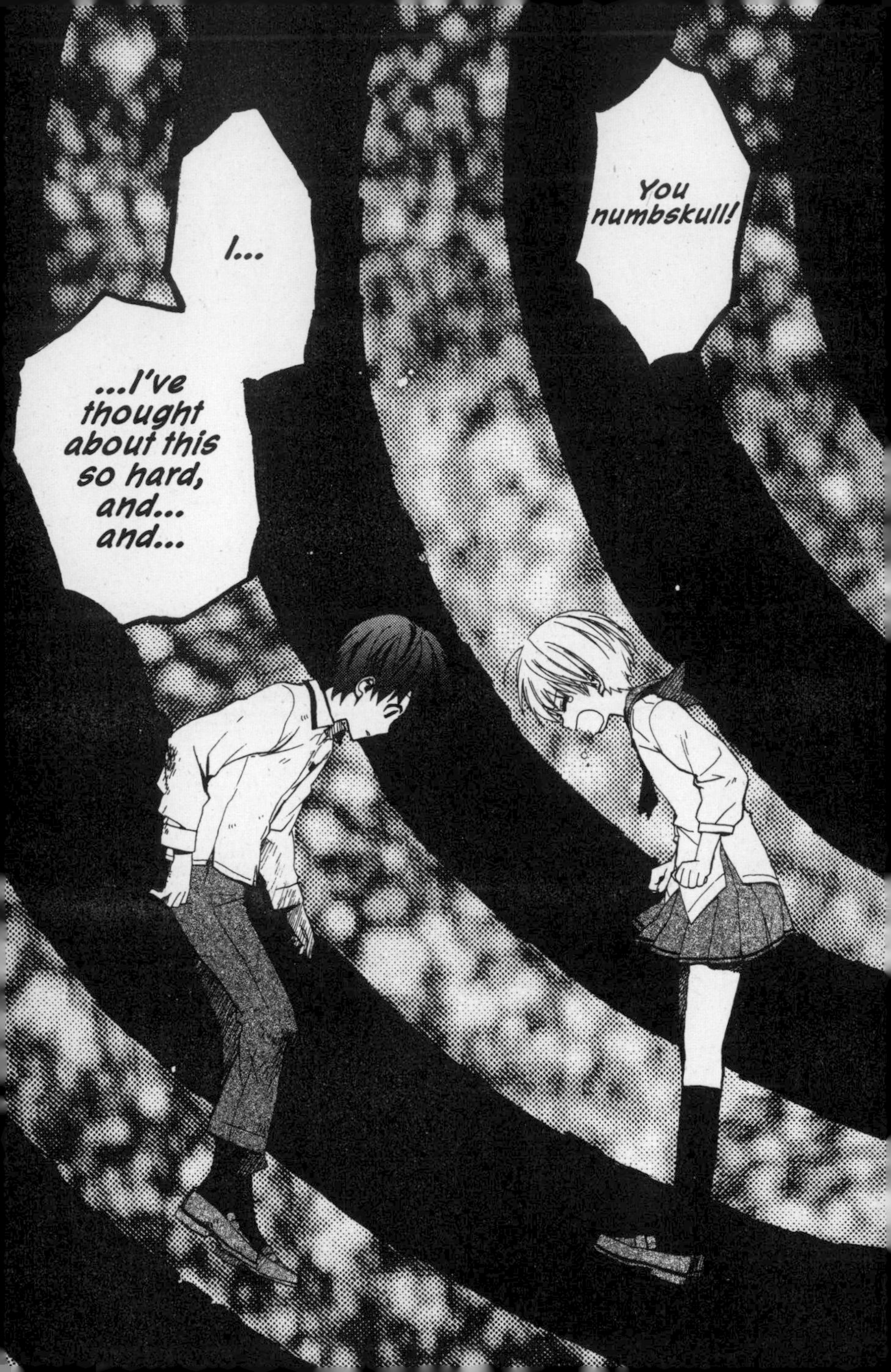
You numbskull!
I...
...I've thought about this so hard, and... and...

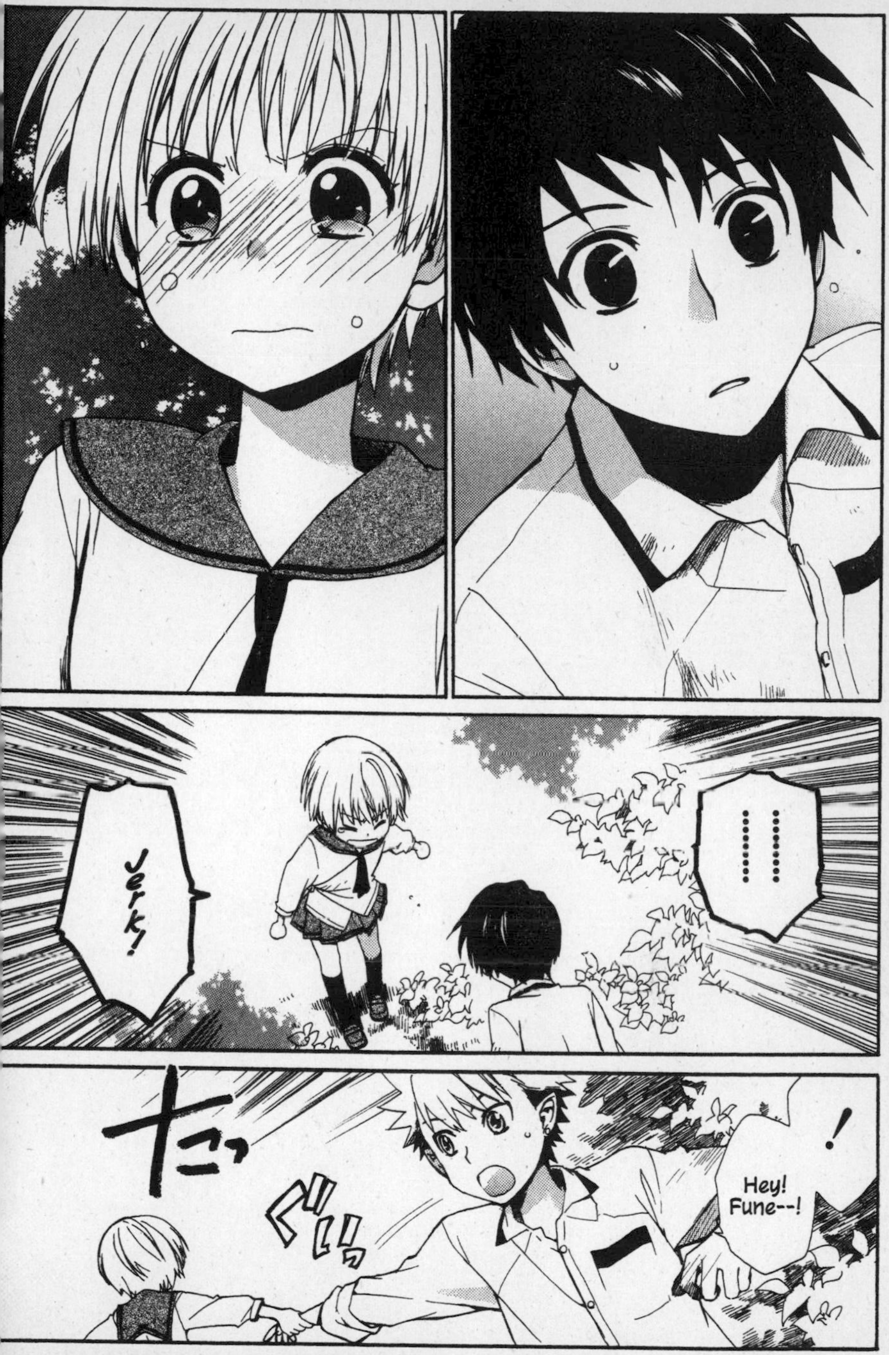
......!!
Jerk!
!
Hey! Fune--!
ぐいっ

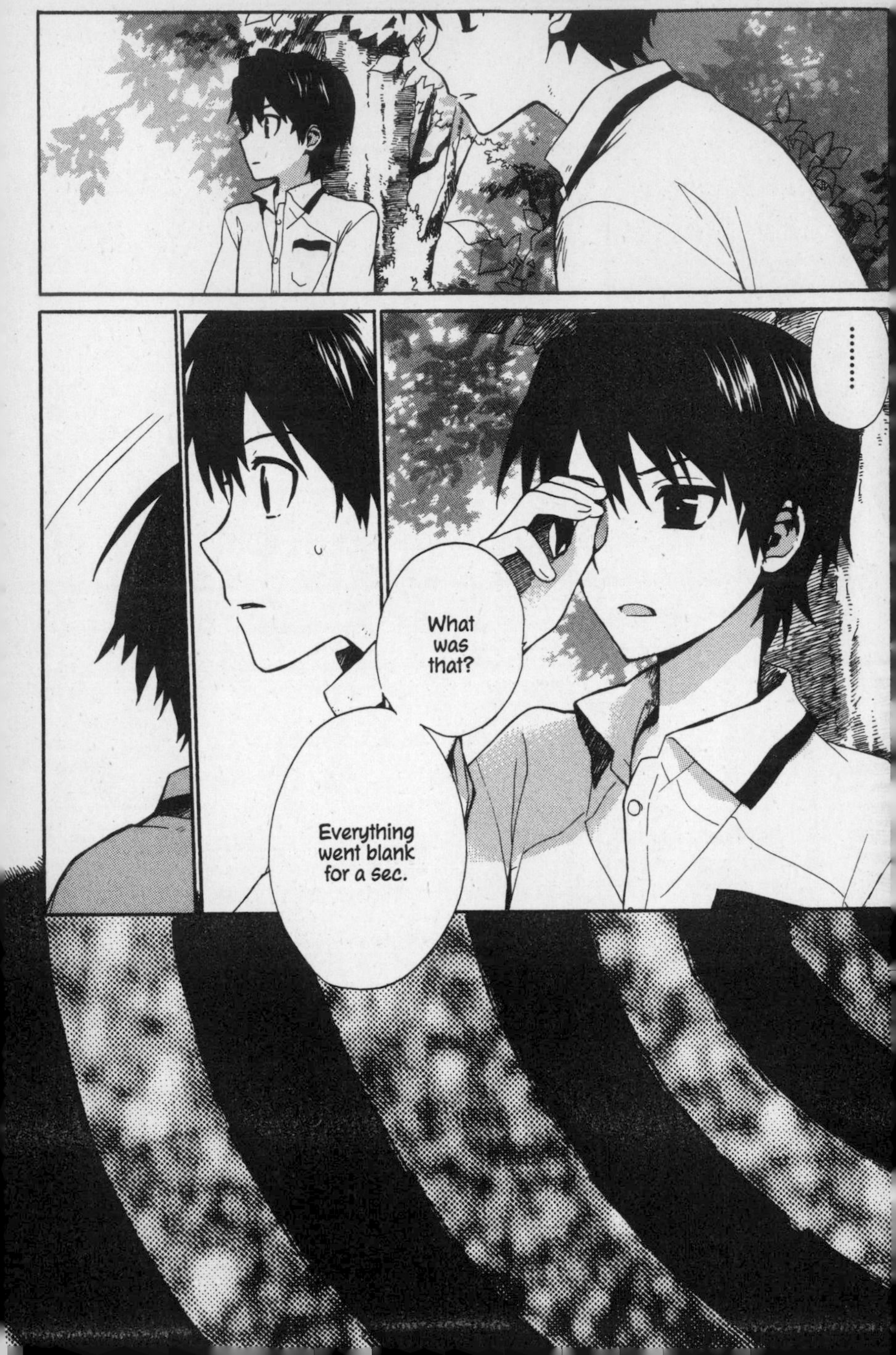
......
What was that?
Everything went blank for a sec.

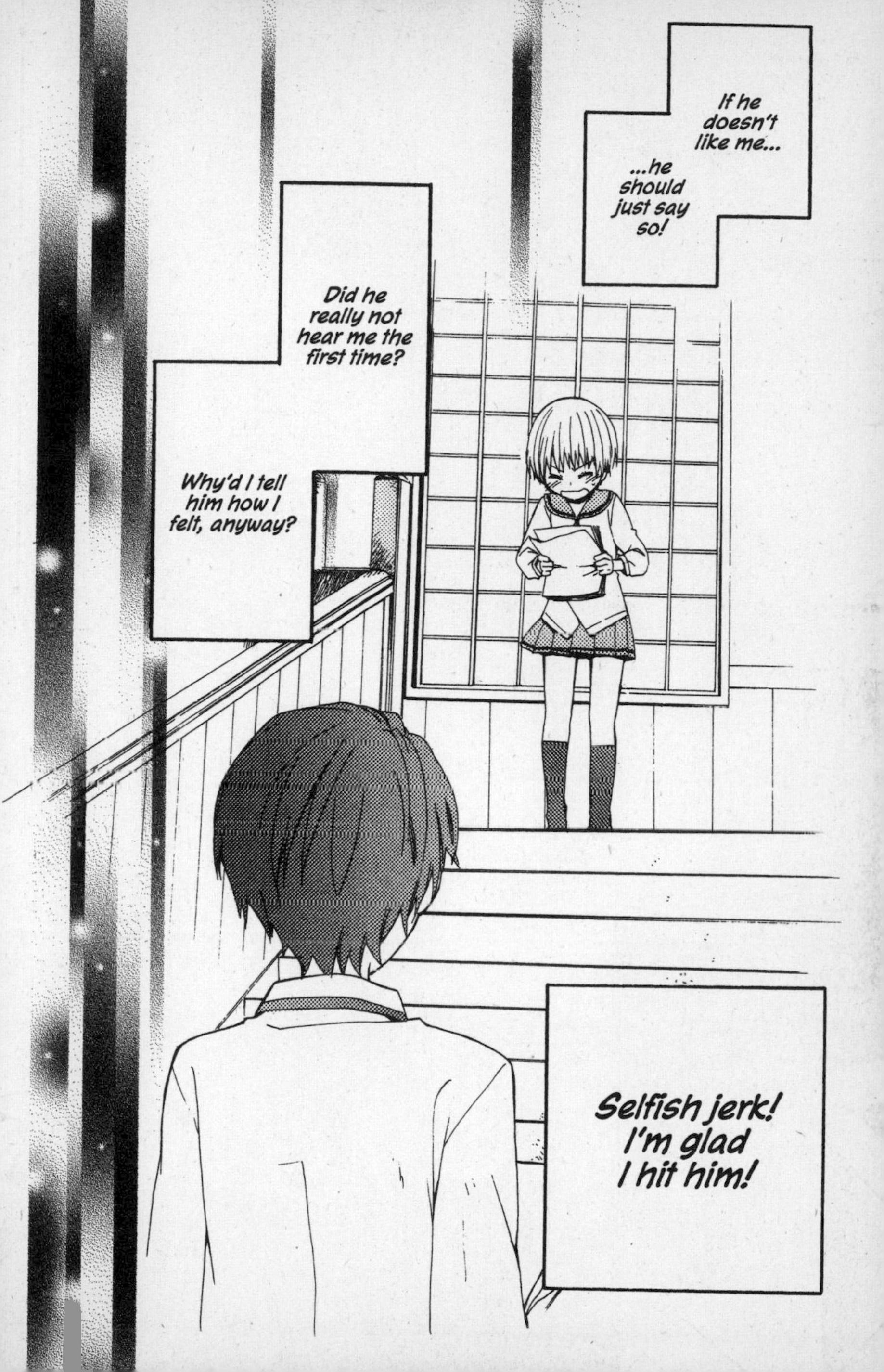
If he doesn't like me...
...he should just say so!
Did he really not hear me the first time?
Why'd I tell him how I felt, anyway?
Selfish jerk! I'm glad I hit him!

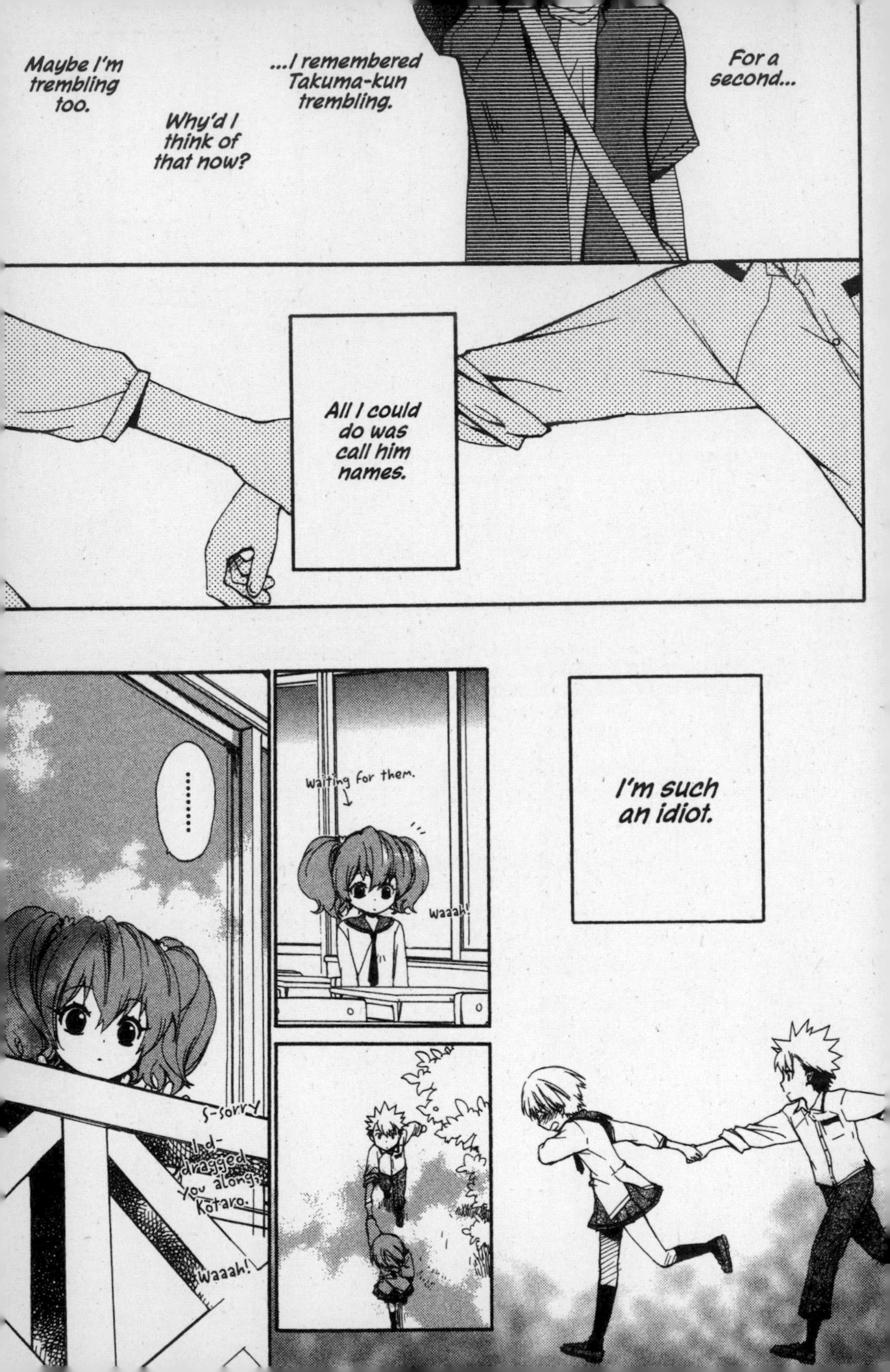
For a second...
...I remembered Takuma-kun trembling.
Why'd I think of that now?
Maybe I'm trembling too.
All I could do was call him names.
I'm such an idiot.
Waiting for them.
Waaah!
......
S-sorry
I-I dragged you along, Kotaro.
Waaah!

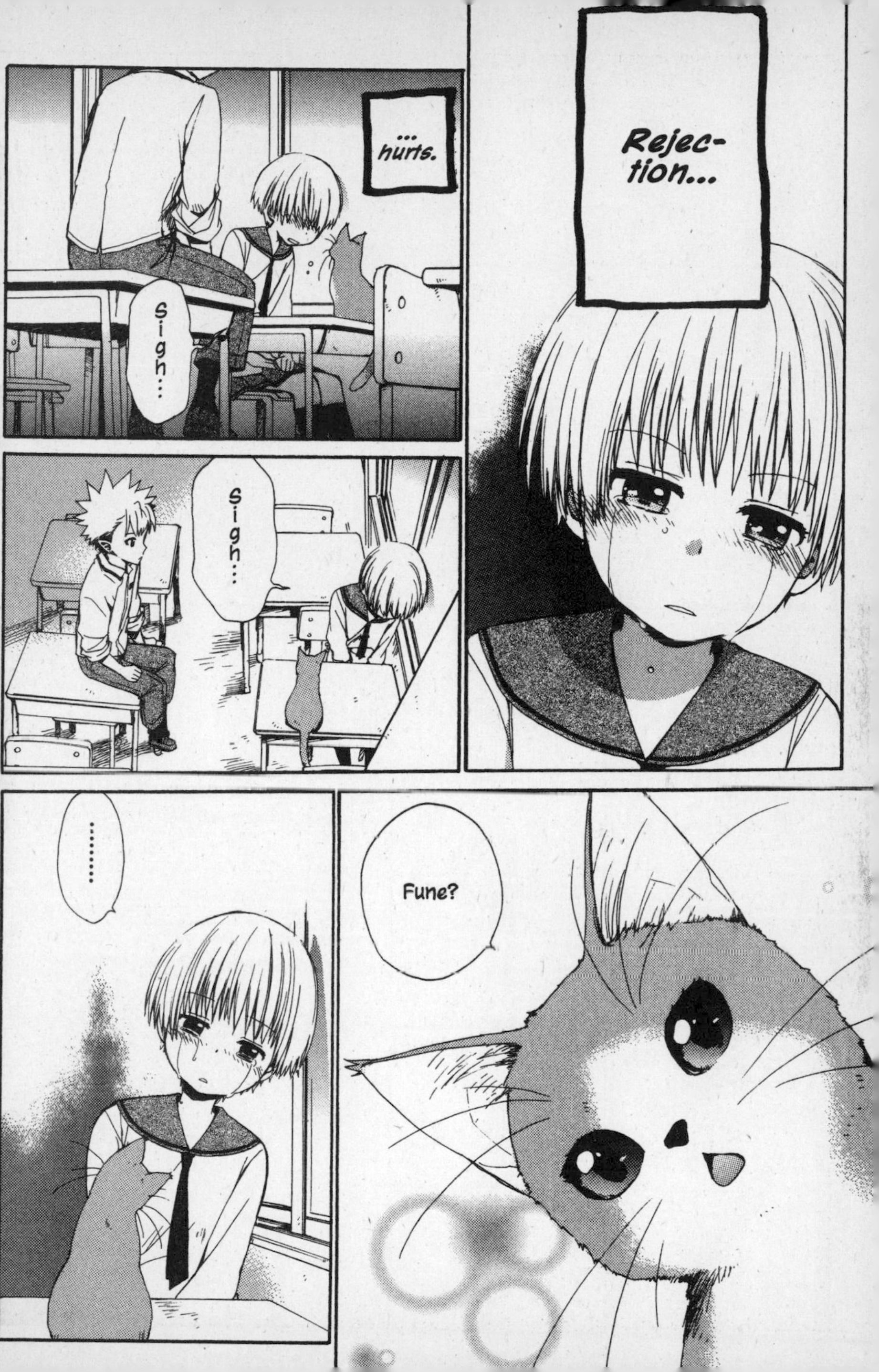
Rejection...
... hurts.
Sigh...
Sigh...
Fune?
....

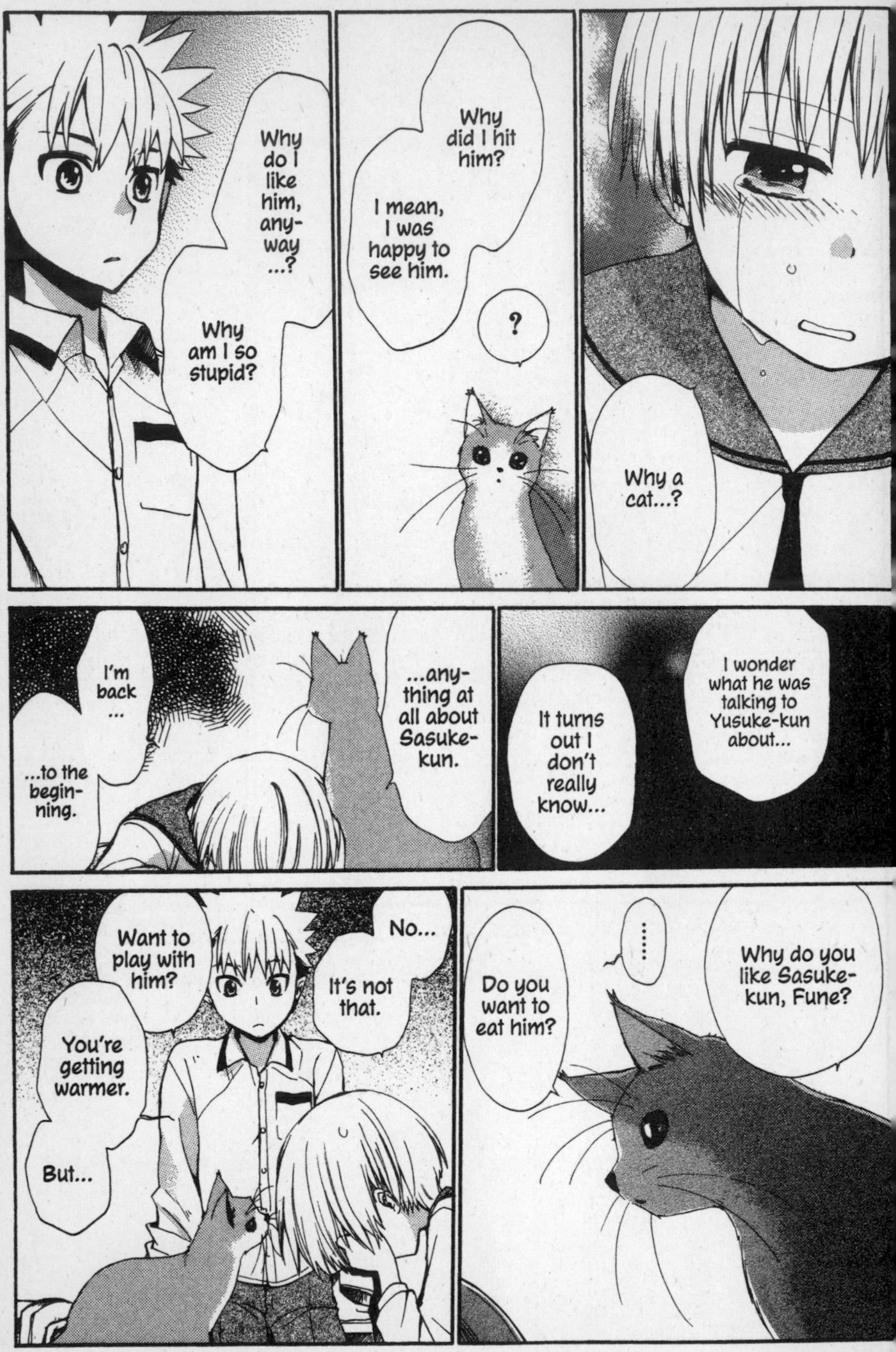
Why a cat...?
Why did I hit him?
I mean, I was happy to see him.
?
Why do I like him, anyway...?
Why am I so stupid?
I wonder what he was talking to Yusuke-kun about...
It turns out I don't really know...
...anything at all about Sasuke-kun.
I'm back...
...to the beginning.
Why do you like Sasuke-kun, Fune?
......
Do you want to eat him?
No...
It's not that.
Want to play with him?
You're getting warmer.
But...

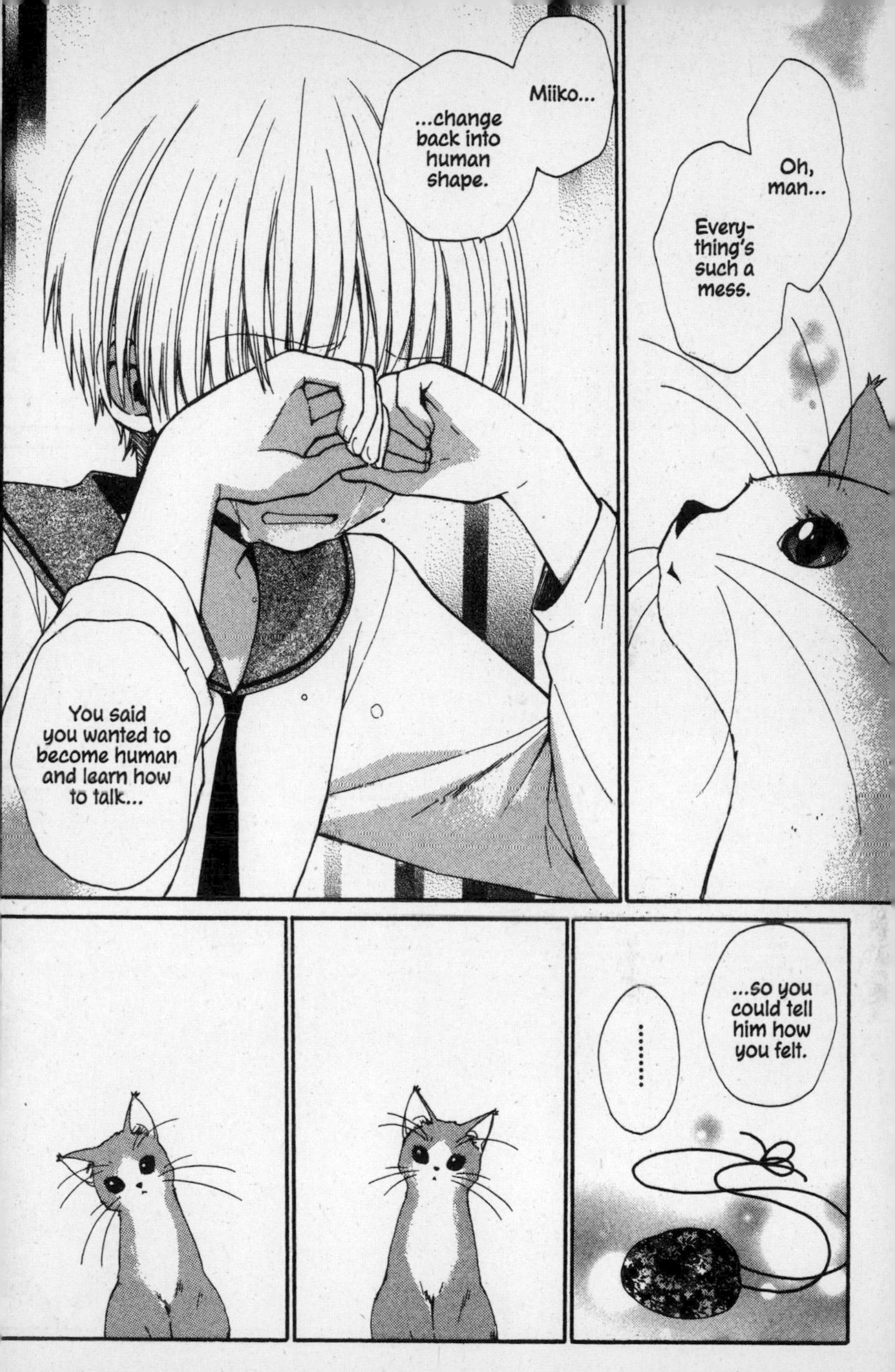
Oh, man...
Every-thing's such a mess.
Miiko...
...change back into human shape.
You said you wanted to become human and learn how to talk...
...so you could tell him how you felt.
......

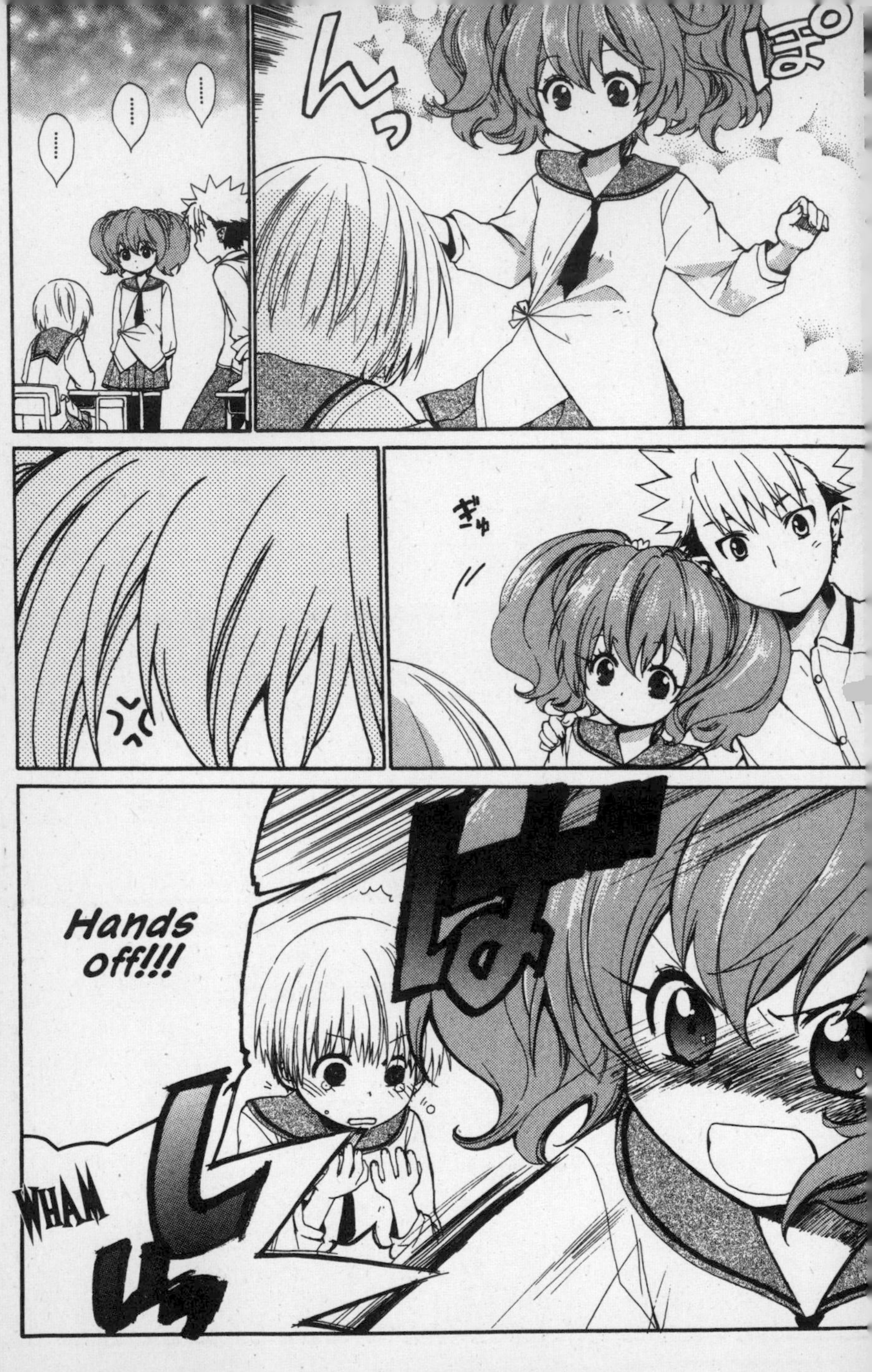

ぽ
んっ
……
……
……
ぎゅ
ば
Hands off!!!
WHAM

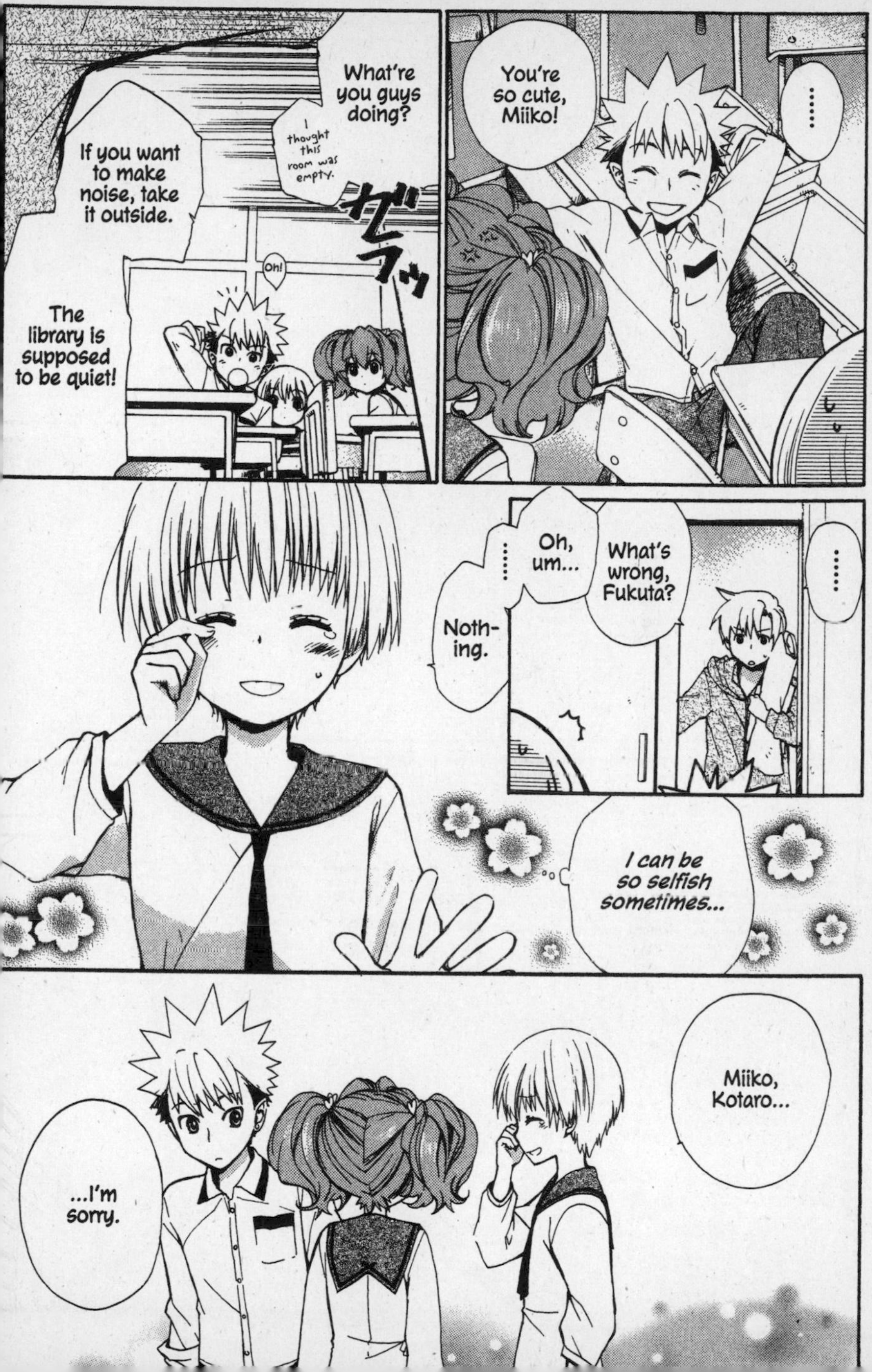
......
You're so cute, Miiko!
What're you guys doing?
I thought this room was empty.
ガラッ
Oh!
If you want to make noise, take it outside.
The library is supposed to be quiet!
......
What's wrong, Fukuta?
Oh, um...
......
Noth-ing.
I can be so selfish sometimes...
Miiko, Kotaro...
...I'm sorry.

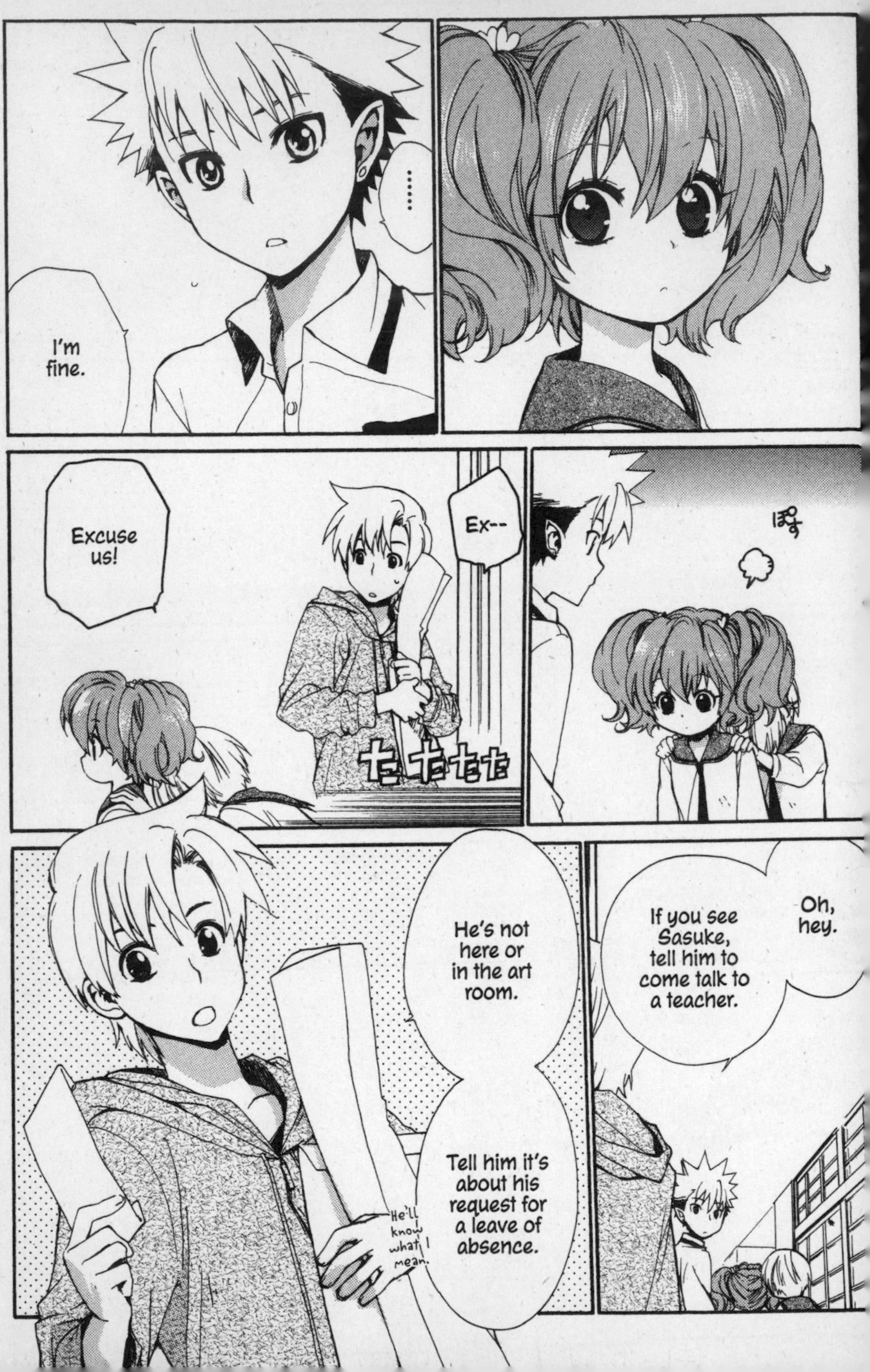
......
I'm fine.
ぽす
Ex--
Excuse us!
たたたた
Oh, hey.
If you see Sasuke, tell him to come talk to a teacher.
He's not here or in the art room.
Tell him it's about his request for a leave of absence.
He'll know what I mean.

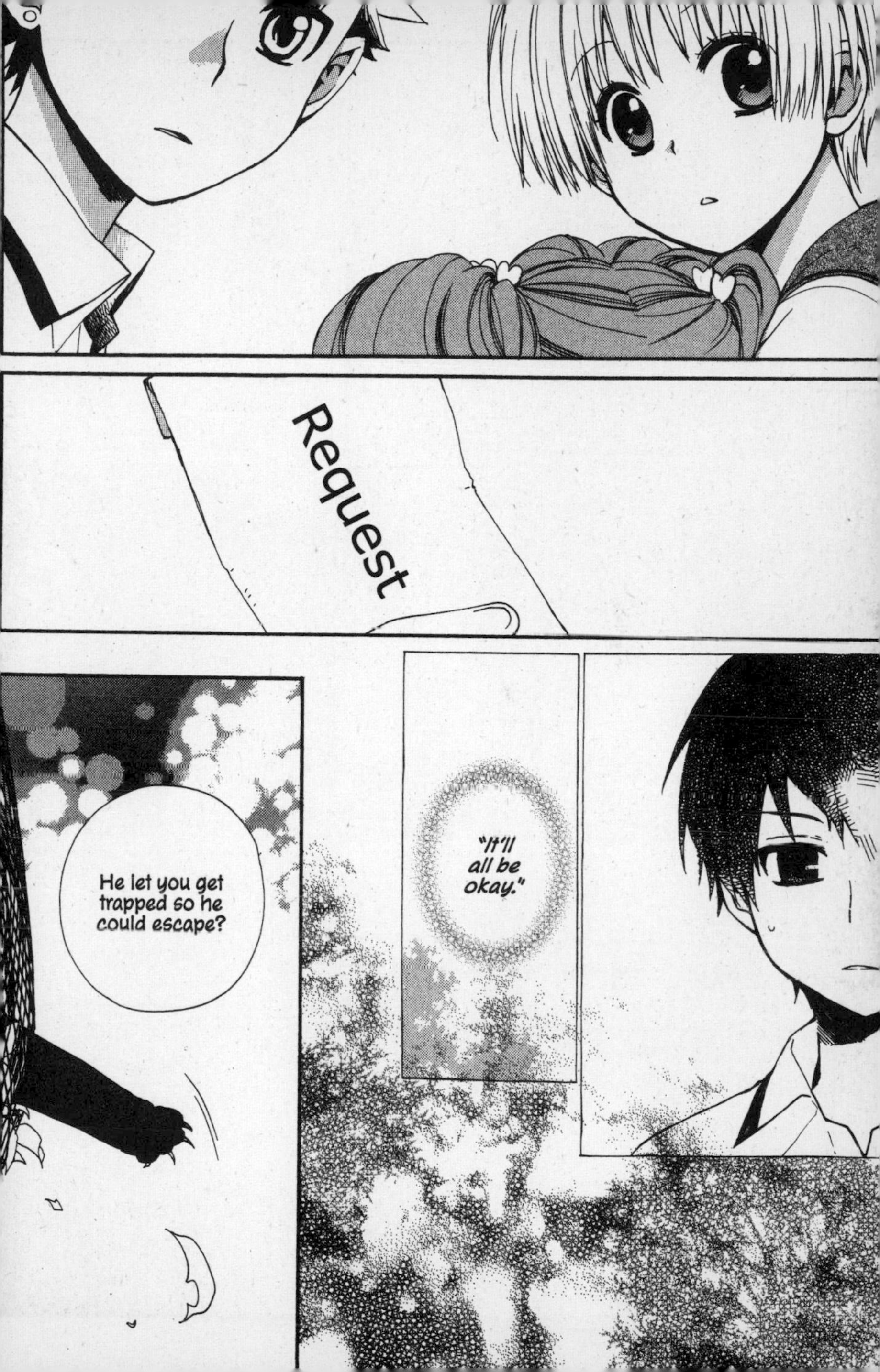
Request
"It'll all be okay."
He let you get trapped so he could escape?

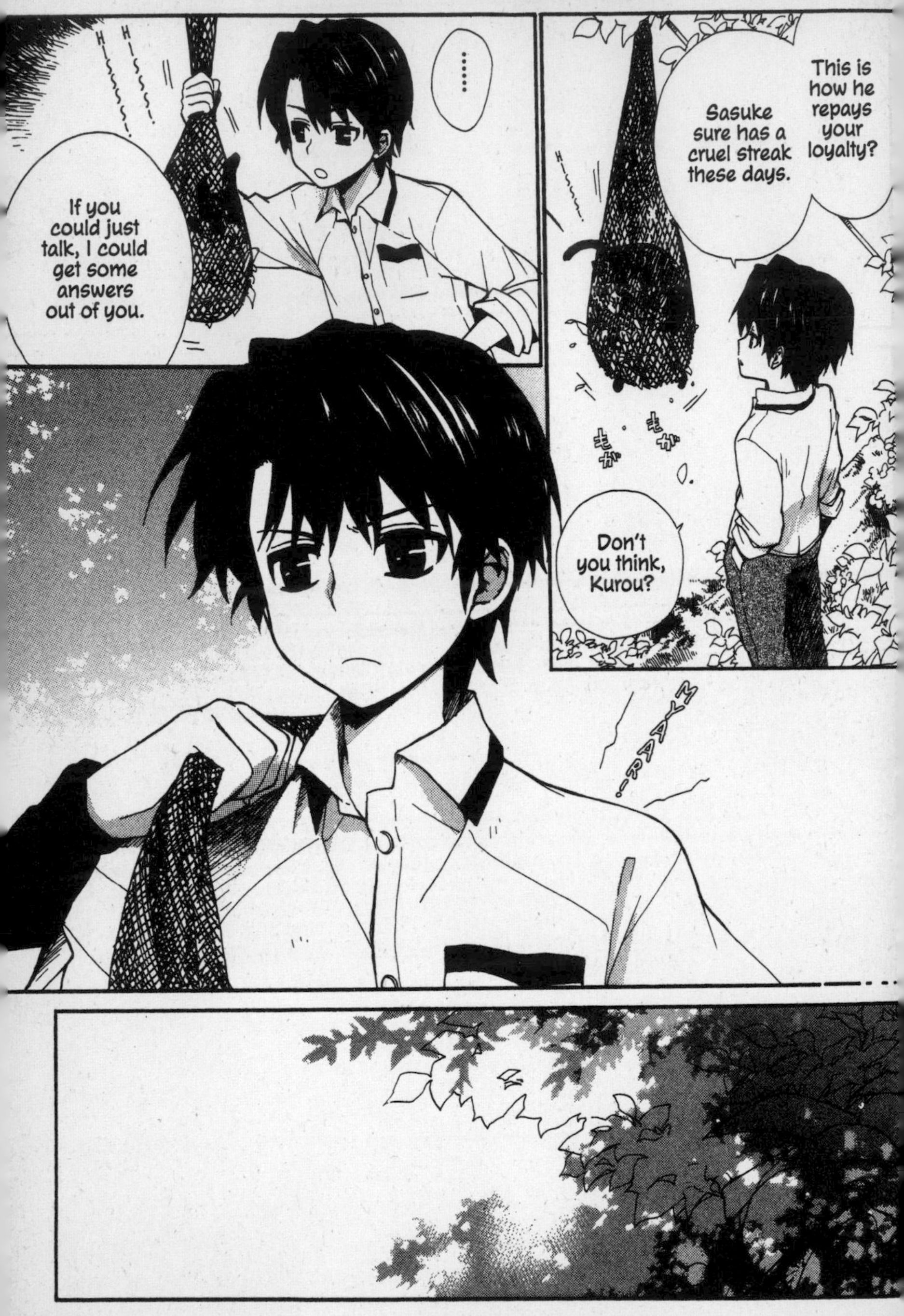

This is how he repays your loyalty?
Sasuke sure has a cruel streak these days.
HISSS.
もが もが
Don't you think, Kurou?
HISSSS!
HISSSSS!
......
If you could just talk, I could get some answers out of you.
MYAAR!

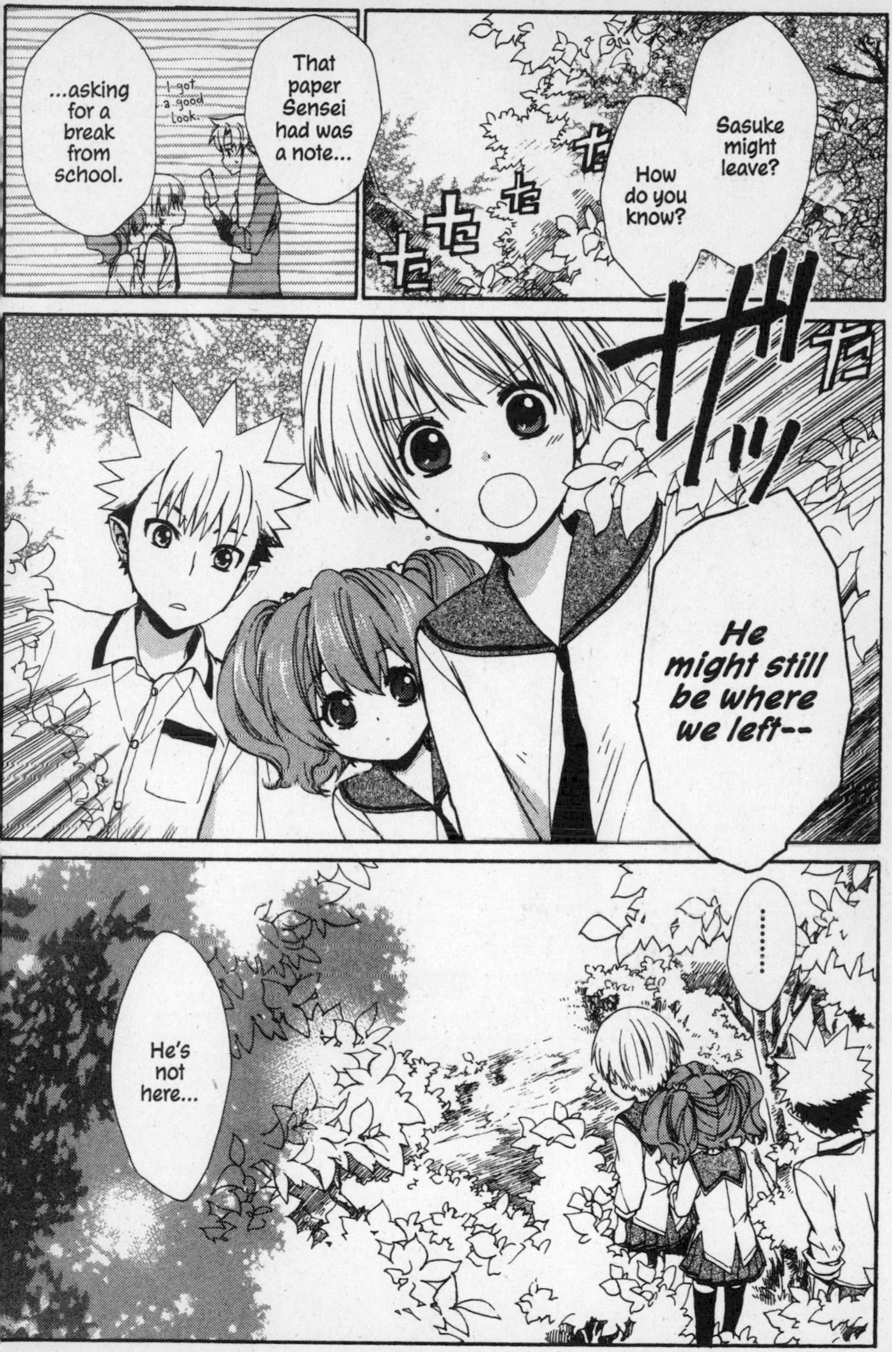
Sasuke might leave?
How do you know?
That paper Sensei had was a note...
I got a good look.
...asking for a break from school.
He might still be where we left--
......
He's not here...

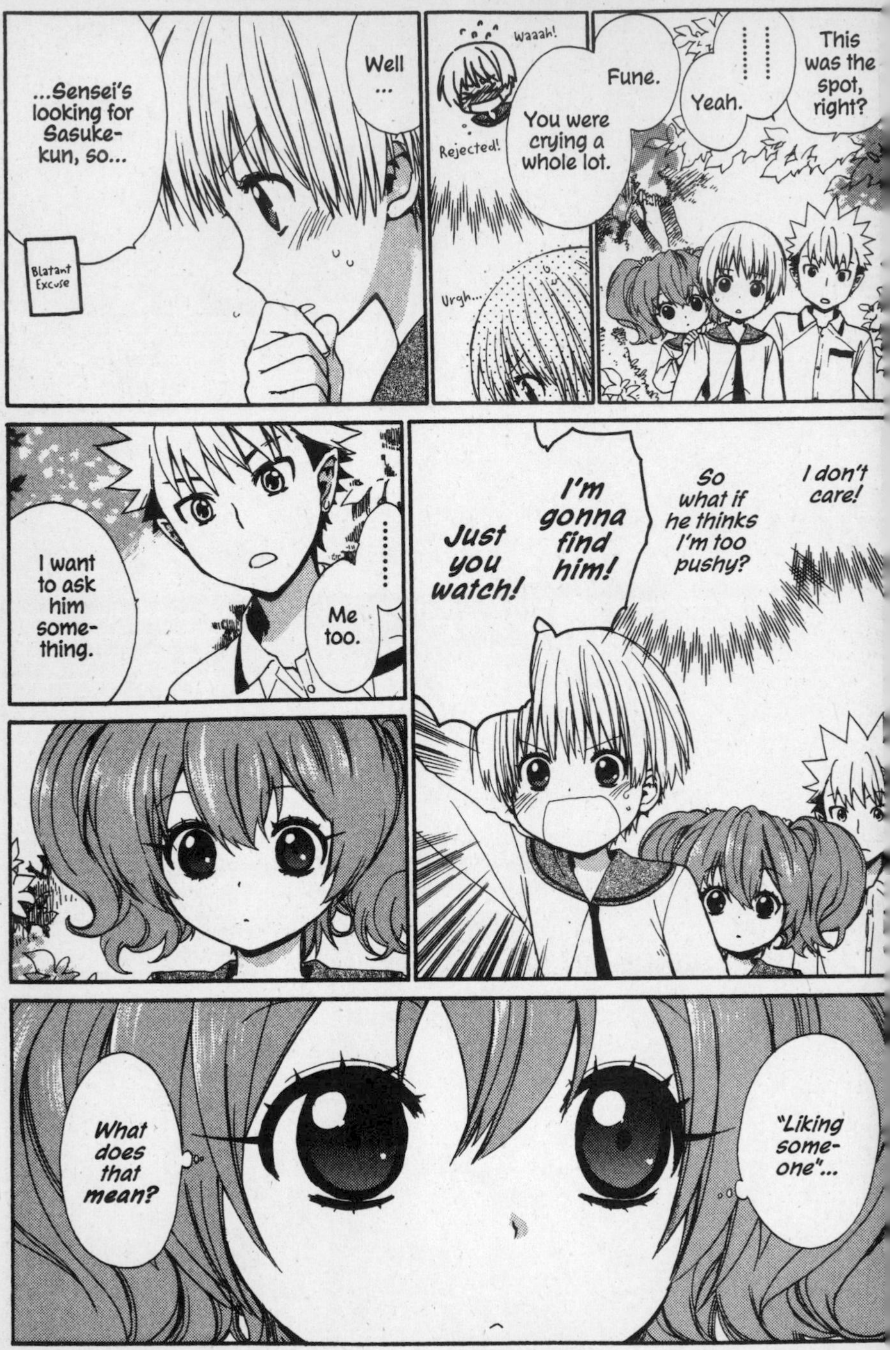
This was the spot, right?
......
Yeah.
Fune.
You were crying a whole lot.
Waaah!
Rejected!
Urgh...
Well ...
...Sensei's looking for Sasuke-kun, so...
Blatant Excuse
I don't care!
So what if he thinks I'm too pushy?
I'm gonna find him!
Just you watch!
......
Me too.
I want to ask him something.
"Liking someone"...
What does that mean?

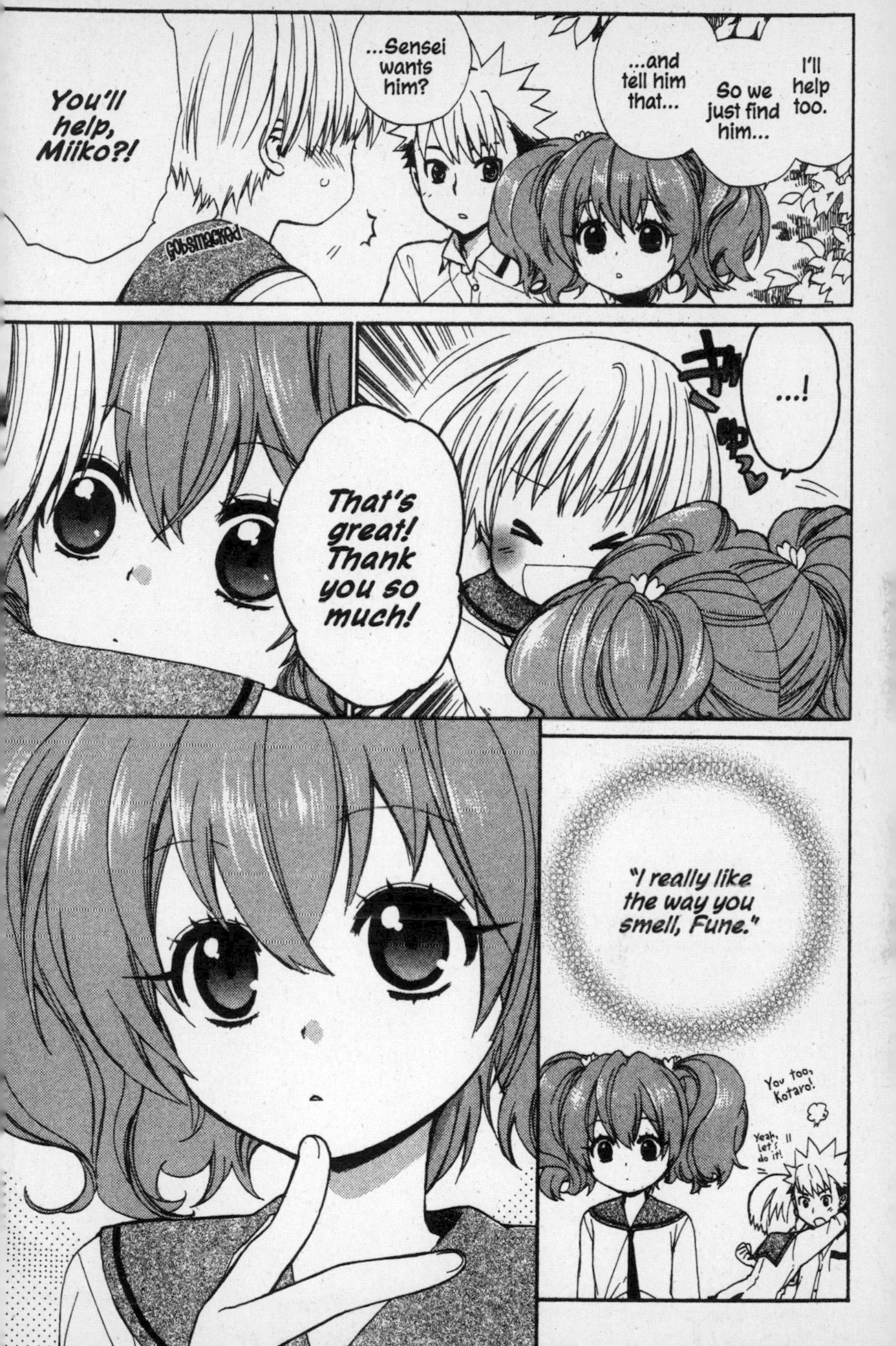
I'll help too.
So we just find him...
...and tell him that...
...Sensei wants him?
You'll help, Miiko?!
GODSMACKED
...!
That's great! Thank you so much!
"I really like the way you smell, Fune."
You too, Kotaro!
Yeah, let's do it!

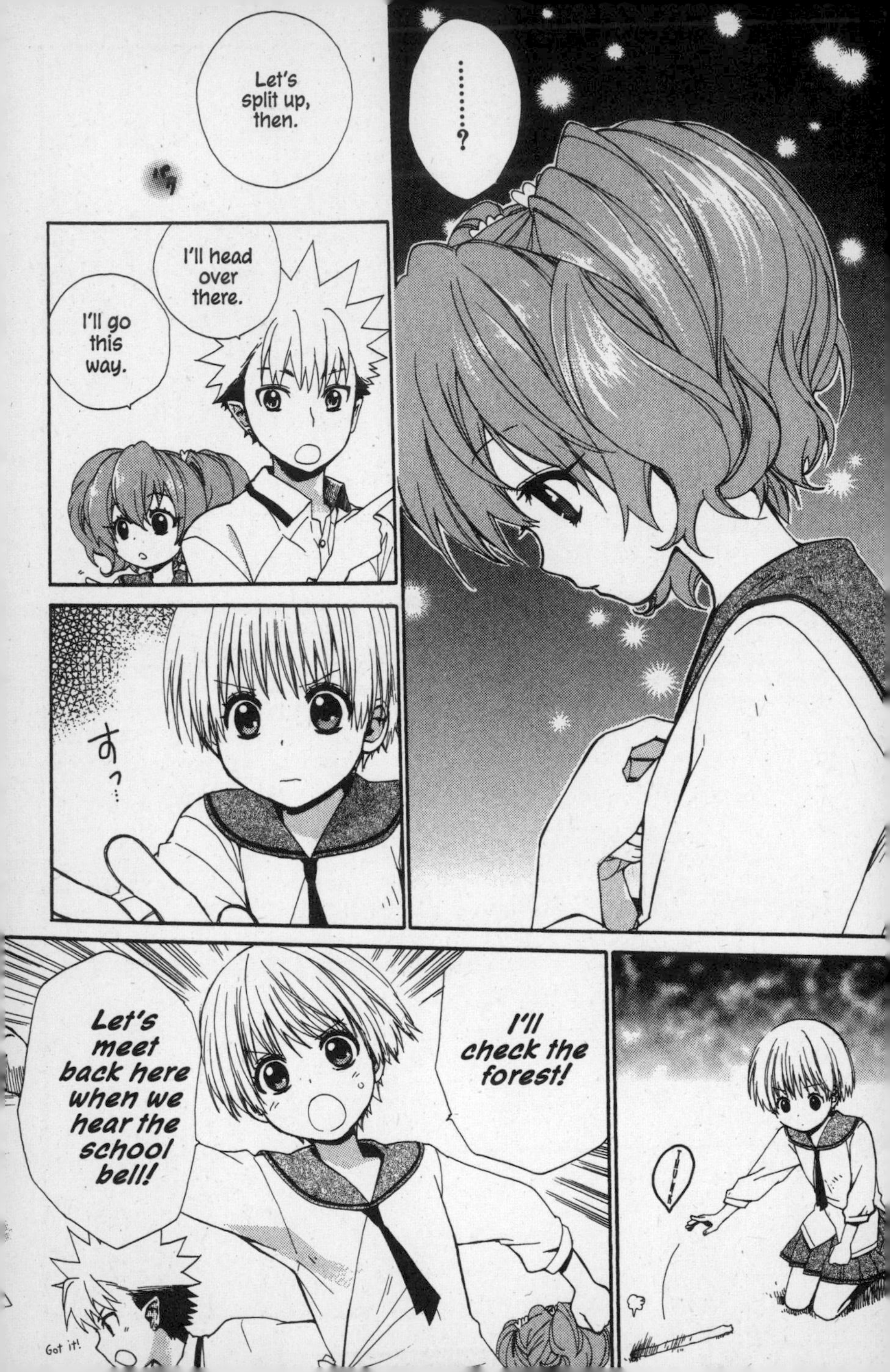

......?
Let's split up, then.
I'll head over there.
I'll go this way.
すっ…
......!
I'll check the forest!
Let's meet back here when we hear the school bell!
Got it!

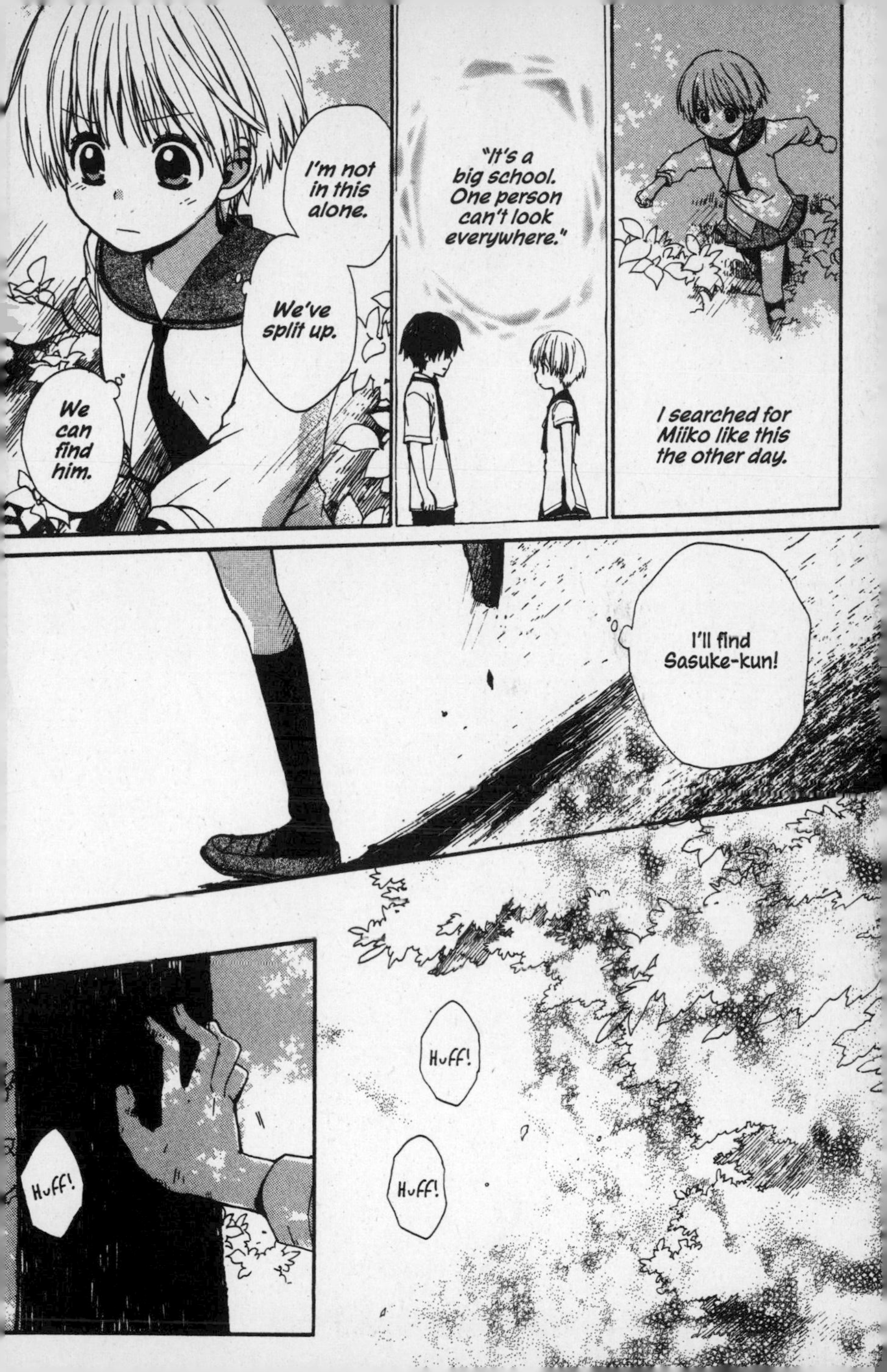
I searched for Miiko like this the other day.
"It's a big school. One person can't look everywhere."
I'm not in this alone.
We've split up.
We can find him.
I'll find Sasuke-kun!
Huff!
Huff!
Huff!

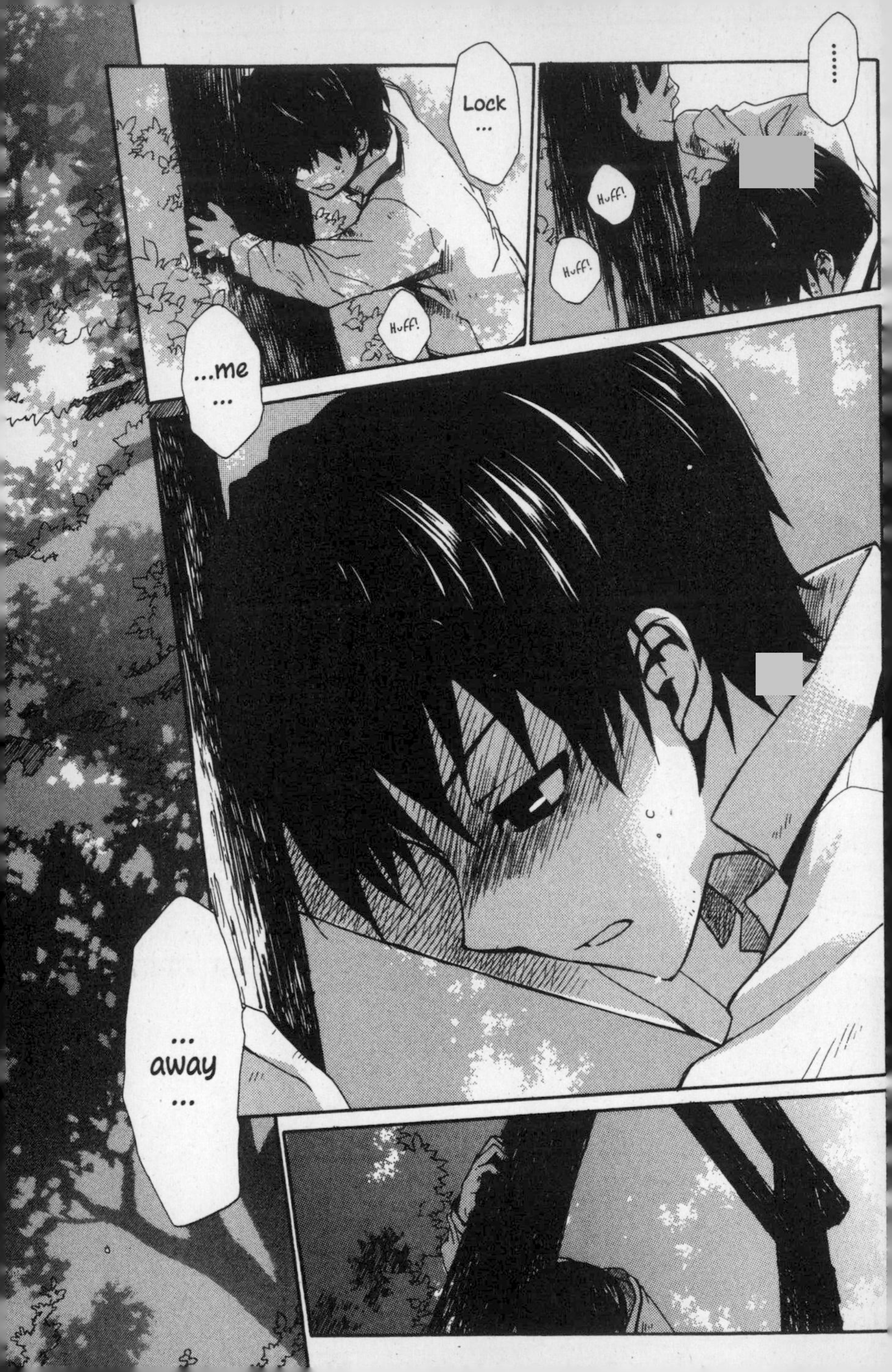
......
Huff!
Huff!
Lock ...
Huff!
...me ...
... away ...

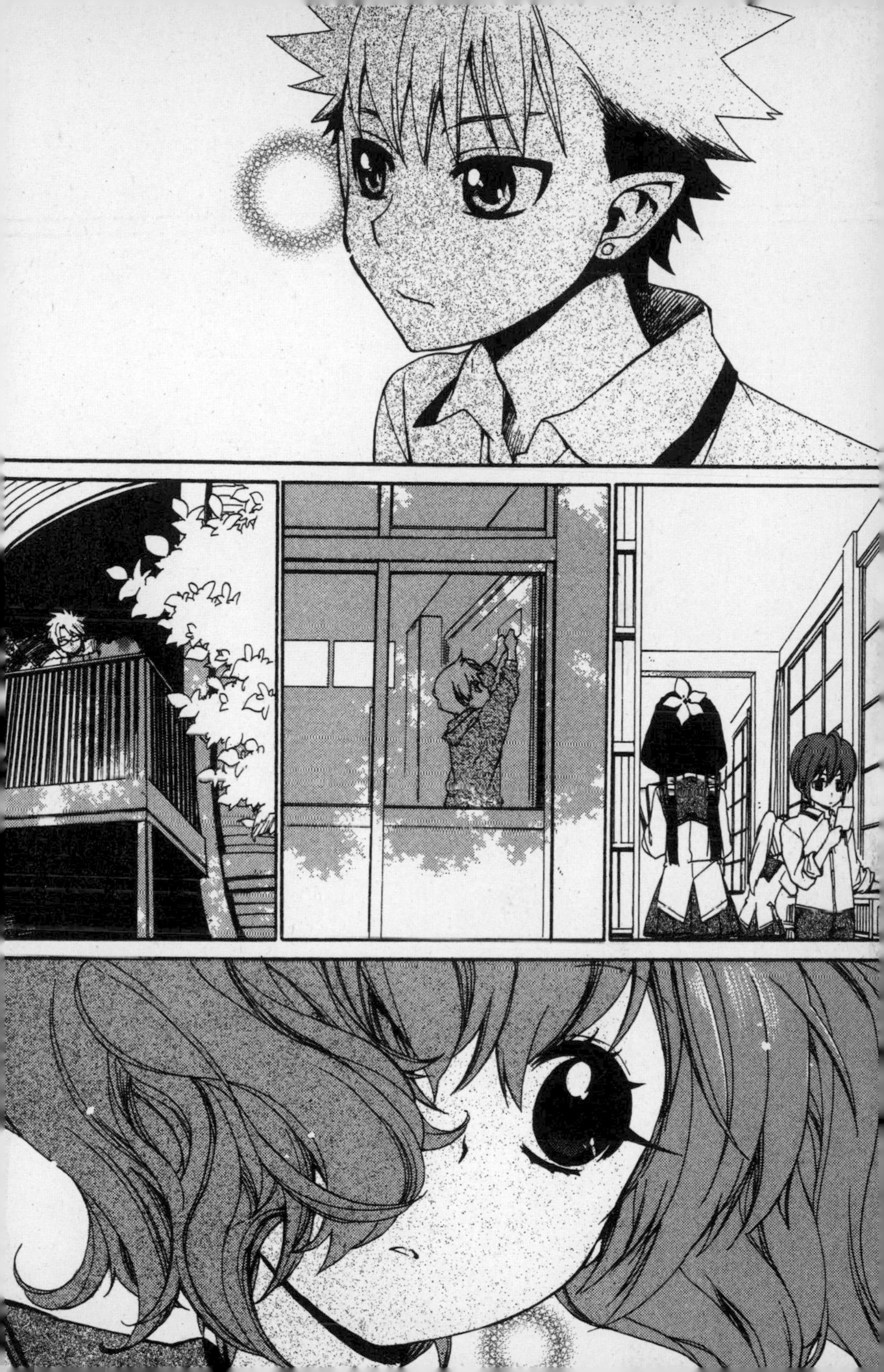

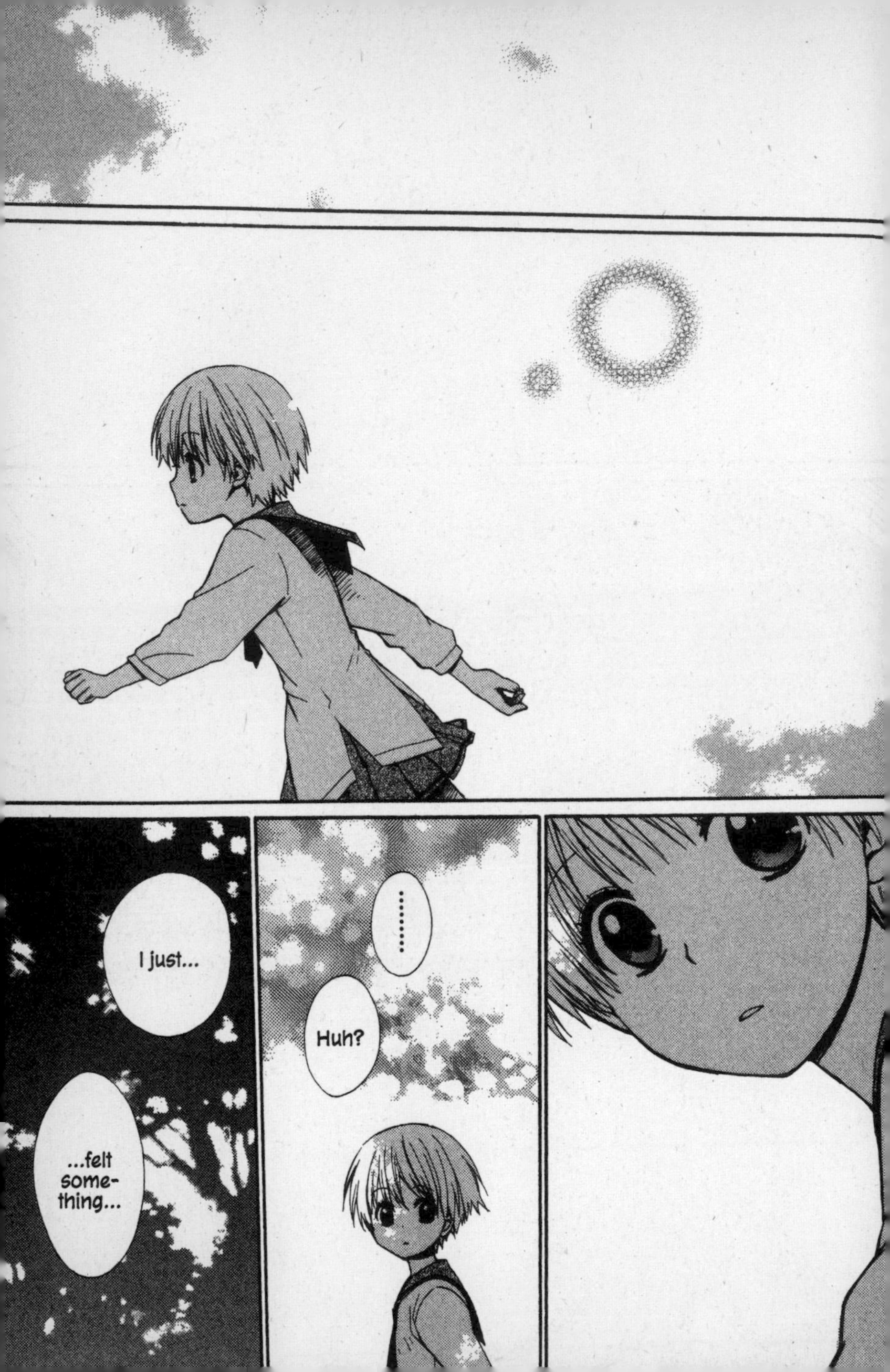
......
Huh?
I just...
...felt something...

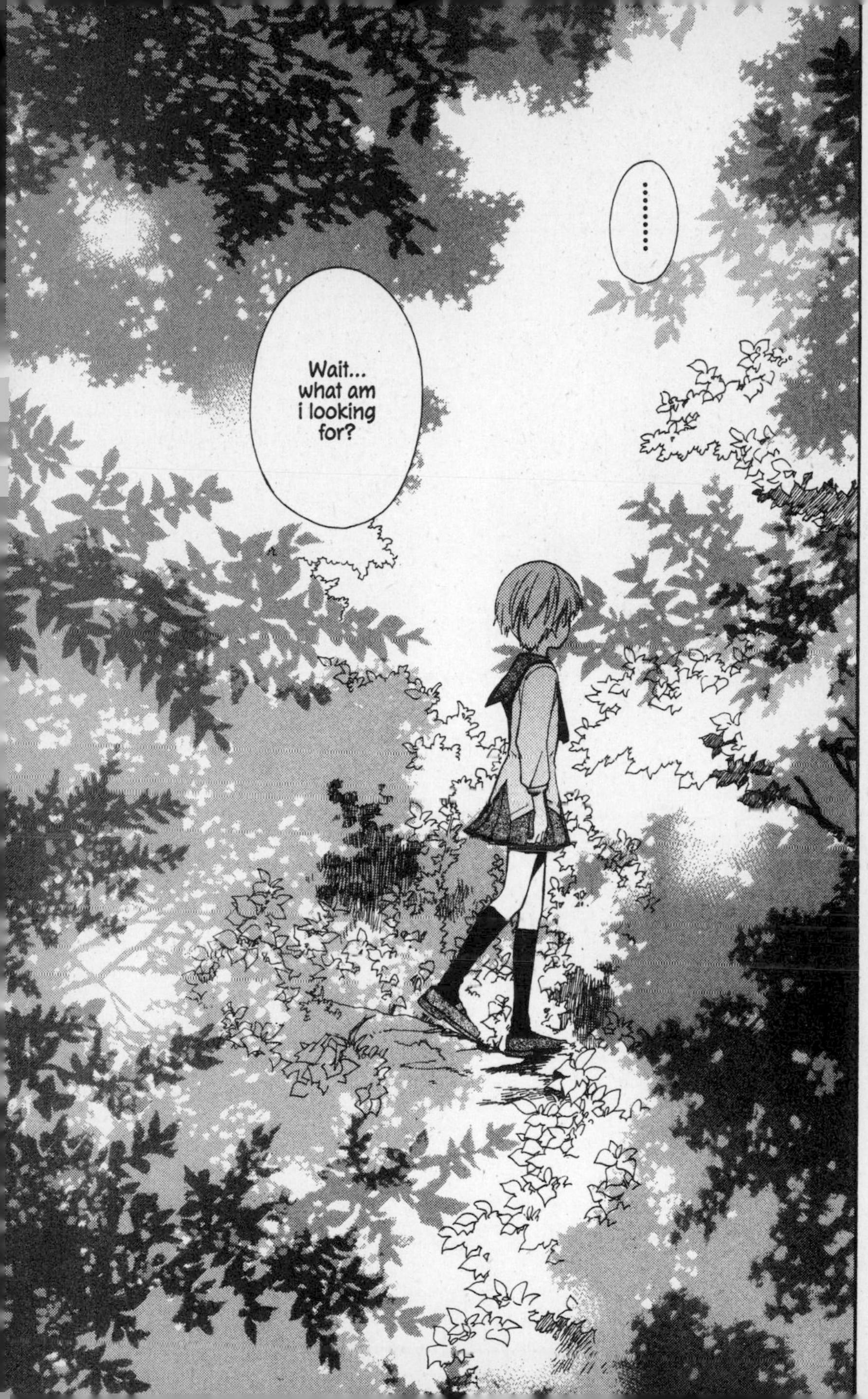
....
Wait... what am i looking for?

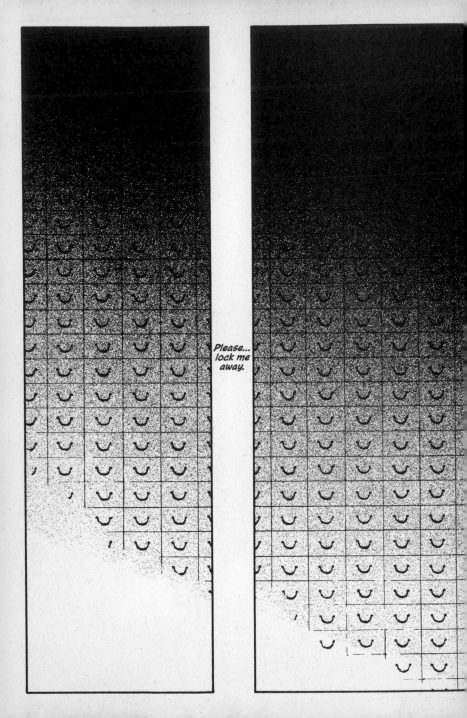

Please... lock me away.

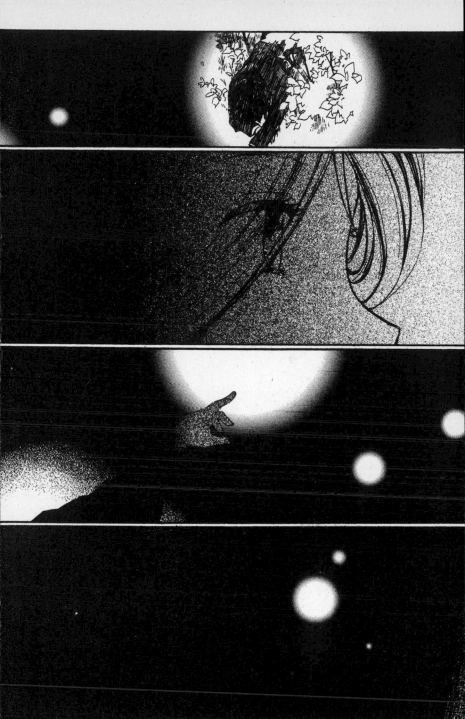

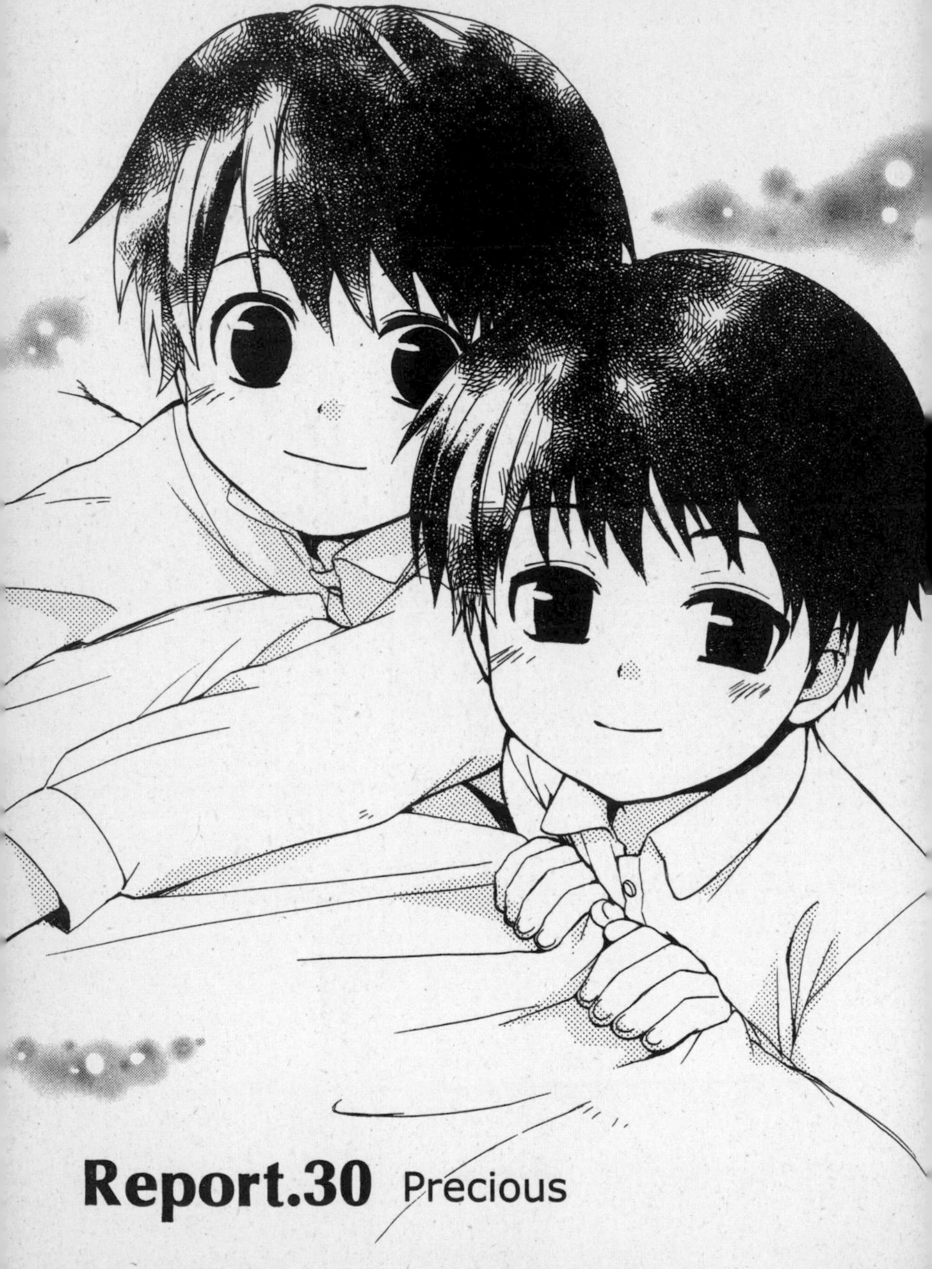

Report.30 Precious

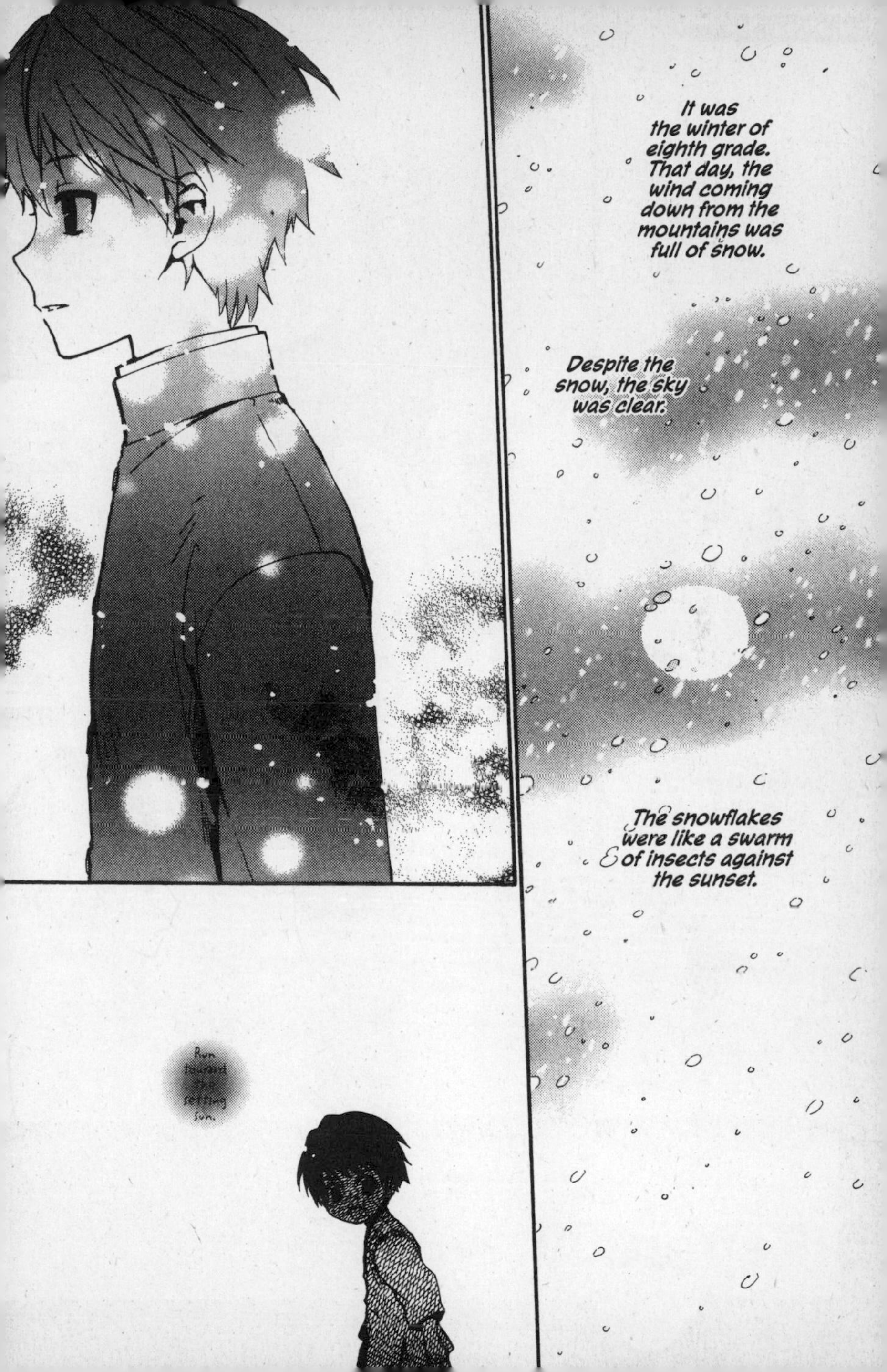
It was the winter of eighth grade. That day, the wind coming down from the mountains was full of snow.
Despite the snow, the sky was clear.
The snowflakes were like a swarm of insects against the sunset.
Run toward the setting sun.

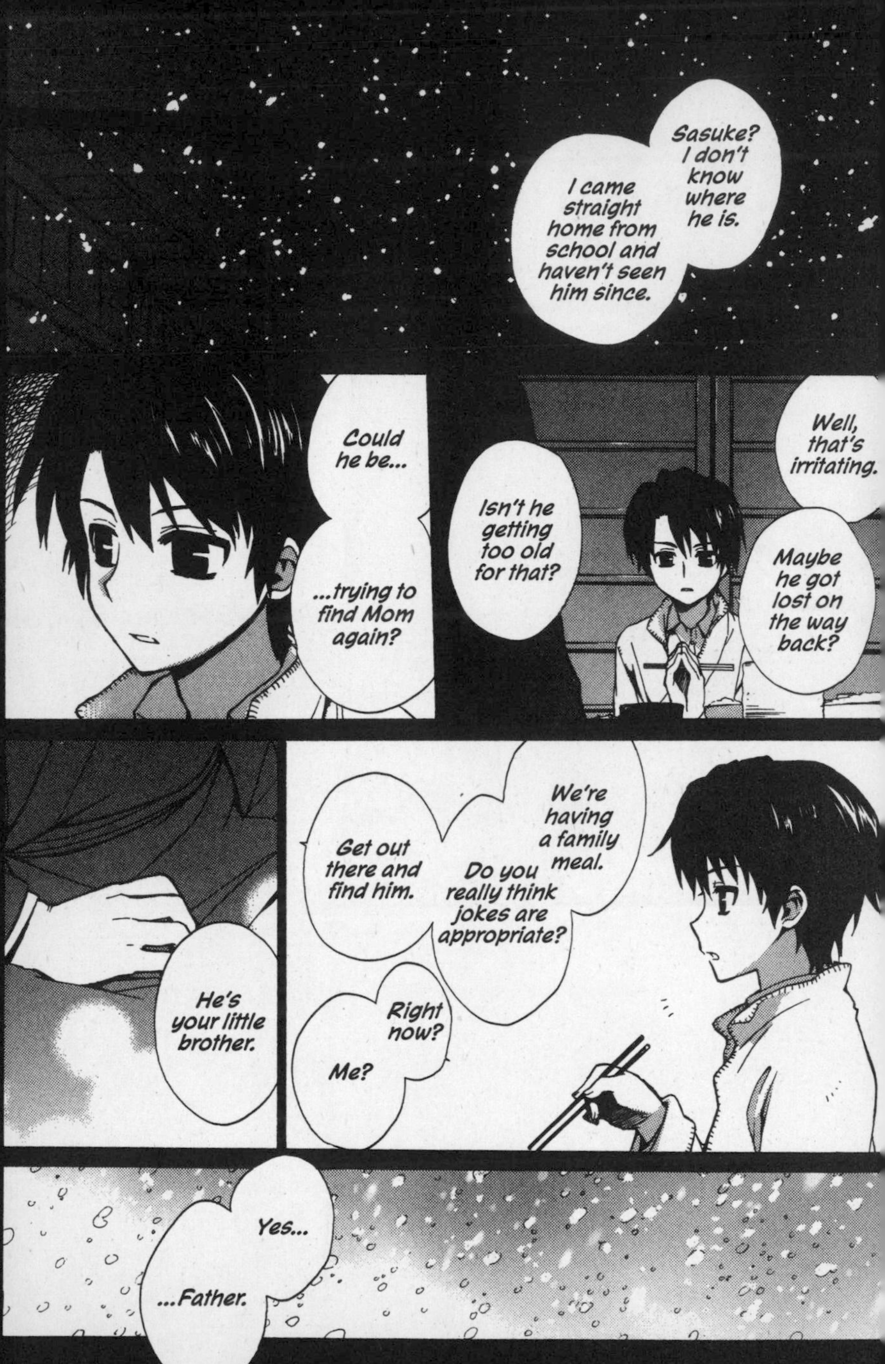
Sasuke? I don't know where he is.
I came straight home from school and haven't seen him since.
Well, that's irritating.
Maybe he got lost on the way back?
Isn't he getting too old for that?
Could he be...
...trying to find Mom again?
We're having a family meal.
Do you really think jokes are appropriate?
Get out there and find him.
Right now?
Me?
He's your little brother.
Yes...
...Father.

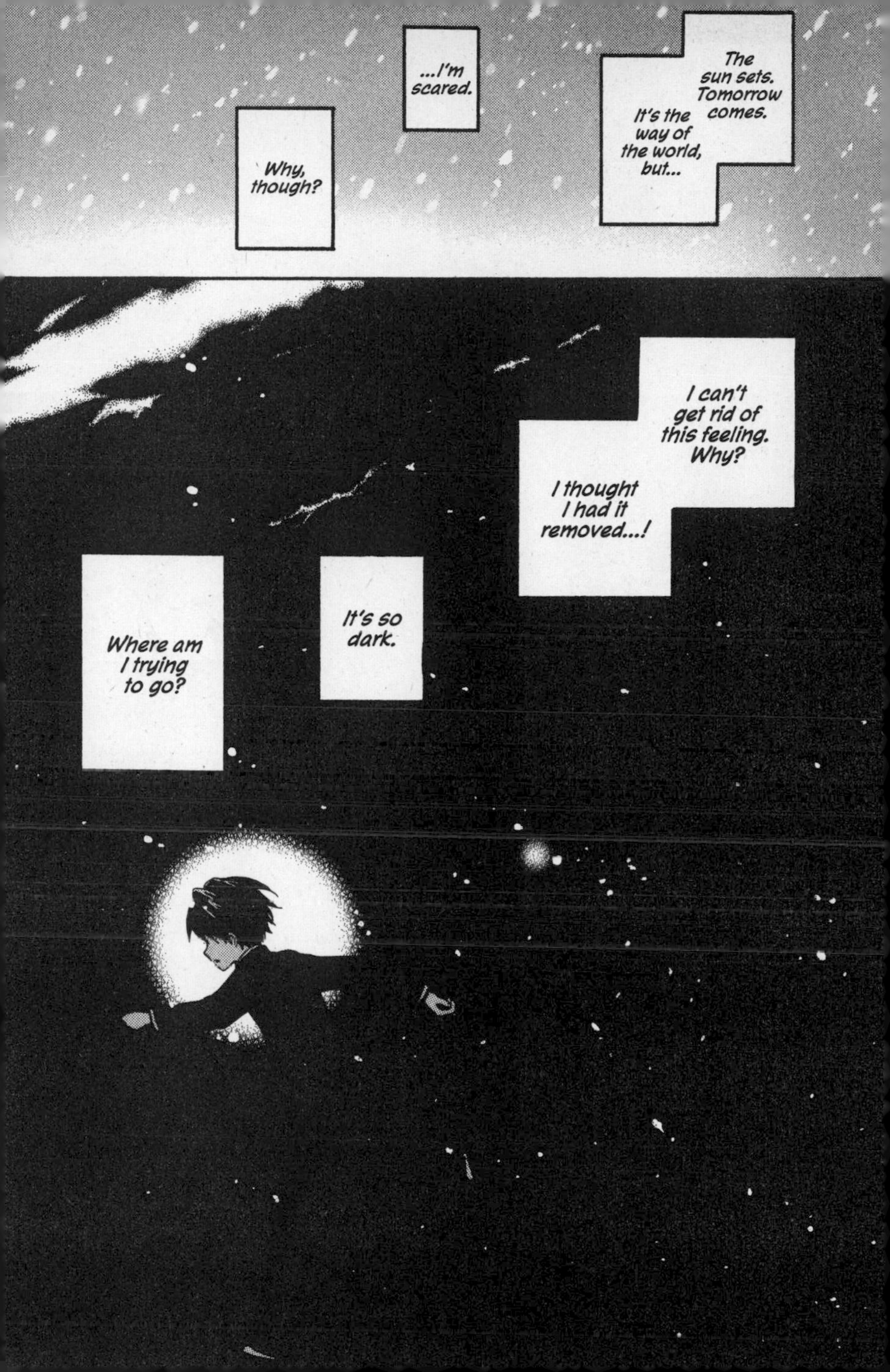
The sun sets. Tomorrow comes.
It's the way of the world, but...
...I'm scared.
Why, though?
I can't get rid of this feeling. Why?
I thought I had it removed...!
It's so dark.
Where am I trying to go?

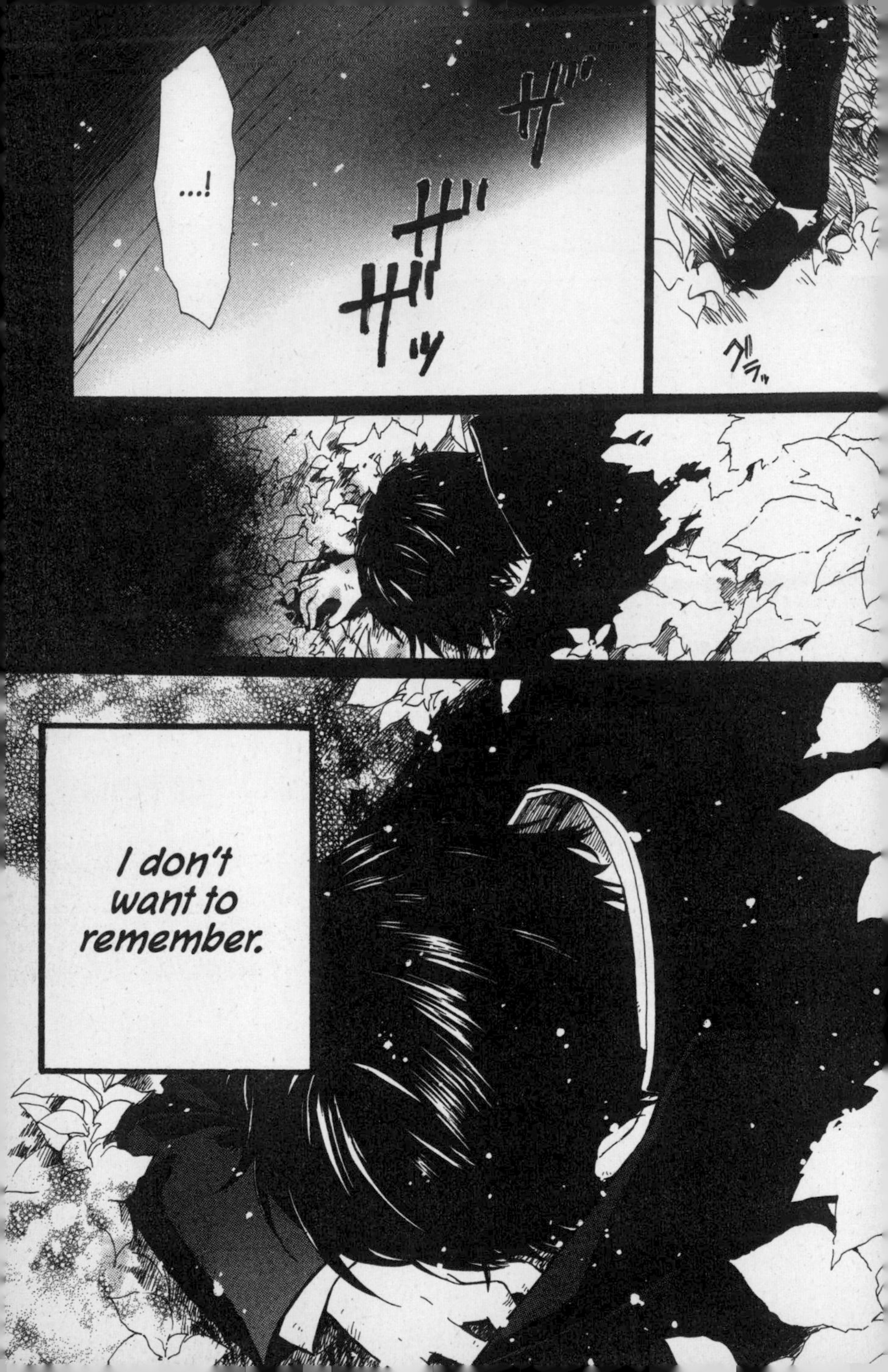
グラッ
...!
I don't want to remember.

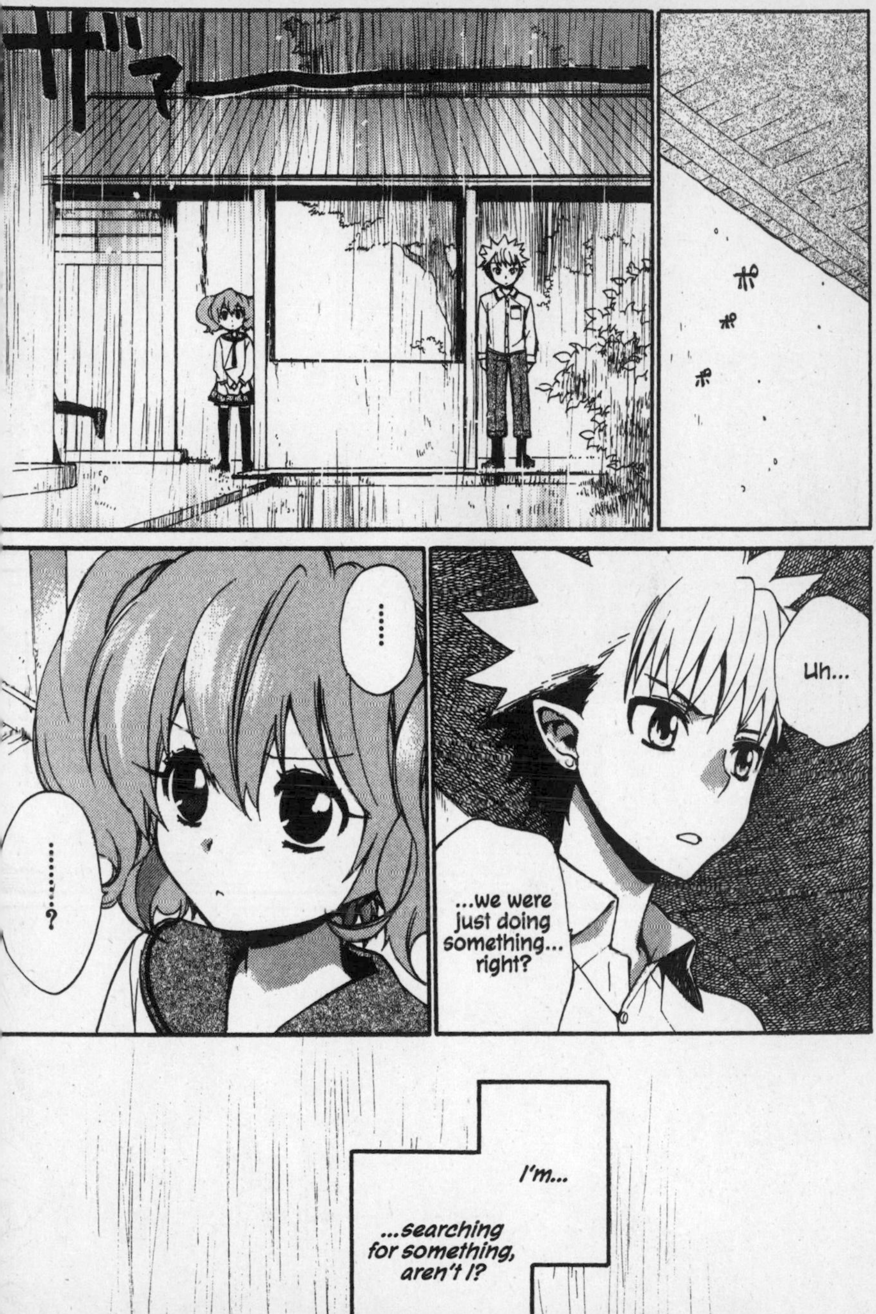
ザァーー
ポ
ポ
ポ
Uh...
...we were just doing something... right?
......
......?
I'm...
...searching for something, aren't I?

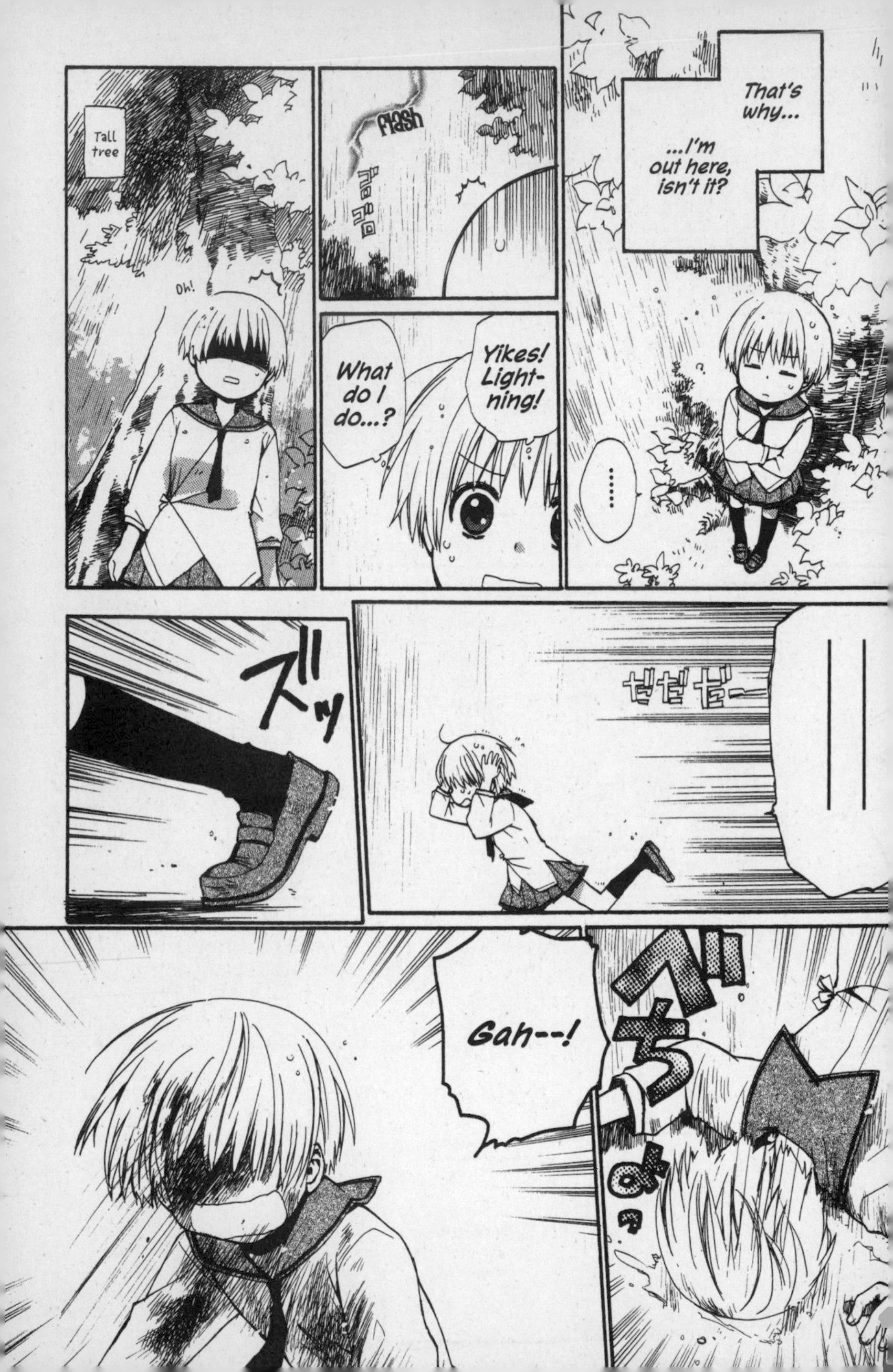
That's why...
...I'm out here, isn't it?
......
Flash
Yikes! Lightning!
What do I do...?
Tall tree
Oh!
ズッ
Gah--!

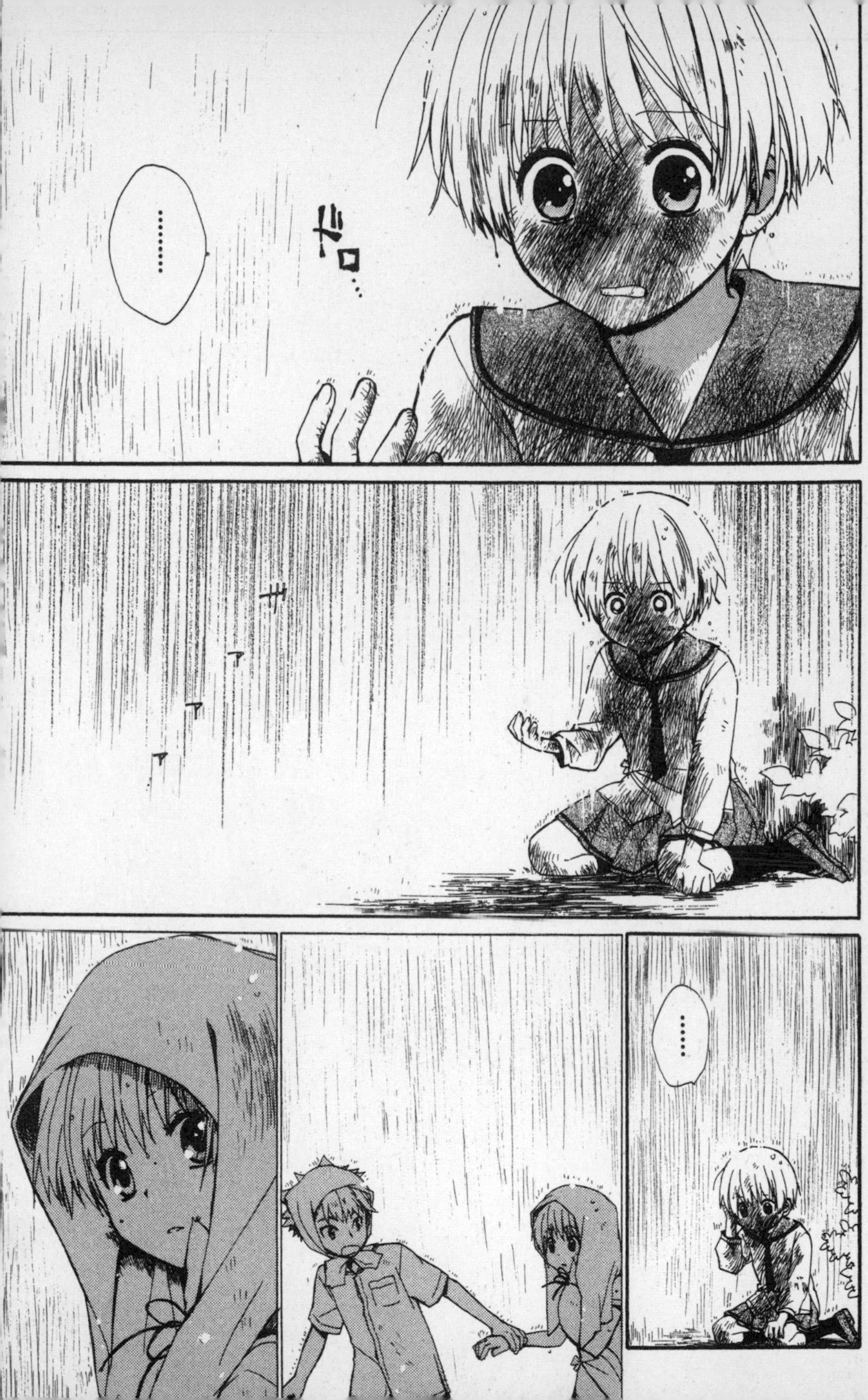
ドロ…
……
ザァァァ
……

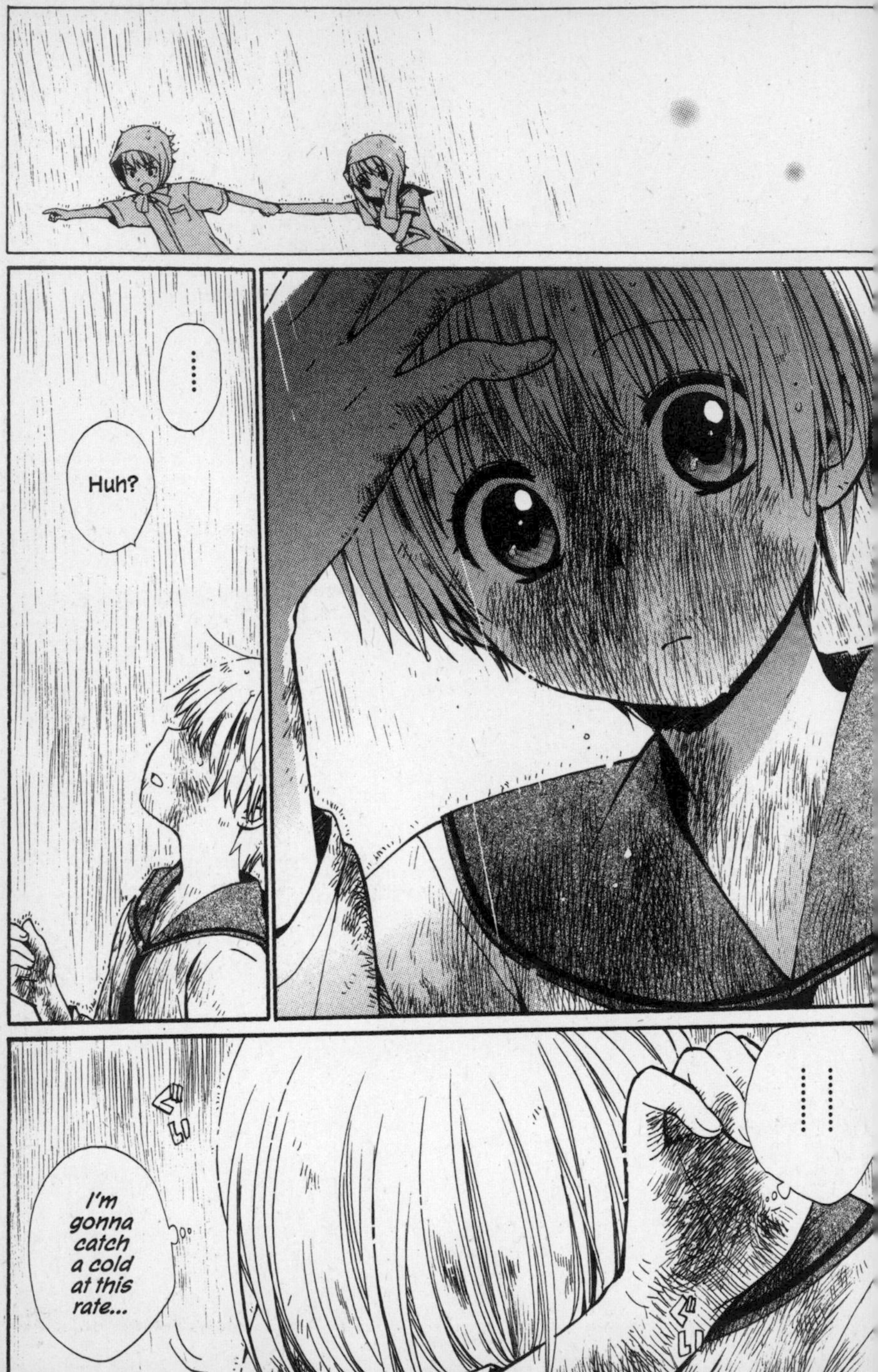

......
Huh?
......
I'm gonna catch a cold at this rate...

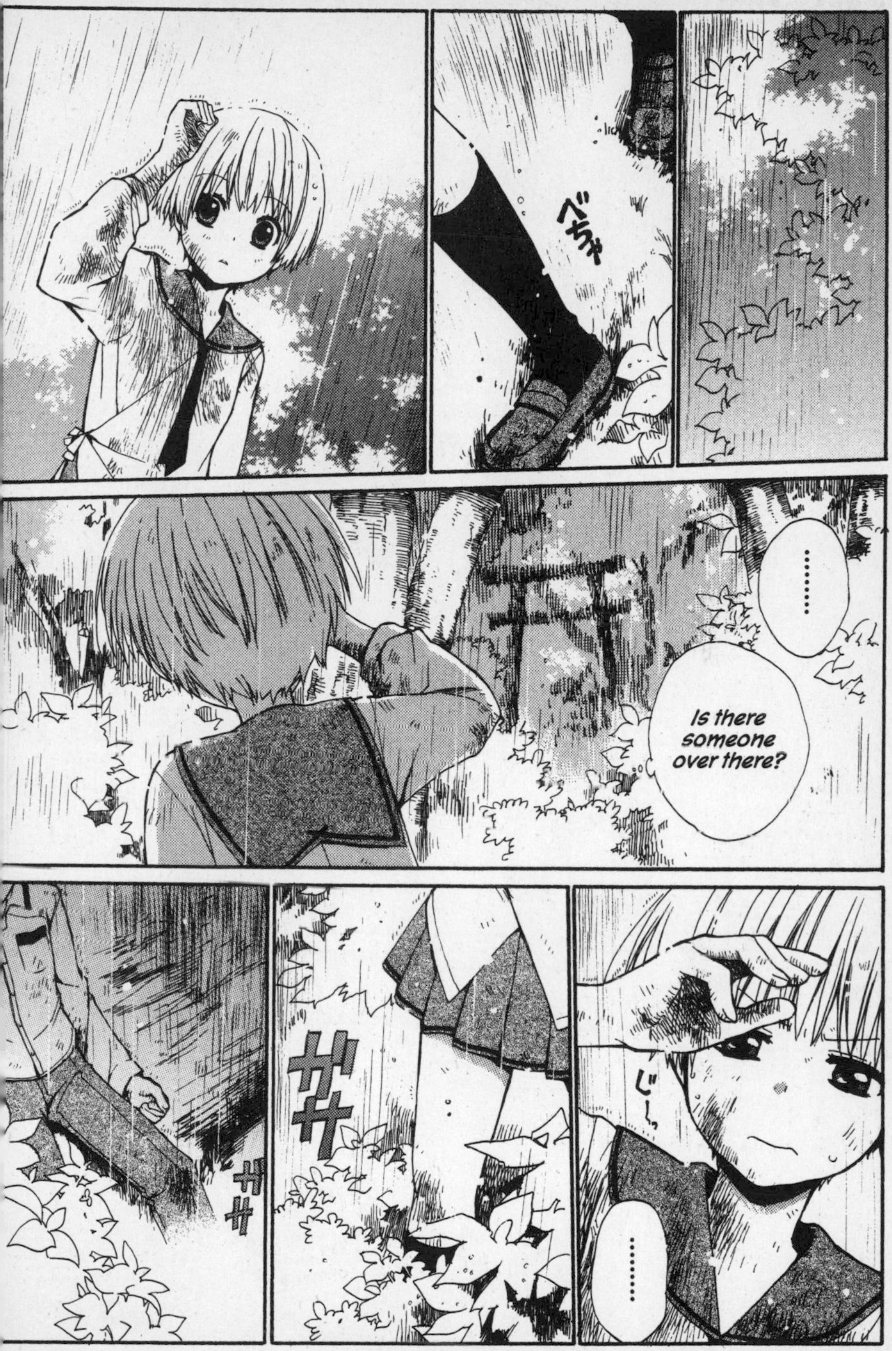

べちゃ
……
Is there someone over there?
じー
……
ガサ
ガサ

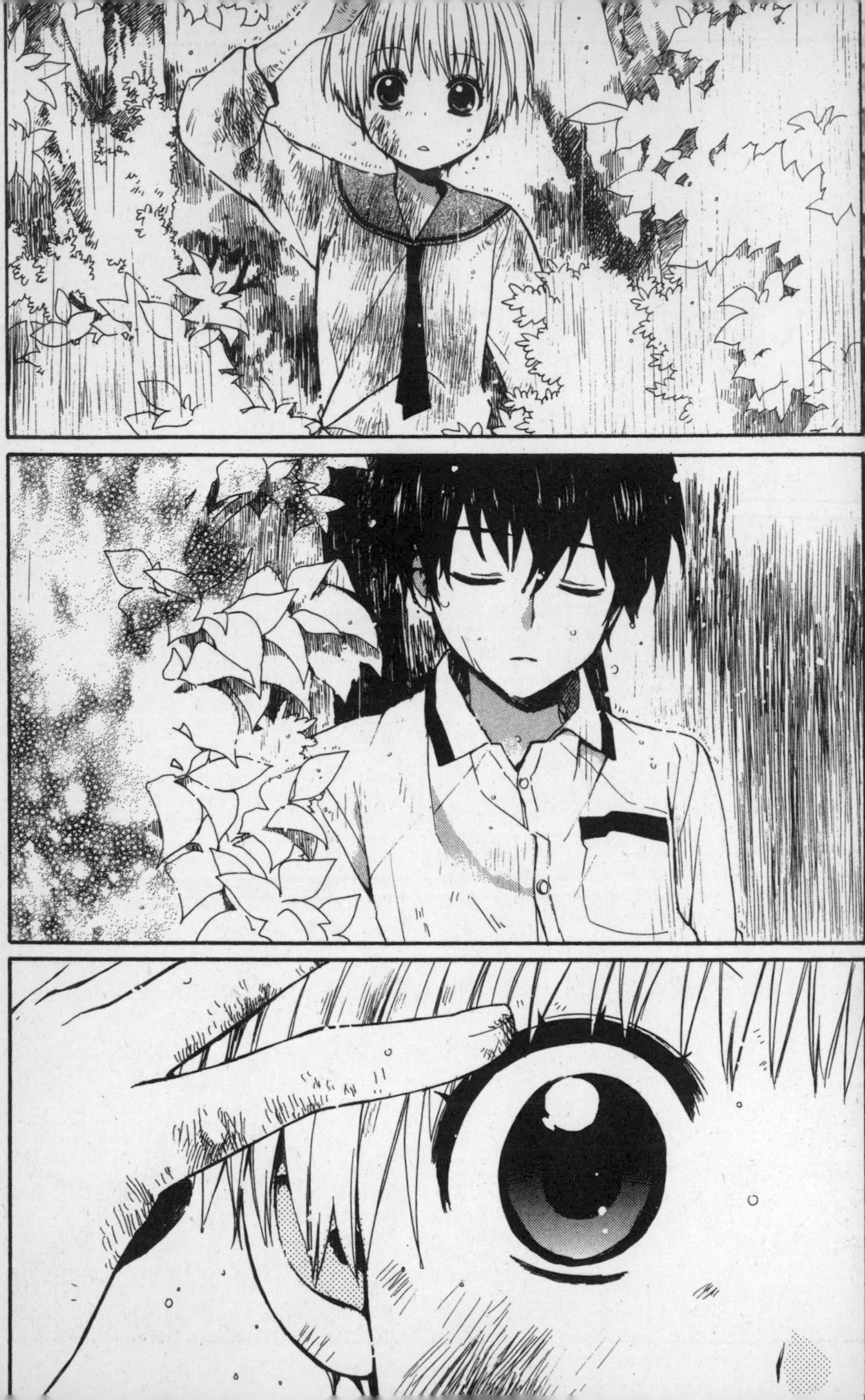

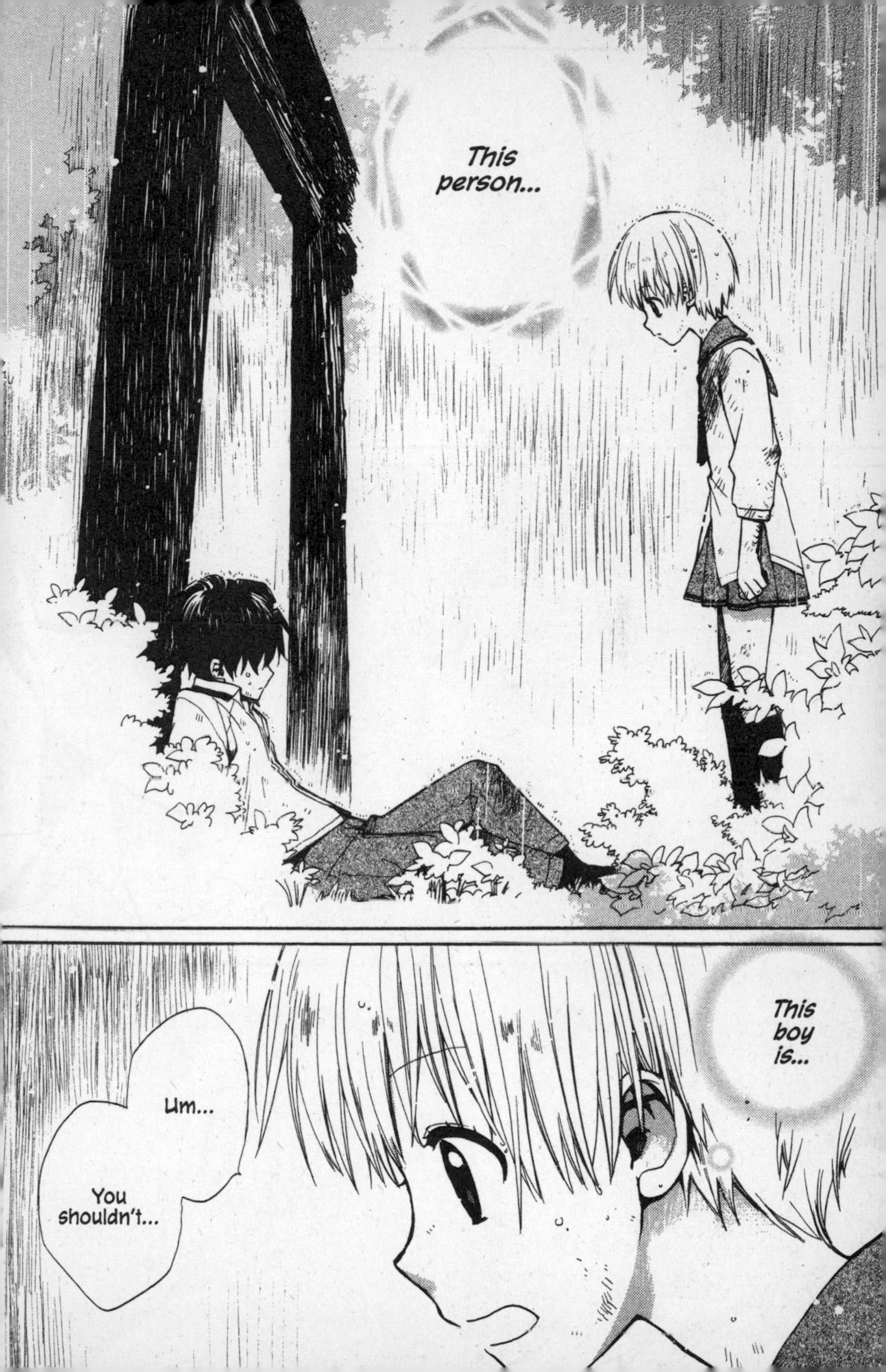
This person...
This boy is...
Um...
You shouldn't...

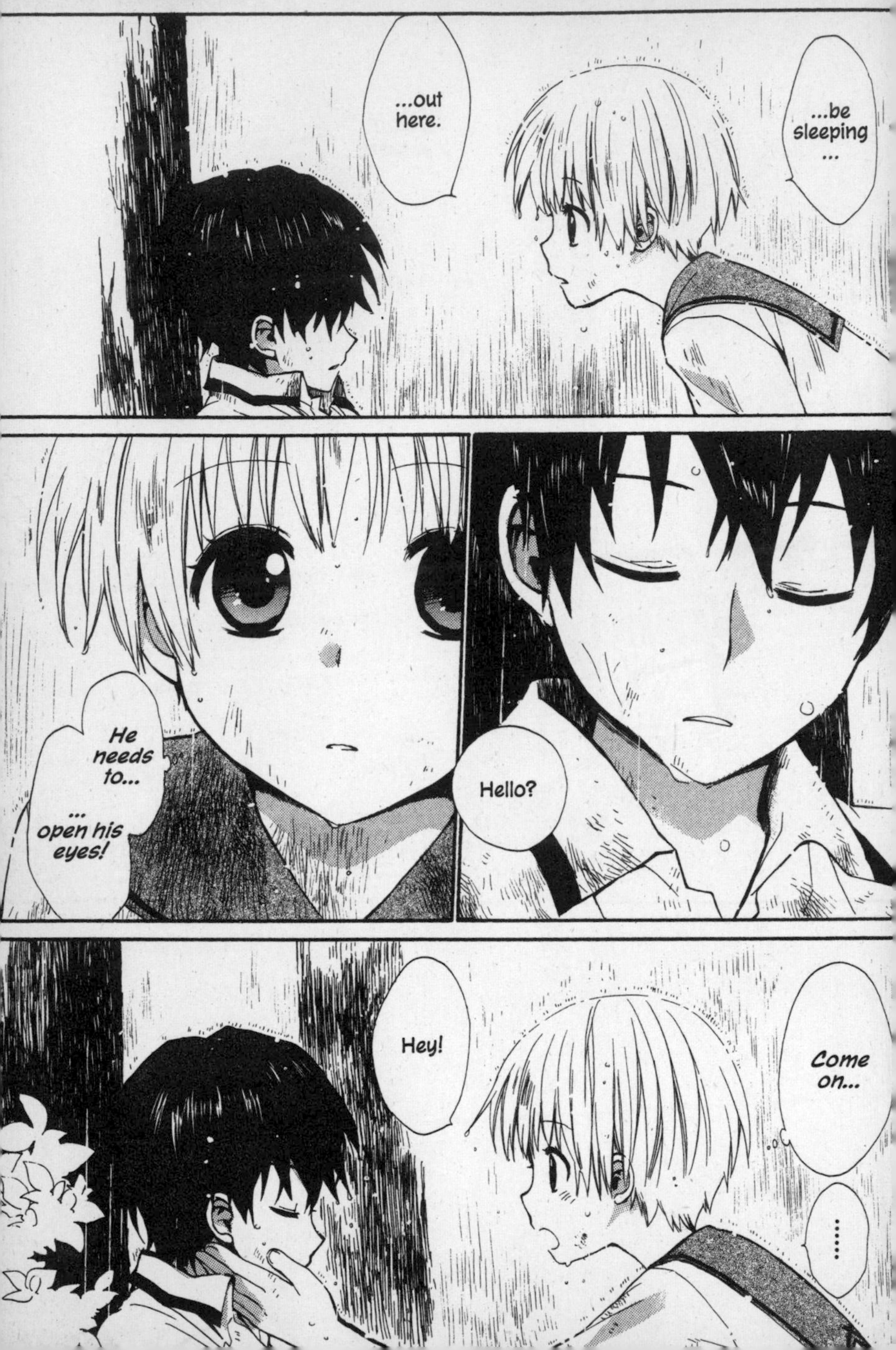
...be sleeping ...
...out here.
Hello?
He needs to...
... open his eyes!
Come on...
......
Hey!

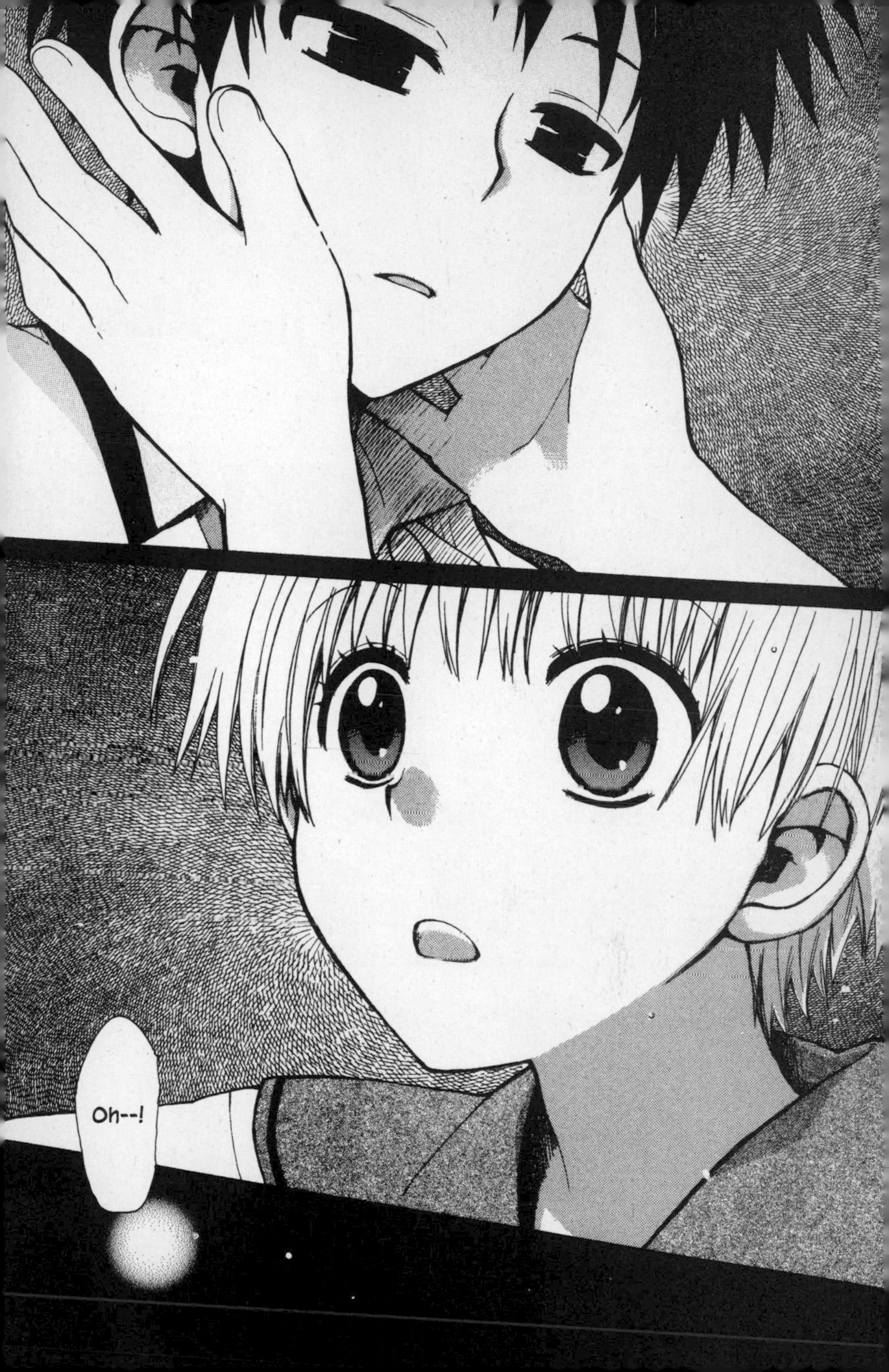
Oh--!

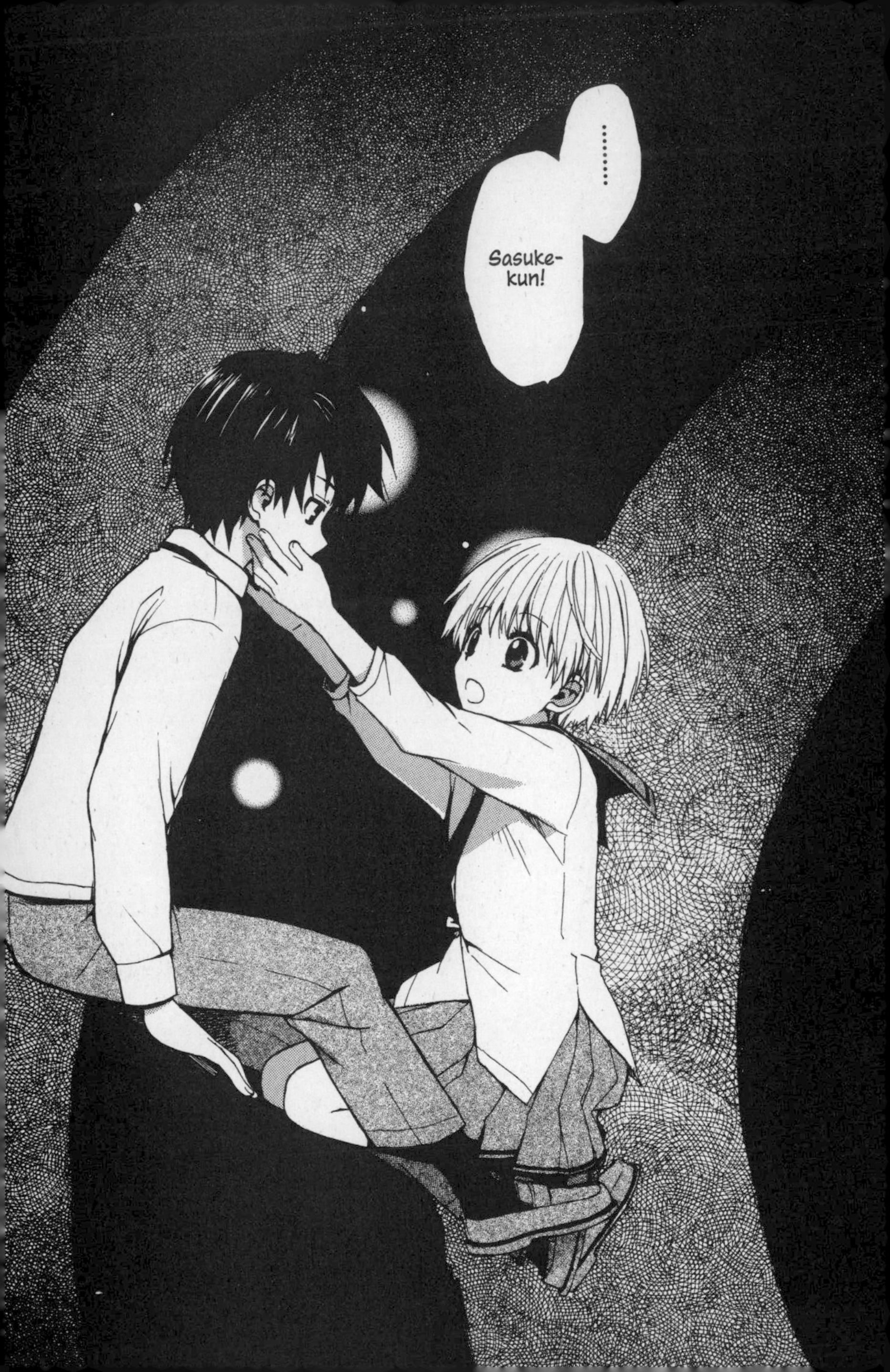
......
Sasuke-kun!

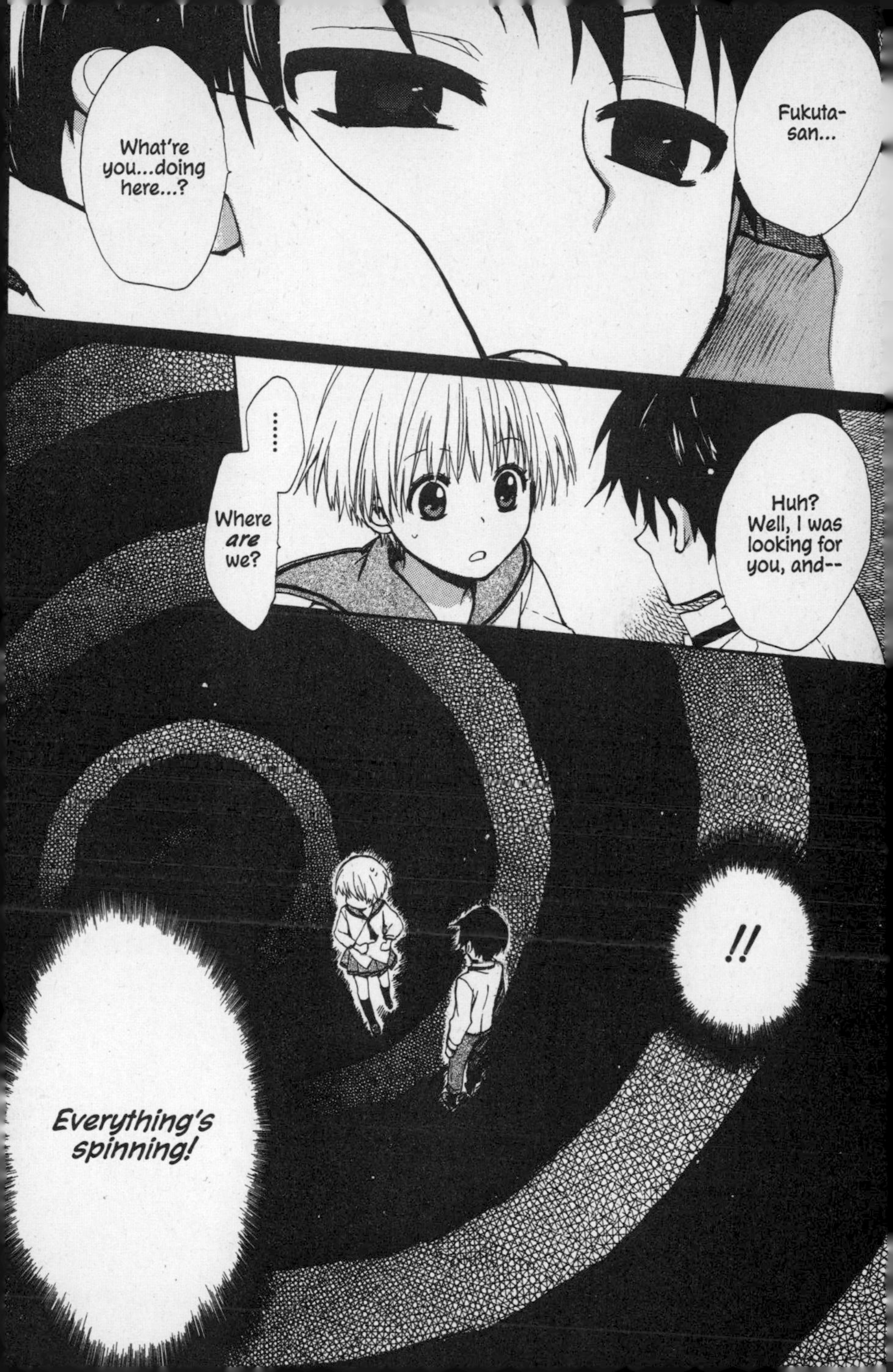

Fukuta-san...
What're you...doing here...?
Huh? Well, I was looking for you, and--
......
Where *are* we?
!!
Everything's spinning!

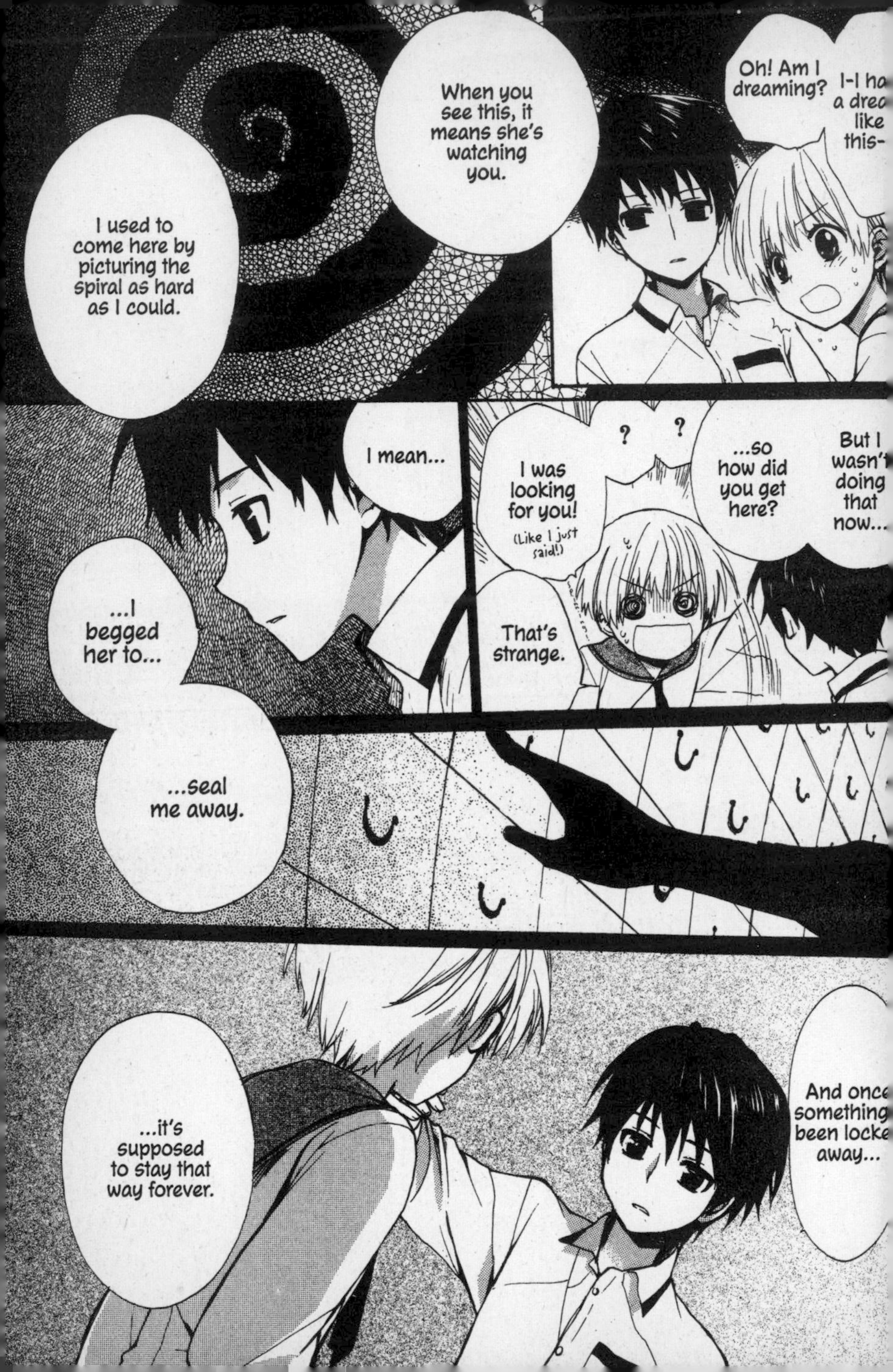

Oh! Am I dreaming?
I-I ha a drea like this-
When you see this, it means she's watching you.
I used to come here by picturing the spiral as hard as I could.
But I wasn't doing that now...
...so how did you get here?
? ?
I was looking for you!
(Like I just said!)
That's strange.
I mean...
...I begged her to...
...seal me away.
And once something been locke away...
...it's supposed to stay that way forever.

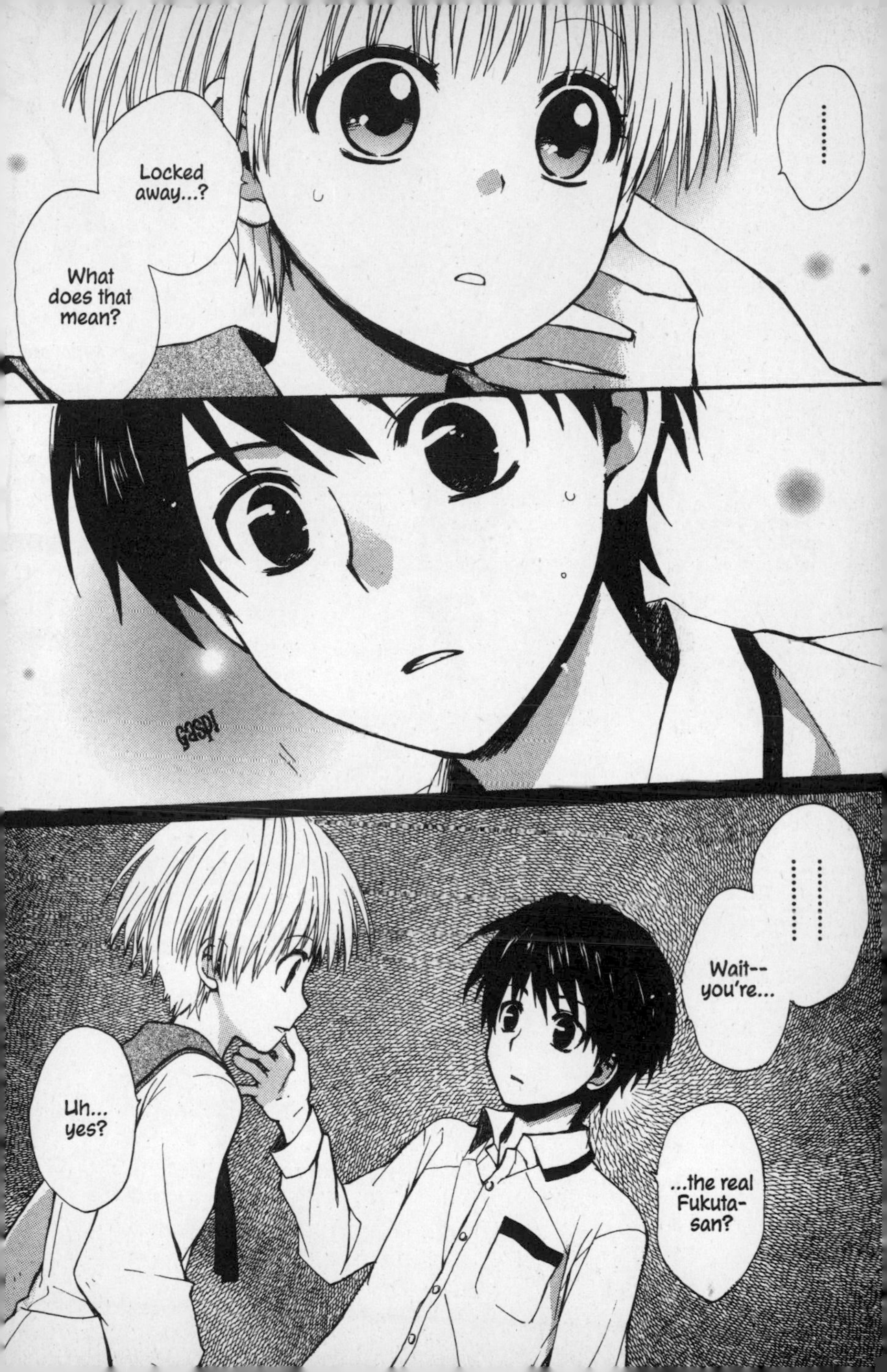
......
Locked away...?
What does that mean?
GASP!
......
Wait-- you're...
...the real Fukuta-san?
Uh... yes?

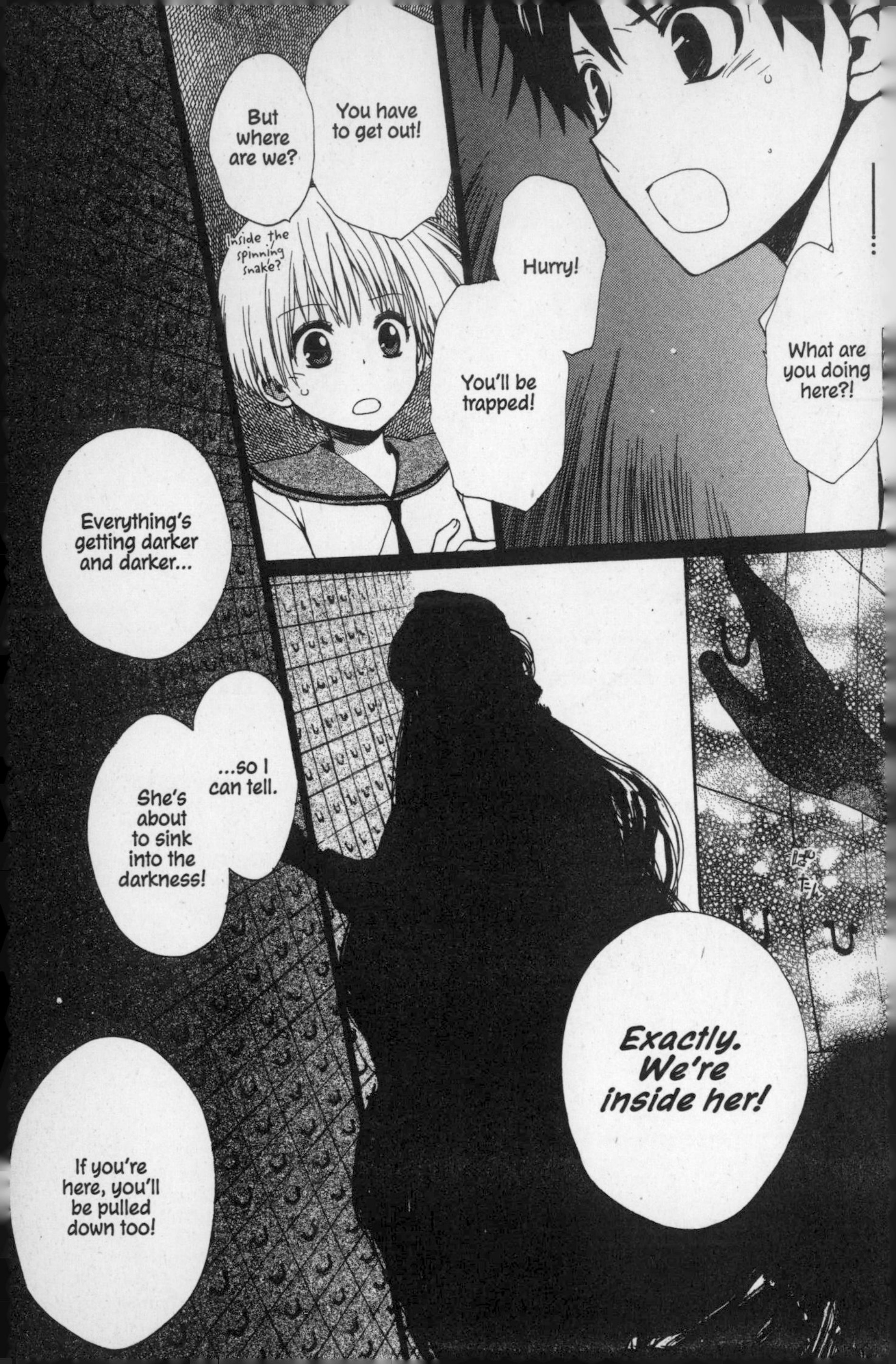
What are you doing here?!
Hurry!
You'll be trapped!
You have to get out!
But where are we?
Inside the spinning snake?
ぱたん
Exactly. We're inside her!
Everything's getting darker and darker...
...so I can tell.
She's about to sink into the darkness!
If you're here, you'll be pulled down too!

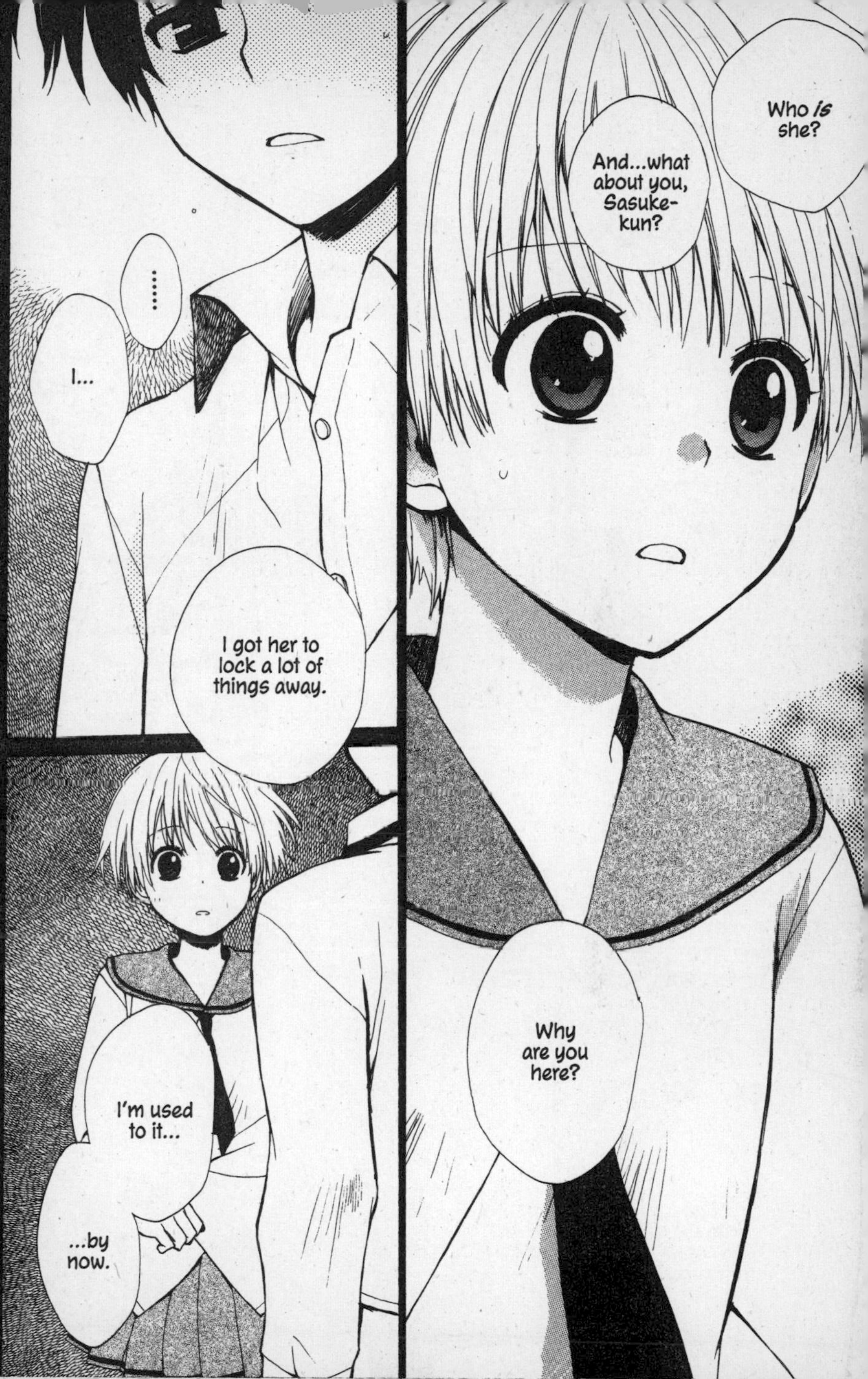
Who *is* she?
And...what about you, Sasuke-kun?
Why are you here?
......
I...
I got her to lock a lot of things away.
I'm used to it...
...by now.

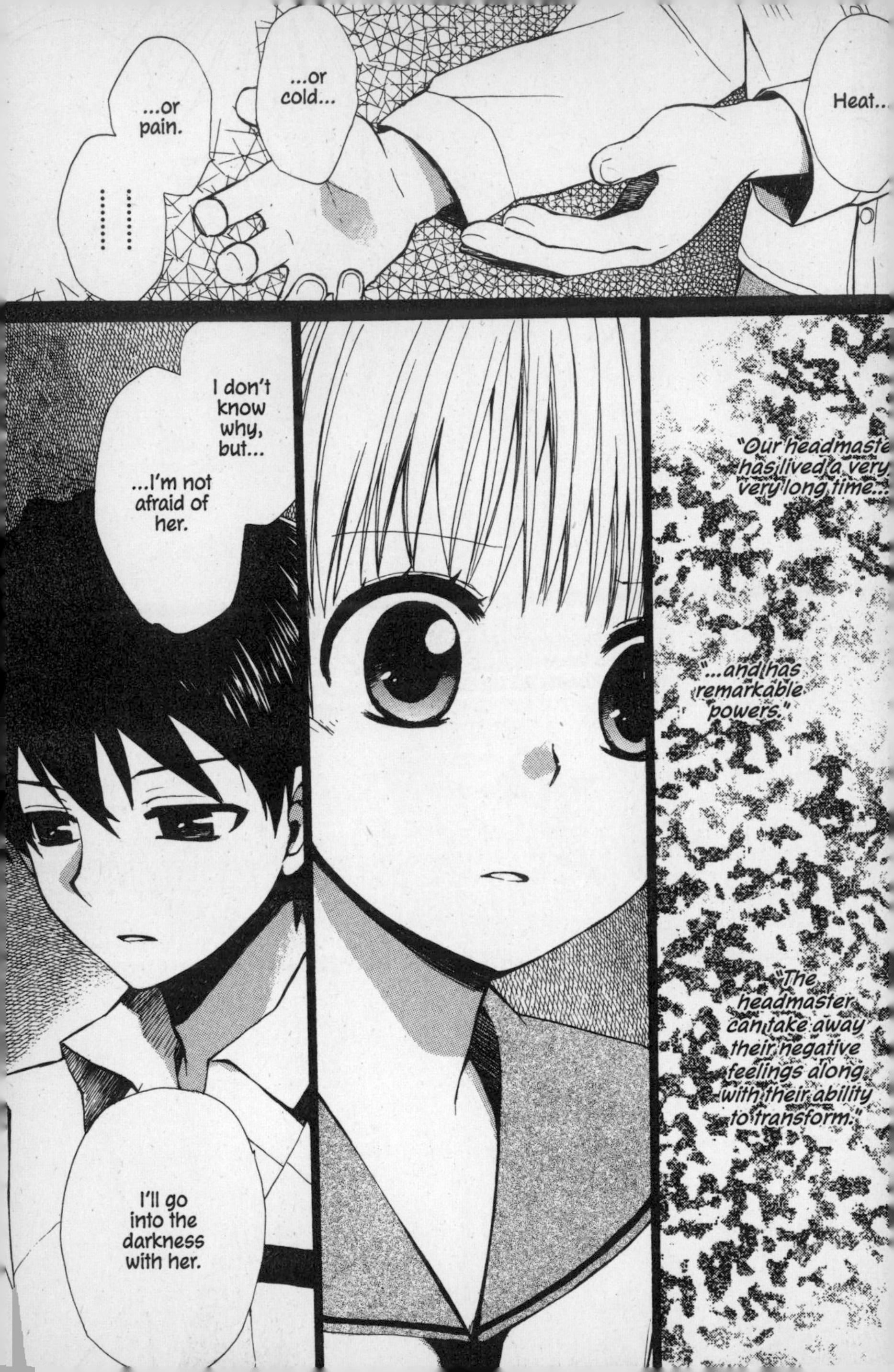
Heat...
...or cold...
...or pain.
......
"Our headmaste has lived a very, very long time..."
"...and has remarkable powers."
"The headmaster can take away their negative feelings along with their ability to transform."
I don't know why, but...
...I'm not afraid of her.
I'll go into the darkness with her.

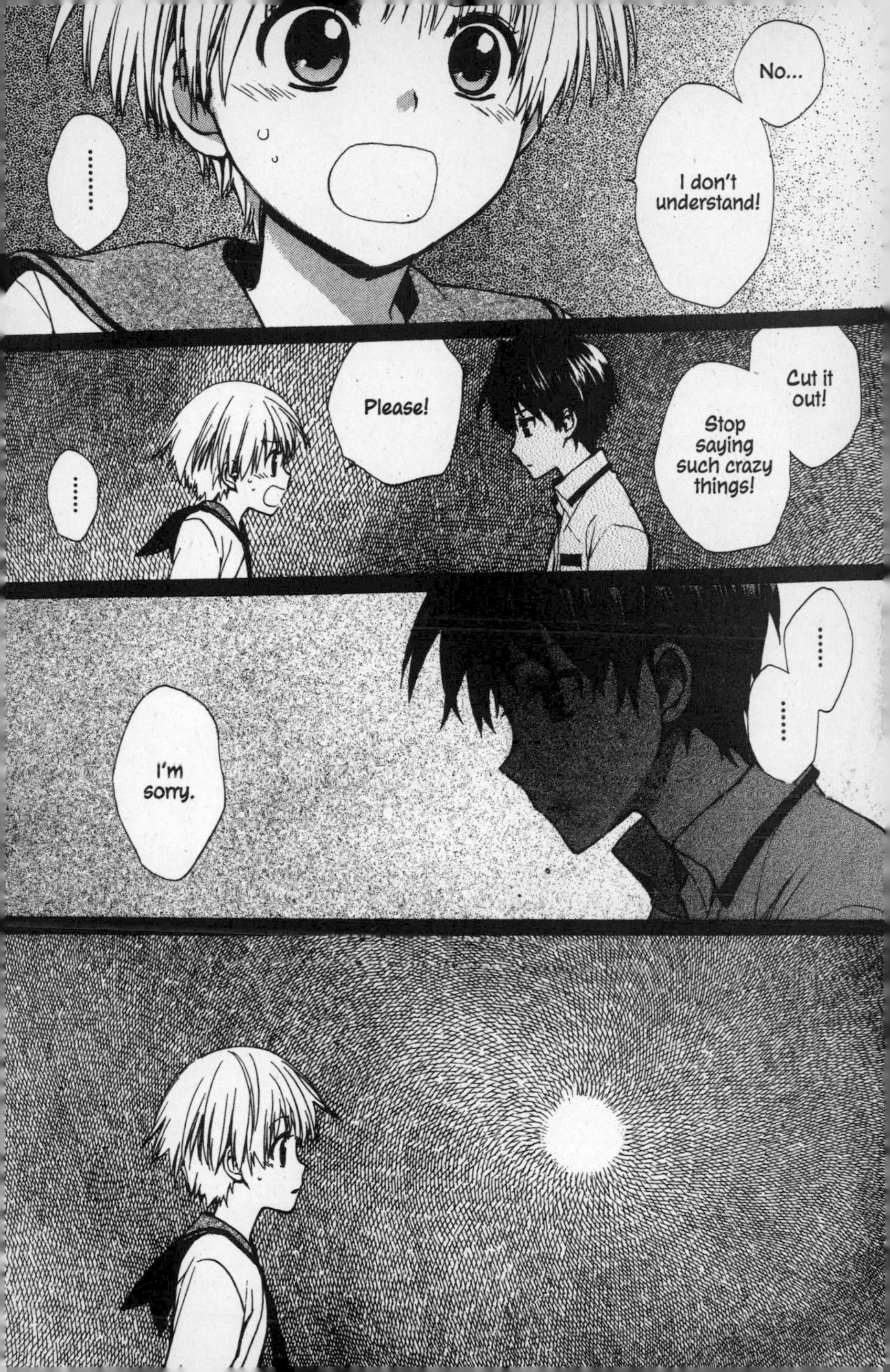
No...
I don't understand!
......
Cut it out!
Stop saying such crazy things!
Please!
......
......
......
I'm sorry.

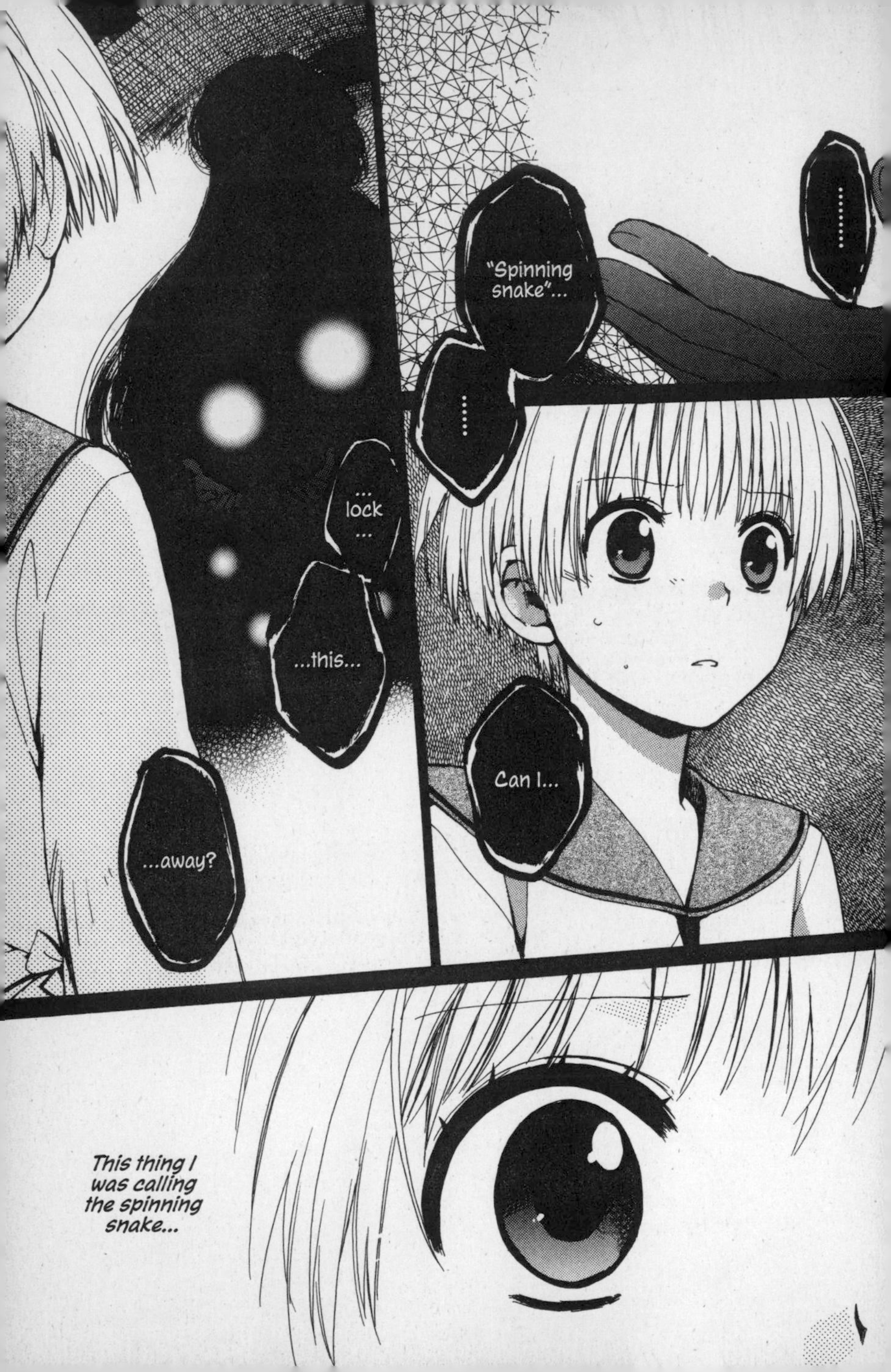
......
"Spinning snake"...
......
Can I...
...lock...
...this...
...away?
This thing I was calling the spinning snake...

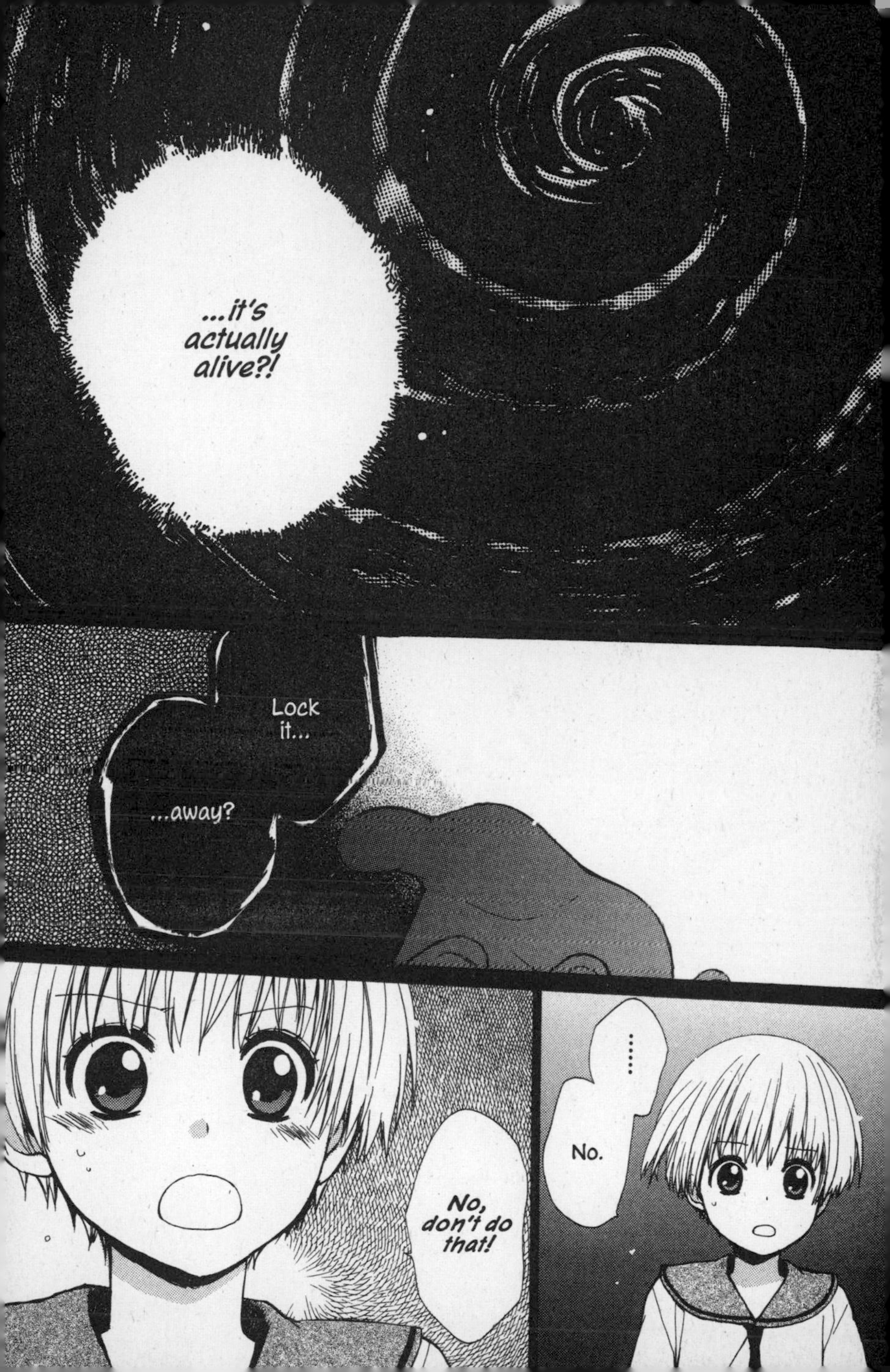
...it's actually alive?!
Lock it...
...away?
......
No.
No, don't do that!

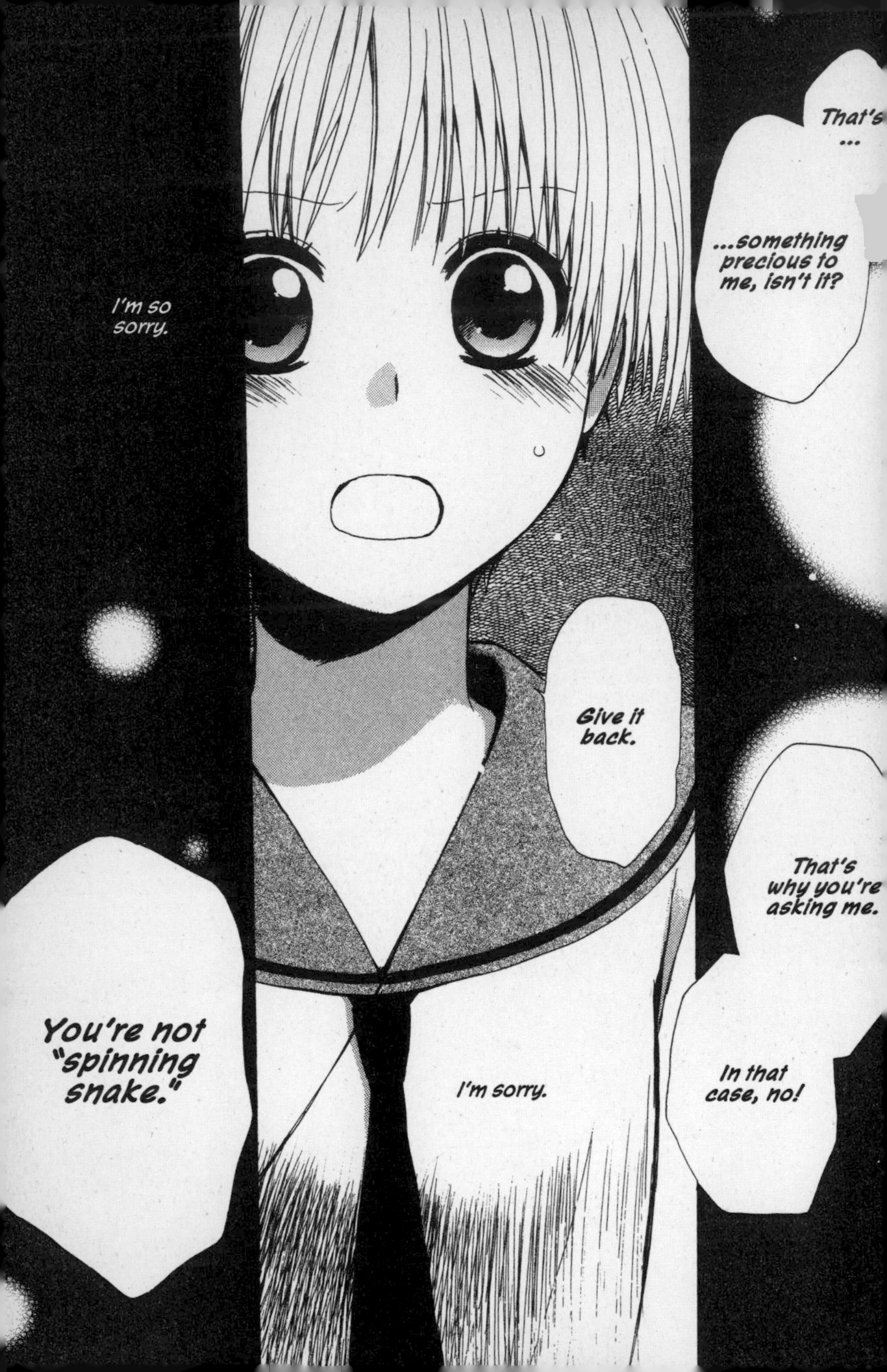
That's ...
...something precious to me, isn't it?
That's why you're asking me.
In that case, no!
Give it back.
I'm sorry.
I'm so sorry.
You're not "spinning snake."

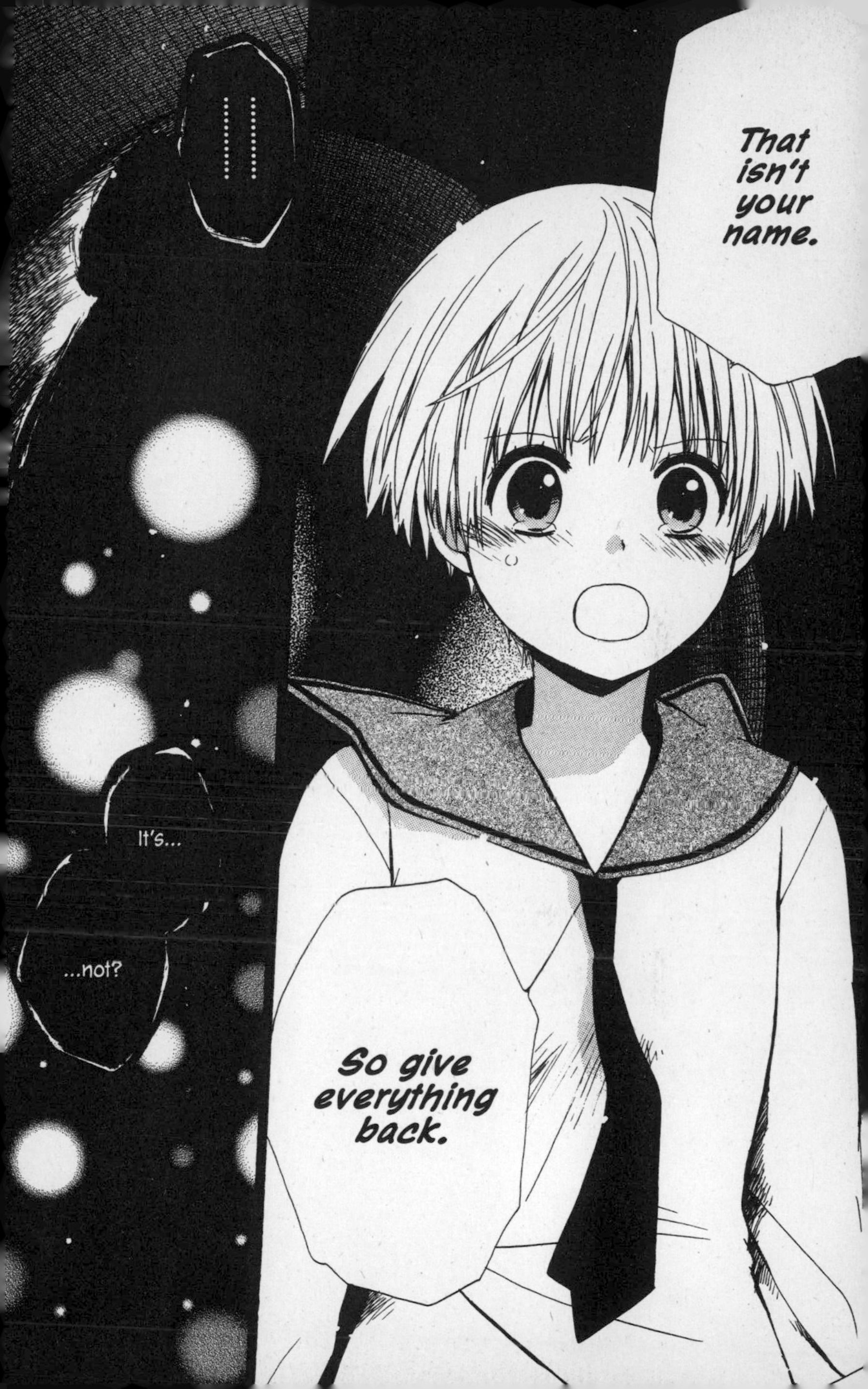
That isn't your name.
It's...
...not?
So give everything back.

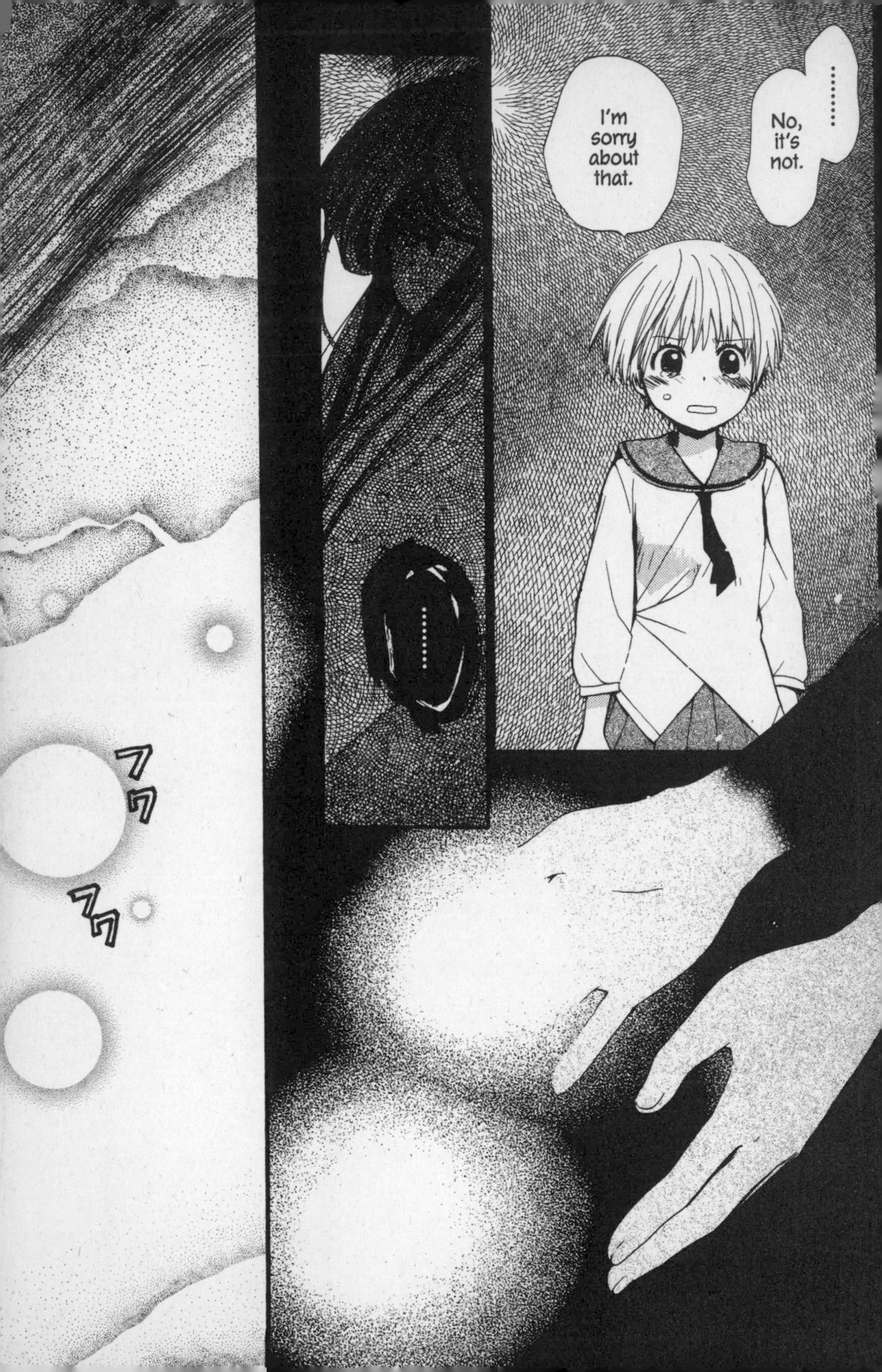
......
No, it's not.
I'm sorry about that.
......

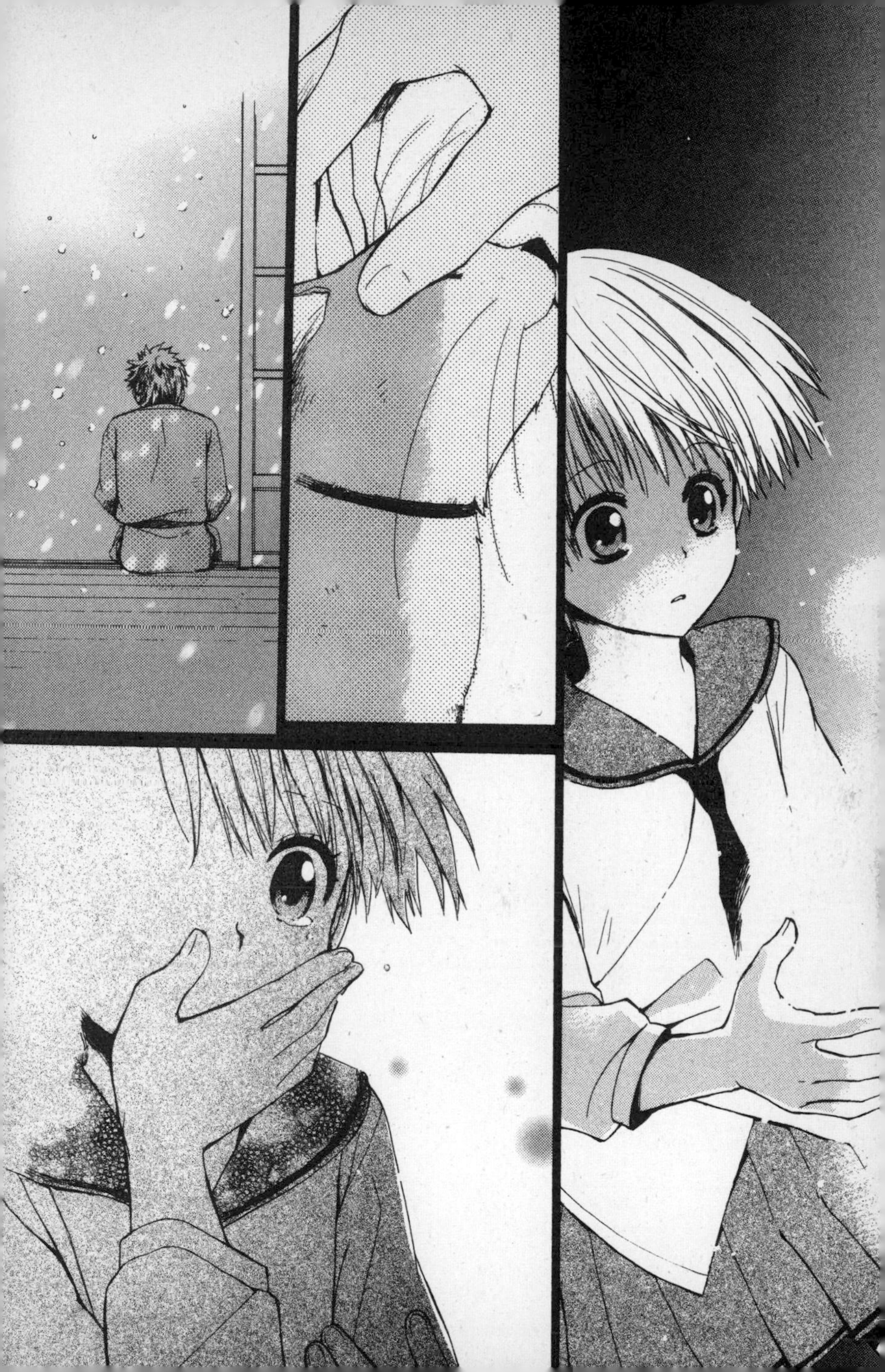

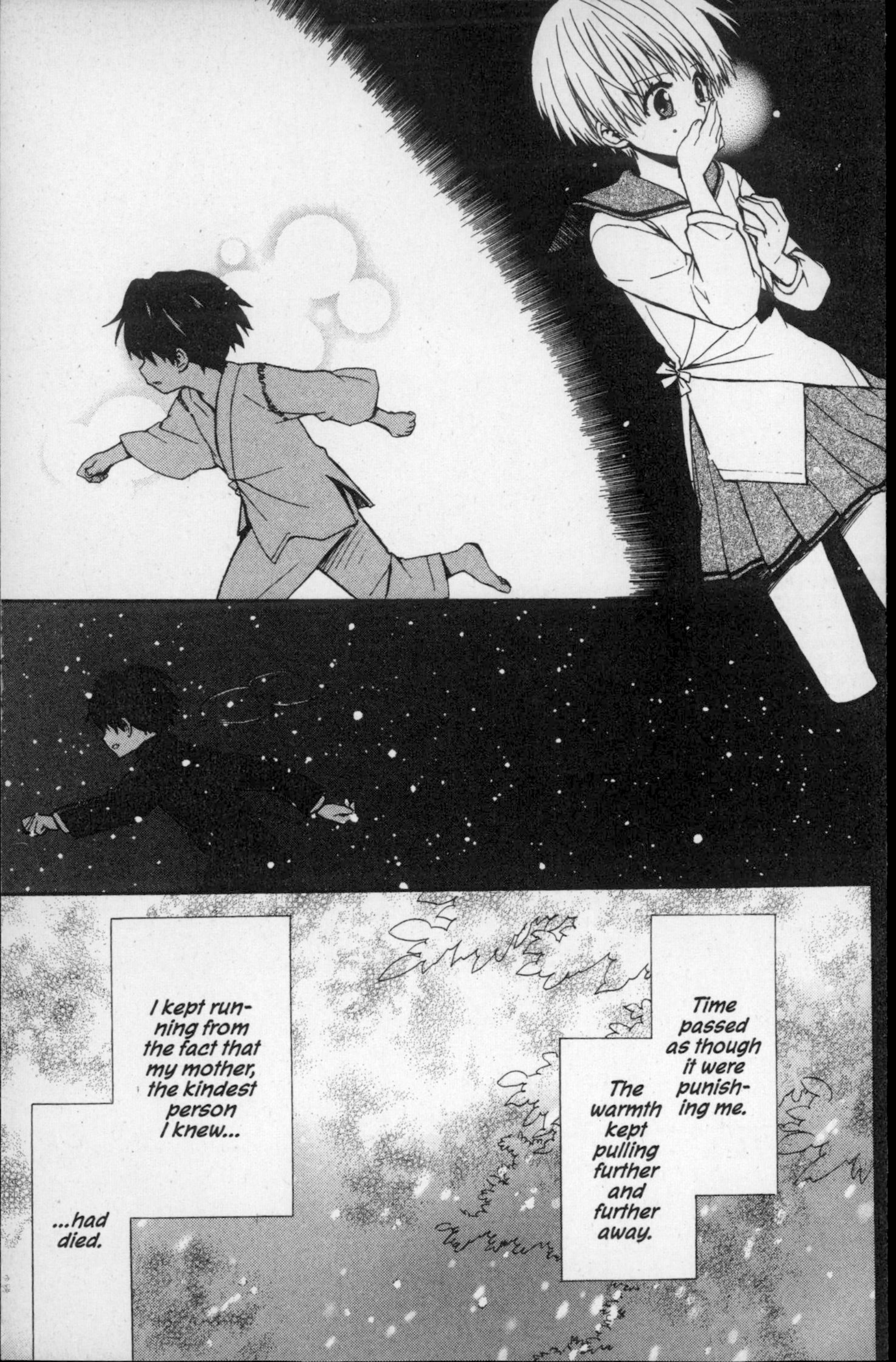
Time passed as though it were punishing me.
The warmth kept pulling further and further away.
I kept running from the fact that my mother, the kindest person I knew...
...had died.

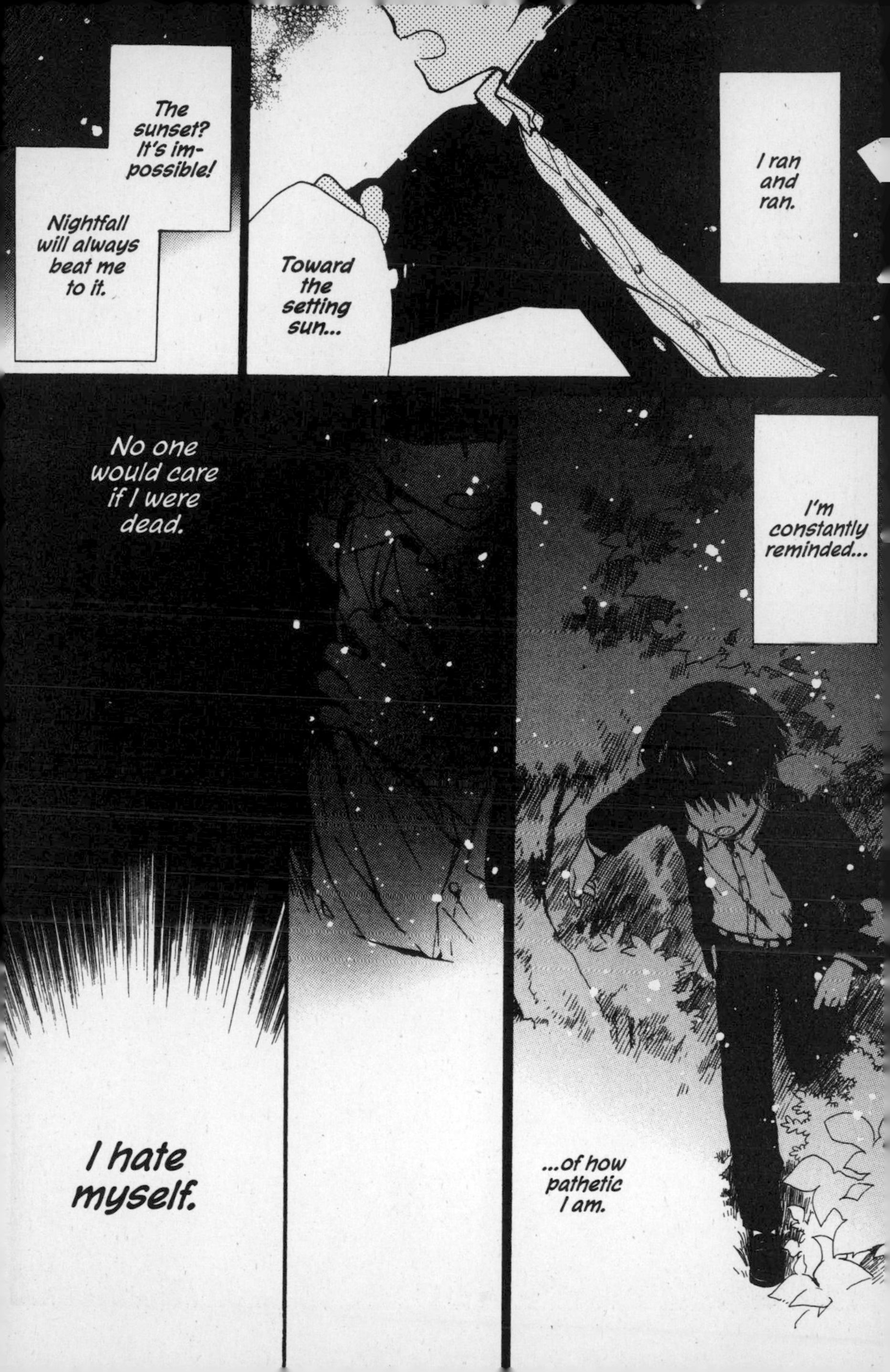
I ran and ran.
Toward the setting sun...
The sunset? It's impossible!
Nightfall will always beat me to it.
I'm constantly reminded...
...of how pathetic I am.
No one would care if I were dead.
I hate myself.

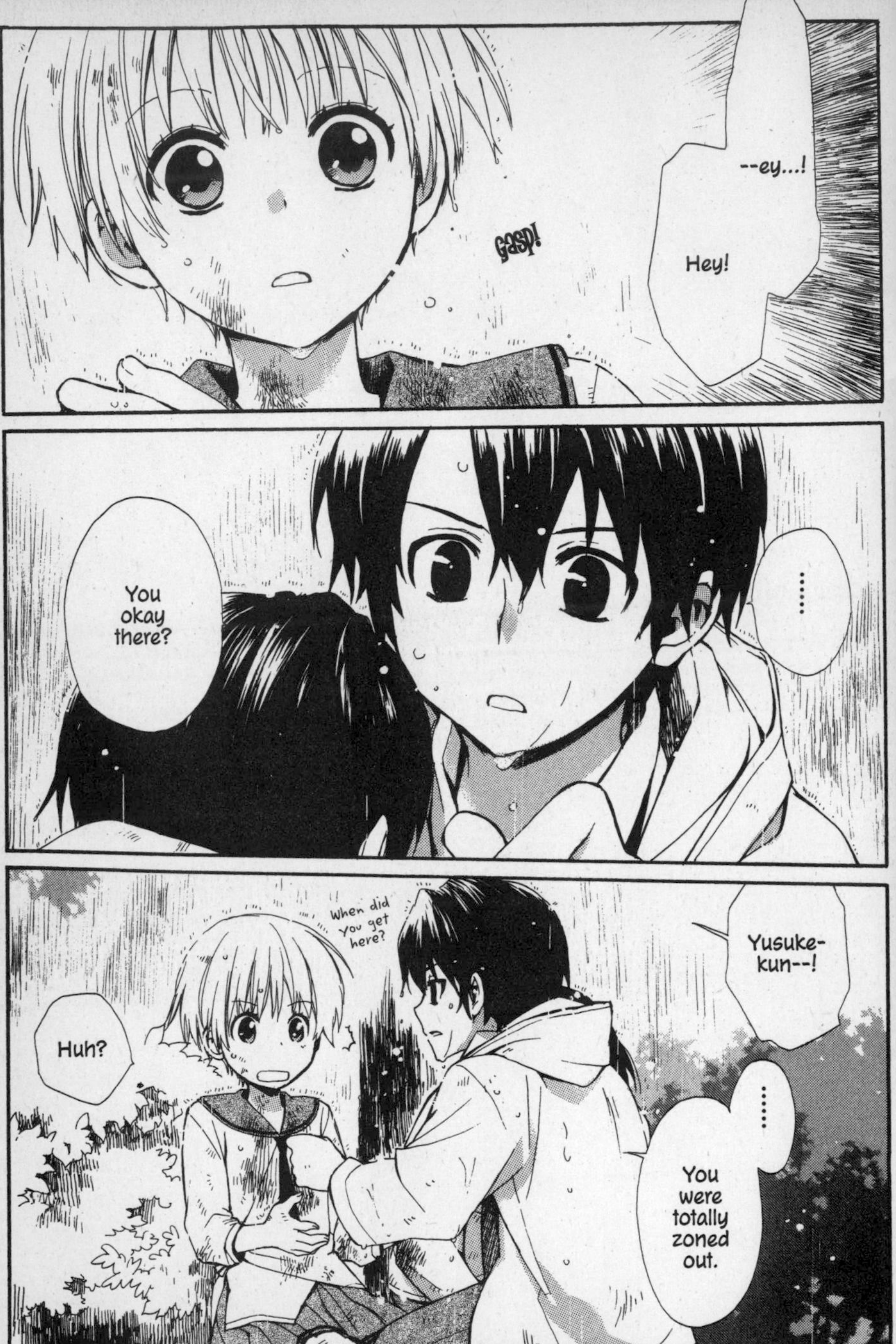
--ey...!
Hey!
GASP!
......
You okay there?
Yusuke-kun--!
......
You were totally zoned out.
When did You get here?
Huh?

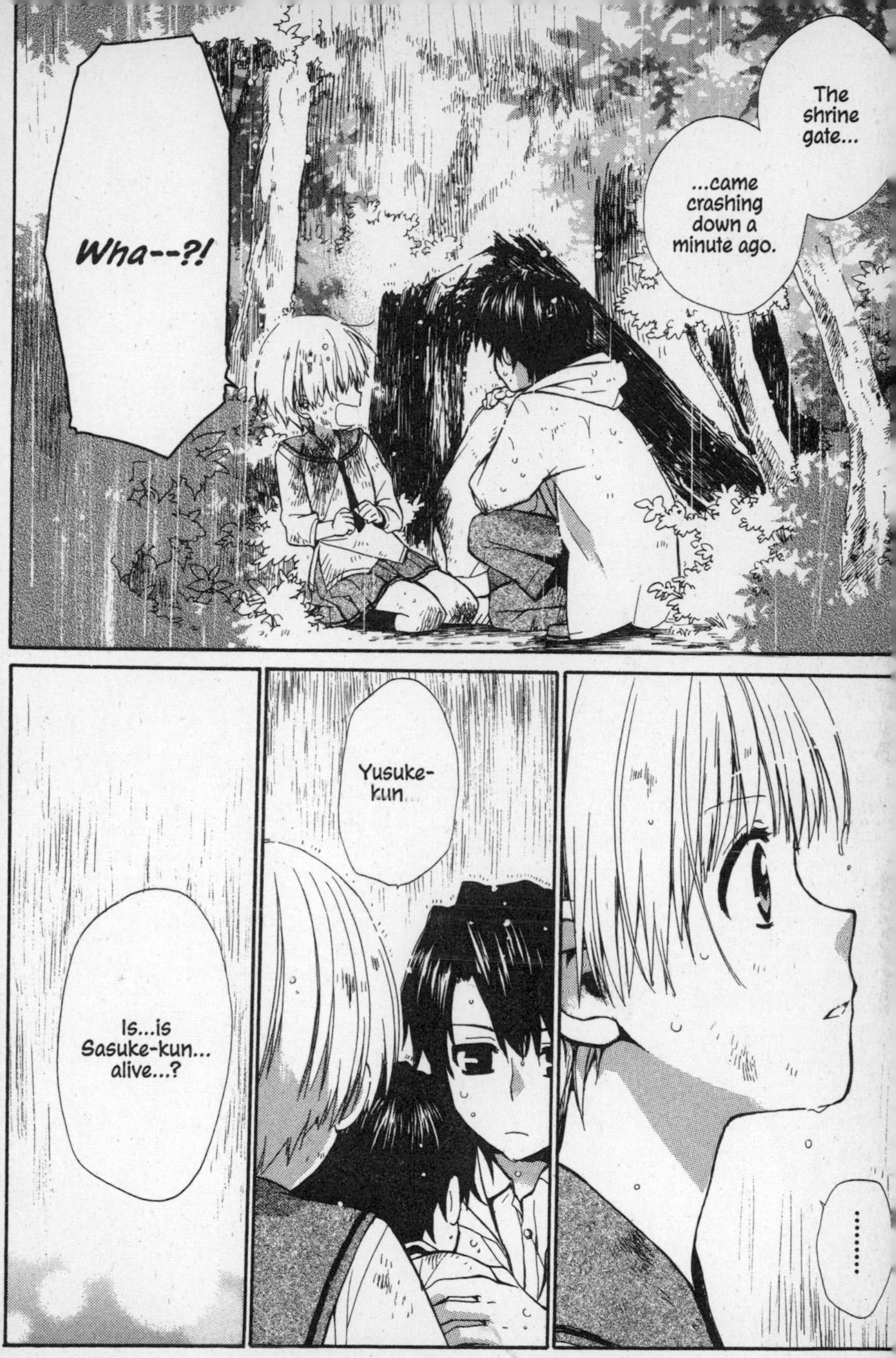
The shrine gate...
...came crashing down a minute ago.
Wha--?!
......
Yusuke-kun...
Is...is Sasuke-kun... alive...?

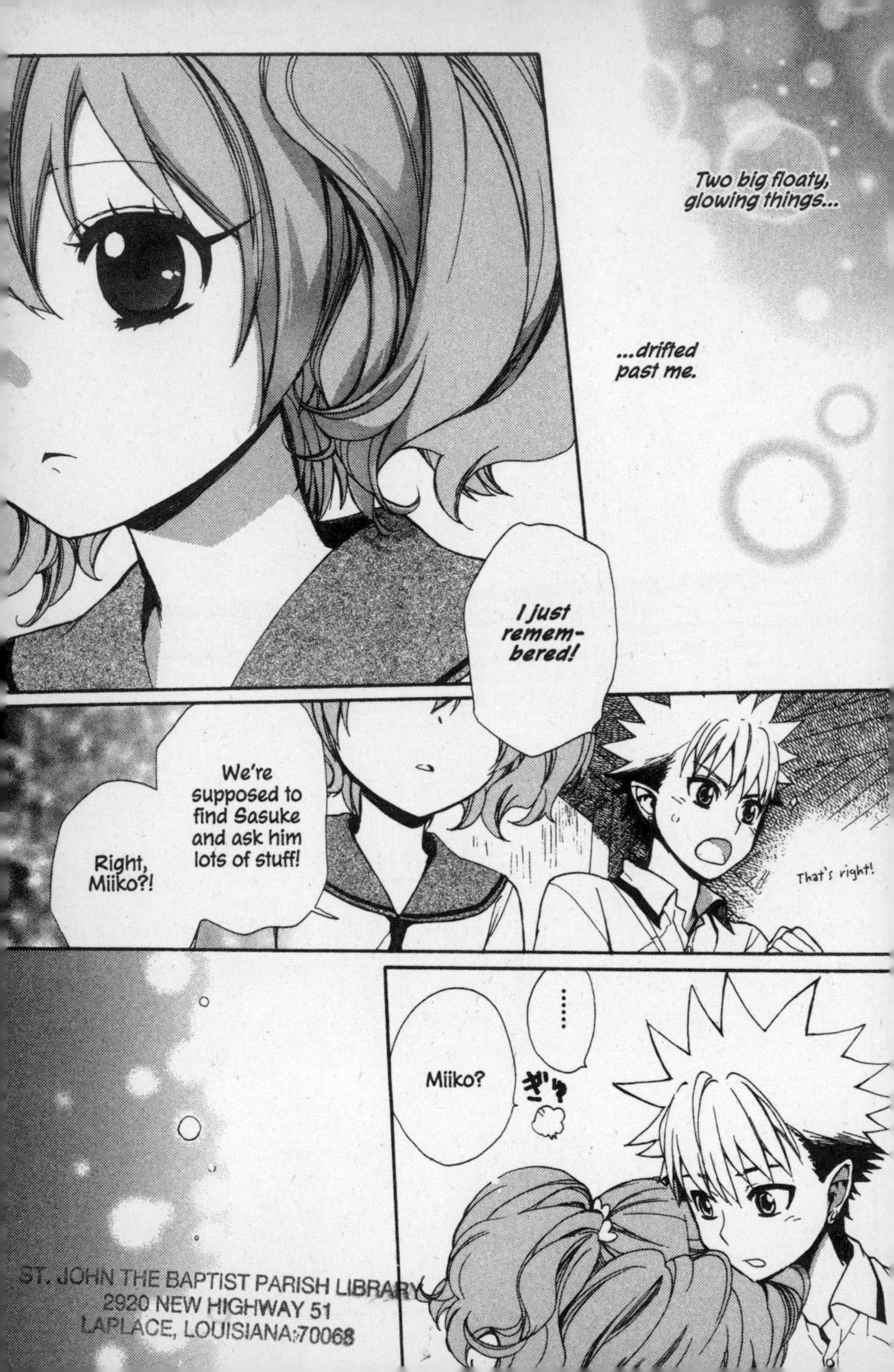
Two big floaty, glowing things...
...drifted past me.
I just remem-bered!
That's right!
We're supposed to find Sasuke and ask him lots of stuff!
Right, Miiko?!
……
Miiko?
ぎゅ

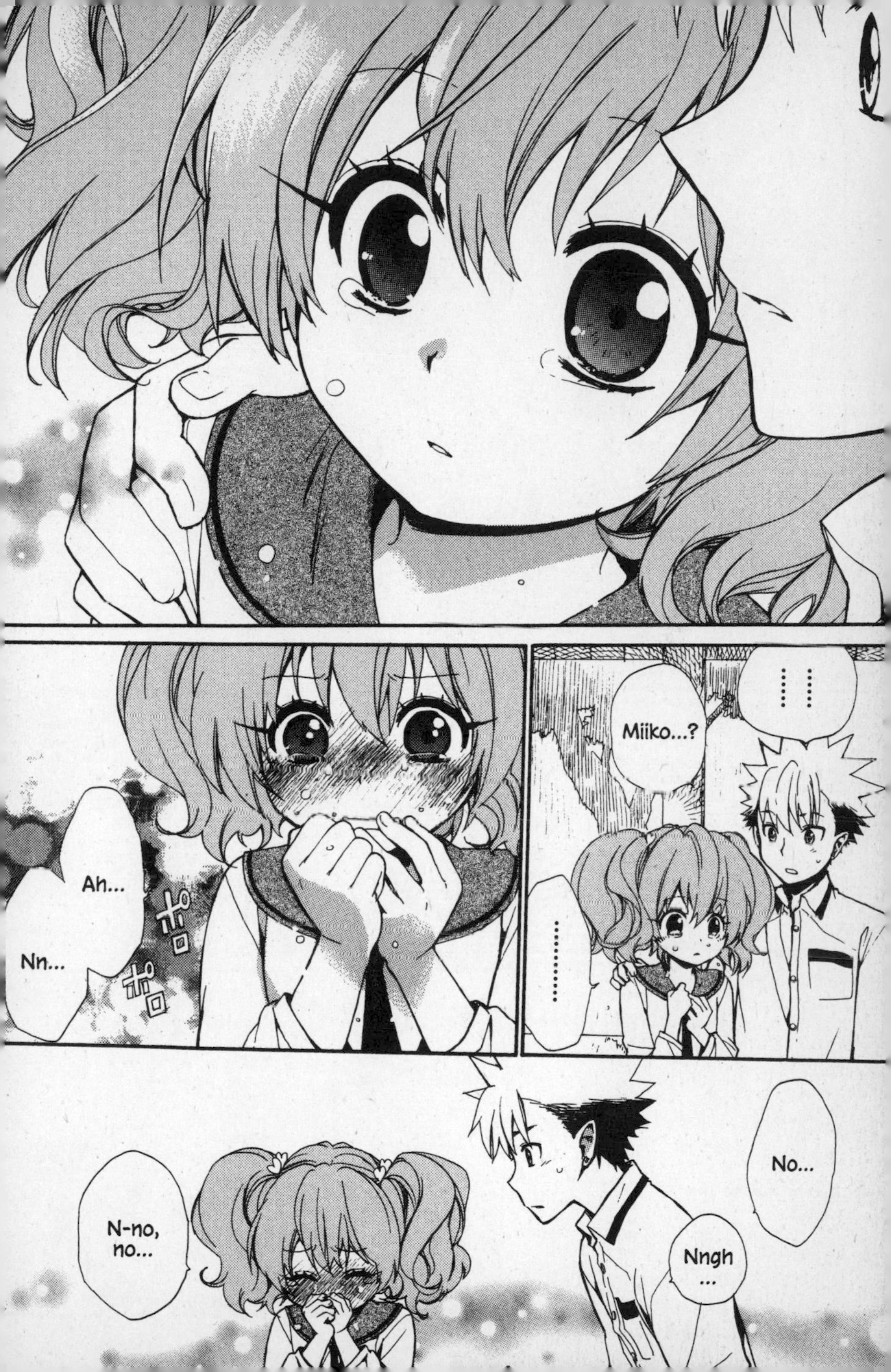
......
Miiko...?
......
Ah... Nn...
ポロ
ポロ
No...
Nngh ...
N-no, no...

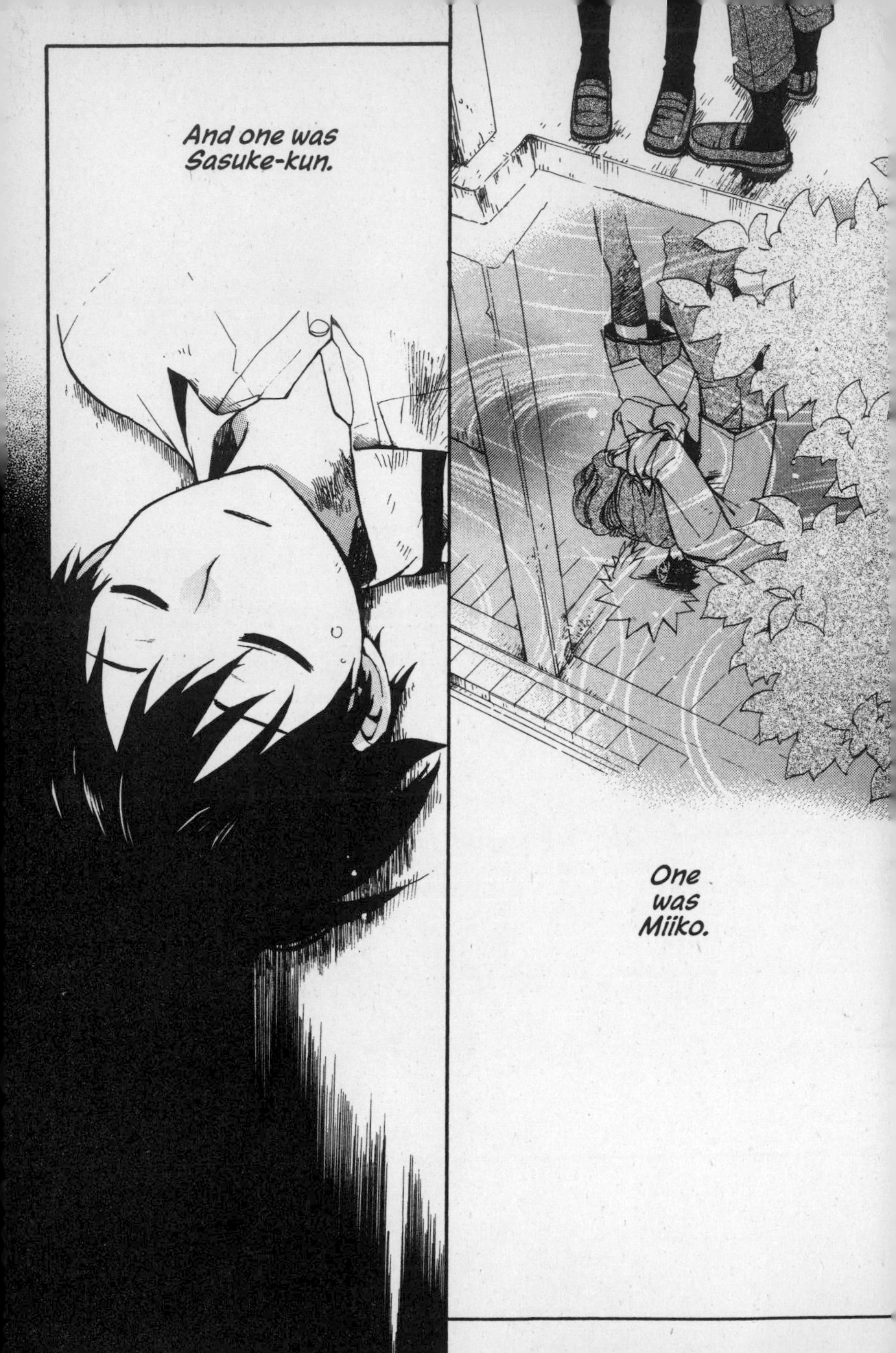
One was Miiko.
And one was Sasuke-kun.

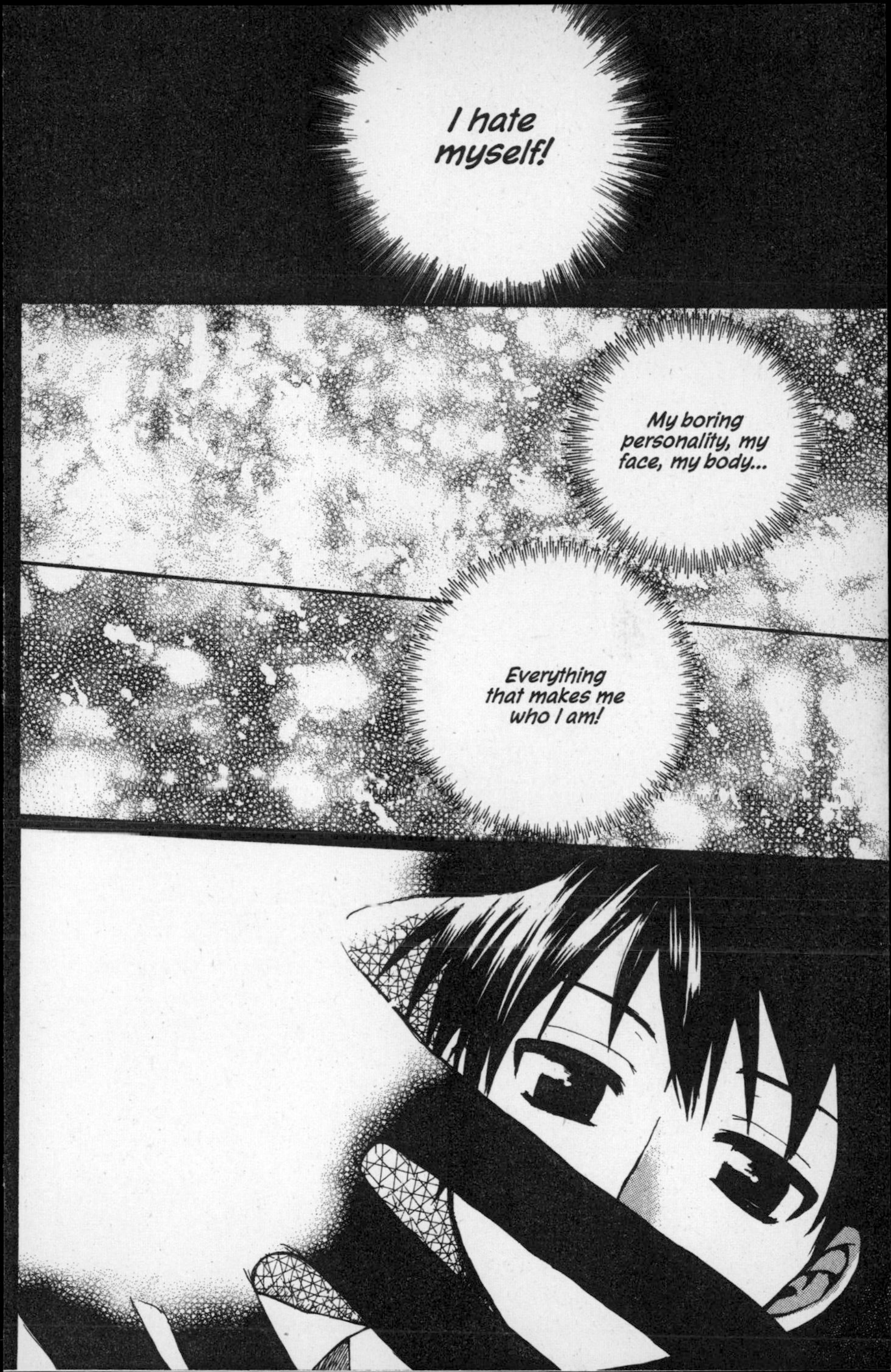
I hate myself!
My boring personality, my face, my body...
Everything that makes me who I am!

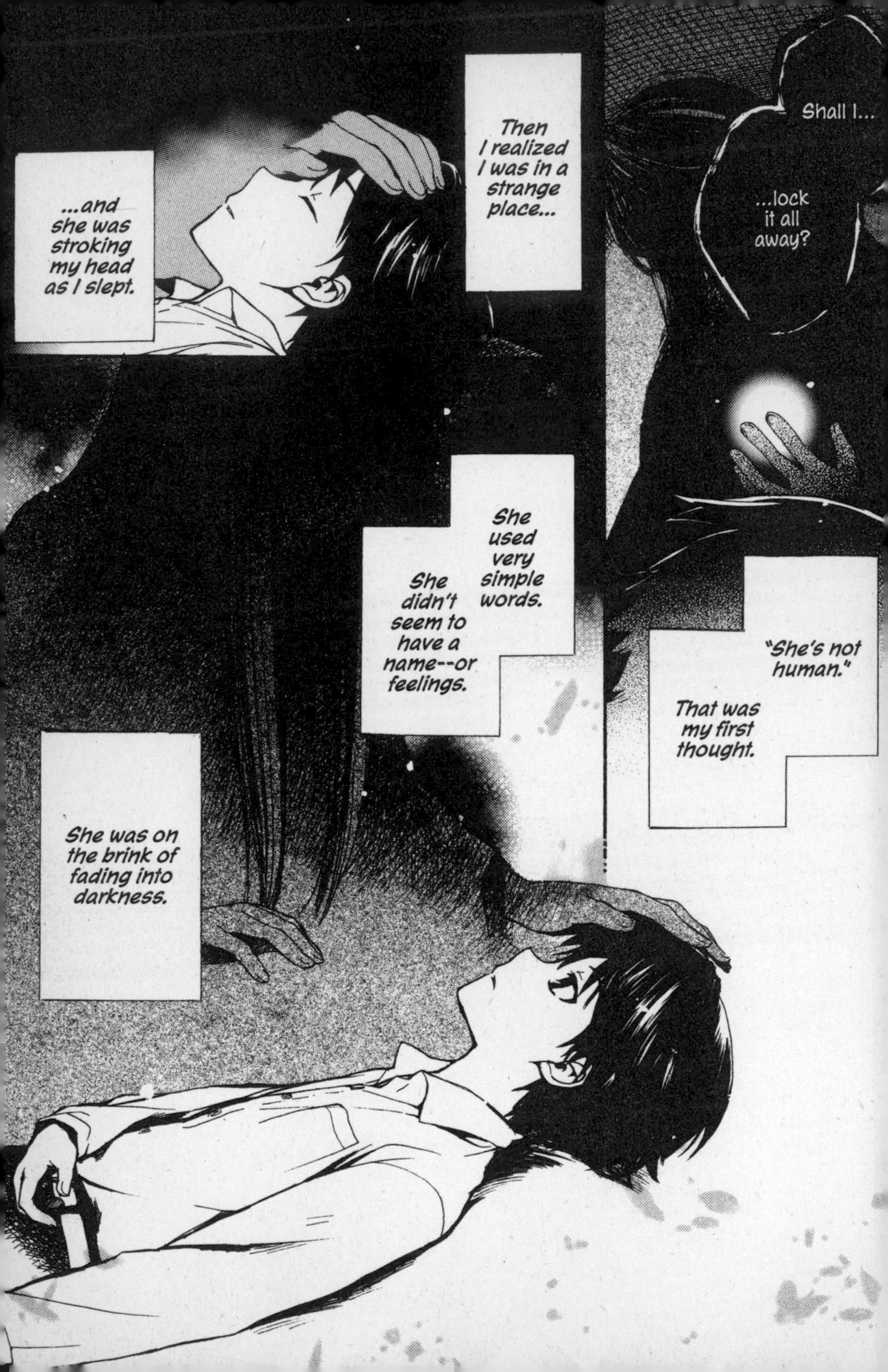
Shall I...
...lock it all away?
"She's not human."
That was my first thought.
Then I realized I was in a strange place...
...and she was stroking my head as I slept.
She used very simple words.
She didn't seem to have a name--or feelings.
She was on the brink of fading into darkness.

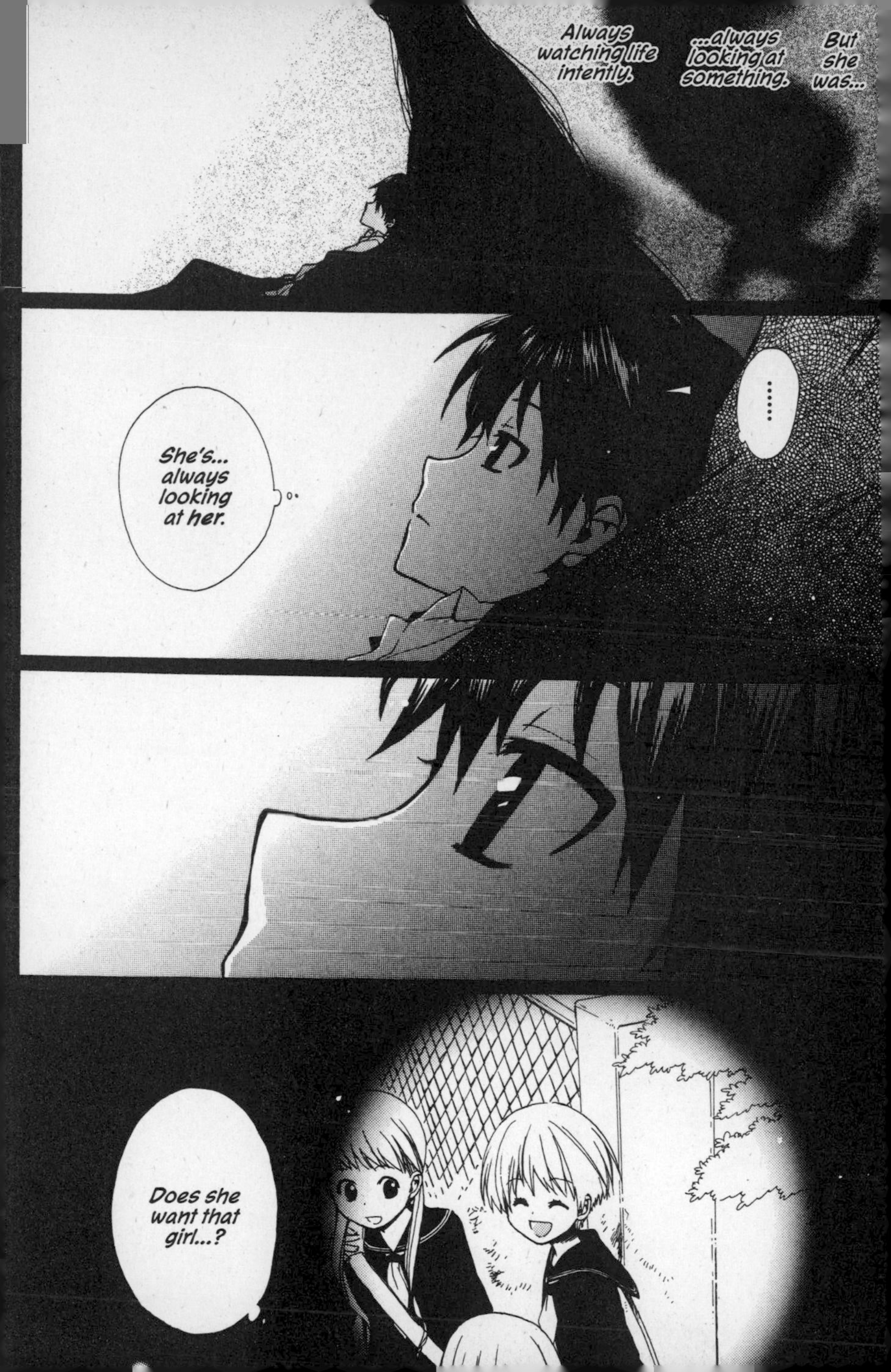
But she was...
...always looking at something.
Always watching life intently.
......
She's... always looking at her.
Does she want that girl...?

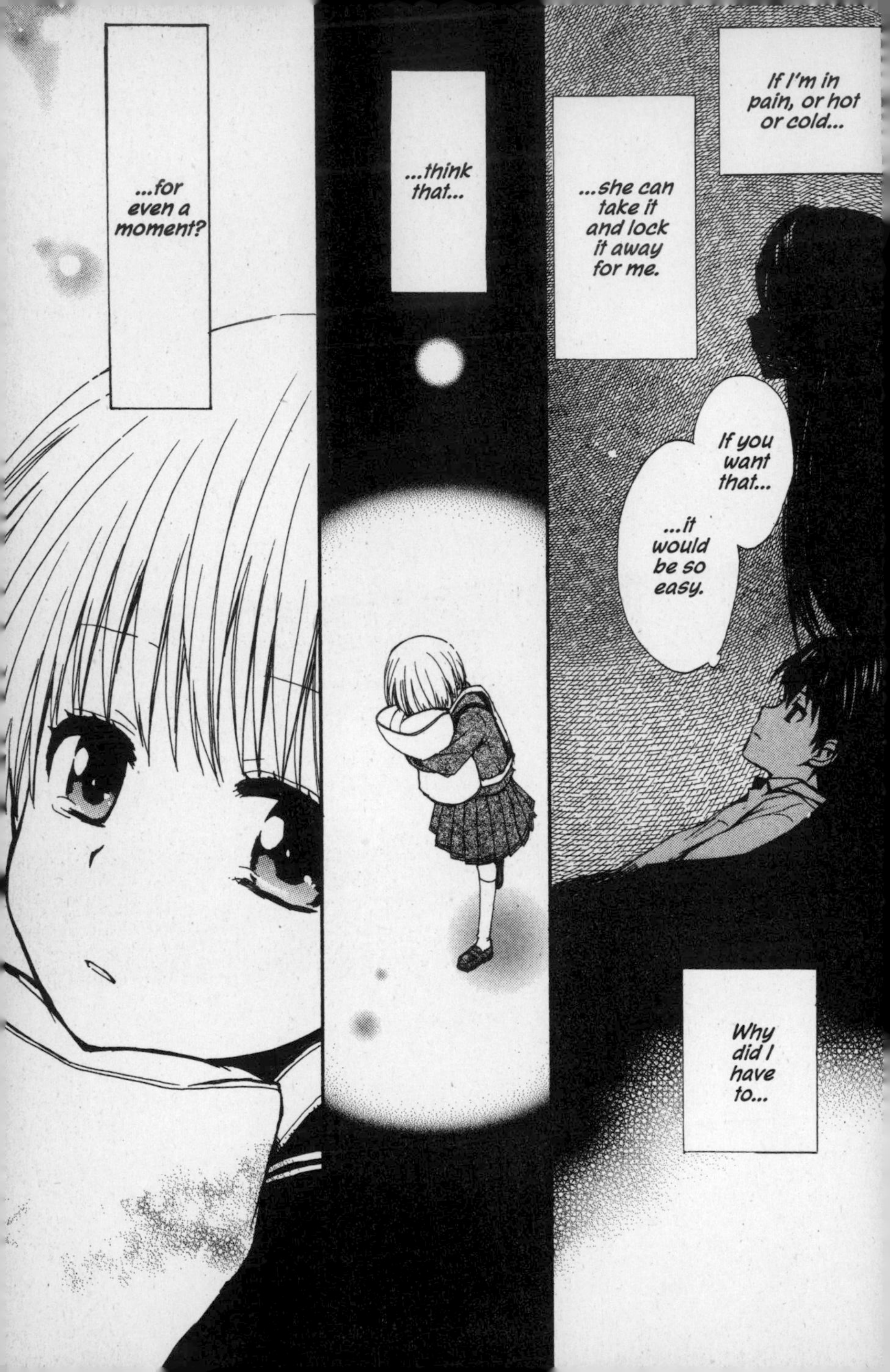

If I'm in pain, or hot or cold...
...she can take it and lock it away for me.
If you want that...
...it would be so easy.
Why did I have to...
...think that...
...for even a moment?

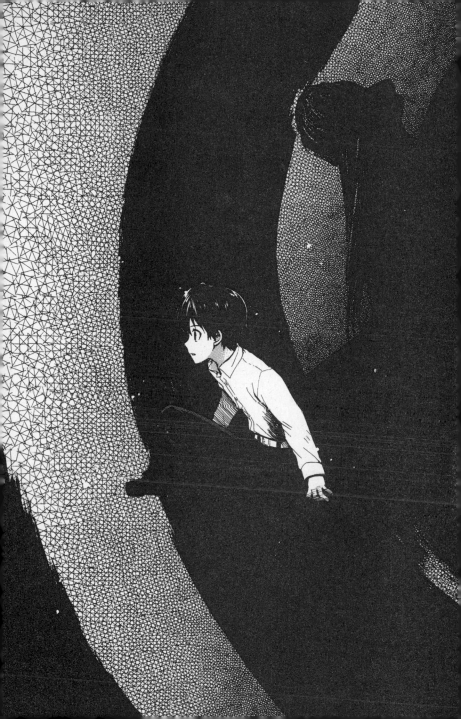

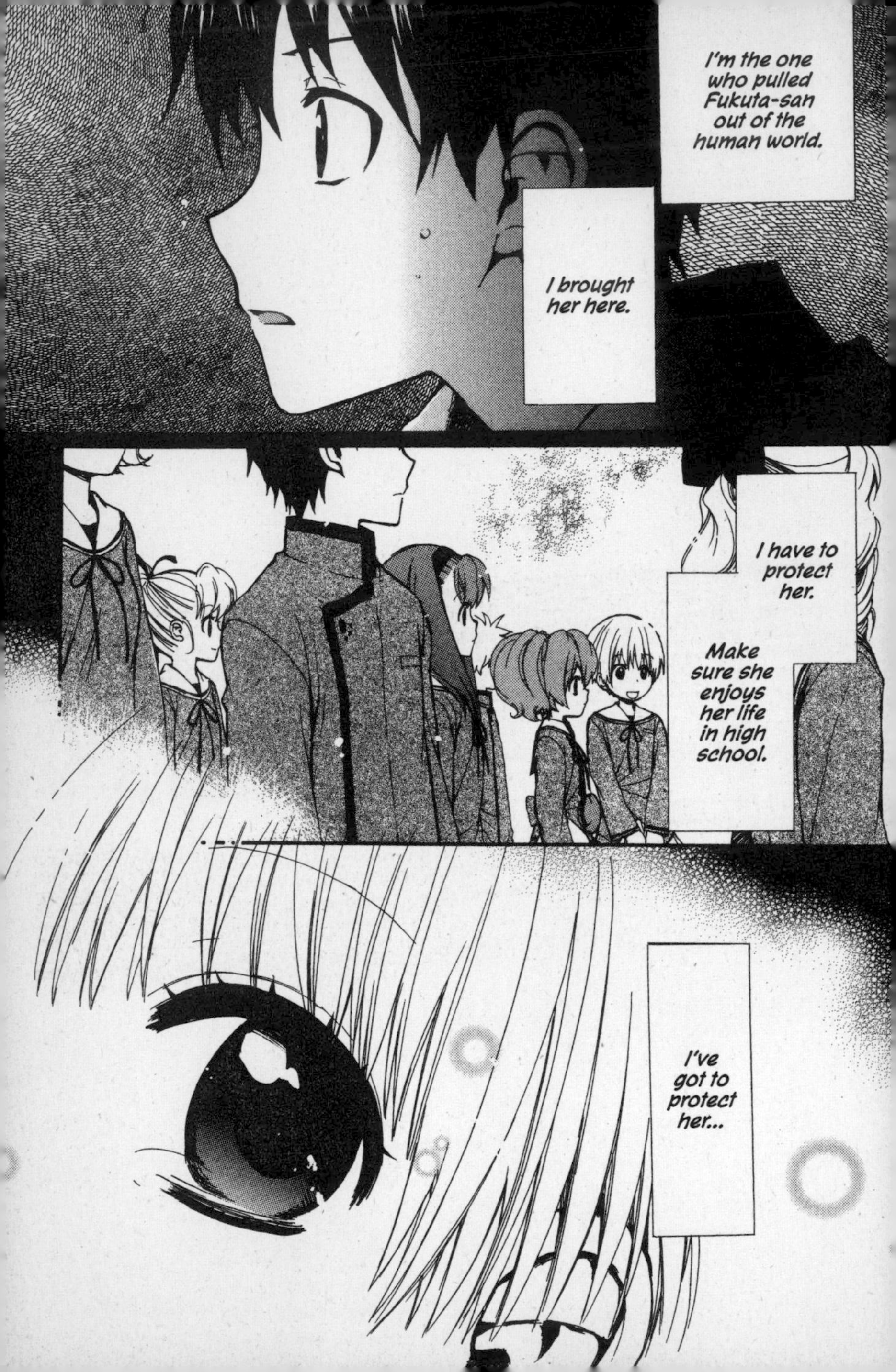
I'm the one who pulled Fukuta-san out of the human world.
I brought her here.
I have to protect her.
Make sure she enjoys her life in high school.
I've got to protect her...

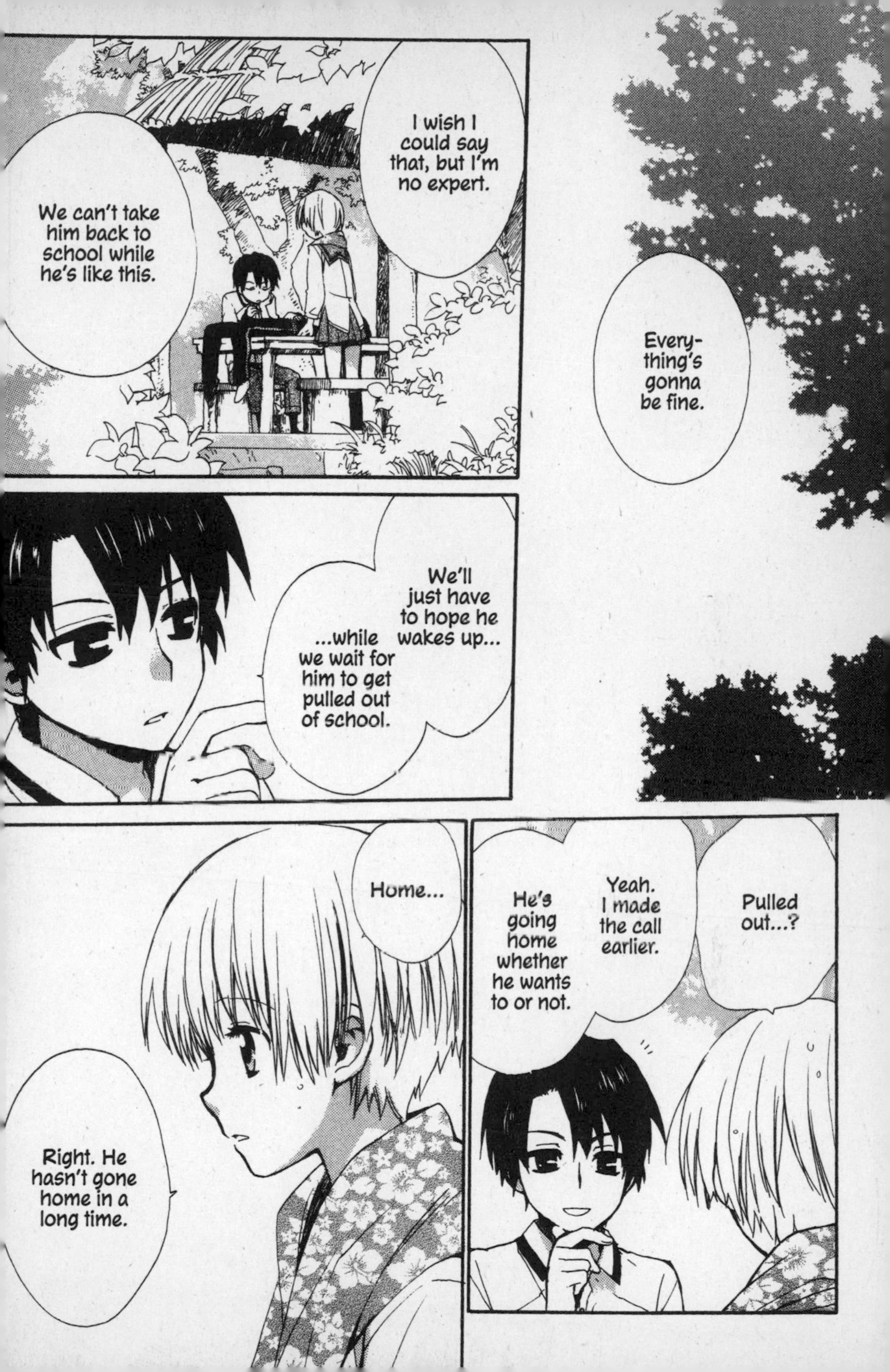
Every-thing's gonna be fine.
I wish I could say that, but I'm no expert.
We can't take him back to school while he's like this.
We'll just have to hope he wakes up...
...while we wait for him to get pulled out of school.
Pulled out...?
Yeah. I made the call earlier.
He's going home whether he wants to or not.
Home...
Right. He hasn't gone home in a long time.

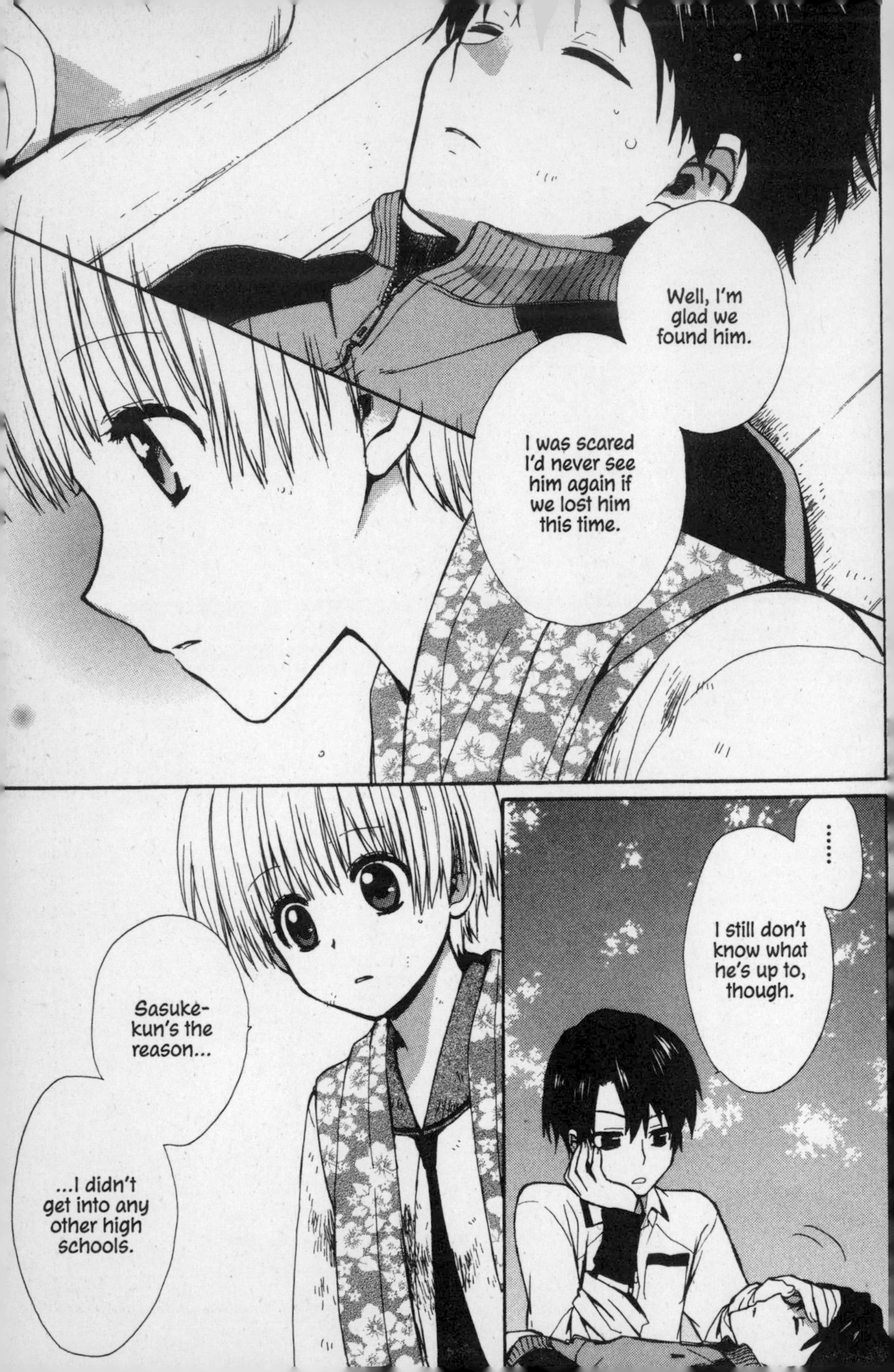
Well, I'm glad we found him.
I was scared I'd never see him again if we lost him this time.
......
I still don't know what he's up to, though.
Sasuke-kun's the reason...
...I didn't get into any other high schools.

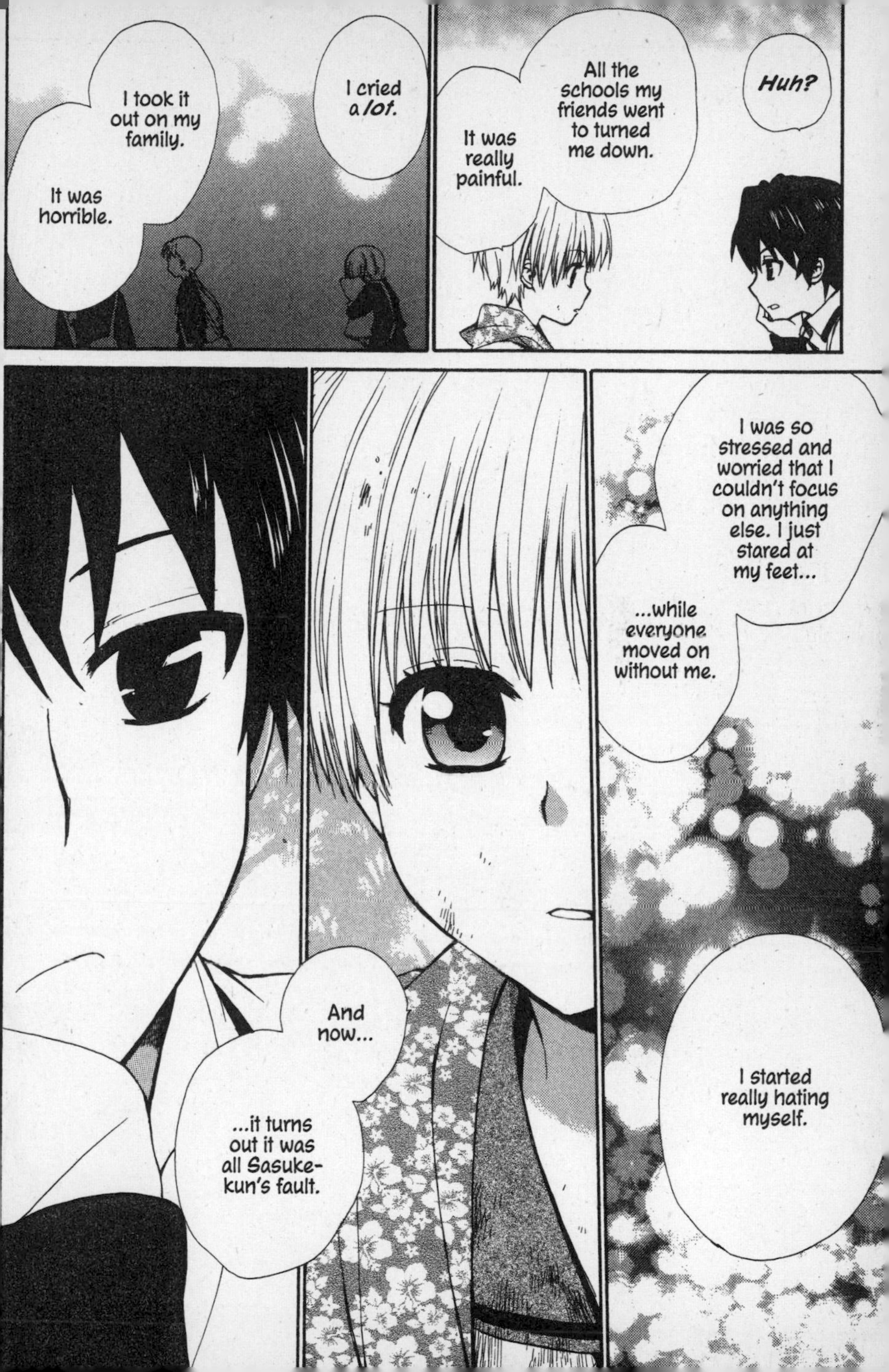
Huh?
All the schools my friends went to turned me down.
It was really painful.
I cried a *lot*.
I took it out on my family.
It was horrible.
I was so stressed and worried that I couldn't focus on anything else. I just stared at my feet...
...while everyone moved on without me.
I started really hating myself.
And now...
...it turns out it was all Sasuke-kun's fault.

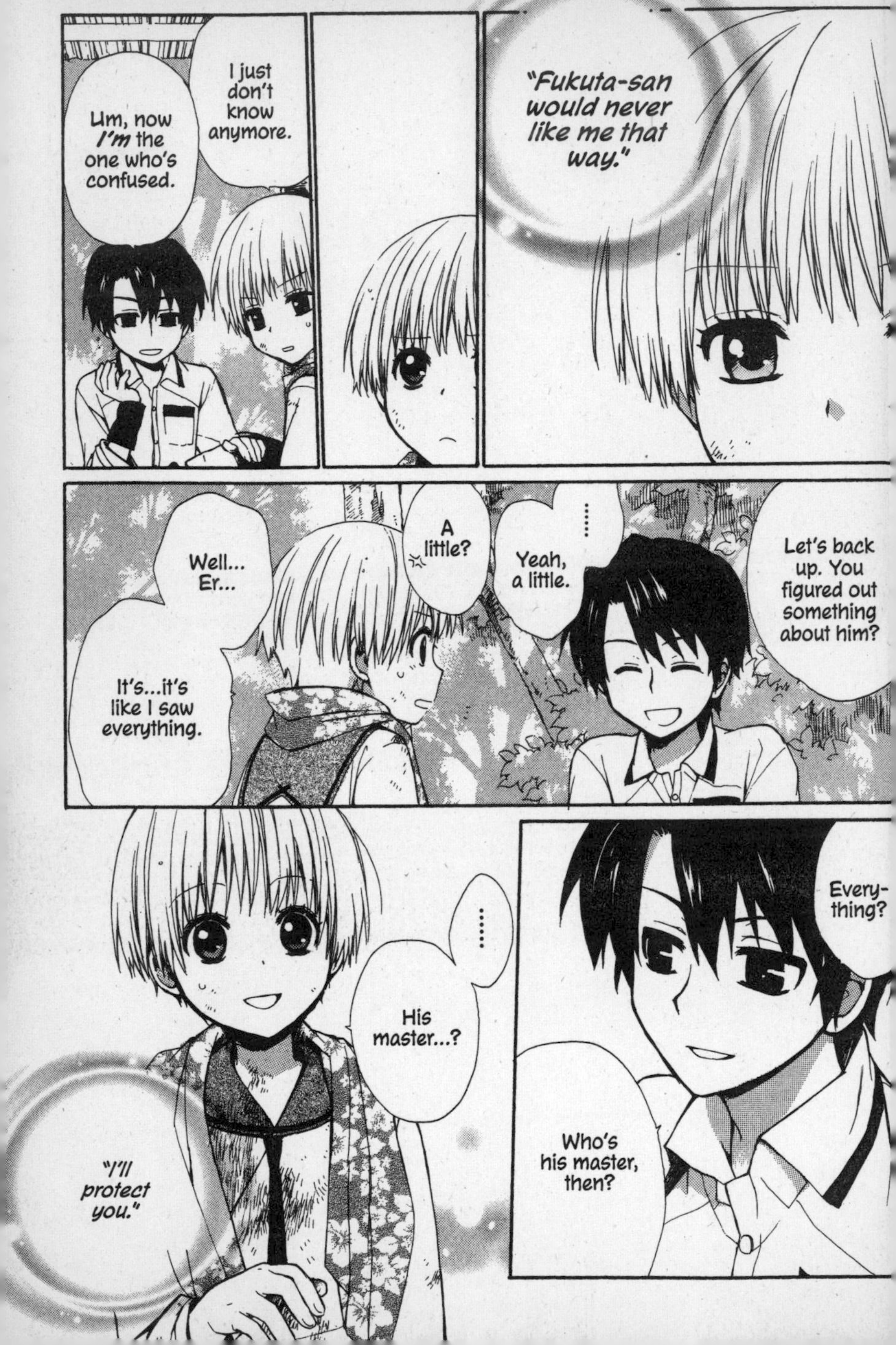
"Fukuta-san would never like me that way."
I just don't know anymore.
Um, now *I'm* the one who's confused.
Let's back up. You figured out something about him?
......
Yeah, a little.
A little?
Well... Er...
It's...it's like I saw everything.
Every-thing?
Who's his master, then?
......
His master...?
"I'll protect you."

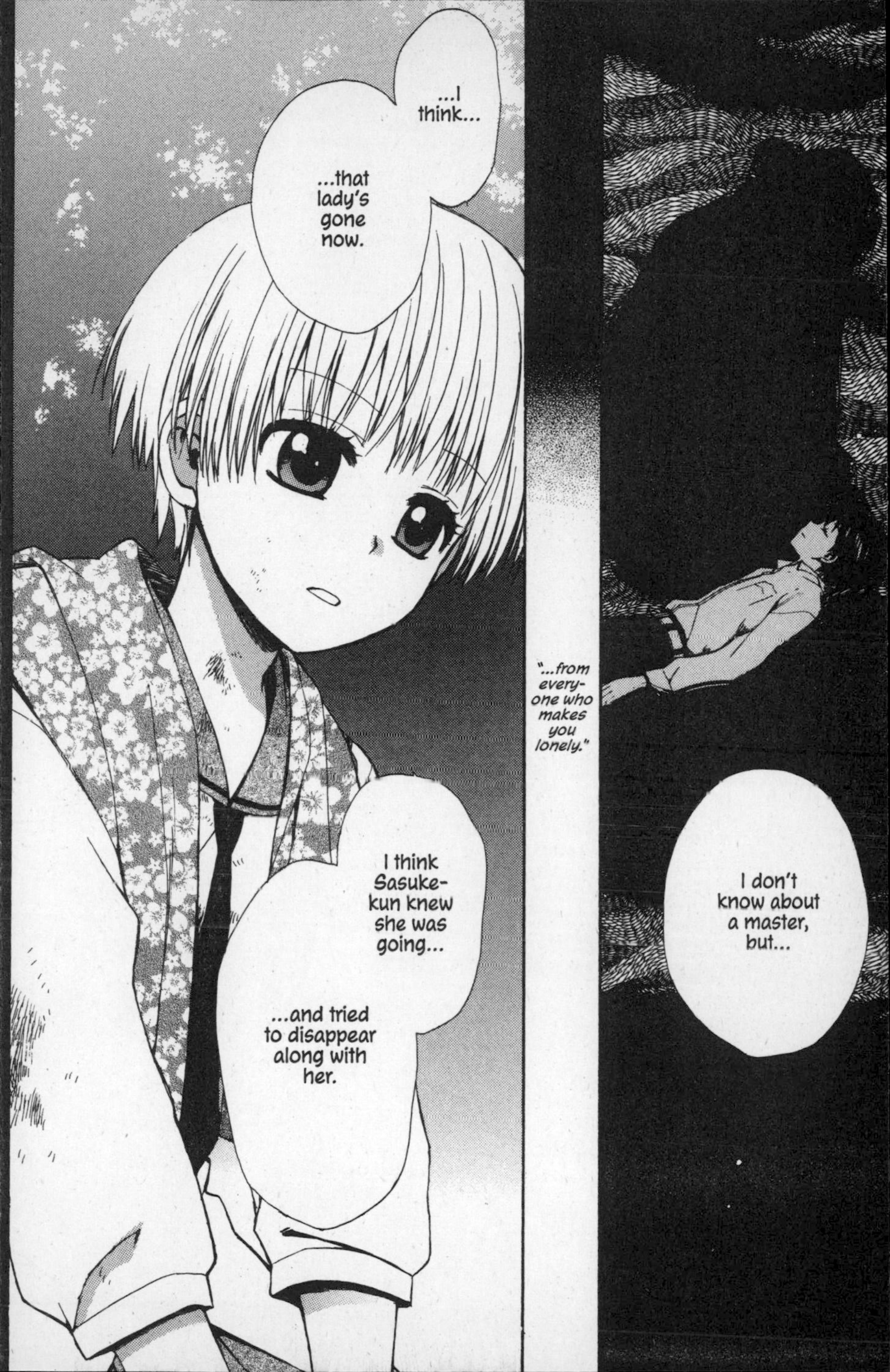
I don't know about a master, but...
"...from everyone who makes you lonely."
...I think...
...that lady's gone now.
I think Sasuke-kun knew she was going...
...and tried to disappear along with her.

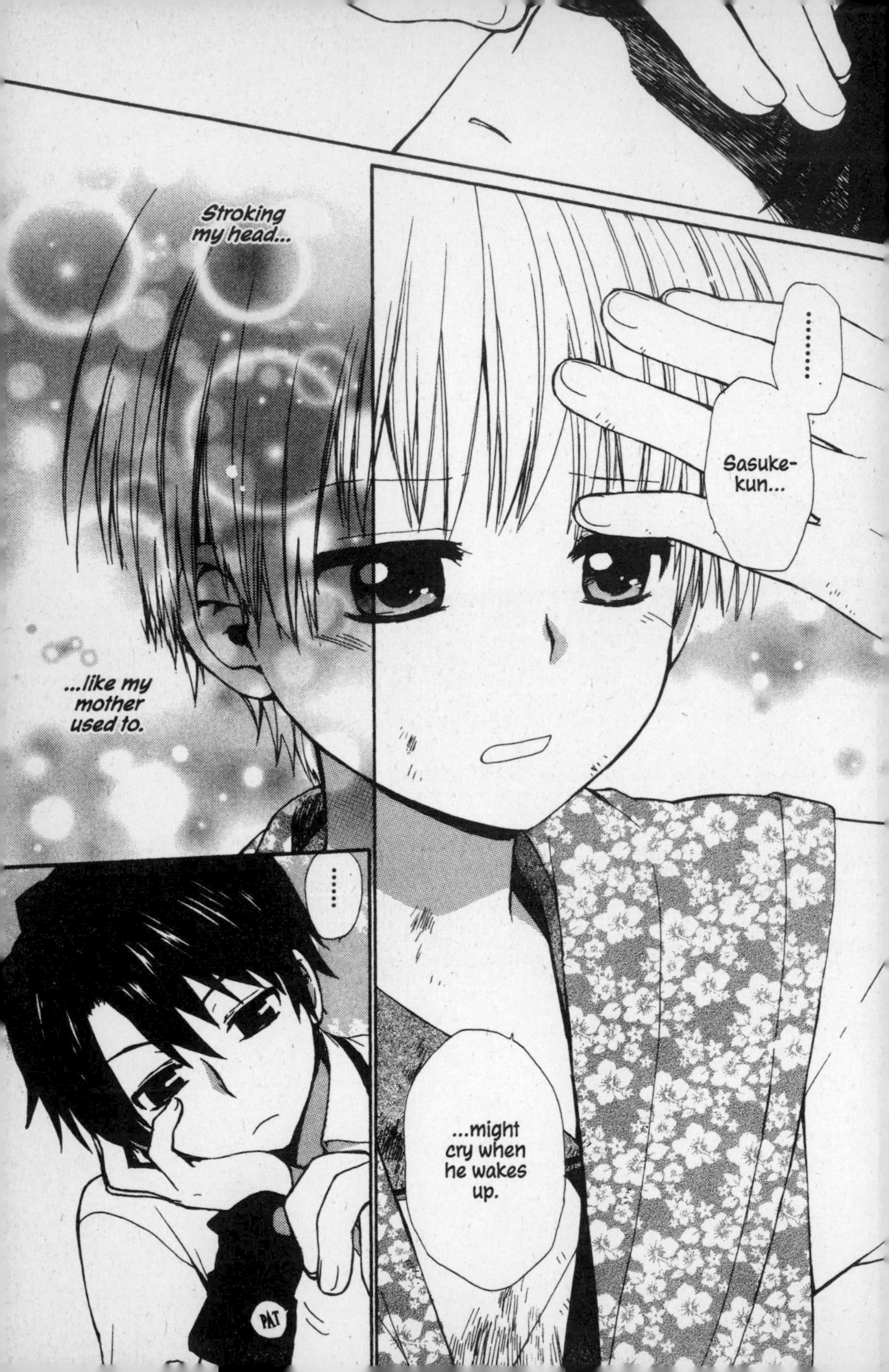

......
Sasuke-kun...
...might cry when he wakes up.
Stroking my head...
...like my mother used to.
......
PAT

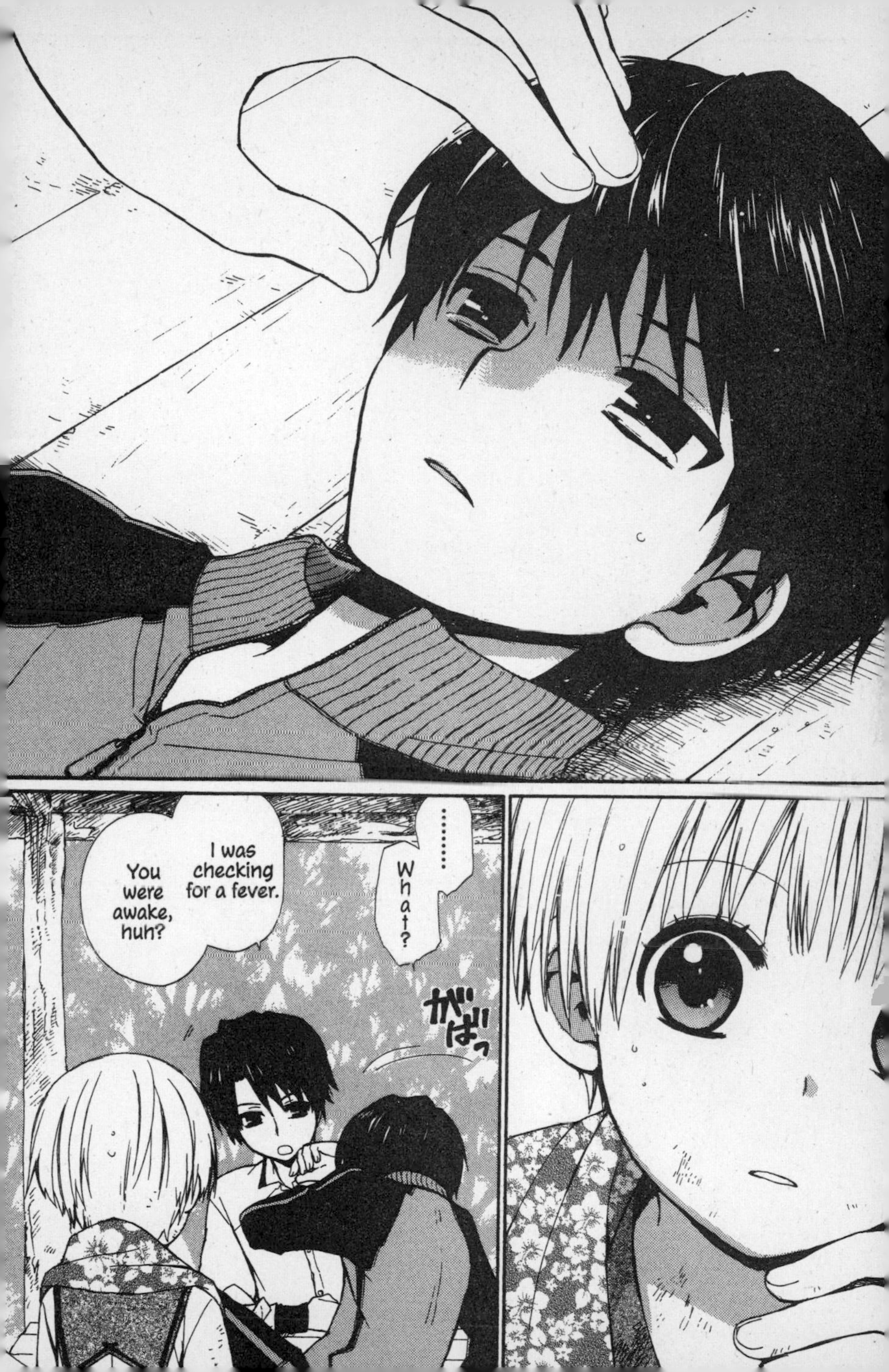

......
What?
I was checking for a fever.
You were awake, huh?
がばっ

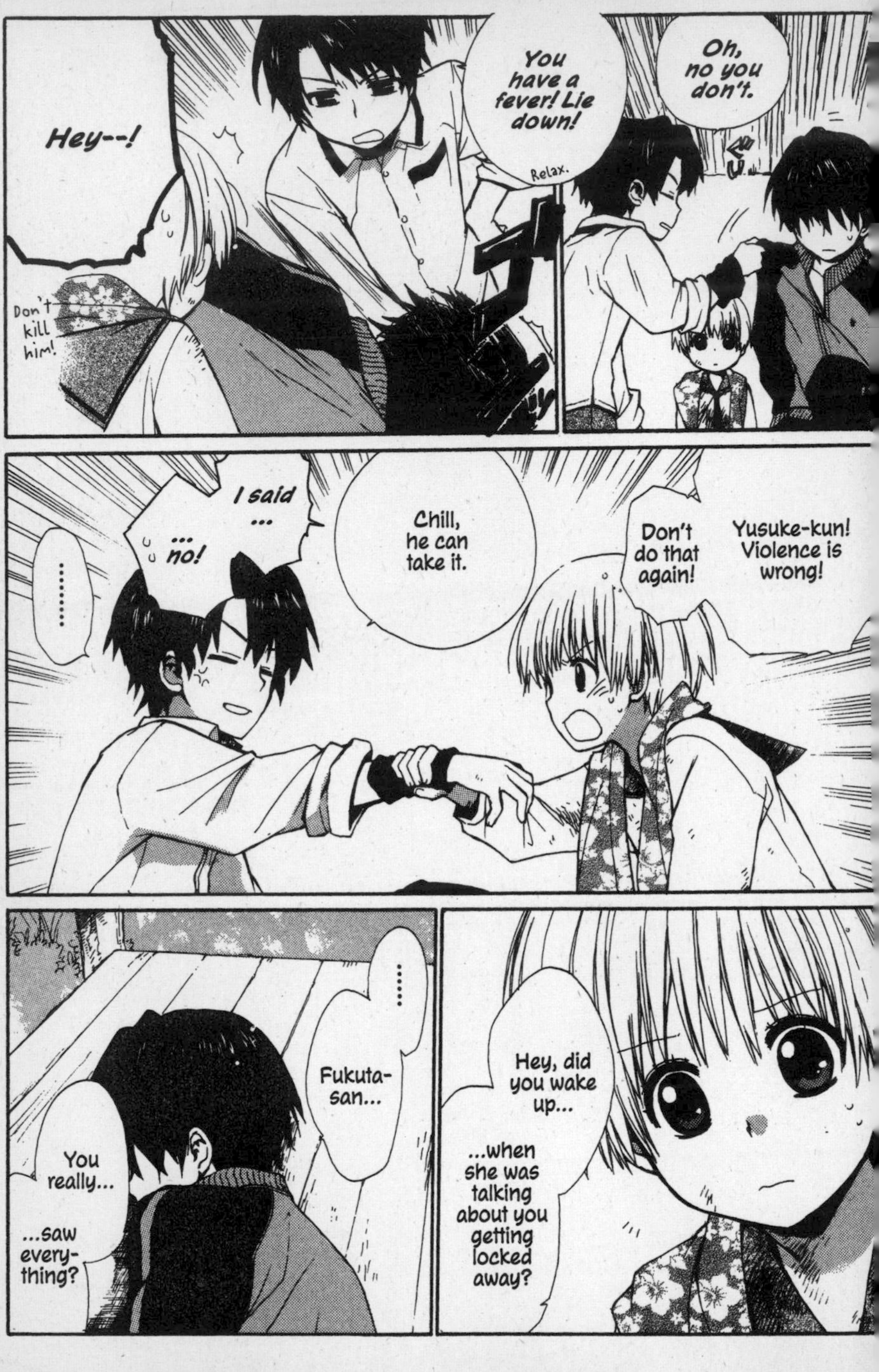
Oh, no you don't.
You have a fever! Lie down!
Relax.
Hey--!
Don't kill him!
Yusuke-kun! Violence is wrong!
Don't do that again!
Chill, he can take it.
I said ...
... no!
......
Hey, did you wake up...
...when she was talking about you getting locked away?
......
Fukuta-san...
You really...
...saw every-thing?

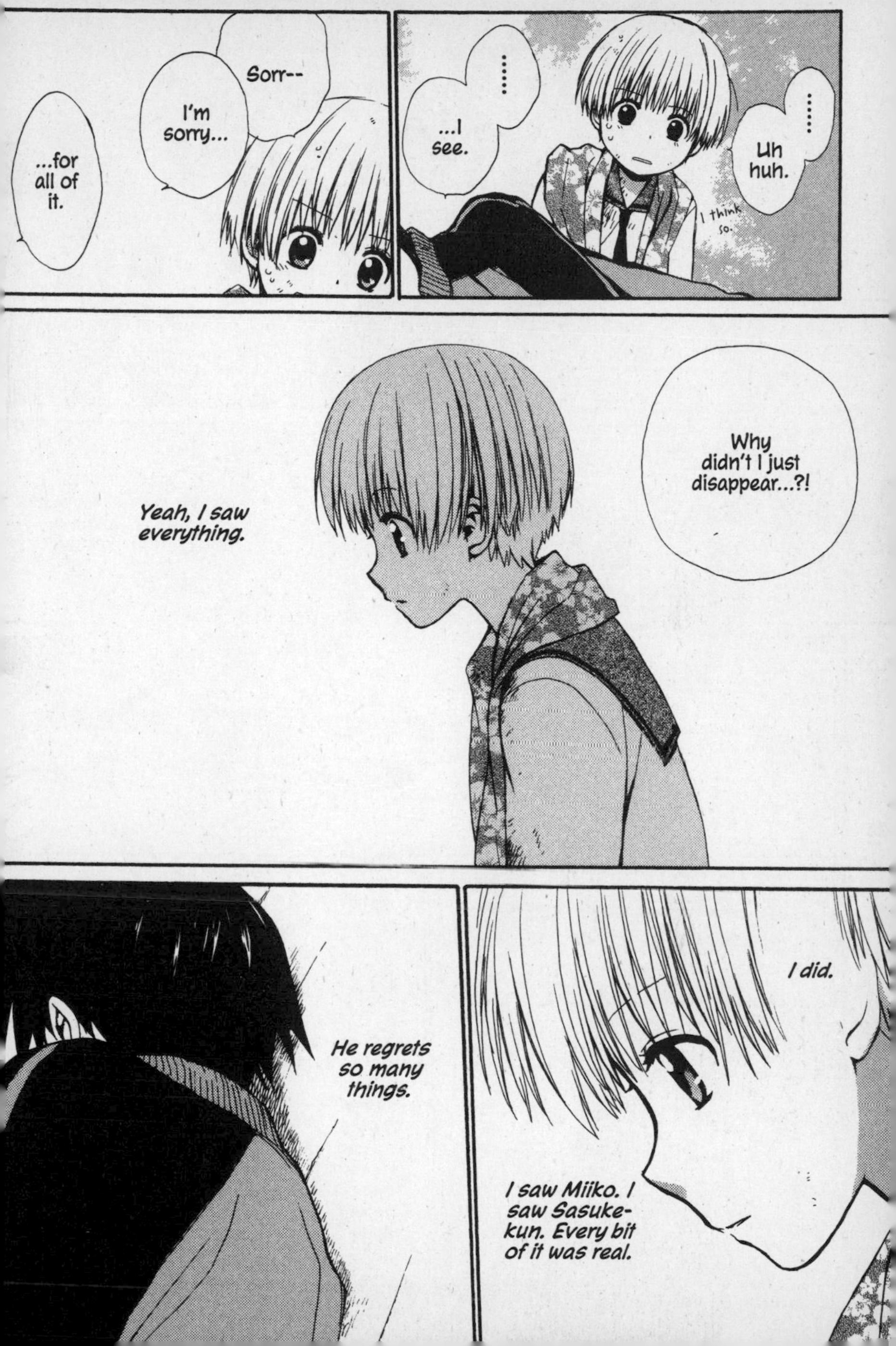
……
Uh huh.
I think so.
……
...I see.
Sorr--
I'm sorry...
...for all of it.
Why didn't I just disappear...?!
Yeah, I saw everything.
I did.
I saw Miiko. I saw Sasuke-kun. Every bit of it was real.
He regrets so many things.

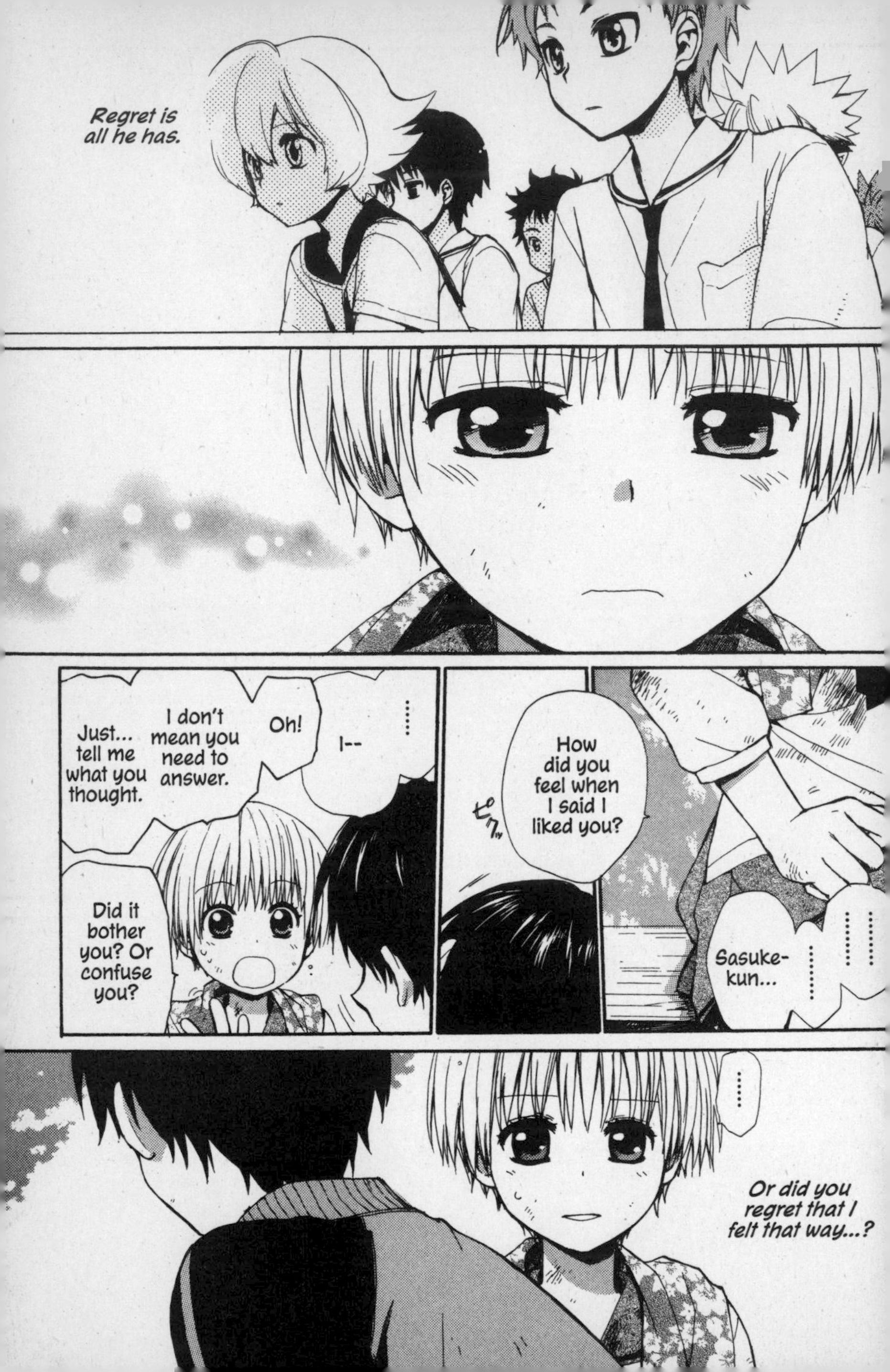

Regret is all he has.
......
Sasuke-kun...
How did you feel when I said I liked you?
ピクッ
......
I--
Oh!
I don't mean you need to answer.
Just... tell me what you thought.
Did it bother you? Or confuse you?
......
Or did you regret that I felt that way...?

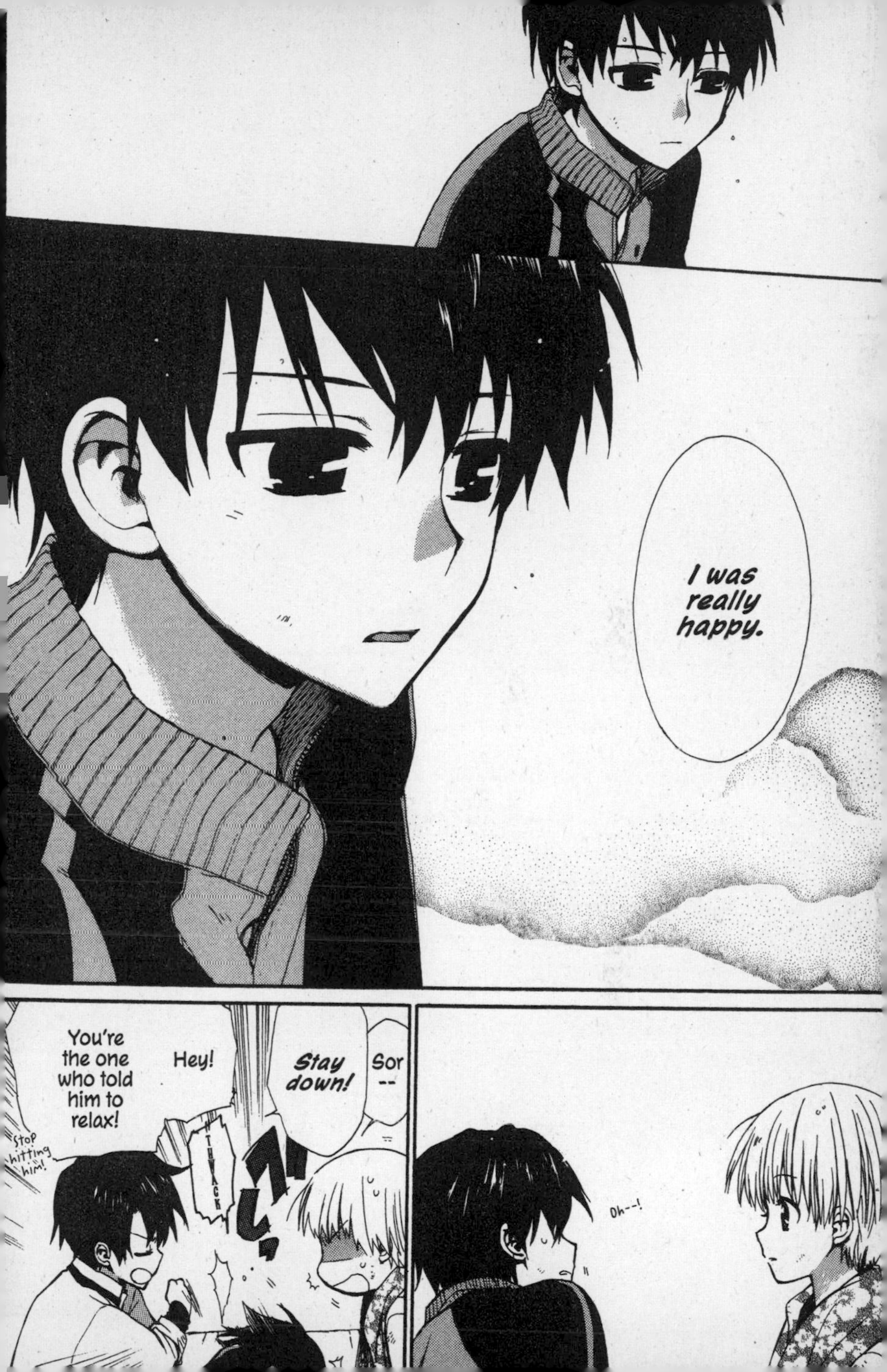
I was really happy.
Oh--!
Sor --
Stay down!
Hey!
You're the one who told him to relax!
THWACK
Stop hitting him!

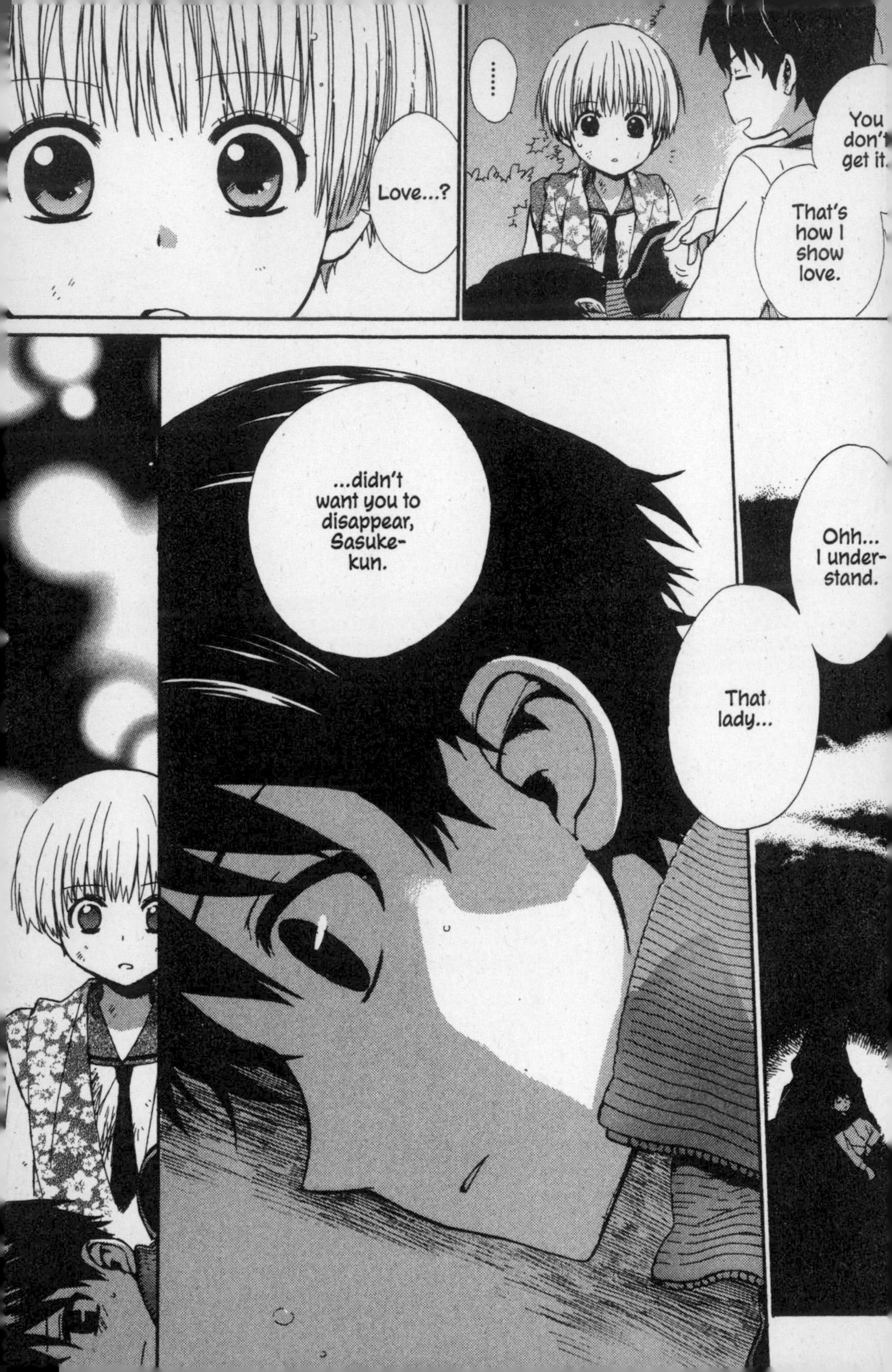
You don't get it.
That's how I show love.
......
Love...?
Ohh... I under-stand.
That lady...
...didn't want you to disappear, Sasuke-kun.

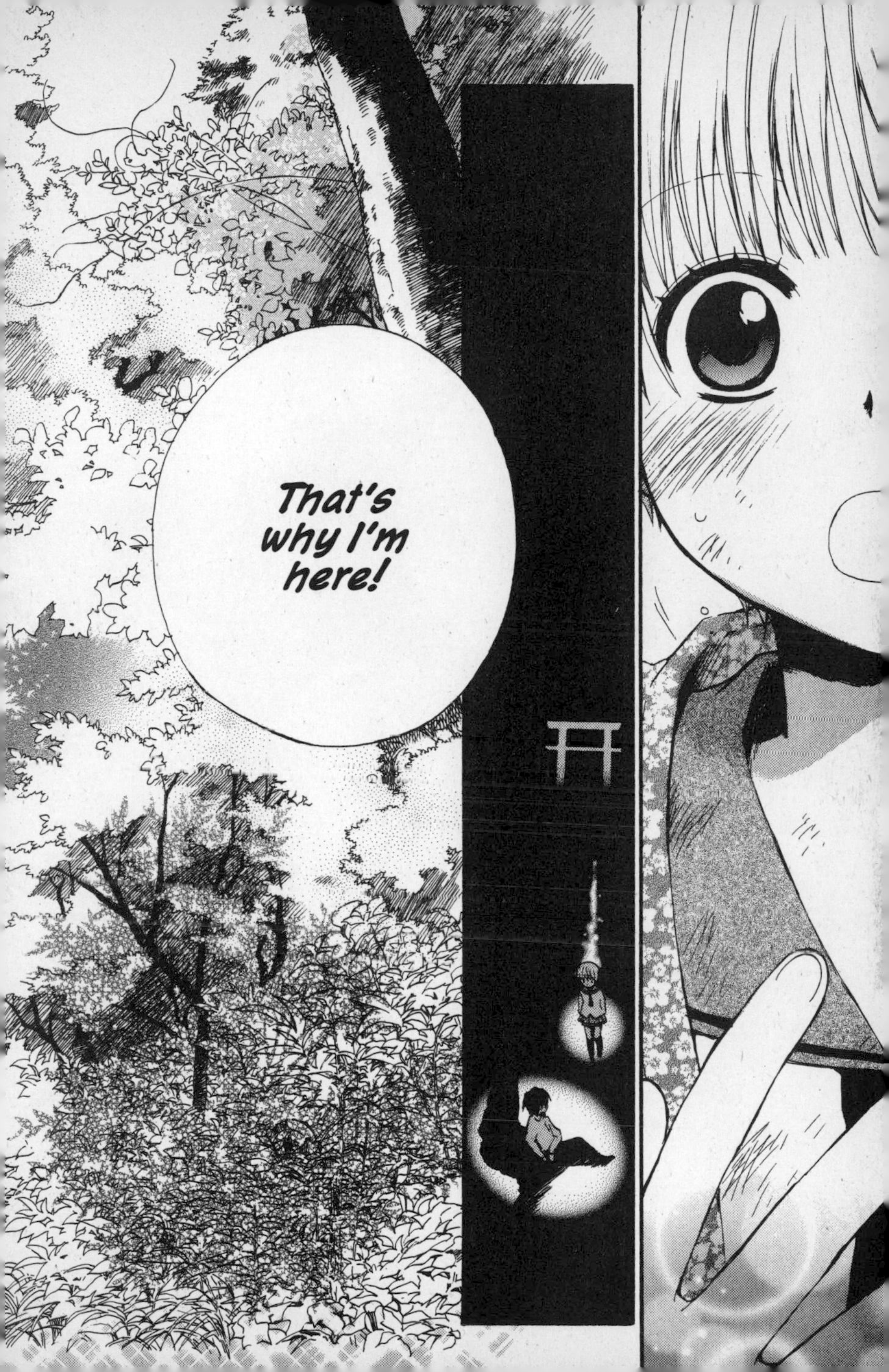
That's why I'm here!

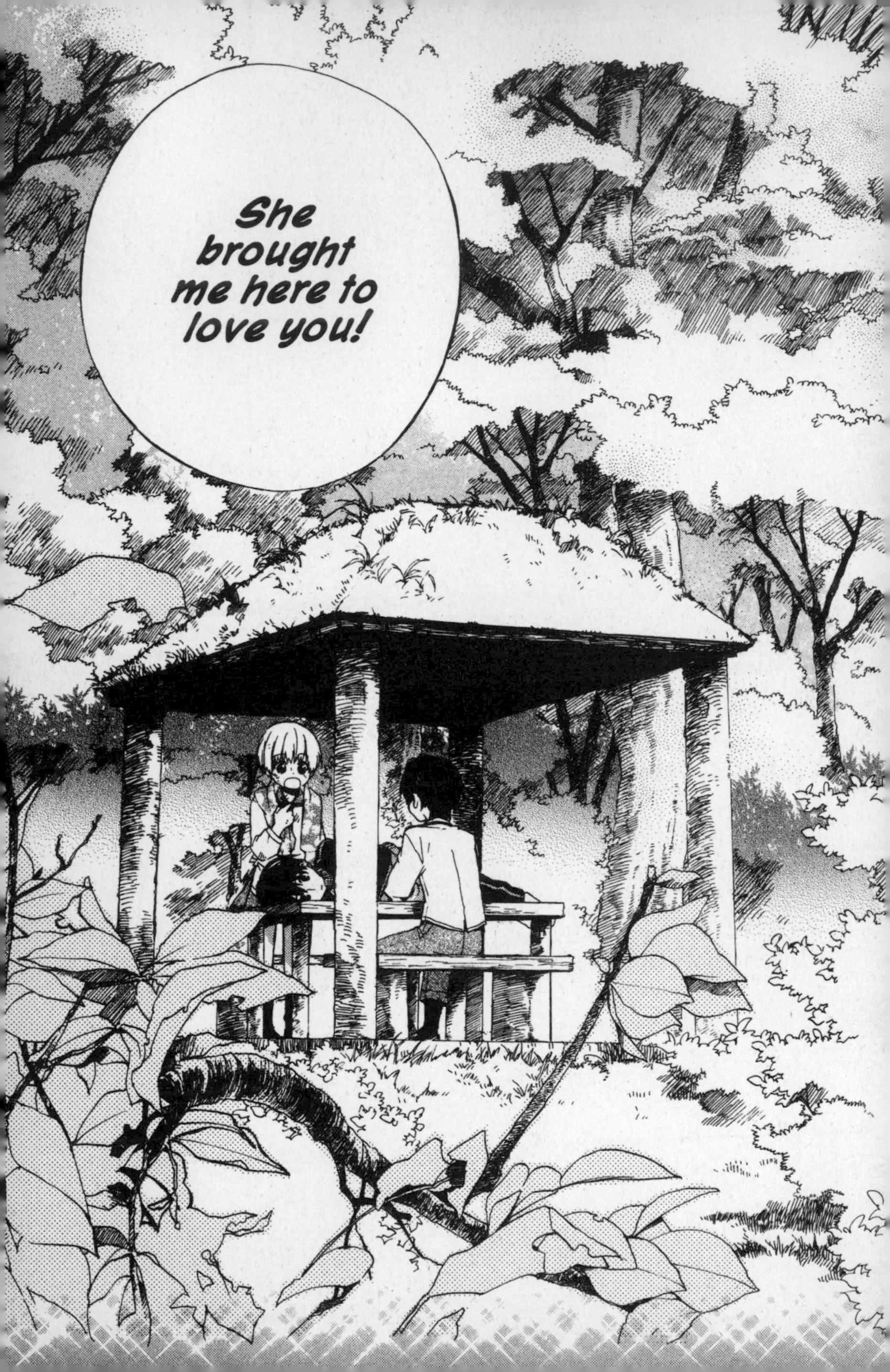
She brought me here to love you!

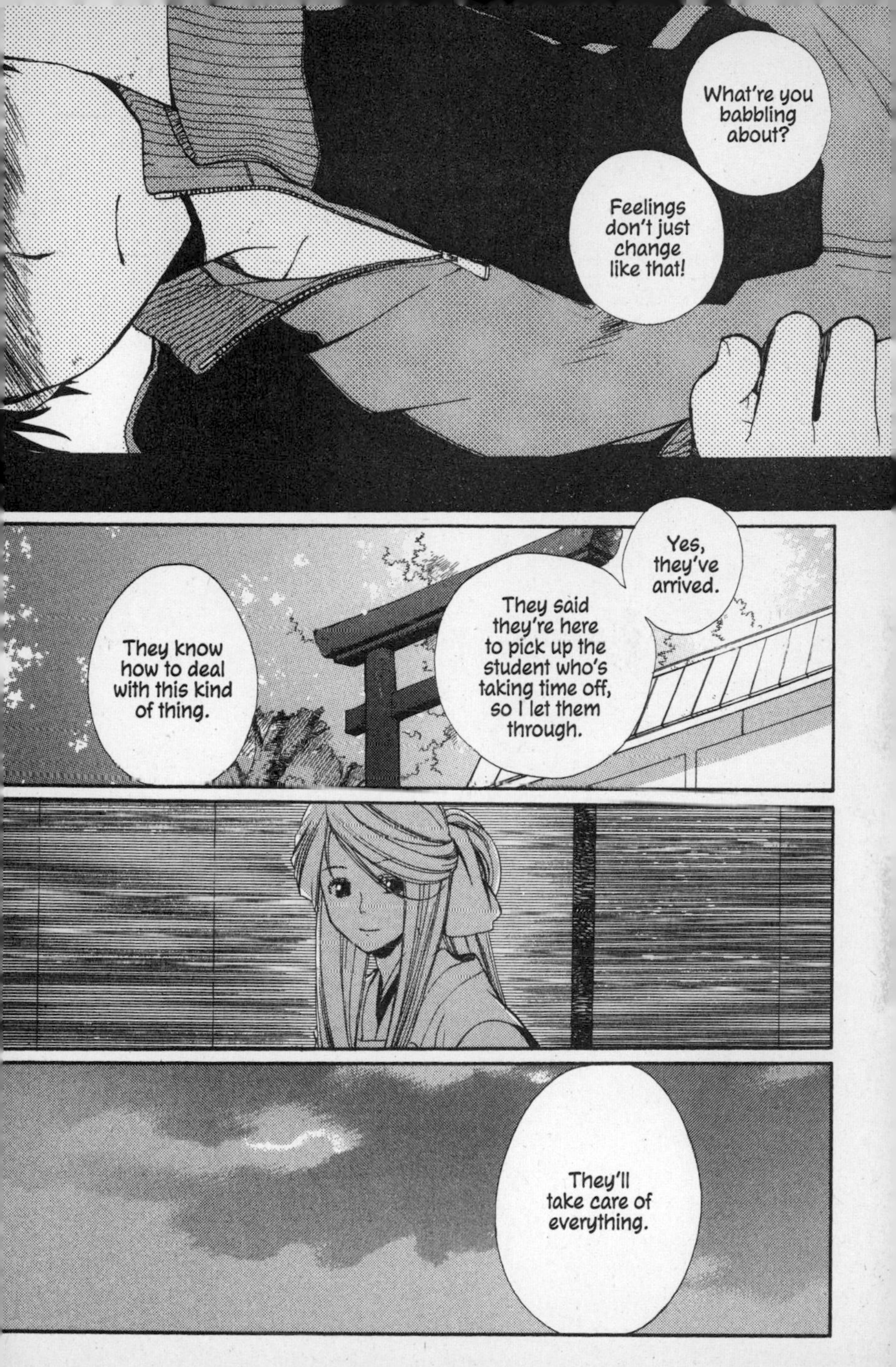
What're you babbling about?
Feelings don't just change like that!
Yes, they've arrived.
They said they're here to pick up the student who's taking time off, so I let them through.
They know how to deal with this kind of thing.
They'll take care of everything.

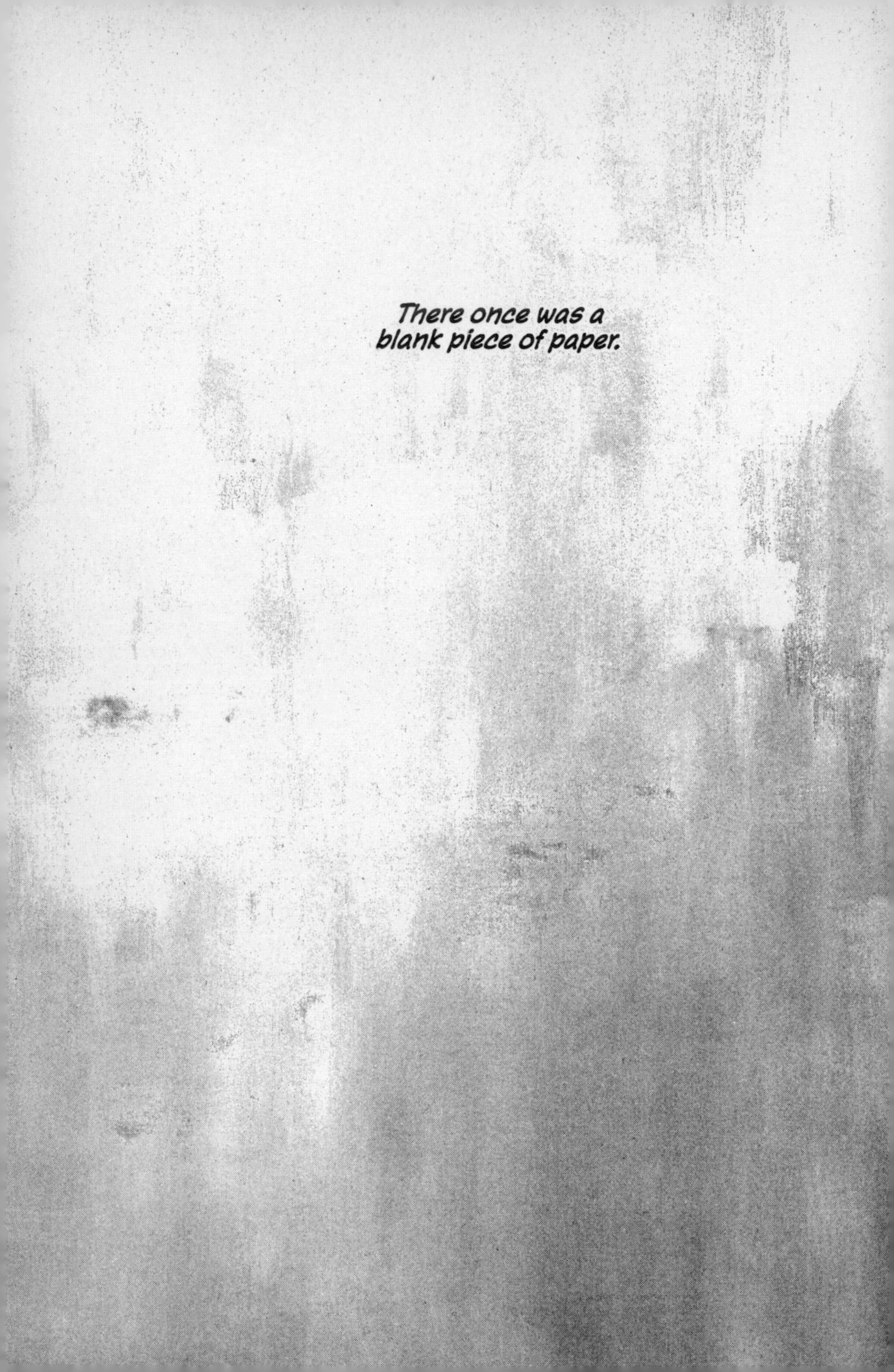
There once was a blank piece of paper.

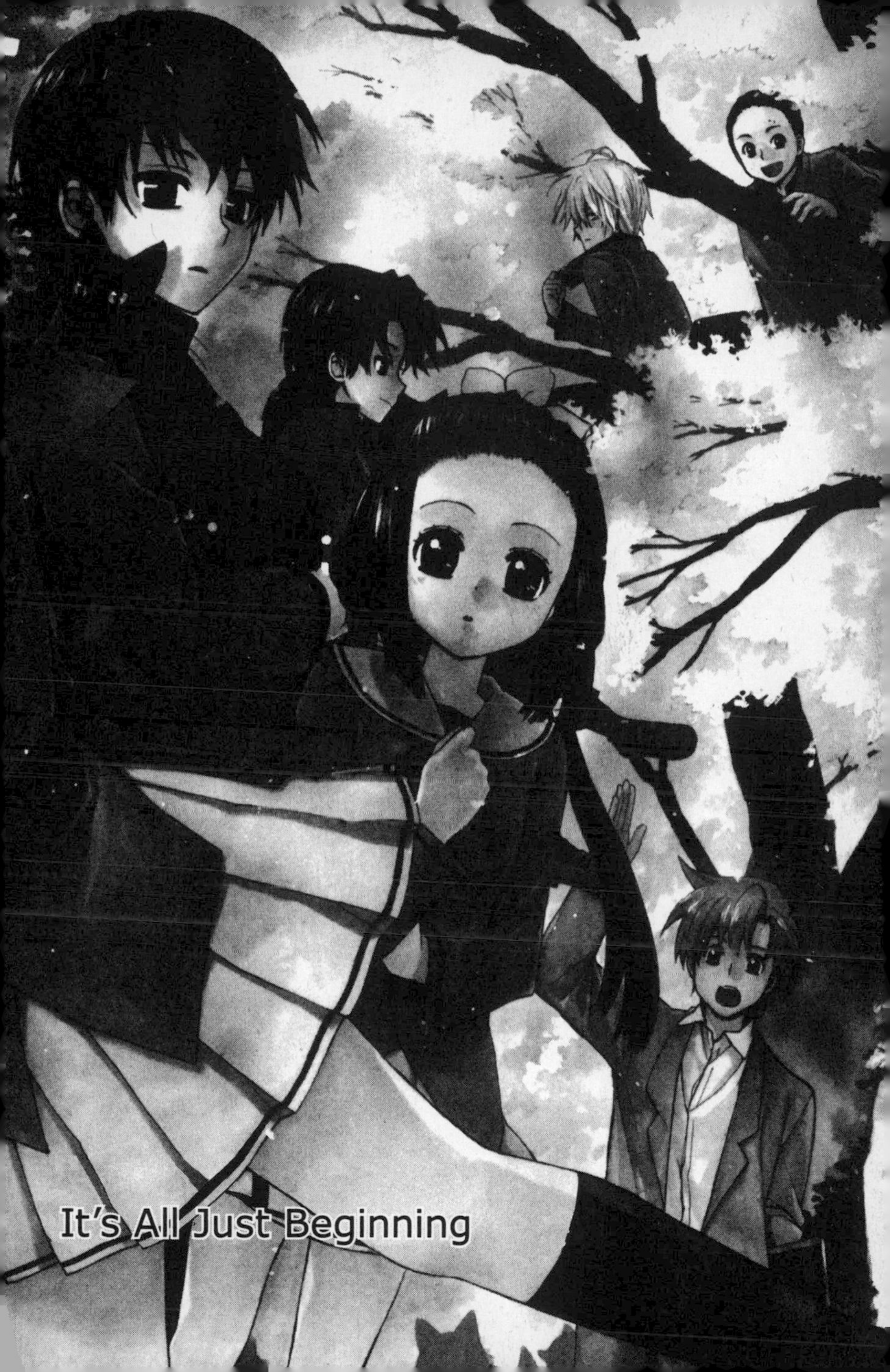
It's All Just Beginning

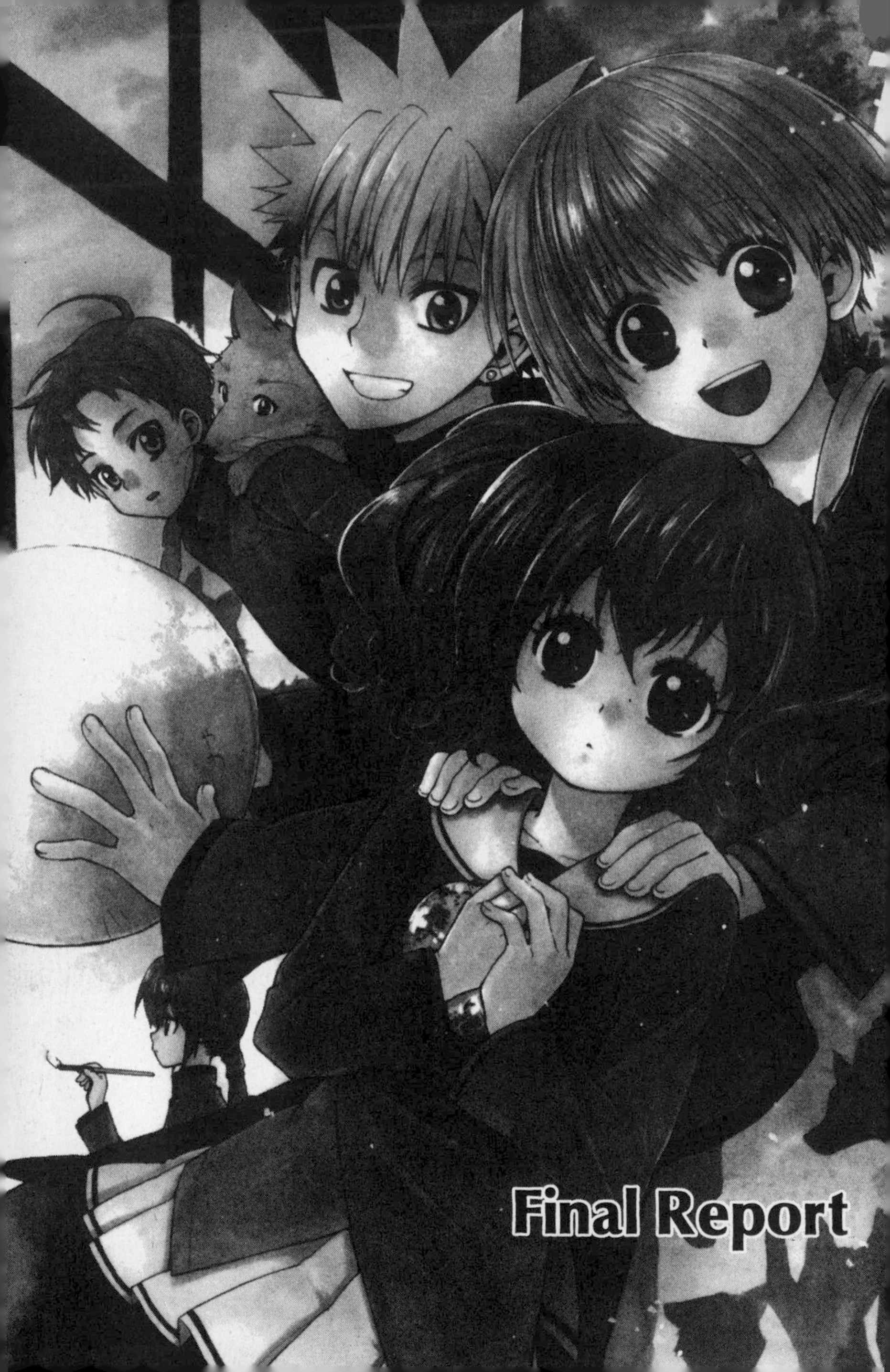
Final Report

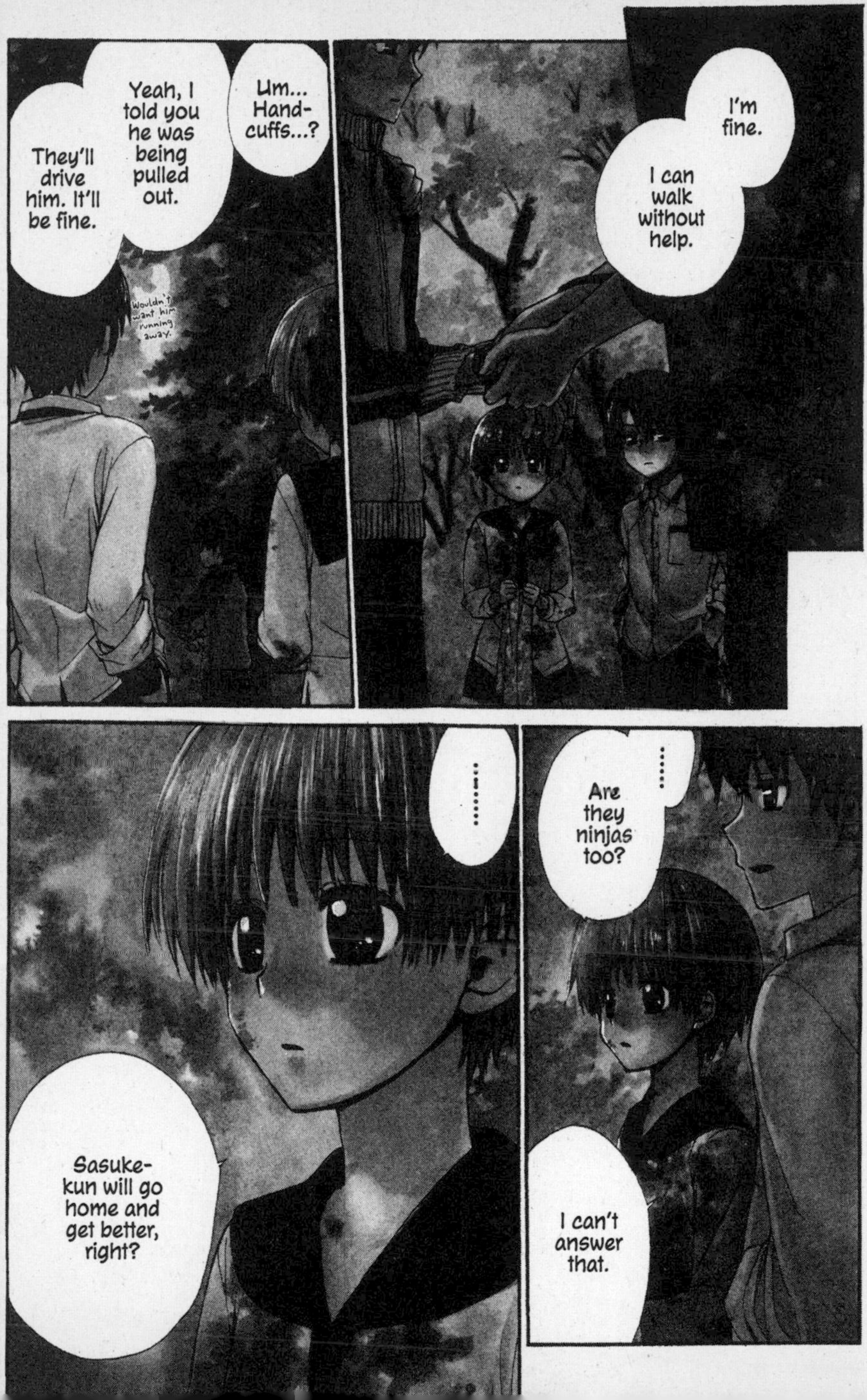
I'm fine.
I can walk without help.
Um... Hand-cuffs...?
Yeah, I told you he was being pulled out.
They'll drive him. It'll be fine.
Wouldn't want him running away.
......
Are they ninjas too?
I can't answer that.
....
Sasuke-kun will go home and get better, right?

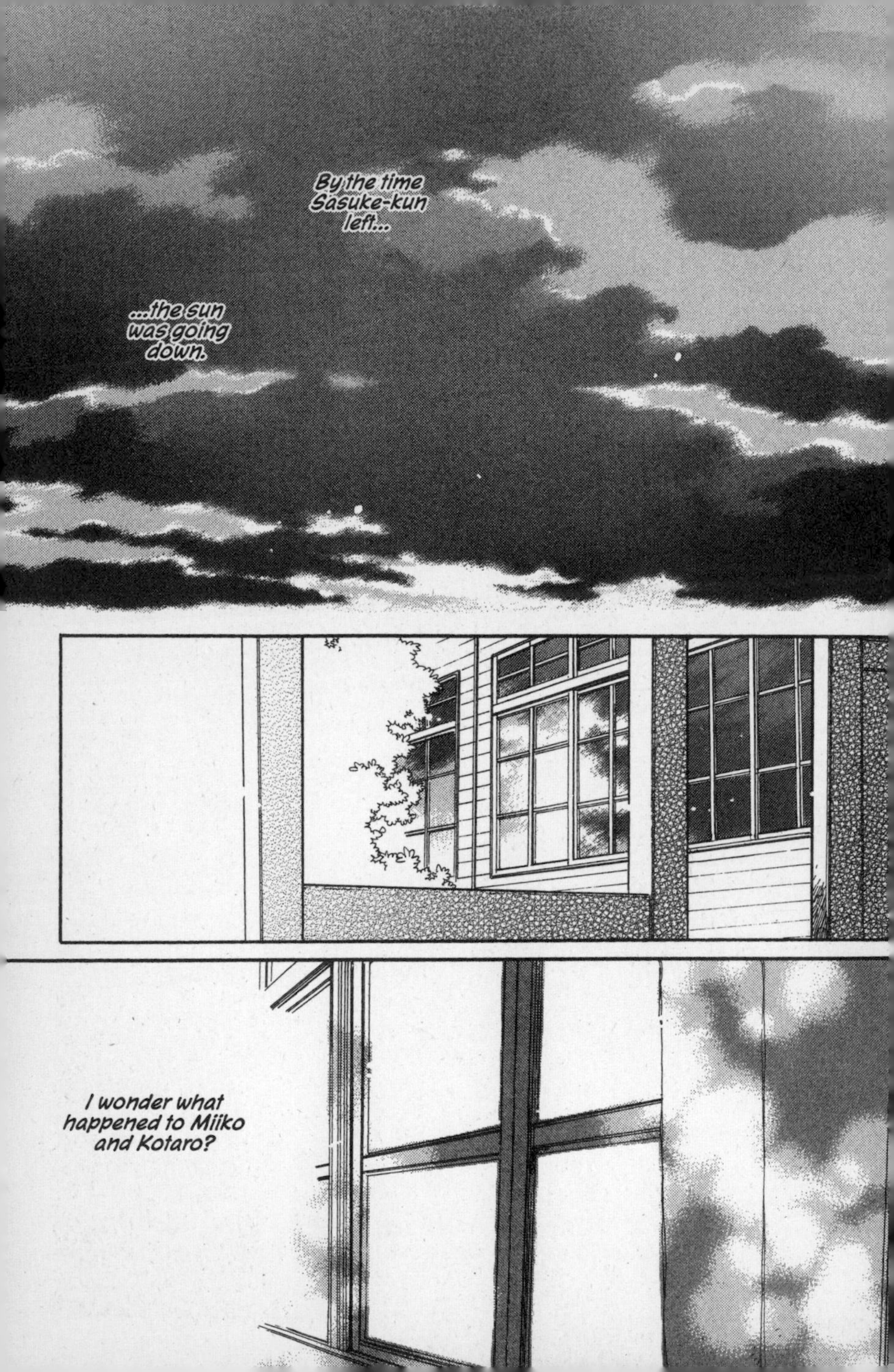
By the time Sasuke-kun left...
...the sun was going down.
I wonder what happened to Miiko and Kotaro?

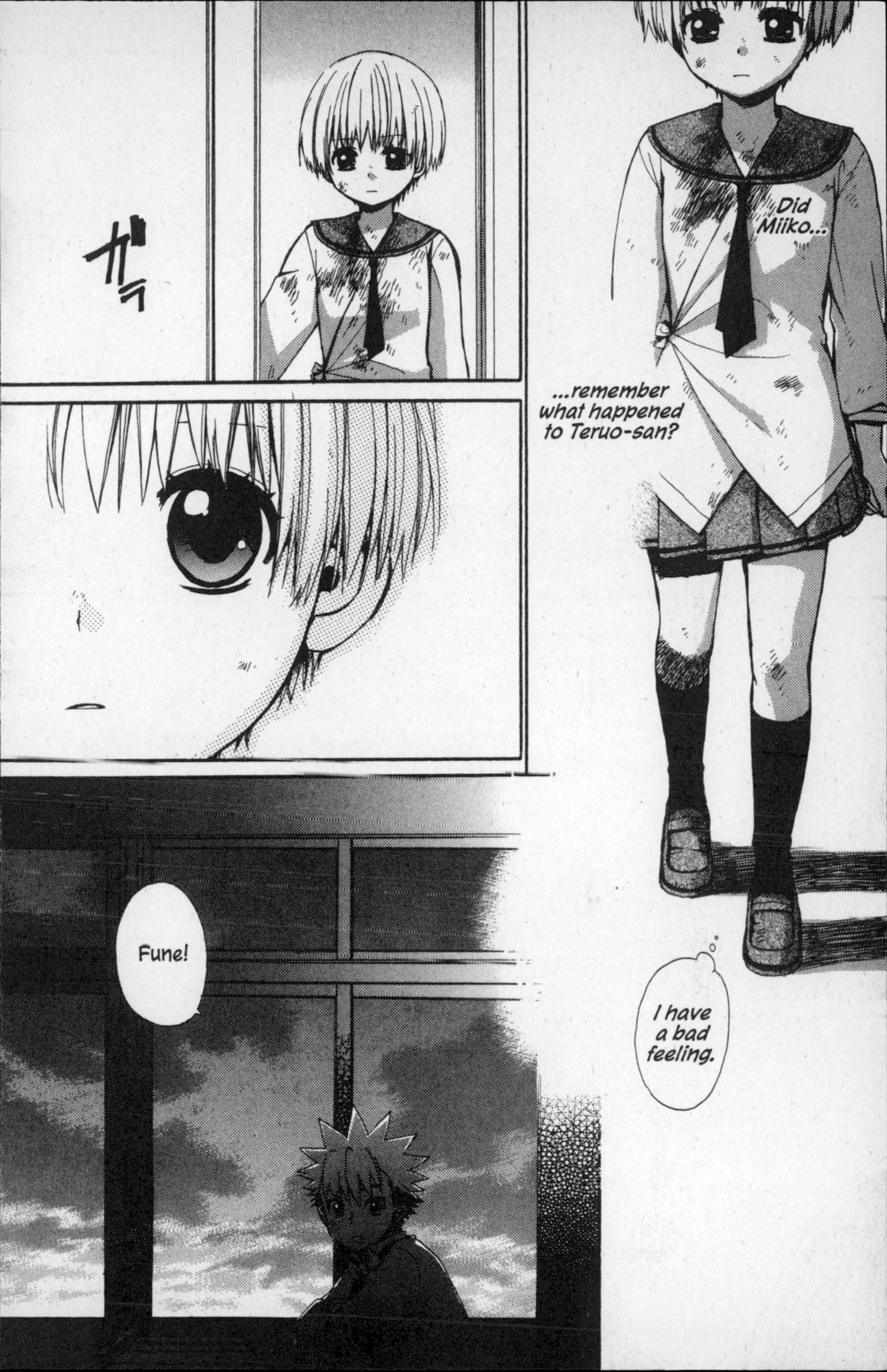
Did Miiko...
...remember what happened to Teruo-san?
I have a bad feeling.
ガラ
Fune!

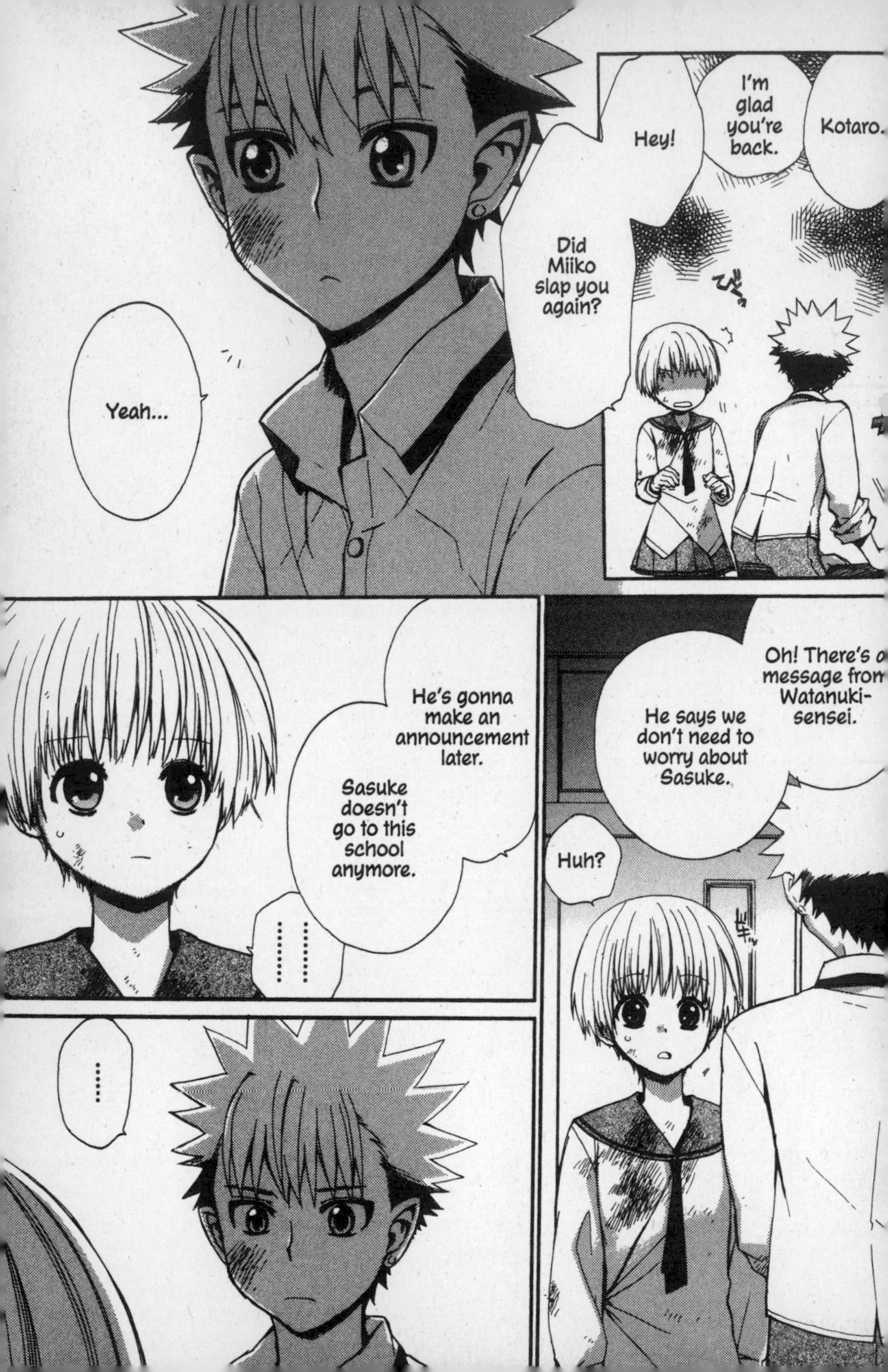
Kotaro.
I'm glad you're back.
Hey!
Did Miiko slap you again?
Yeah...
Oh! There's a message from Watanuki-sensei.
He says we don't need to worry about Sasuke.
Huh?
He's gonna make an announcement later.
Sasuke doesn't go to this school anymore.
......
......

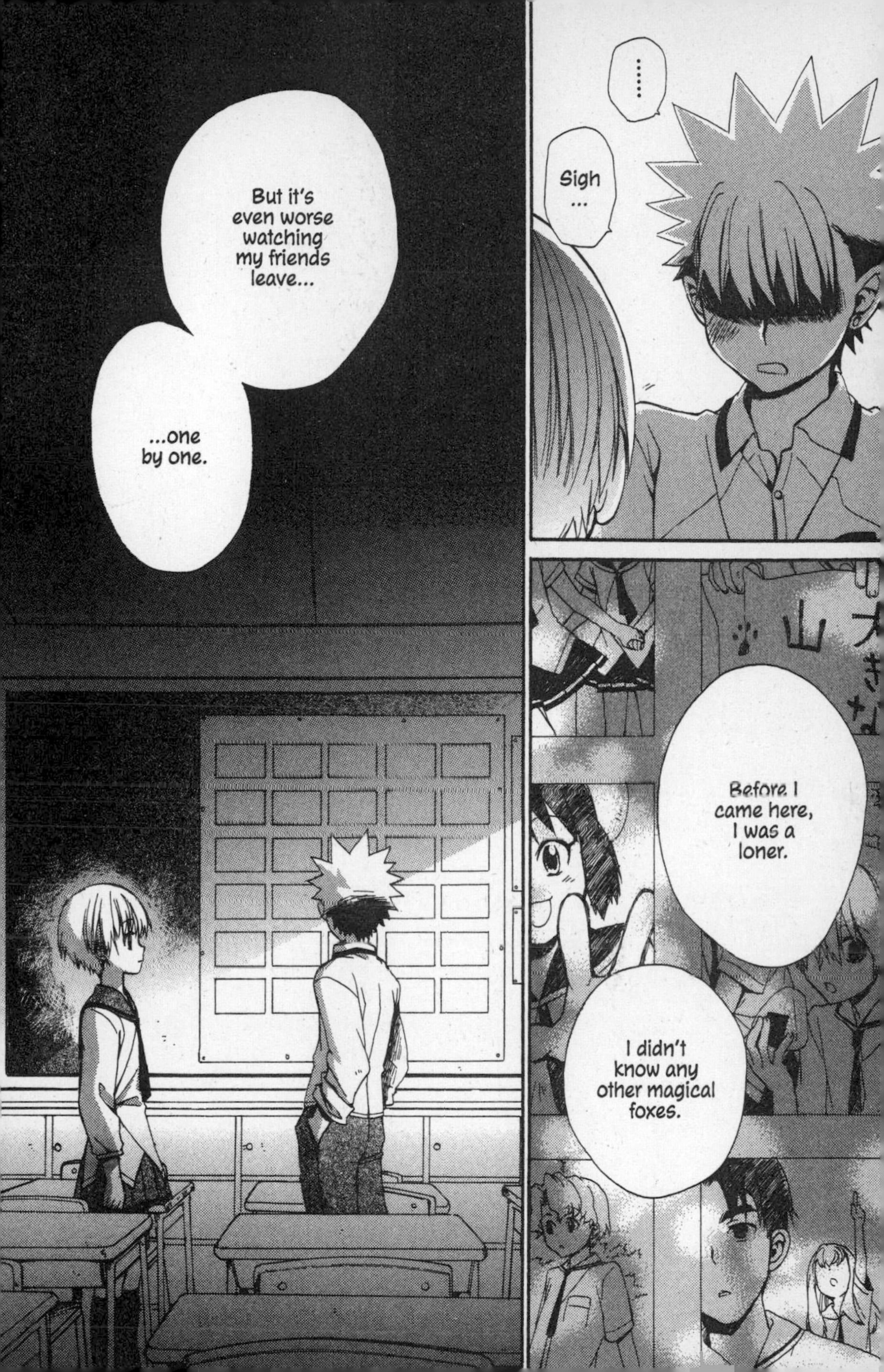
……
Sigh ...
Before I came here, I was a loner.
I didn't know any other magical foxes.
But it's even worse watching my friends leave...
...one by one.

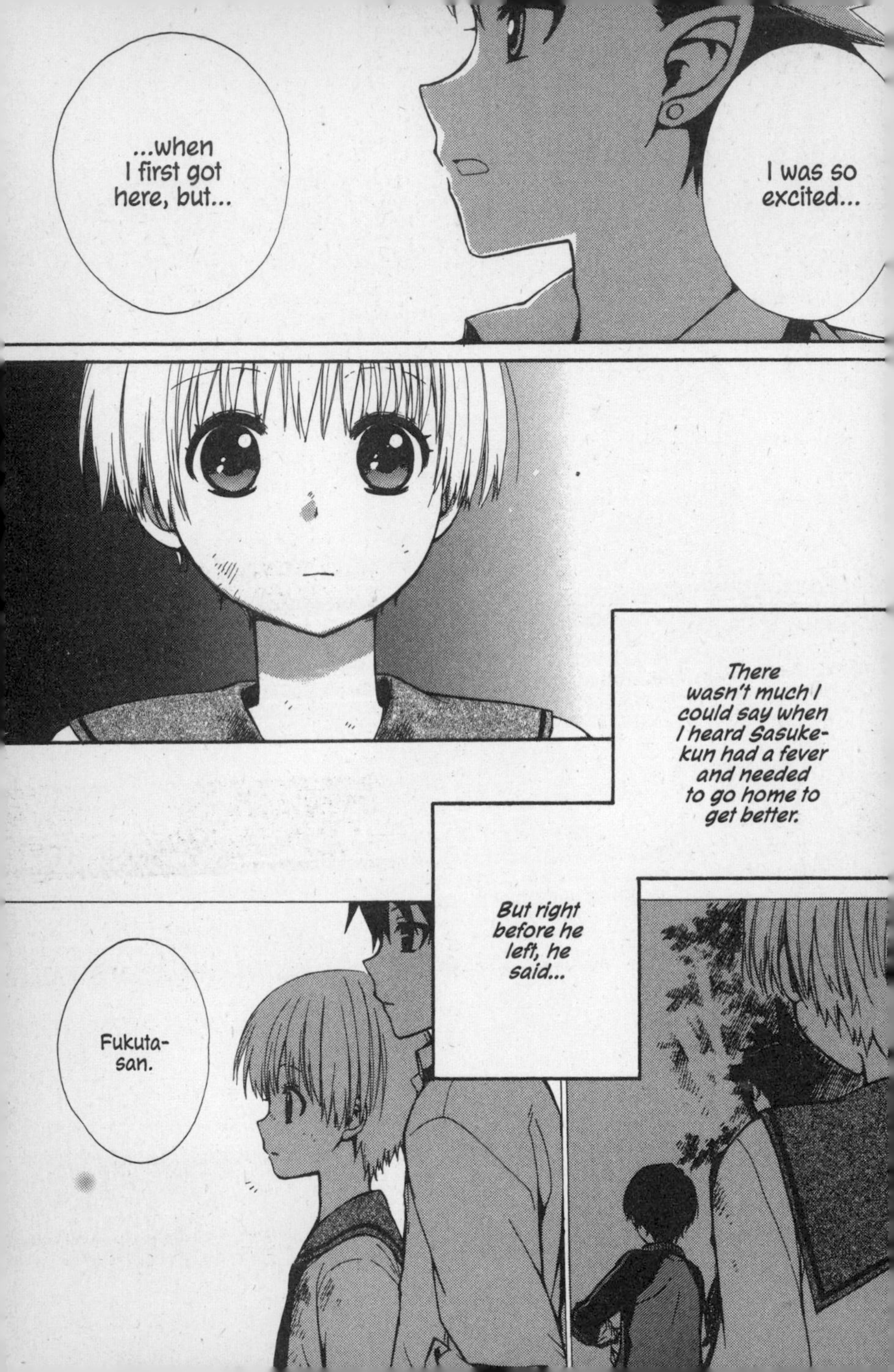
I was so excited...
...when I first got here, but...
There wasn't much I could say when I heard Sasuke-kun had a fever and needed to go home to get better.
But right before he left, he said...
Fukuta-san.

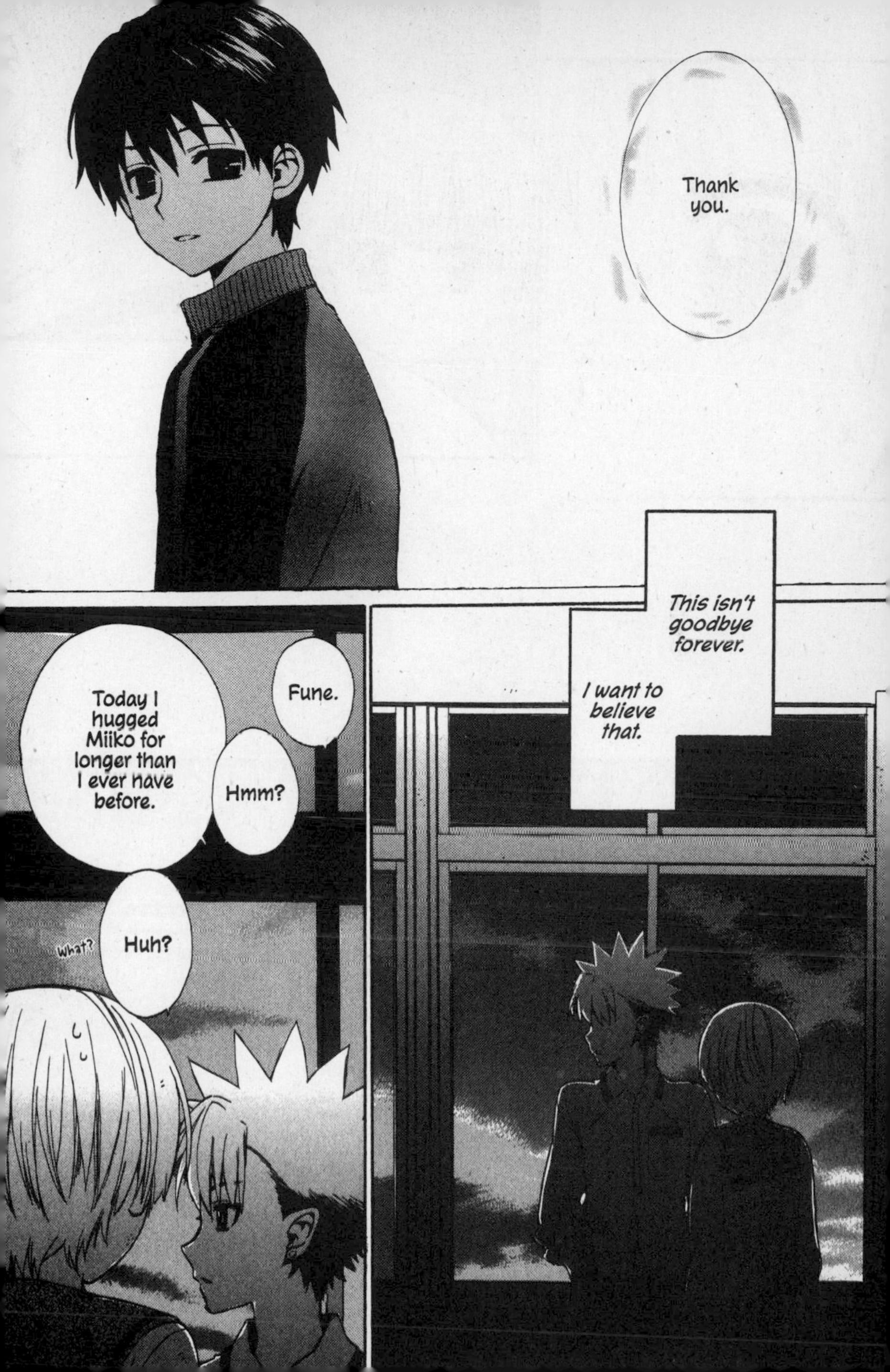
Thank you.
This isn't goodbye forever.
I want to believe that.
Fune.
Hmm?
Today I hugged Miiko for longer than I ever have before.
Huh?
What?

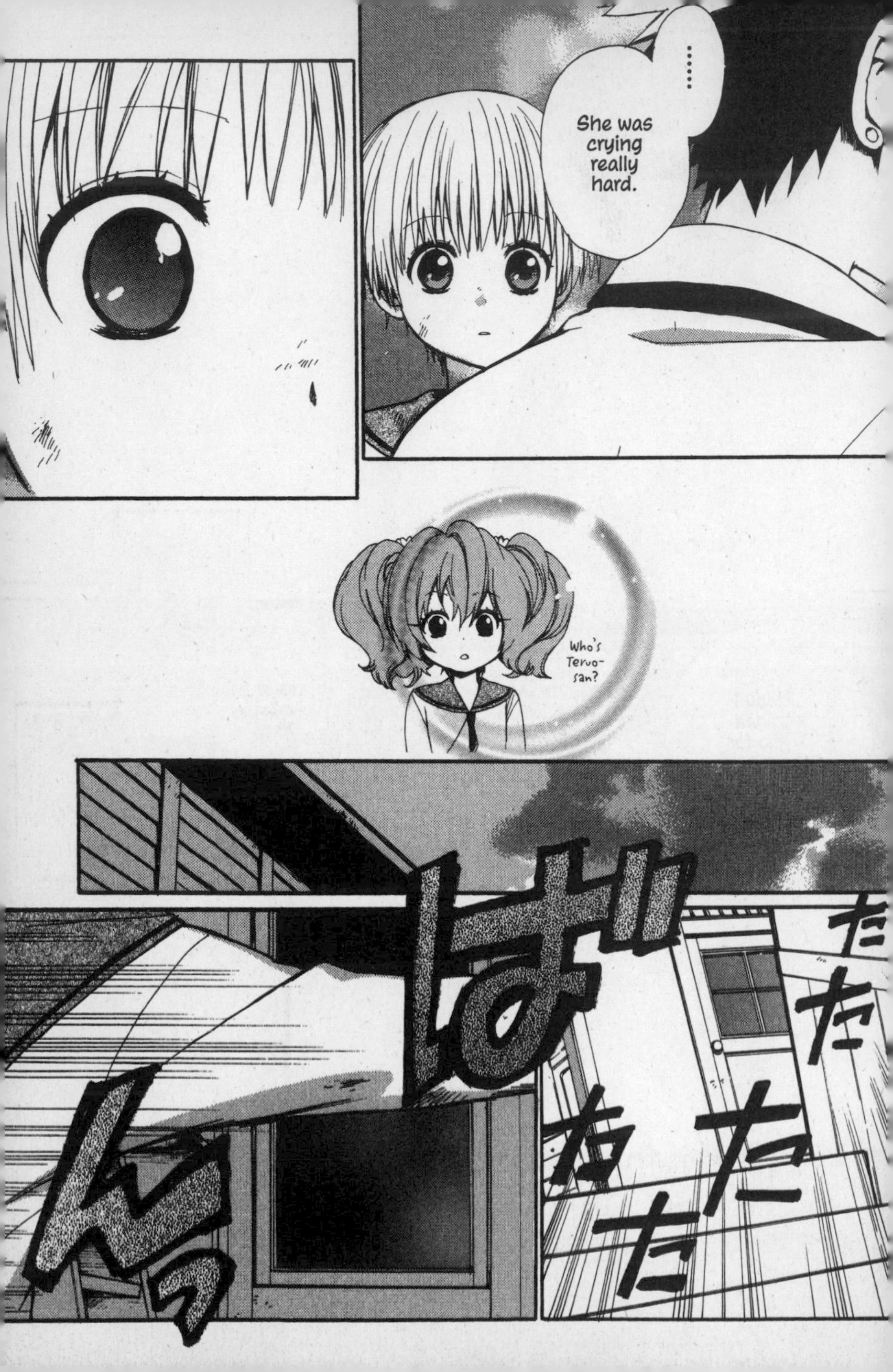

......
She was crying really hard.
Who's Teruo-san?
たたた
たたた
ばんっ

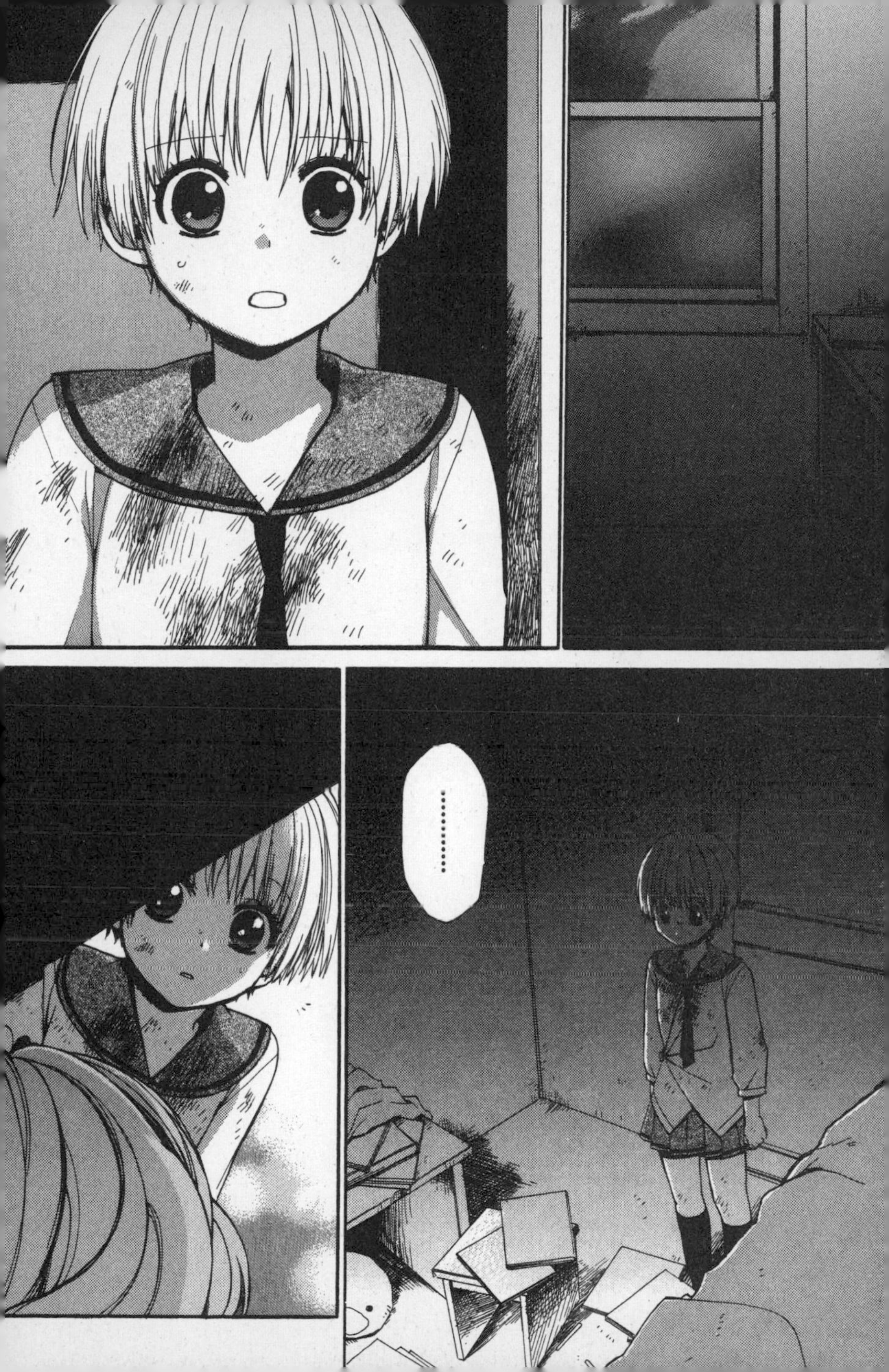
……

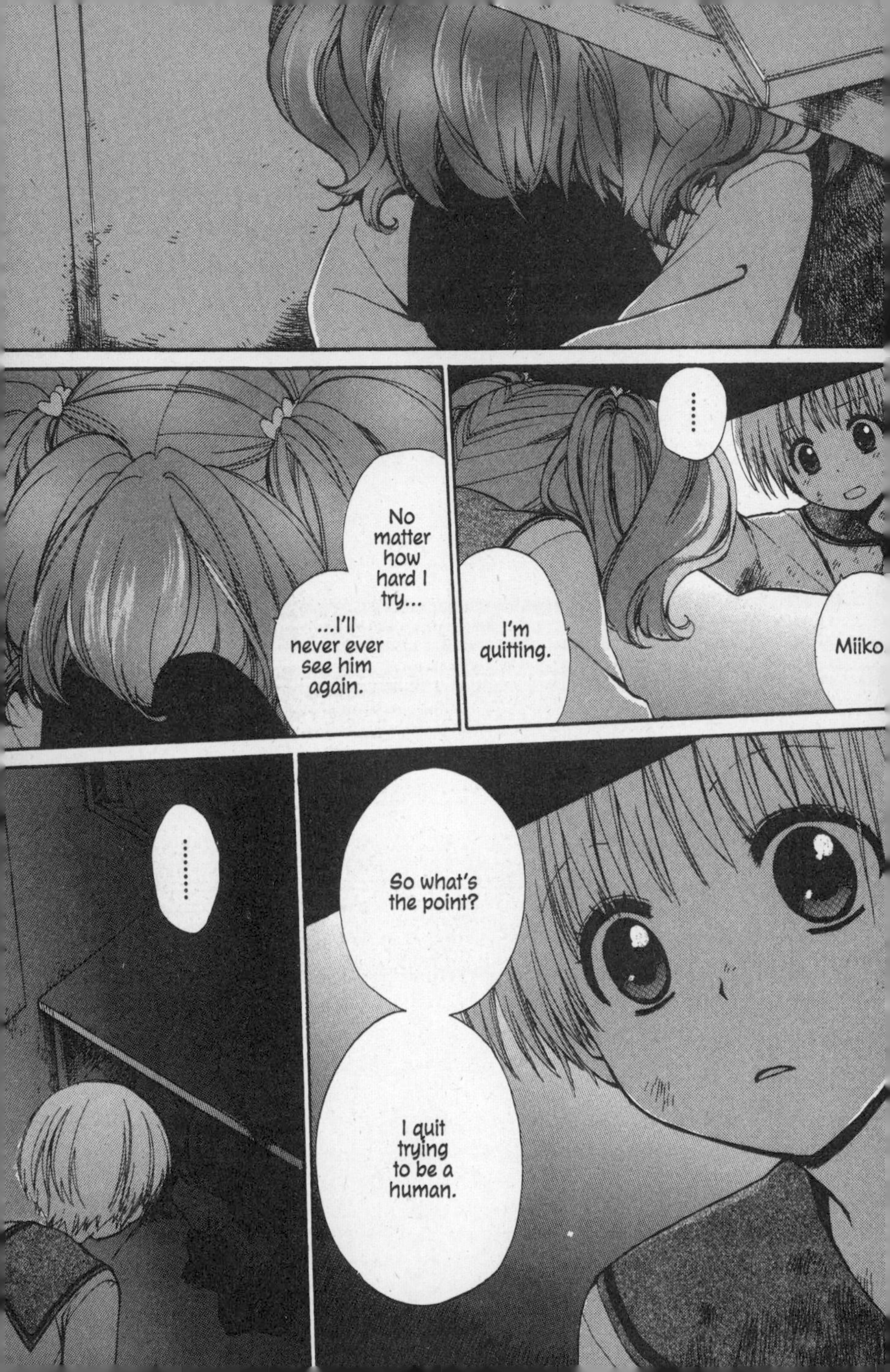
......
Miiko
I'm quitting.
No matter how hard I try...
...I'll never ever see him again.
So what's the point?
I quit trying to be a human.
......

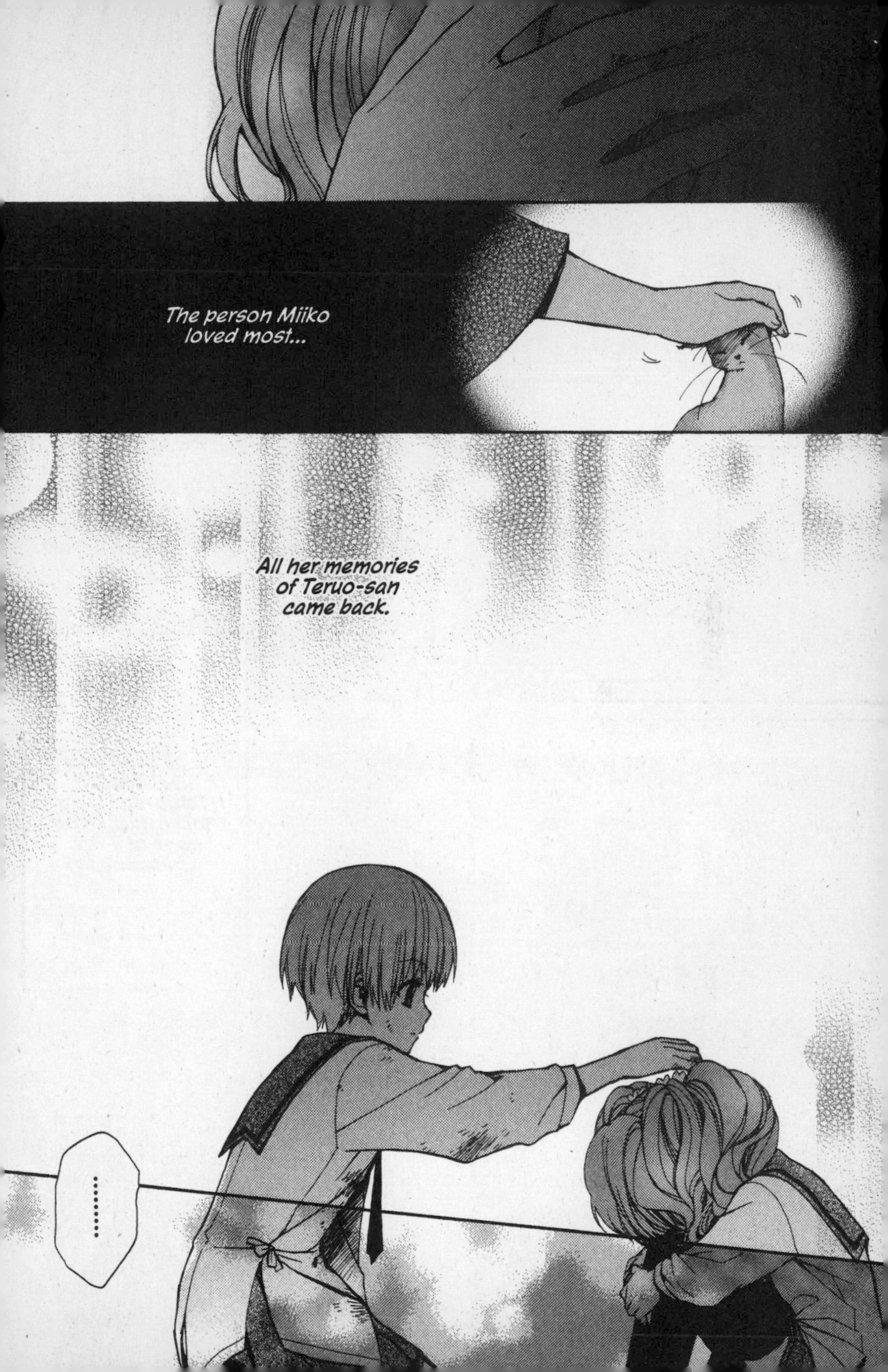
The person Miiko loved most...
All her memories of Teruo-san came back.
......

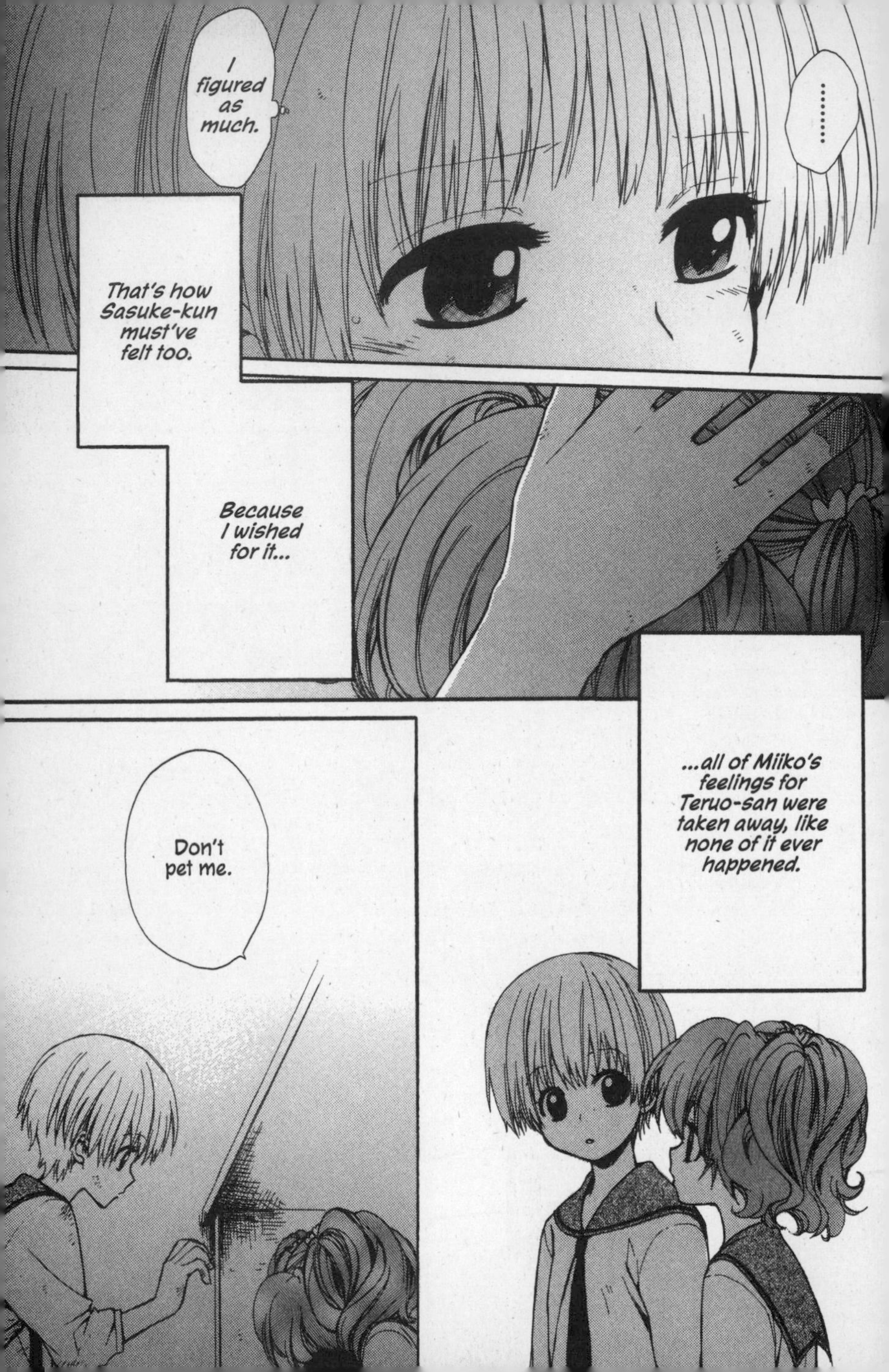
......
I figured as much.
That's how Sasuke-kun must've felt too.
Because I wished for it...
...all of Miiko's feelings for Teruo-san were taken away, like none of it ever happened.
Don't pet me.

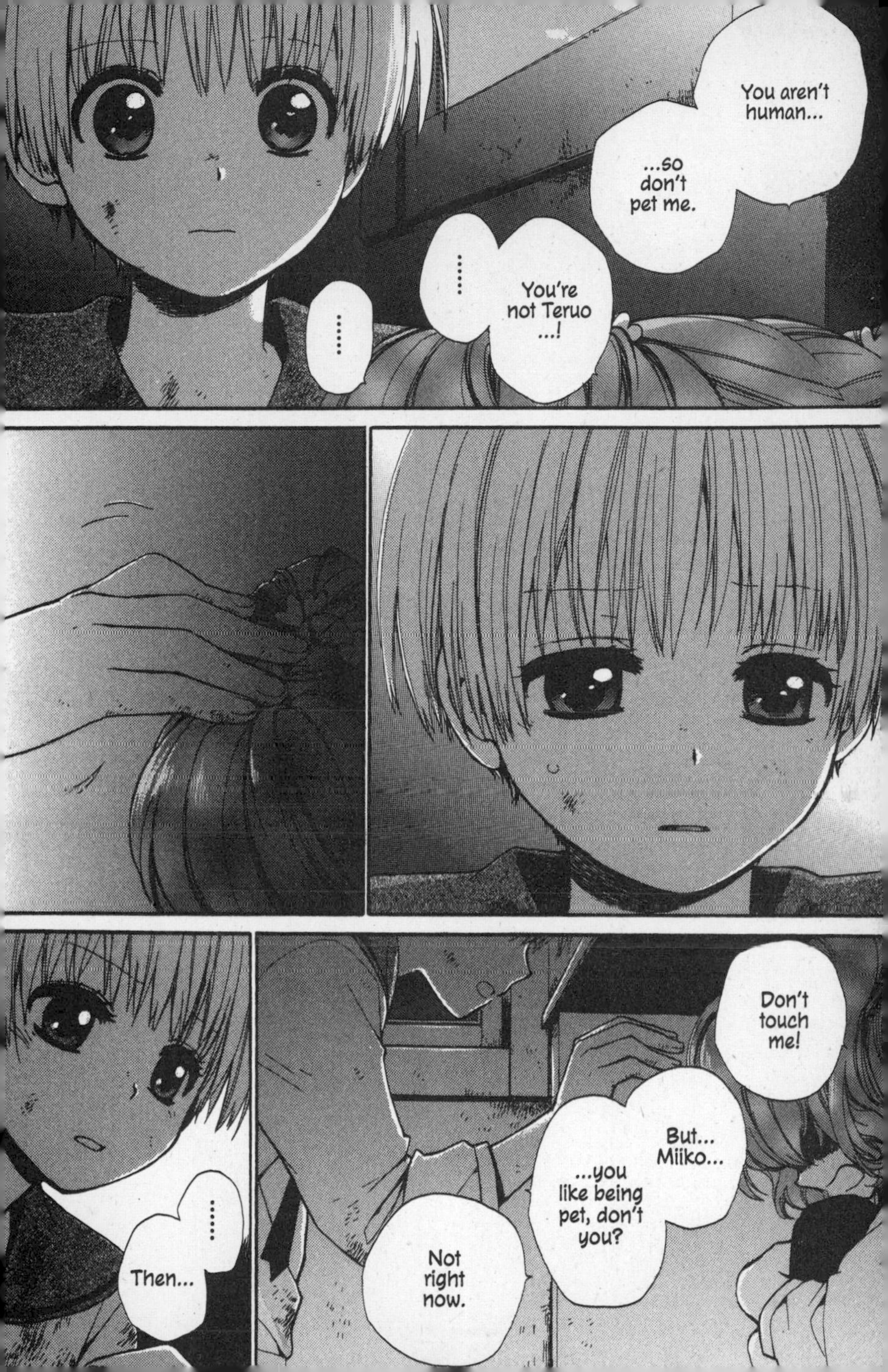
You aren't human...
...so don't pet me.
......
You're not Teruo ...!
......
Don't touch me!
But... Miiko...
...you like being pet, don't you?
Not right now.
......
Then...

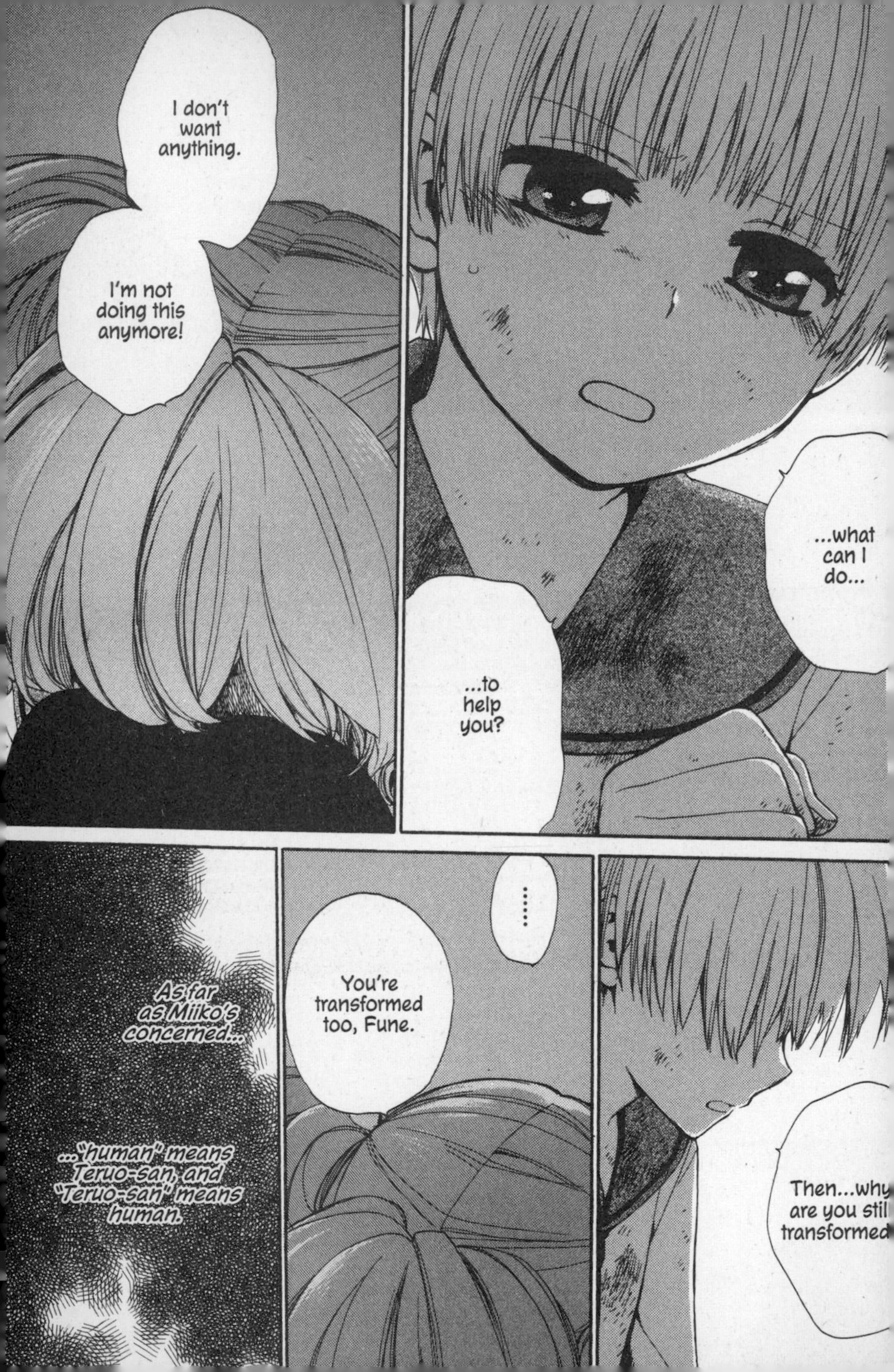
...what can I do...
...to help you?
I don't want anything.
I'm not doing this anymore!
Then...why are you stil transformed
......
You're transformed too, Fune.
As far as Miiko's concerned...
..."human" means Teruo-san, and "Teruo-san" means human.

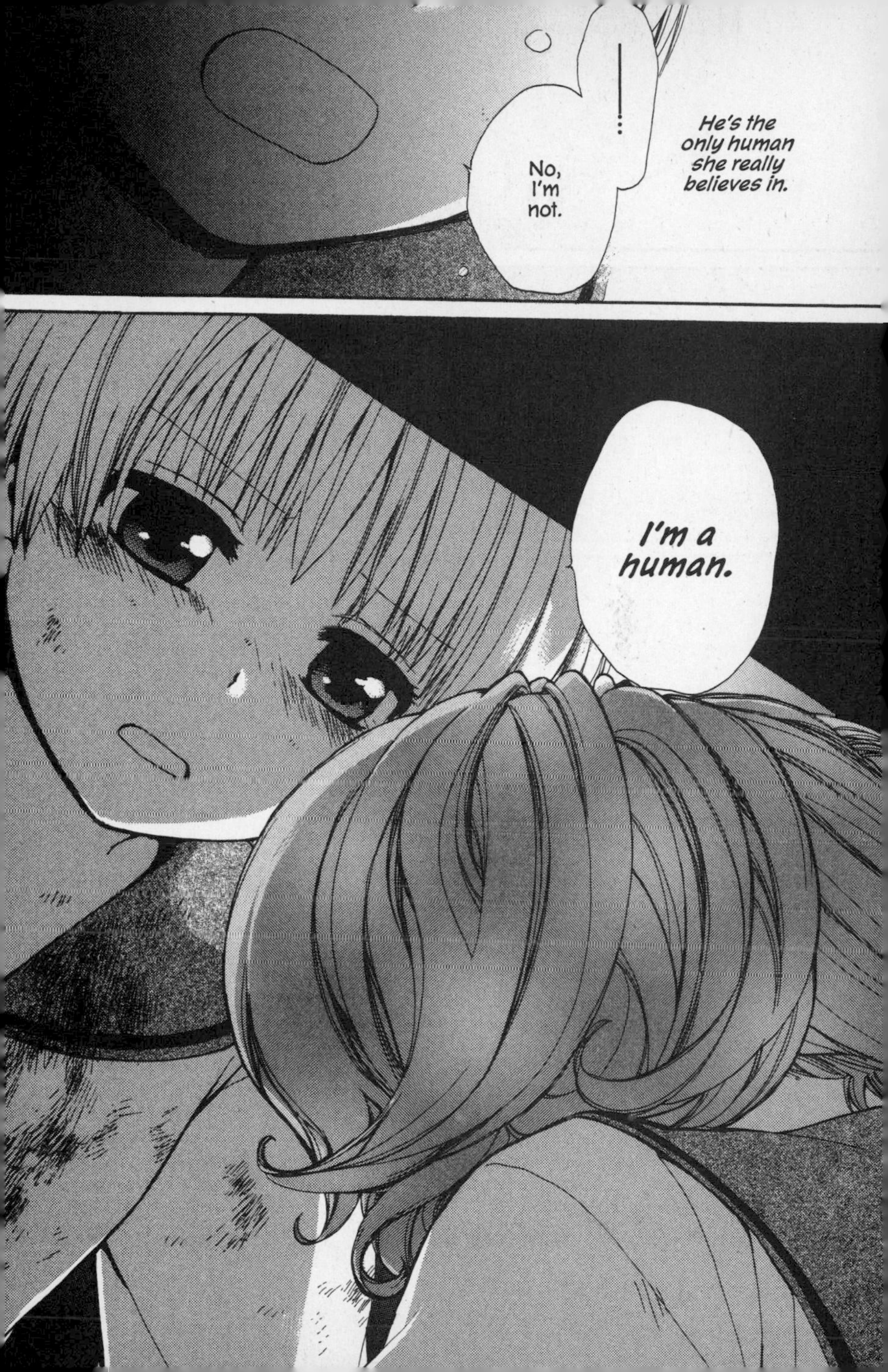
He's the only human she really believes in.
—!… No, I'm not.
I'm a human.

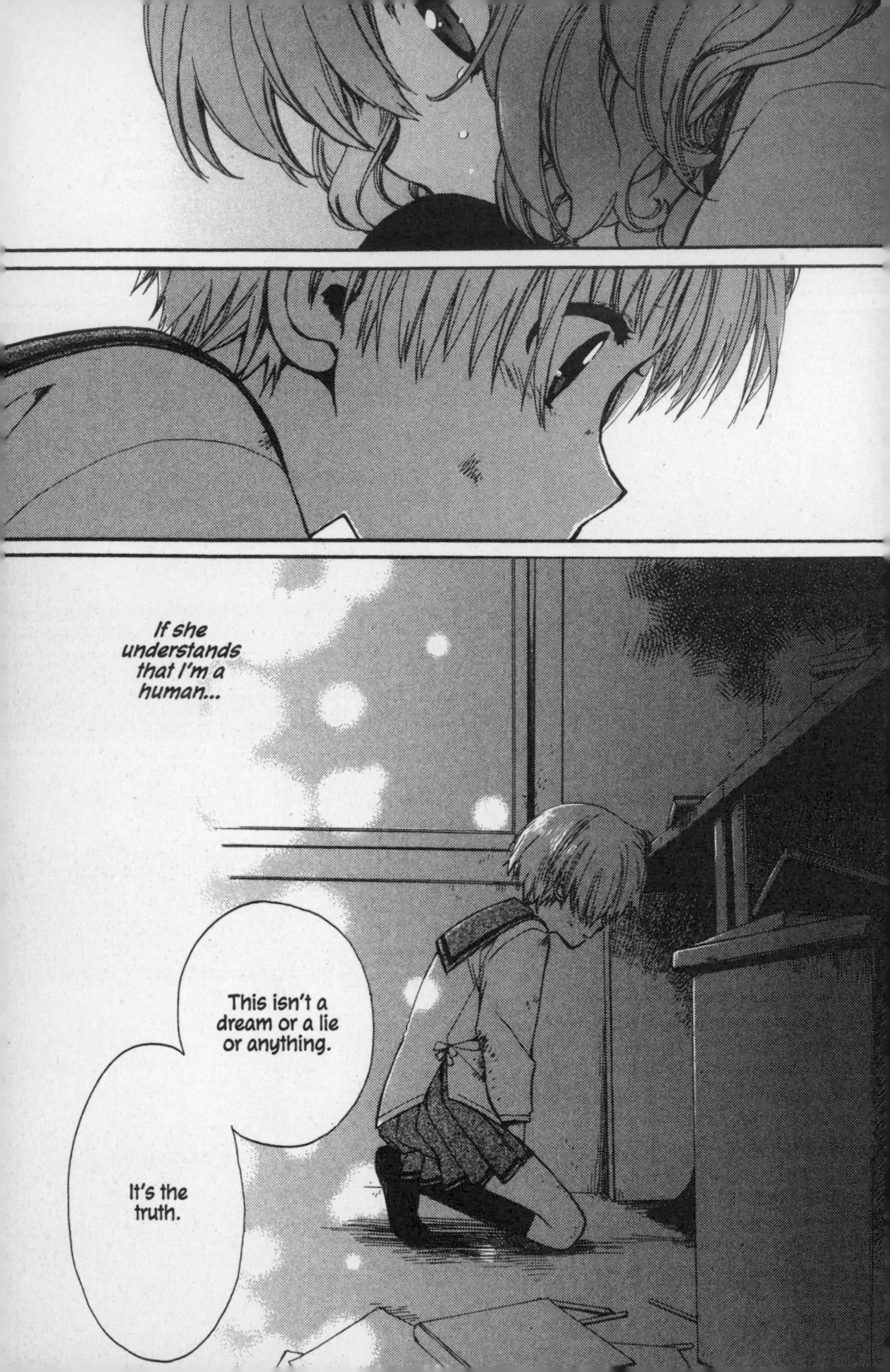
If she understands that I'm a human...
This isn't a dream or a lie or anything.
It's the truth.

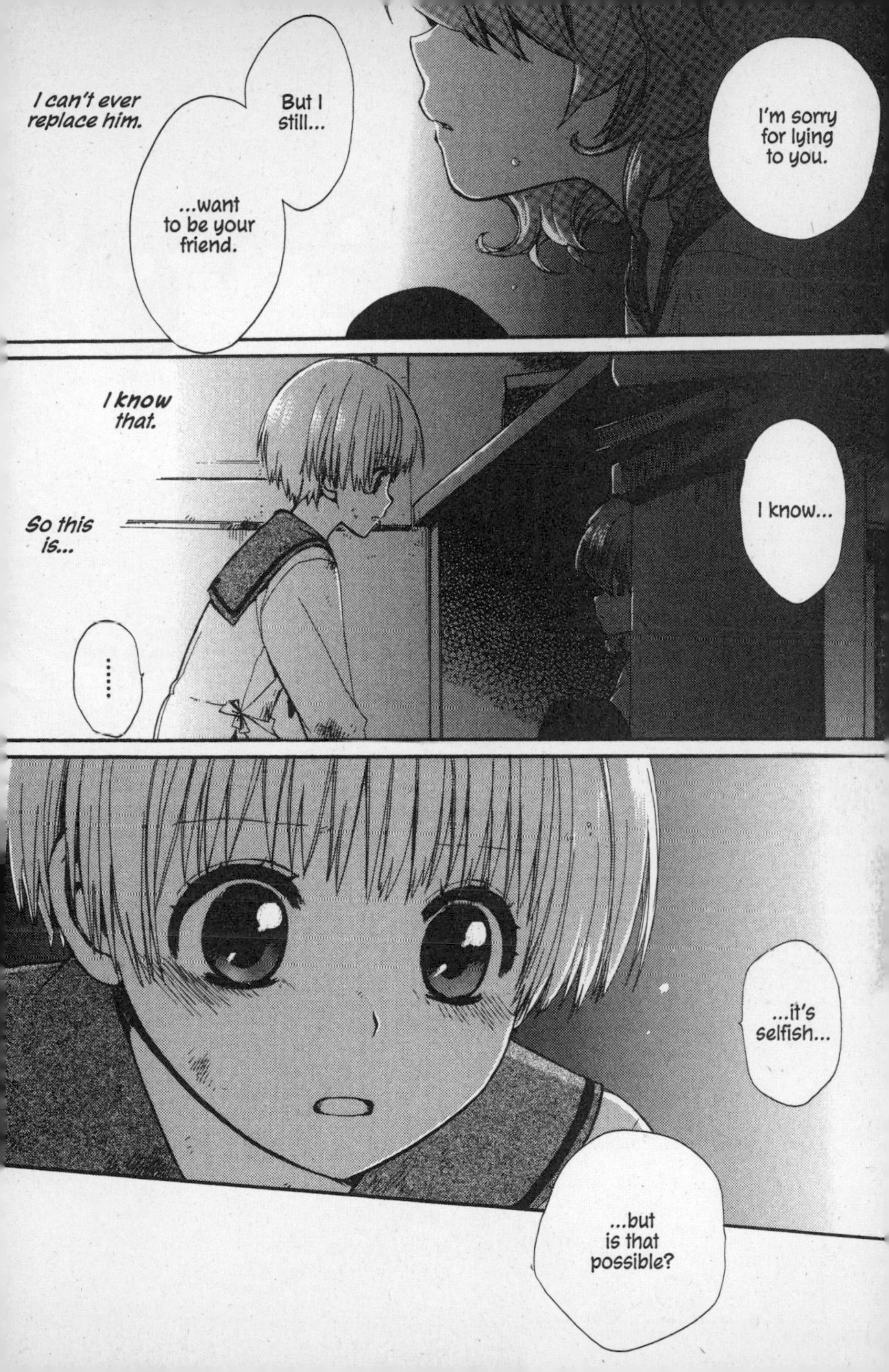
I'm sorry for lying to you.
But I still...
...want to be your friend.
I can't ever replace him.
I know...
I know that.
So this is...
......
...it's selfish...
...but is that possible?

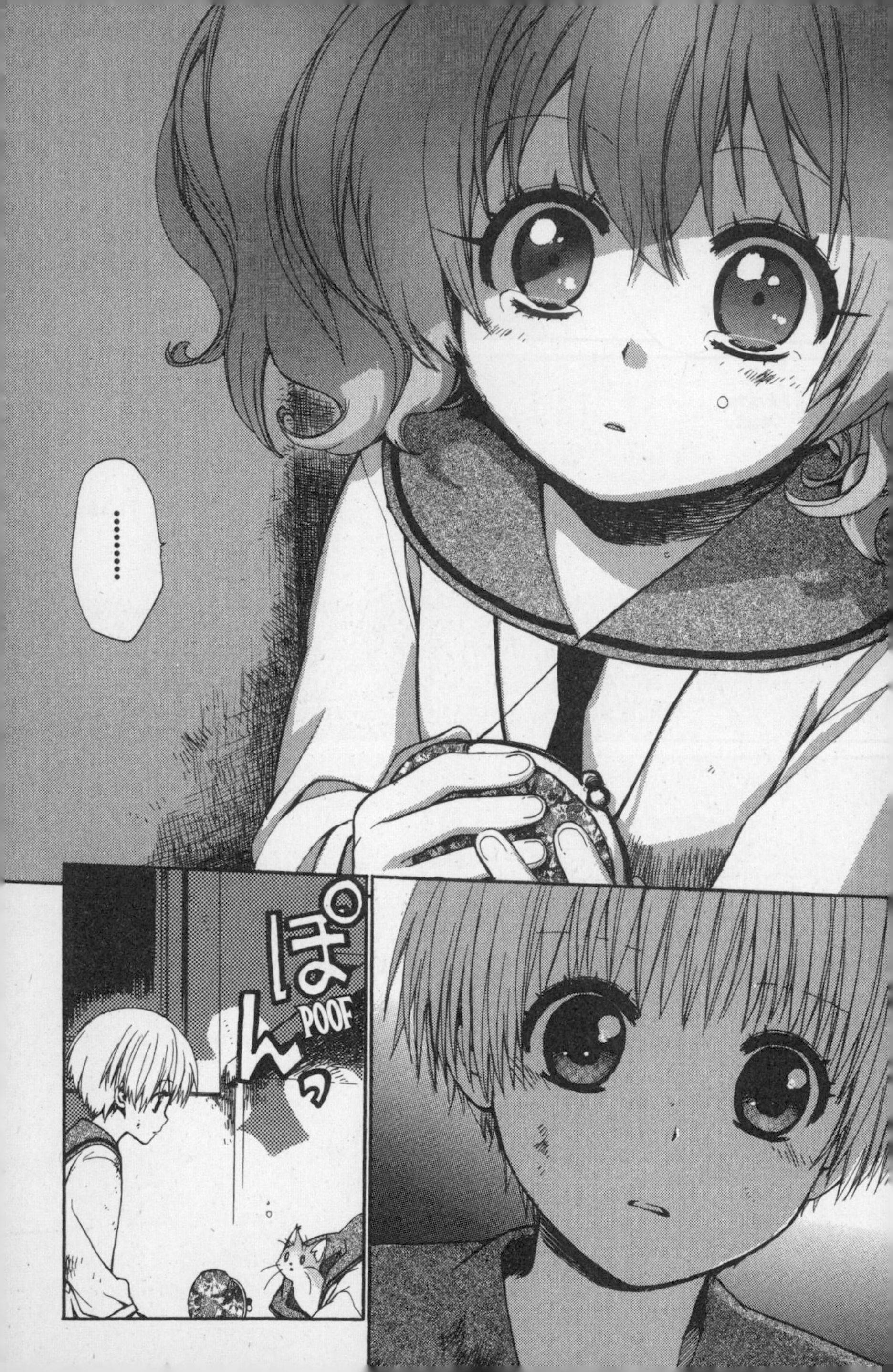
……
ぽんっ
POOF

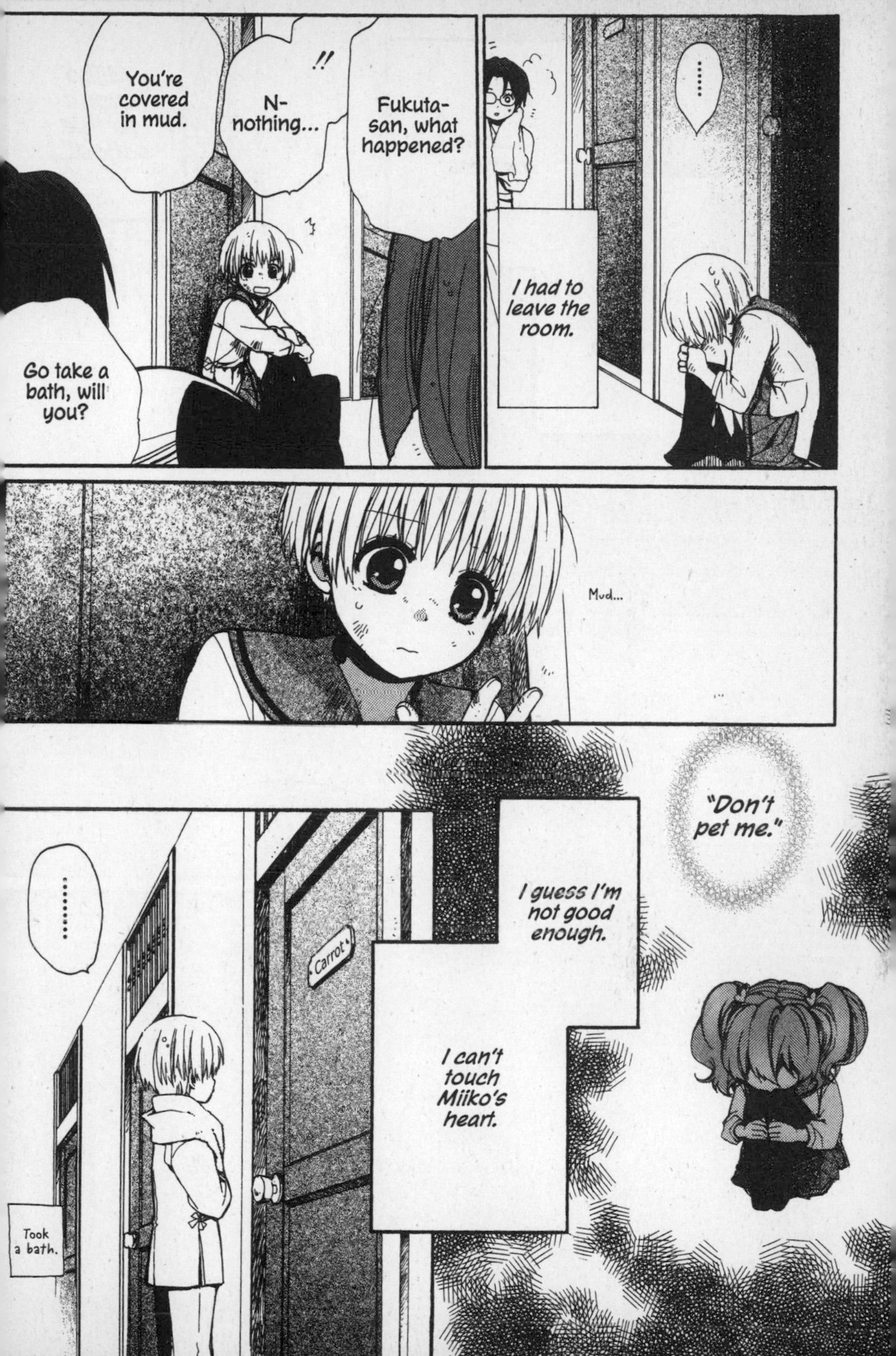
……
I had to leave the room.
Fukuta-san, what happened?
!!
N-nothing...
You're covered in mud.
Go take a bath, will you?
Mud...
...
"Don't pet me."
I guess I'm not good enough.
I can't touch Miiko's heart.
Carrot
……
Took a bath.

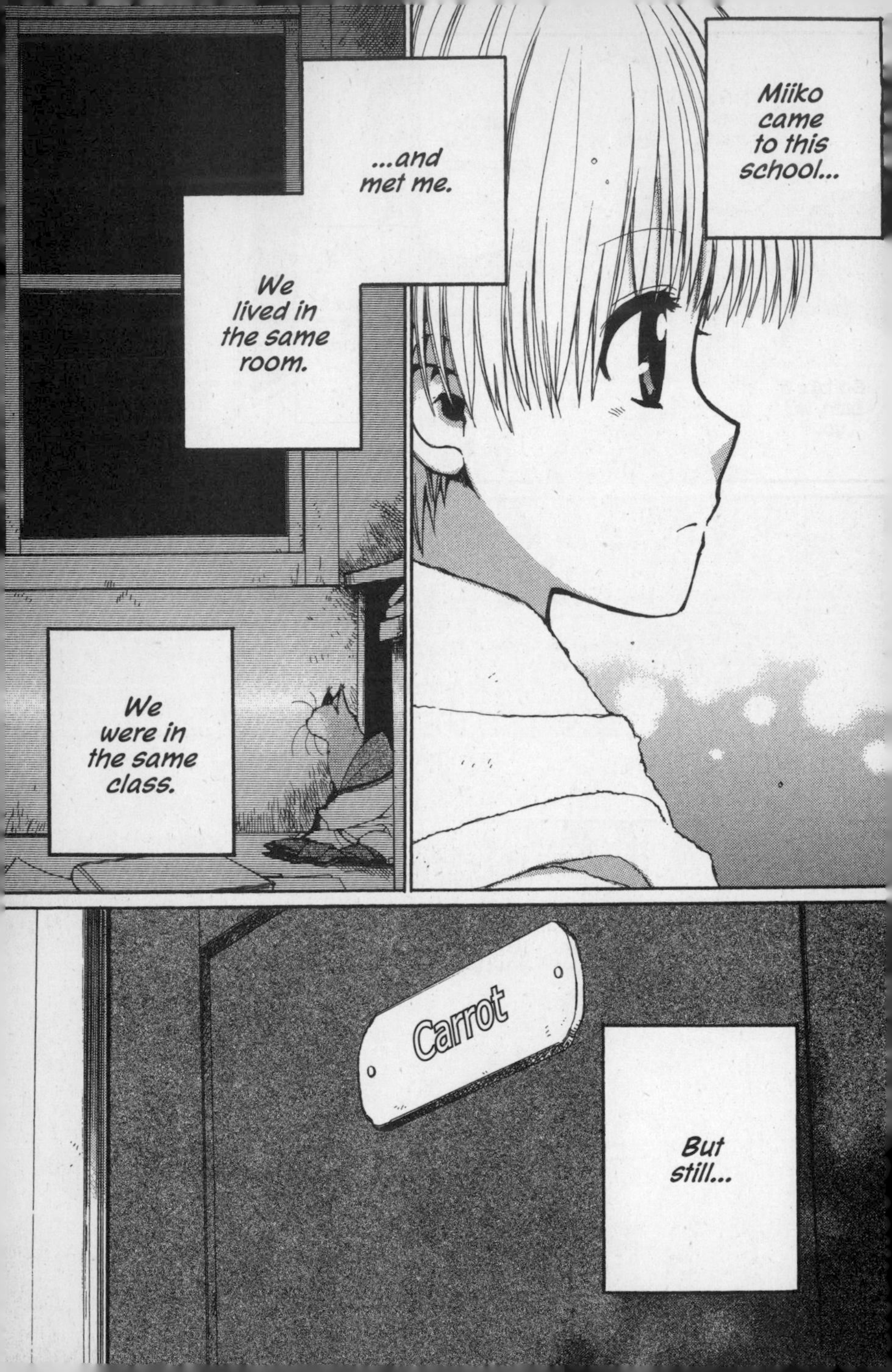
Miiko came to this school...
...and met me.
We lived in the same room.
We were in the same class.
Carrot
But still...

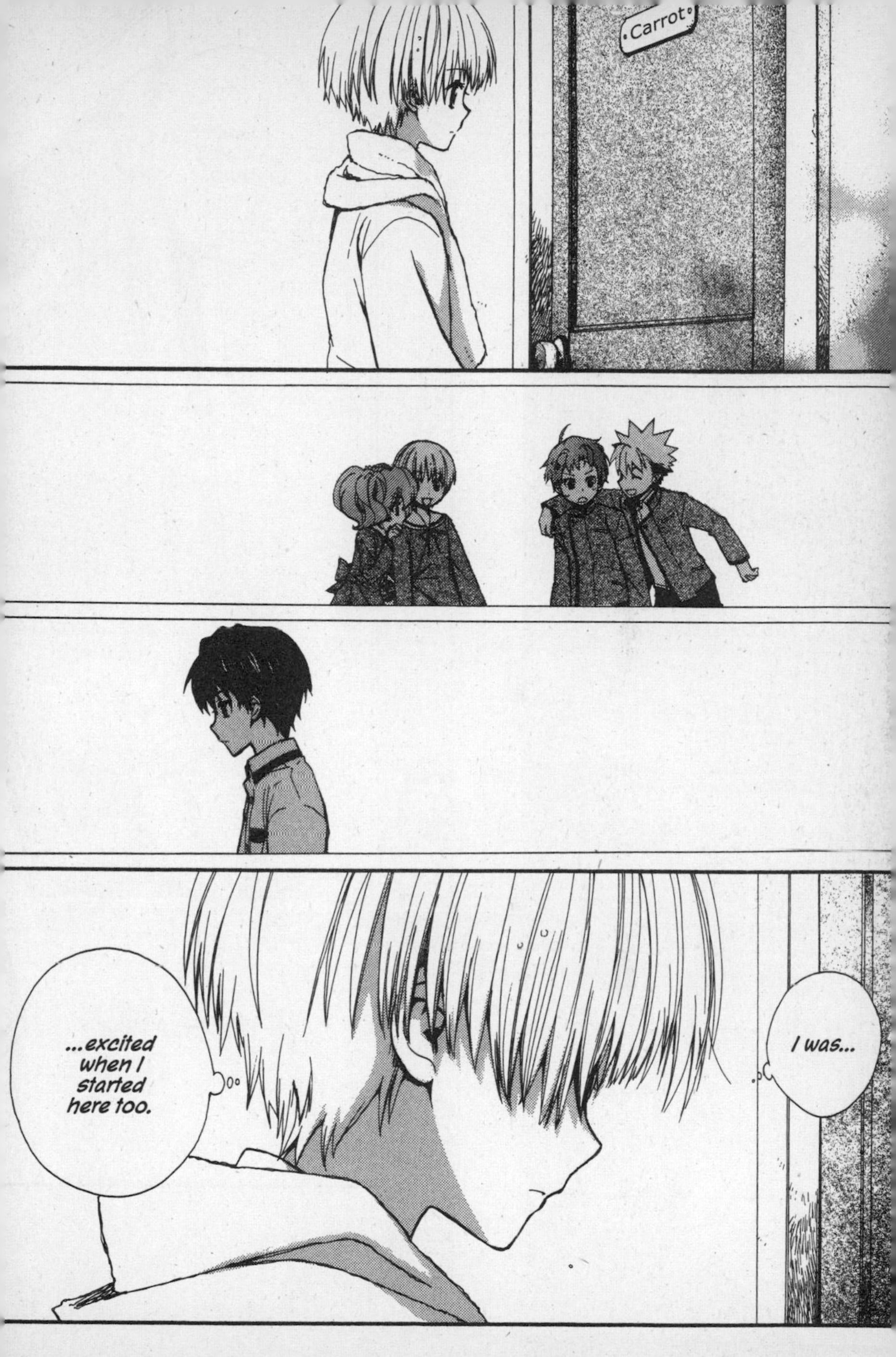
Carrot
I was...
...excited when I started here too.

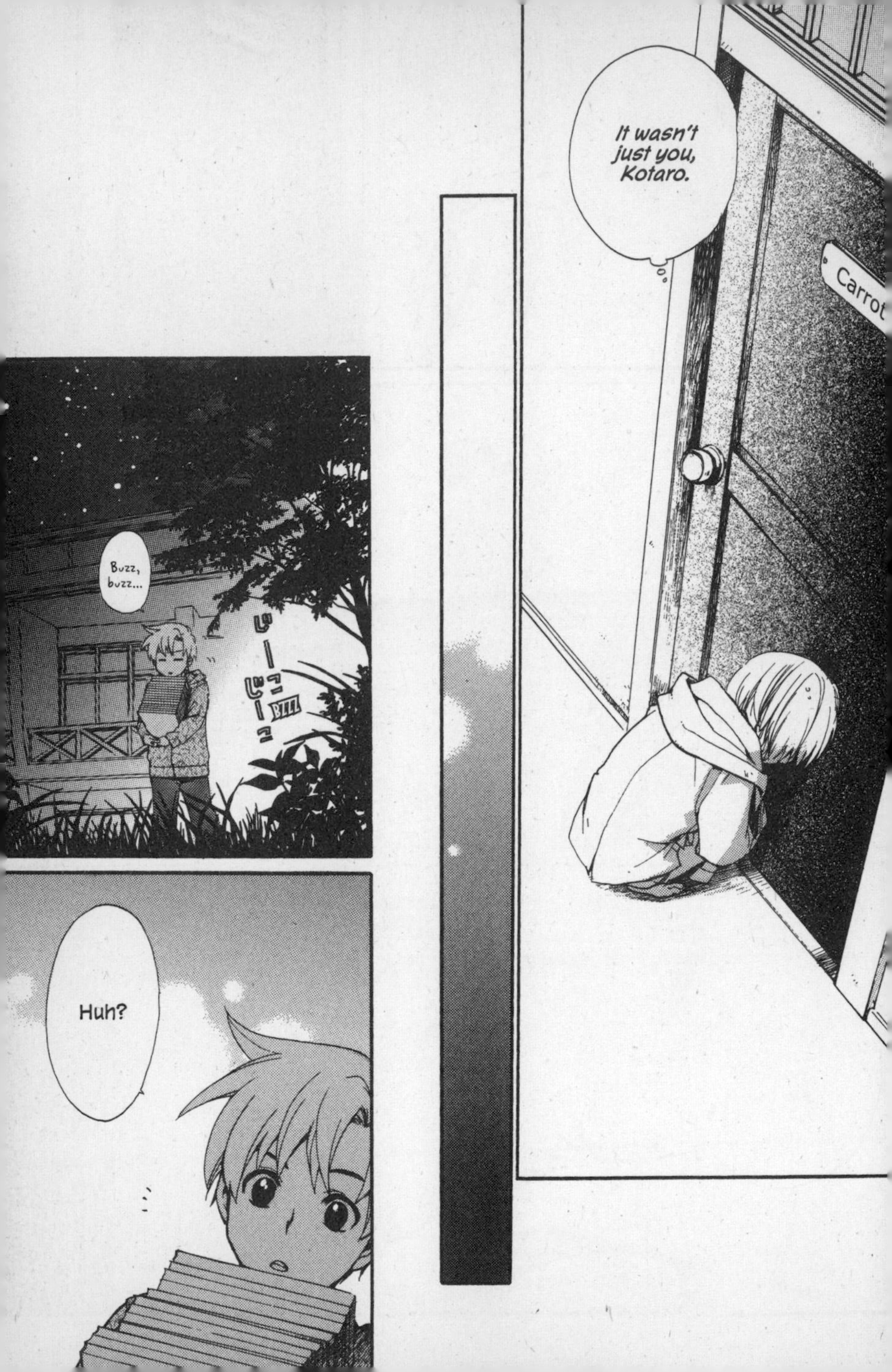
It wasn't just you, Kotaro.
Carrot
Buzz, buzz...
BZZZ
Huh?

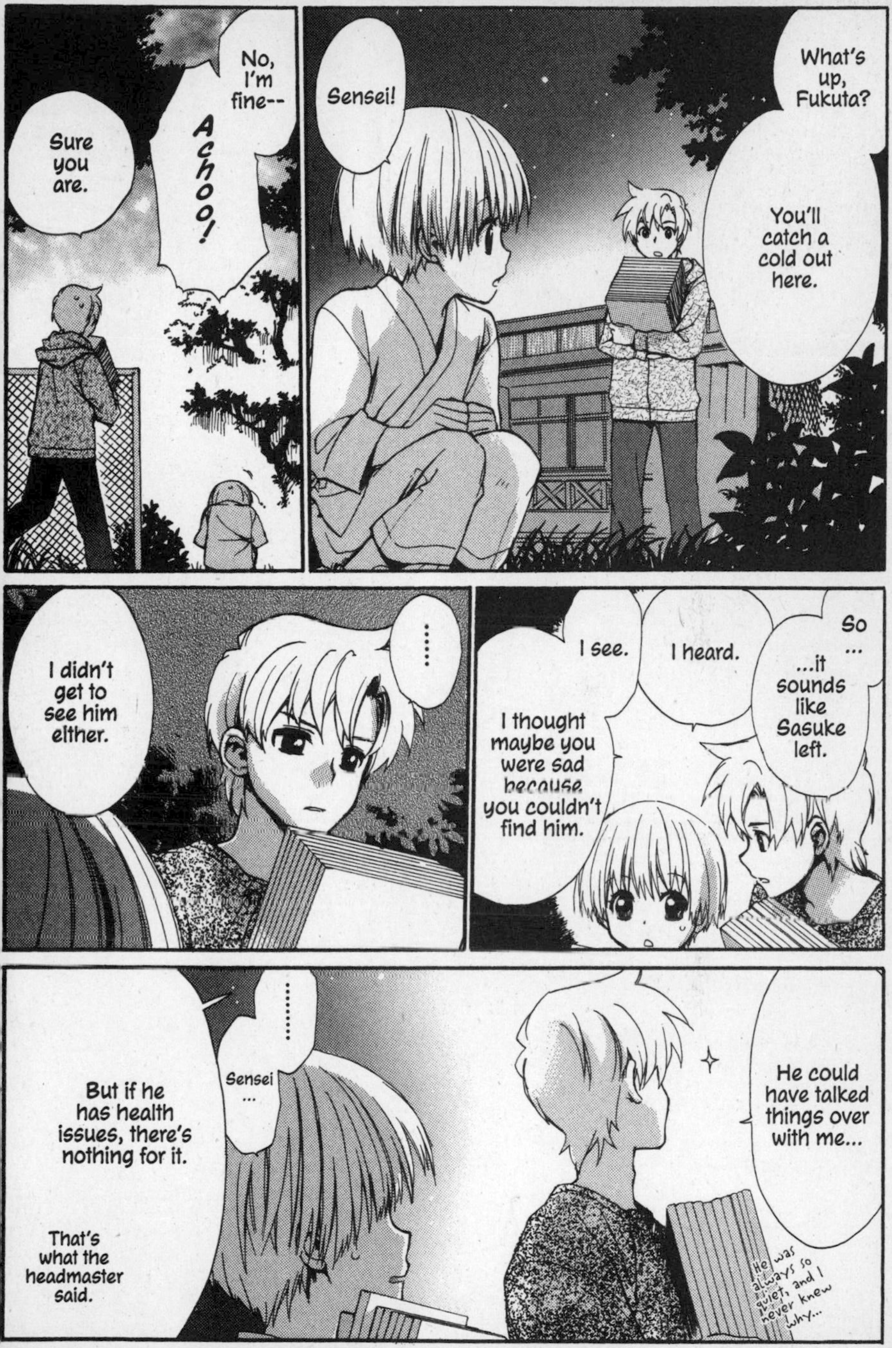

What's up, Fukuta?
Sensei!
You'll catch a cold out here.
No, I'm fine--
Achoo!
Sure you are.
So ... ...it sounds like Sasuke left.
I heard.
I see.
I thought maybe you were sad because you couldn't find him.
......
I didn't get to see him either.
He could have talked things over with me...
He was always so quiet, and I never knew why...
......
Sensei ...
But if he has health issues, there's nothing for it.
That's what the headmaster said.

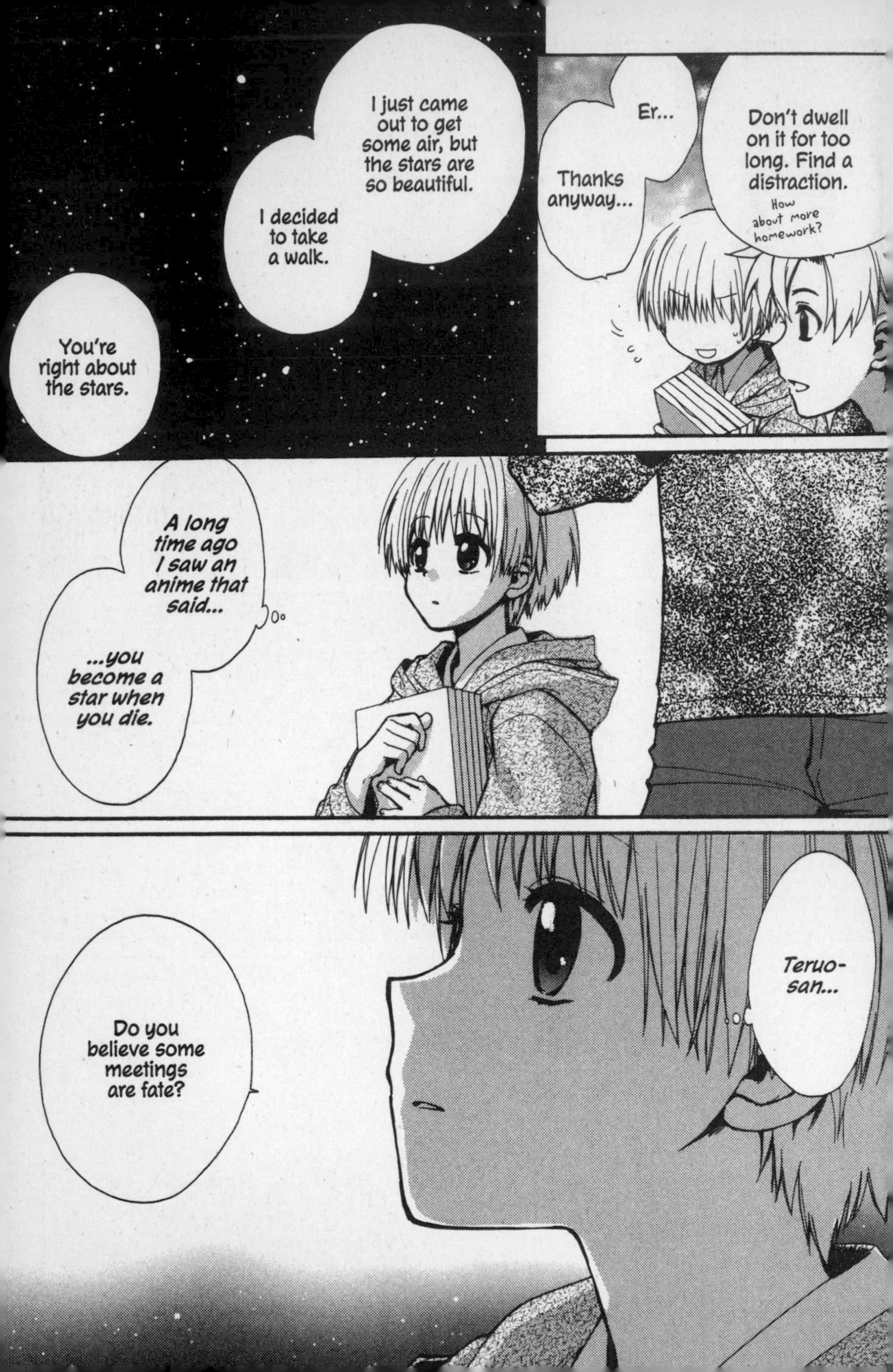
Don't dwell on it for too long. Find a distraction.
How about more homework?
Er...
Thanks anyway...
I just came out to get some air, but the stars are so beautiful.
I decided to take a walk.
You're right about the stars.
A long time ago I saw an anime that said...
...you become a star when you die.
Teruo-san...
Do you believe some meetings are fate?

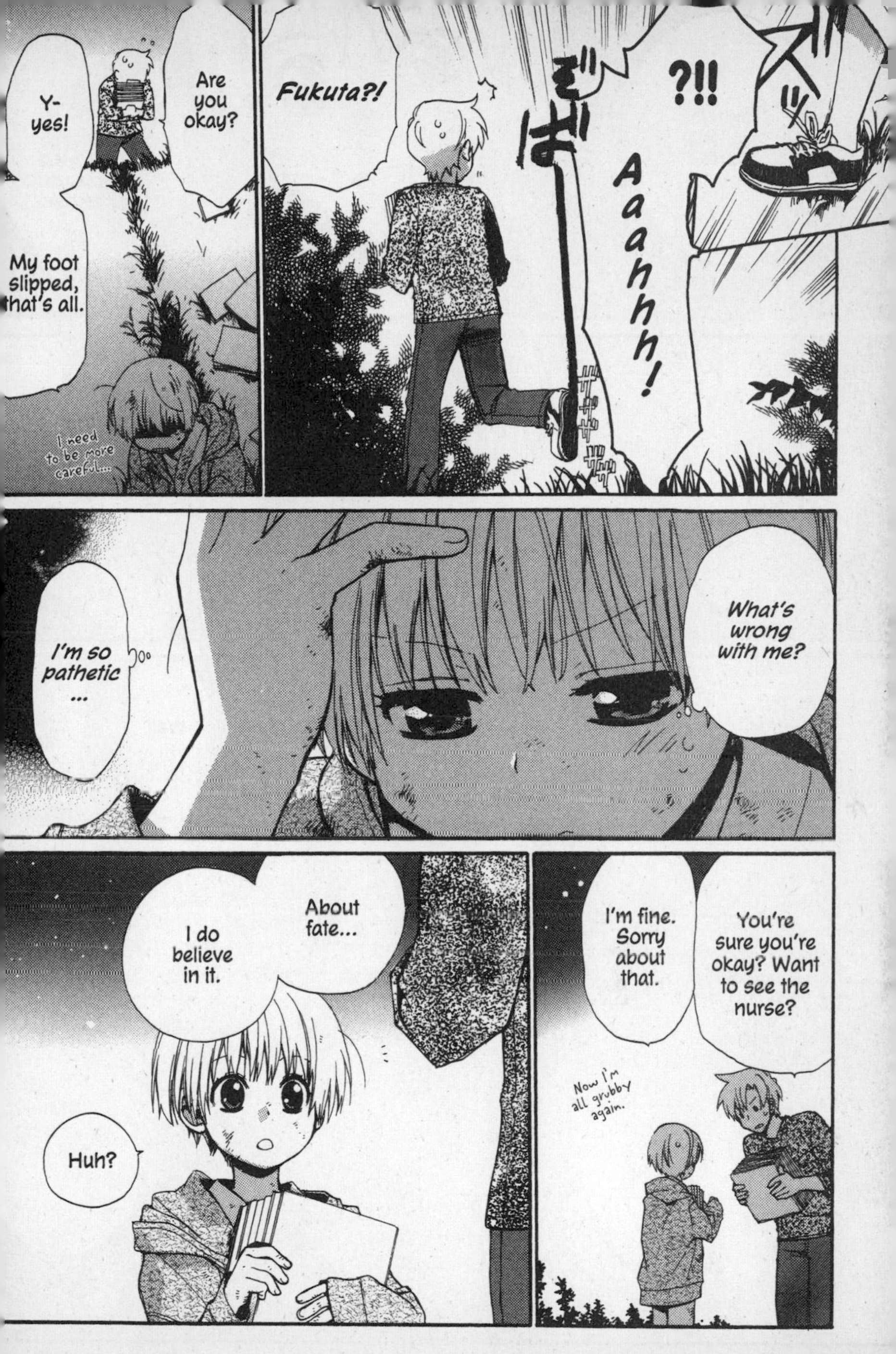

?!!
Aaahhh!
Fukuta?!
Are you okay?
Y-yes!
My foot slipped, that's all.
I need to be more careful...
What's wrong with me?
I'm so pathetic...
You're sure you're okay? Want to see the nurse?
I'm fine. Sorry about that.
Now I'm all grubby again.
About fate...
I do believe in it.
Huh?

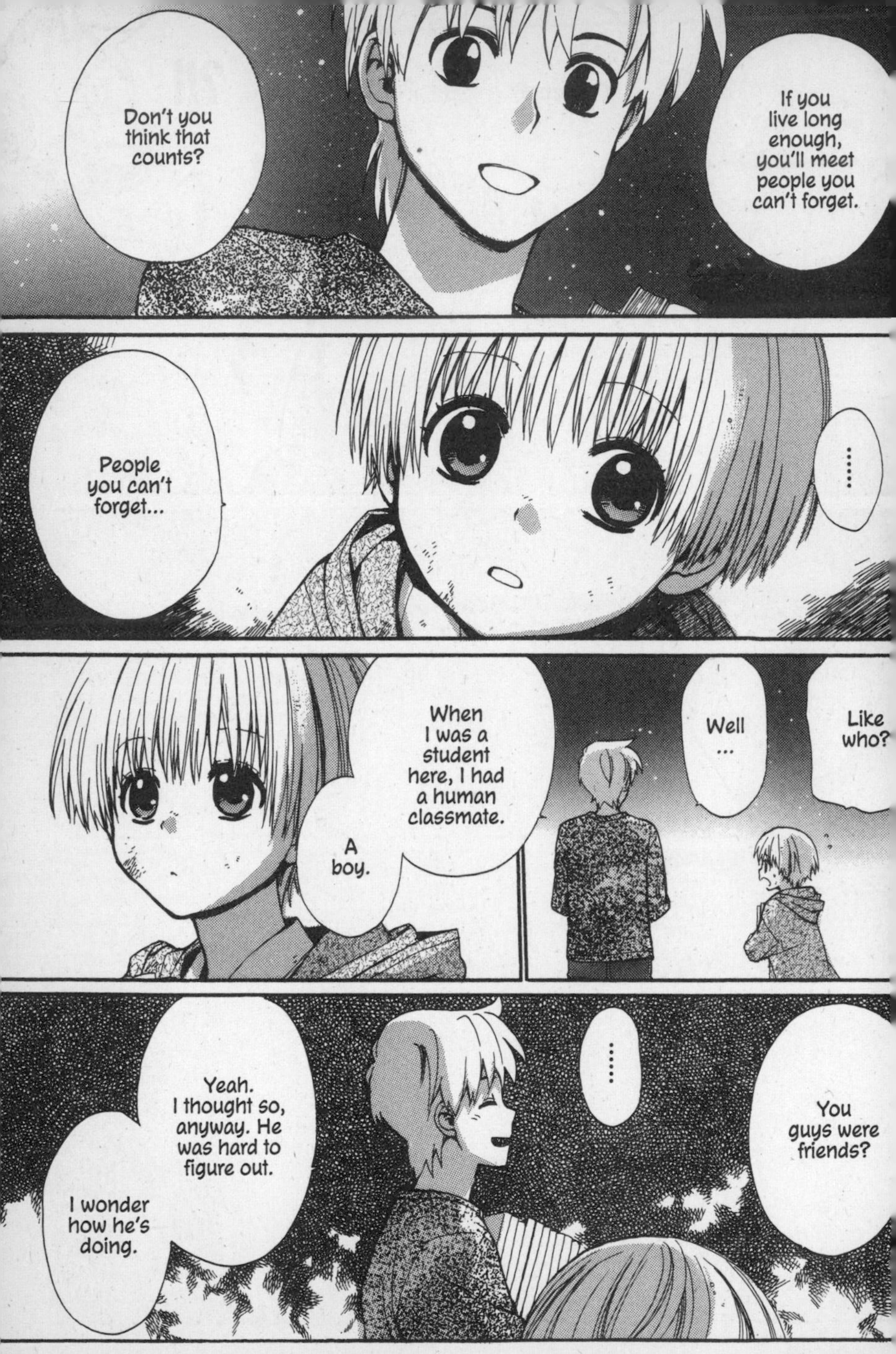
If you live long enough, you'll meet people you can't forget.
Don't you think that counts?
......
People you can't forget...
Like who?
Well ...
When I was a student here, I had a human classmate.
A boy.
......
You guys were friends?
Yeah. I thought so, anyway. He was hard to figure out.
I wonder how he's doing.

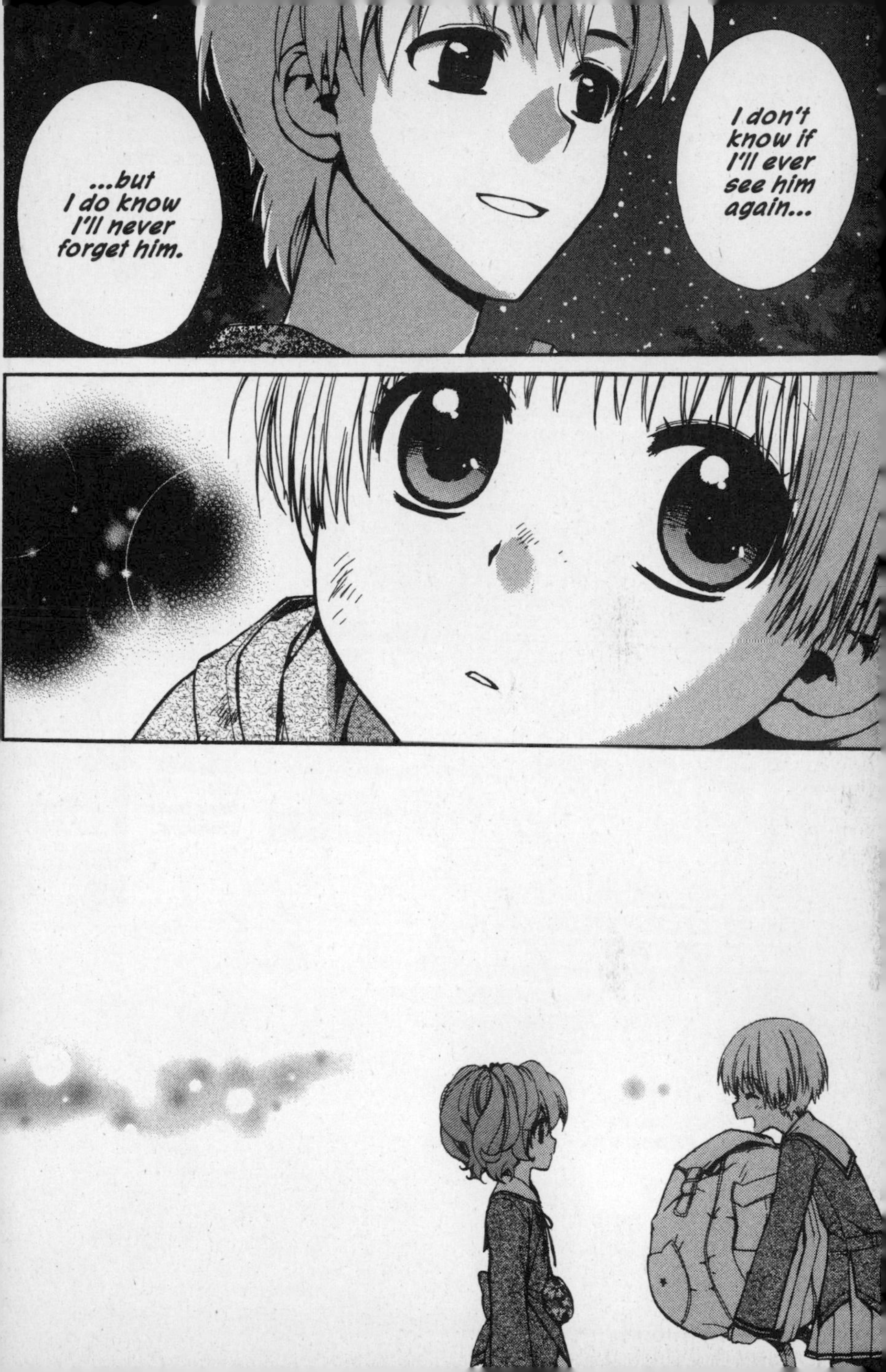
I don't know if I'll ever see him again...
...but I do know I'll never forget him.

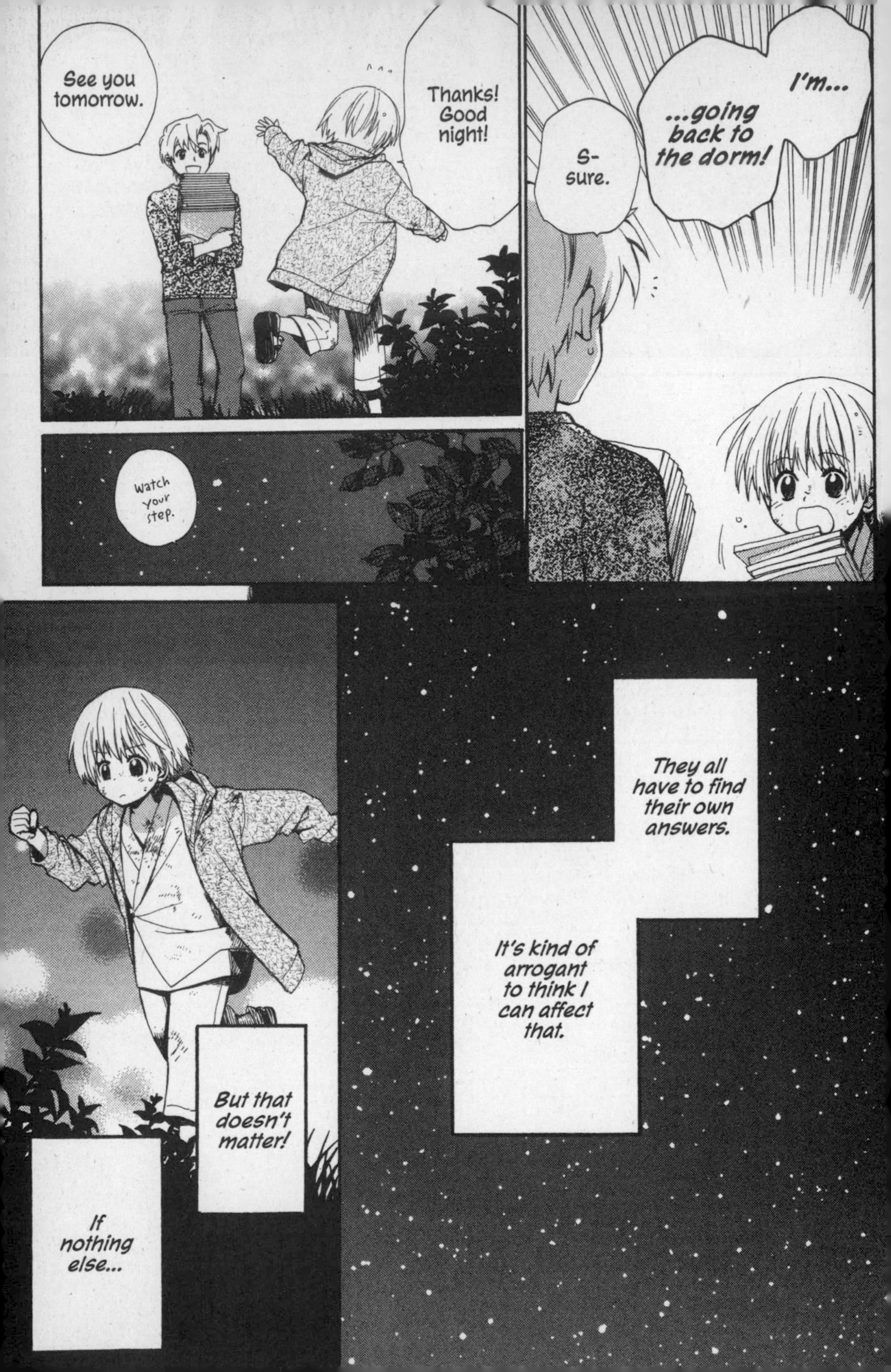
I'm...
...going back to the dorm!
S-sure.
Thanks! Good night!
See you tomorrow.
Watch your step.
They all have to find their own answers.
It's kind of arrogant to think I can affect that.
But that doesn't matter!
If nothing else...

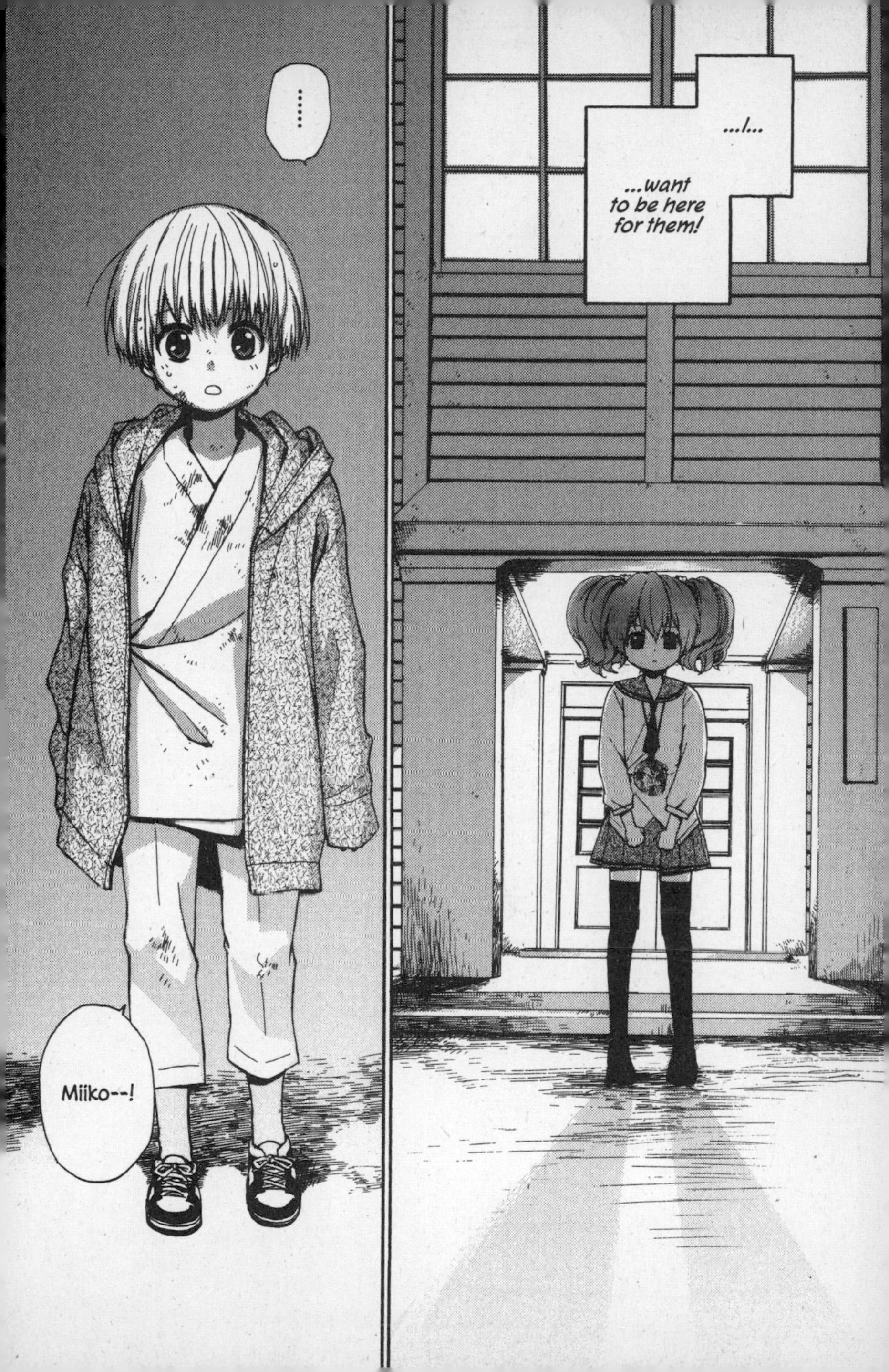
...I...
...want to be here for them!
......
Miiko--!

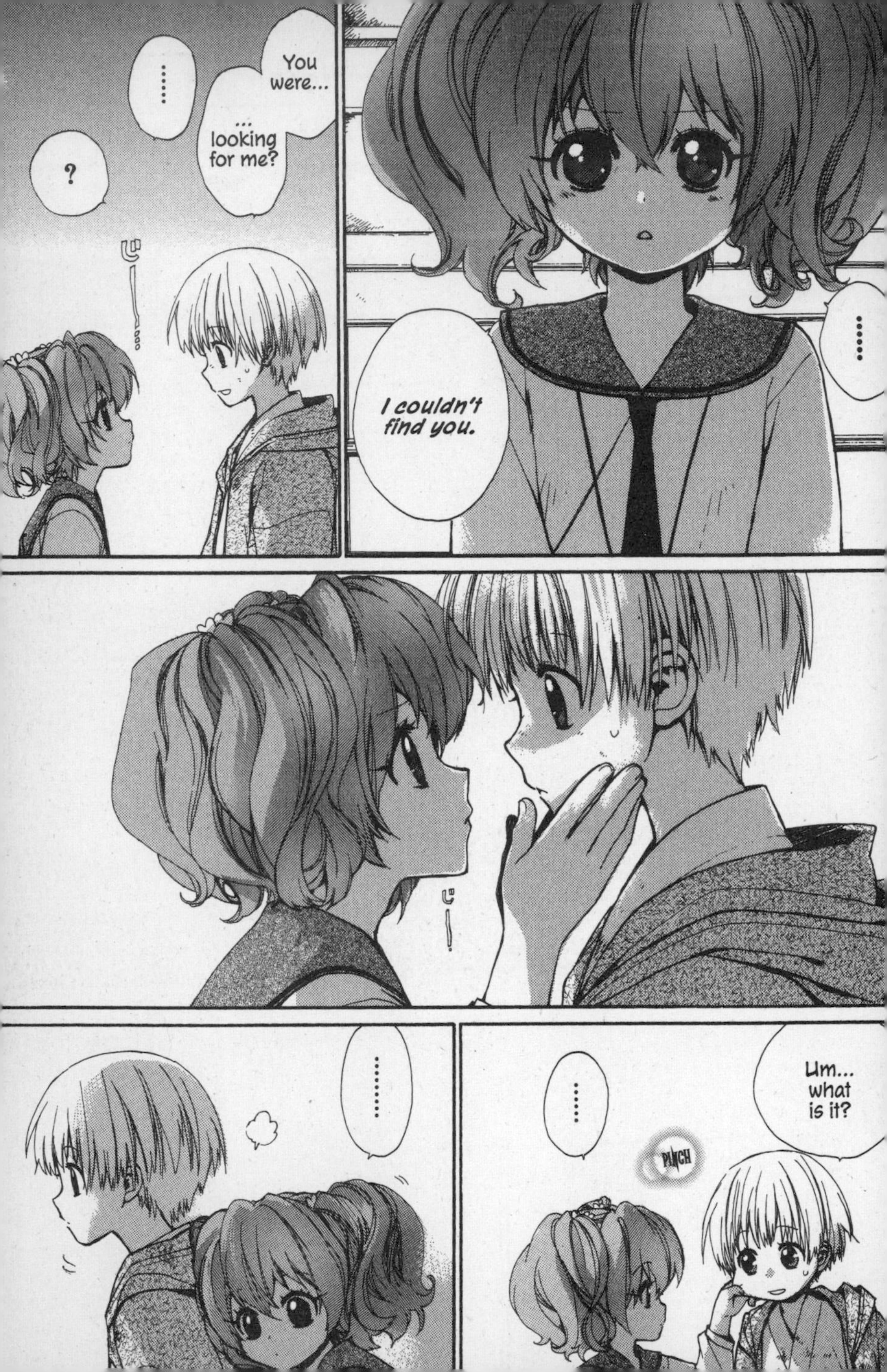
......
I couldn't find you.
You were...
... looking for me?
......
?
Um... what is it?
......
PINCH
......

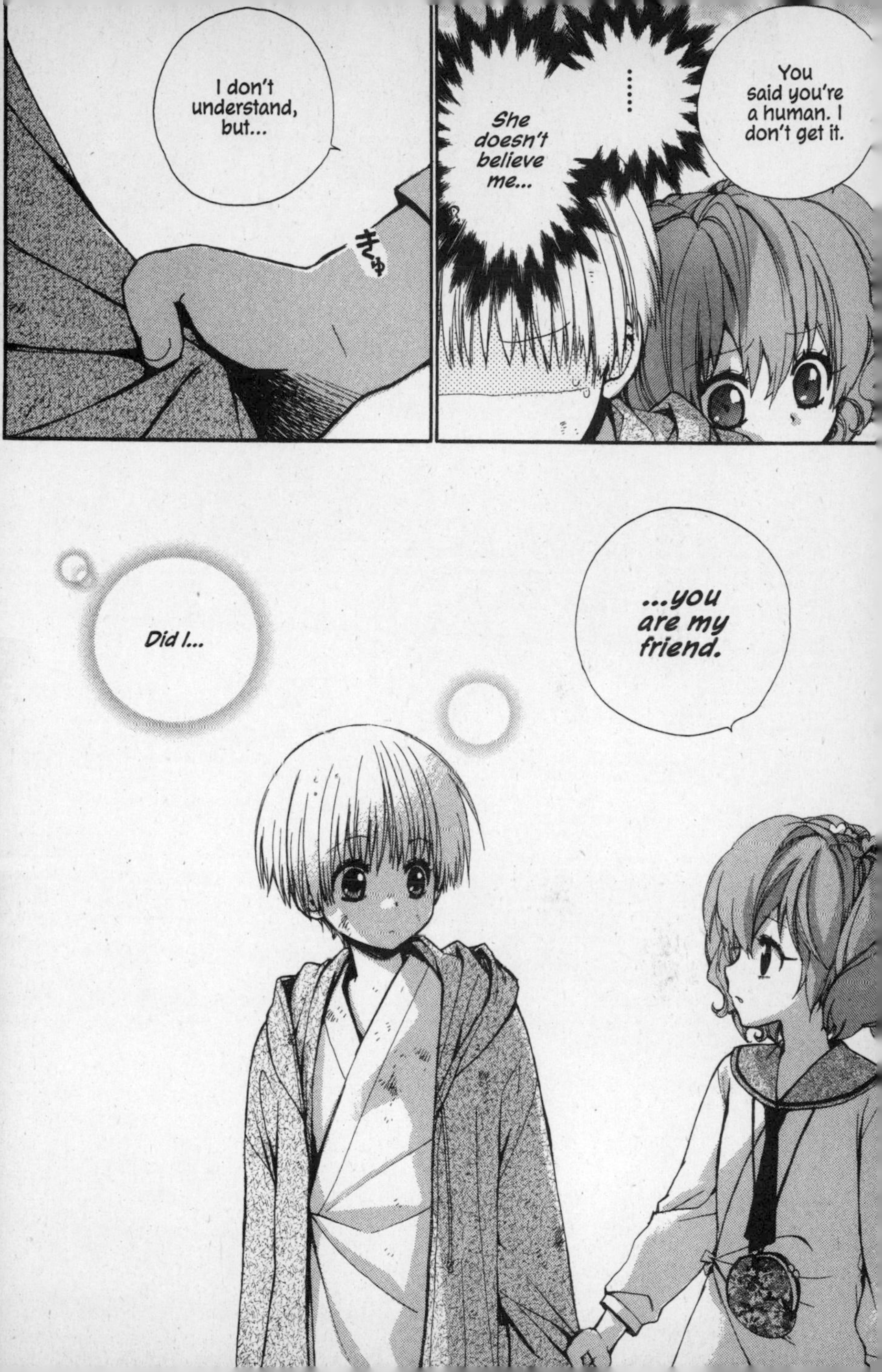
You said you're a human. I don't get it.
......
She doesn't believe me...
きゅ
I don't understand, but...
...you are my friend.
Did I...

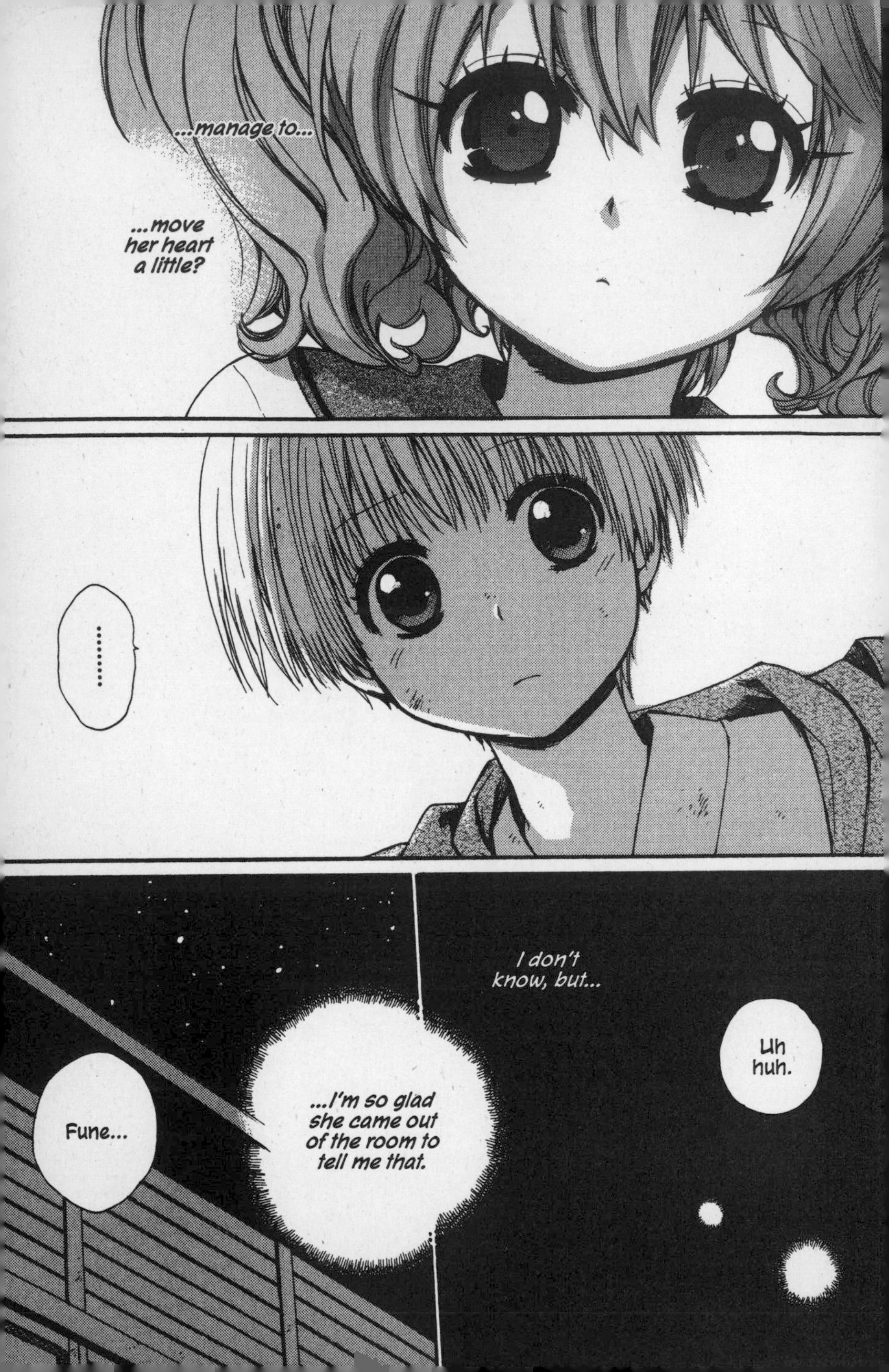
...manage to...
...move her heart a little?
....
I don't know, but...
Uh huh.
...I'm so glad she came out of the room to tell me that.
Fune...

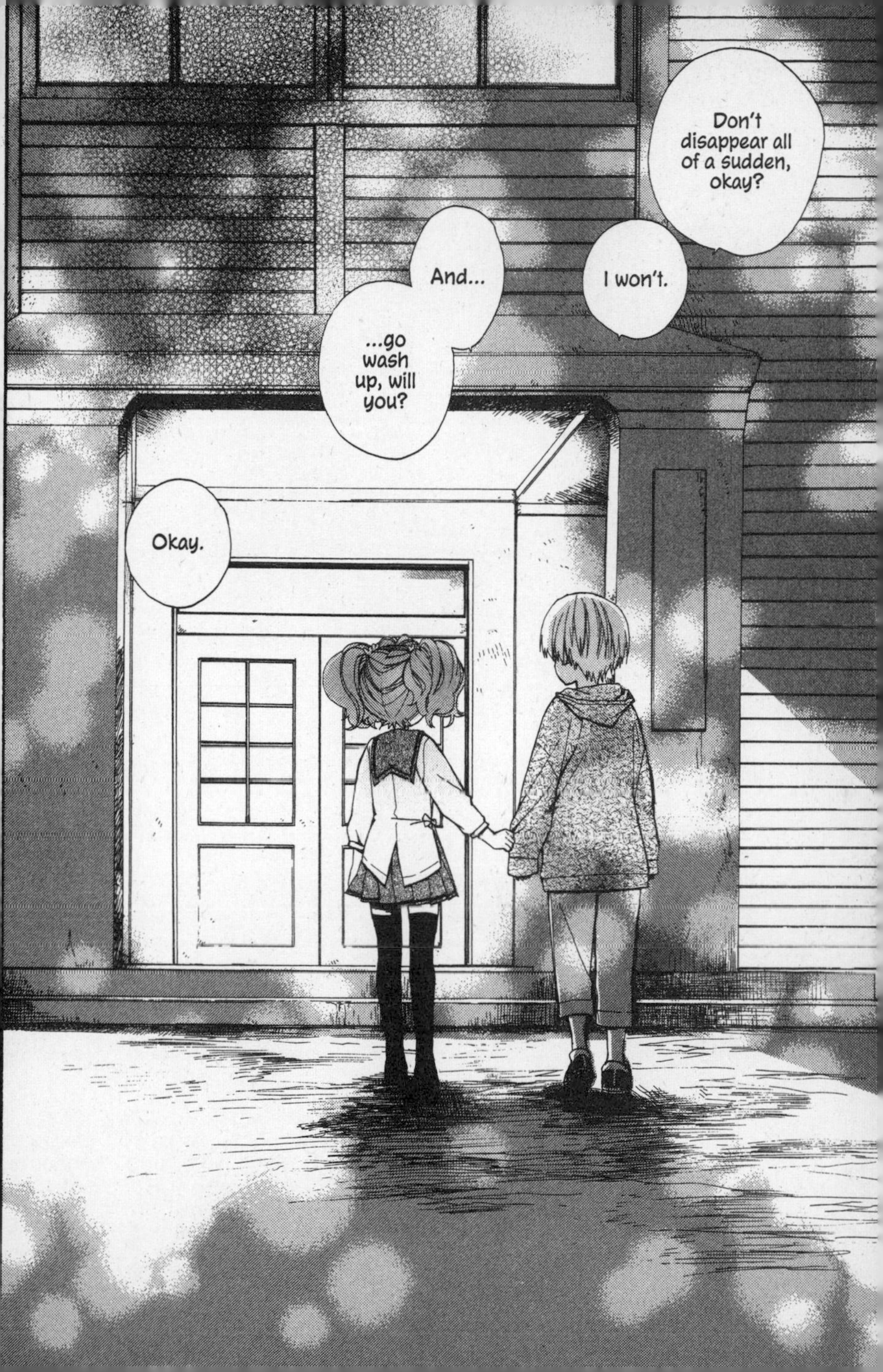
Don't disappear all of a sudden, okay?
I won't.
And...
...go wash up, will you?
Okay.

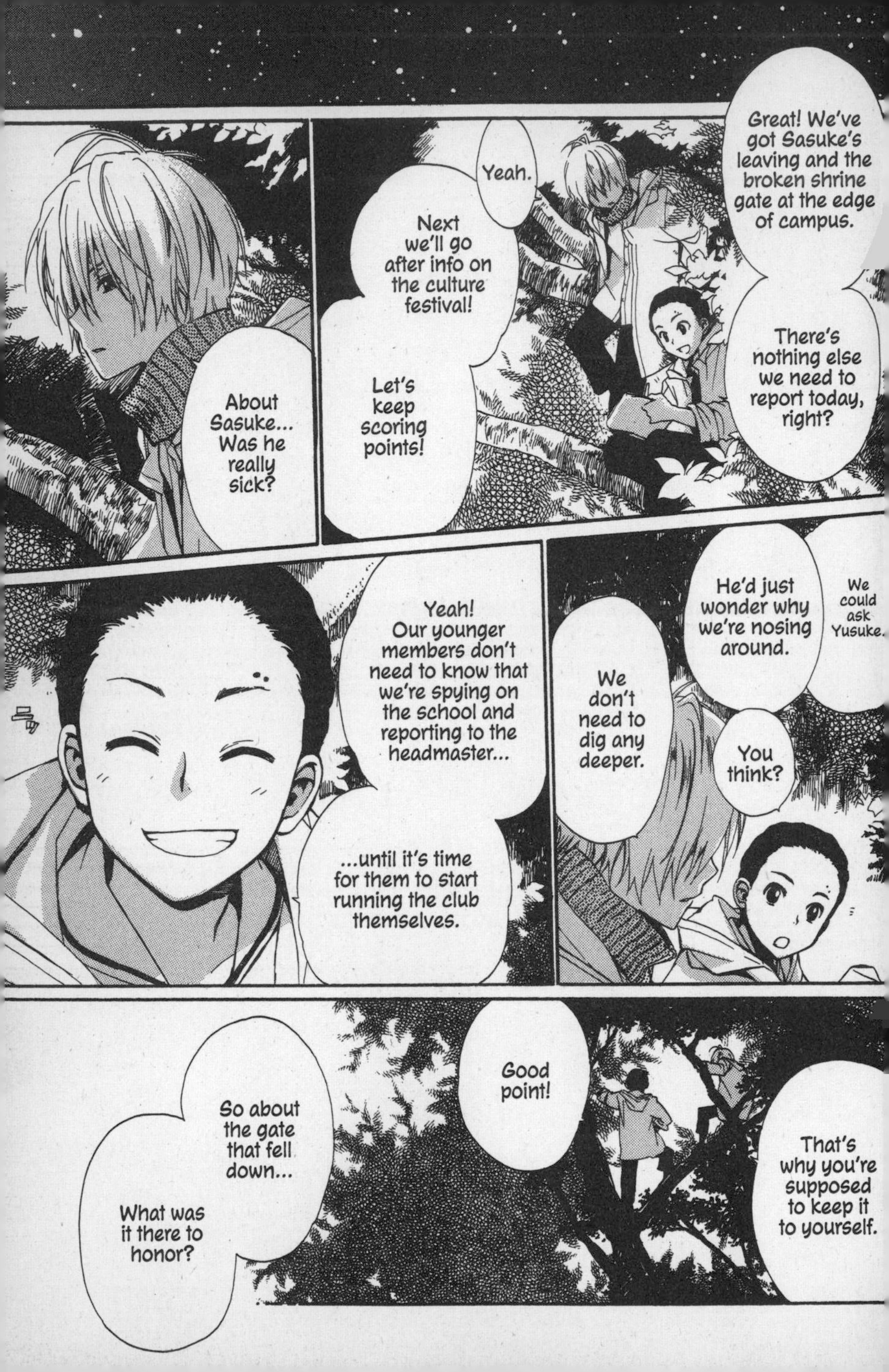
Great! We've got Sasuke's leaving and the broken shrine gate at the edge of campus.
There's nothing else we need to report today, right?
Yeah.
Next we'll go after info on the culture festival!
Let's keep scoring points!
About Sasuke... Was he really sick?
We could ask Yusuke.
He'd just wonder why we're nosing around.
We don't need to dig any deeper.
You think?
Yeah! Our younger members don't need to know that we're spying on the school and reporting to the headmaster...
...until it's time for them to start running the club themselves.
That's why you're supposed to keep it to yourself.
Good point!
So about the gate that fell down...
What was it there to honor?

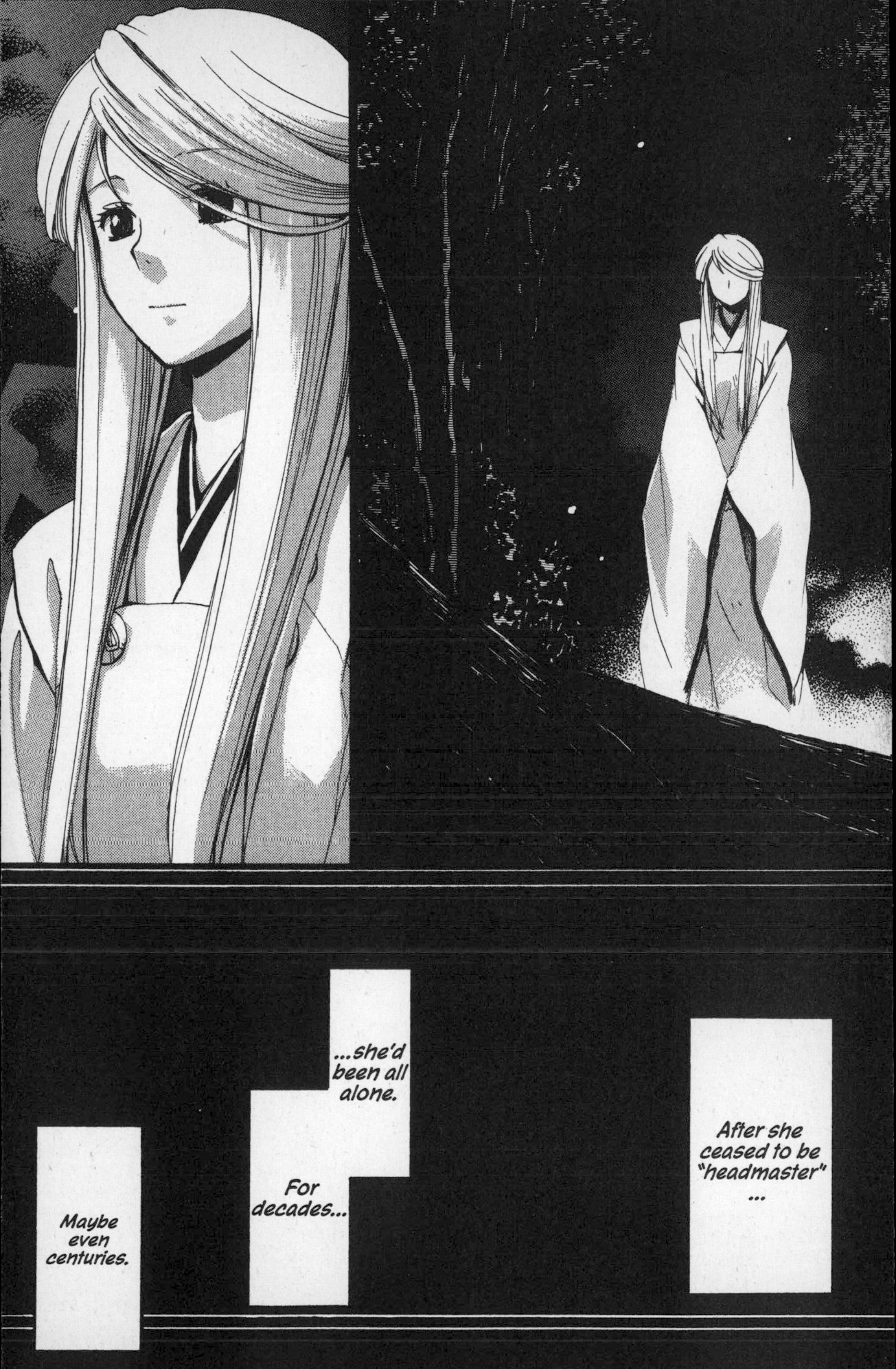
After she ceased to be "headmaster" ...
...she'd been all alone.
For decades...
Maybe even centuries.

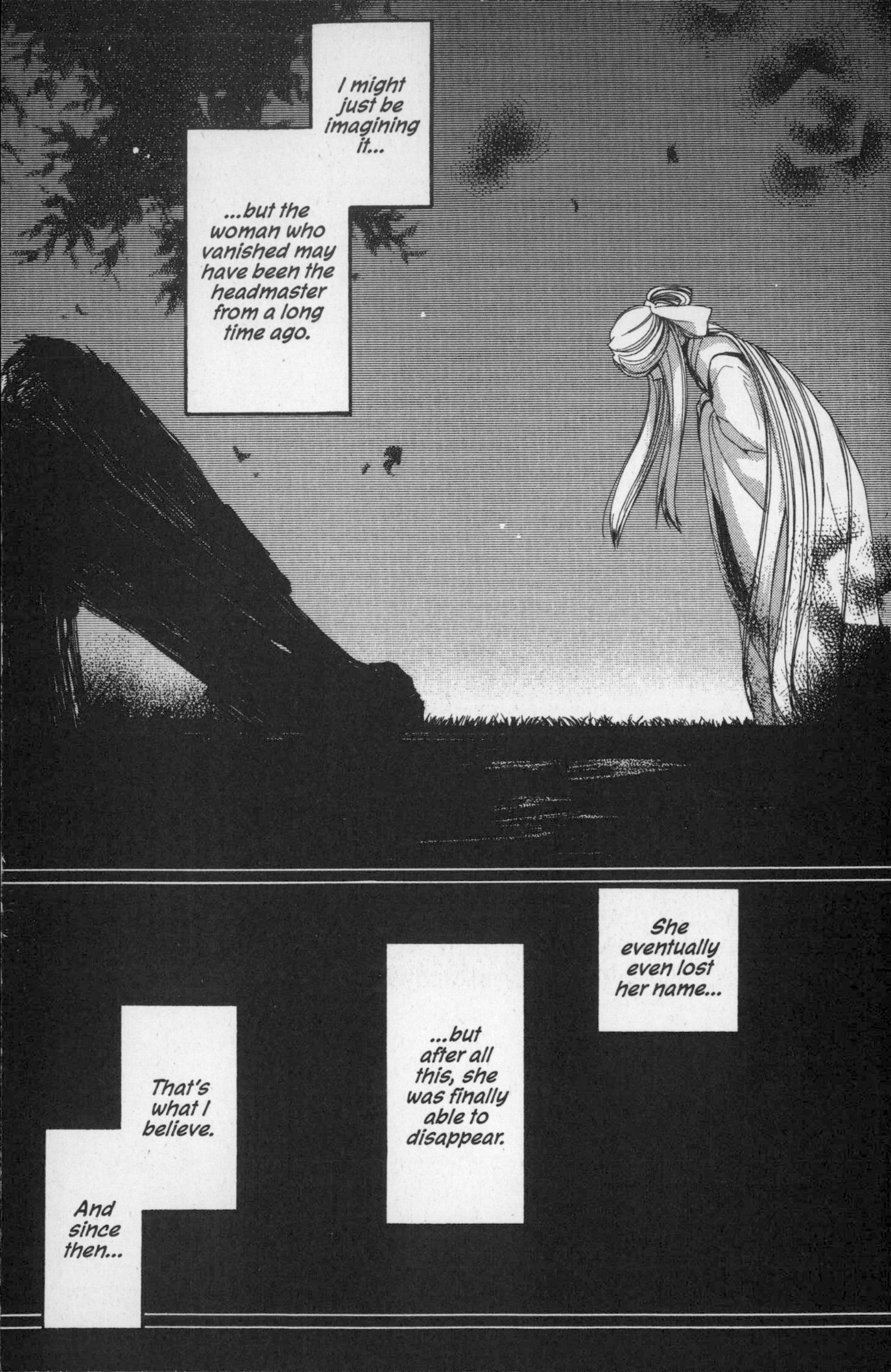
I might just be imagining it...
...but the woman who vanished may have been the headmaster from a long time ago.
She eventually even lost her name...
...but after all this, she was finally able to disappear.
That's what I believe.
And since then...

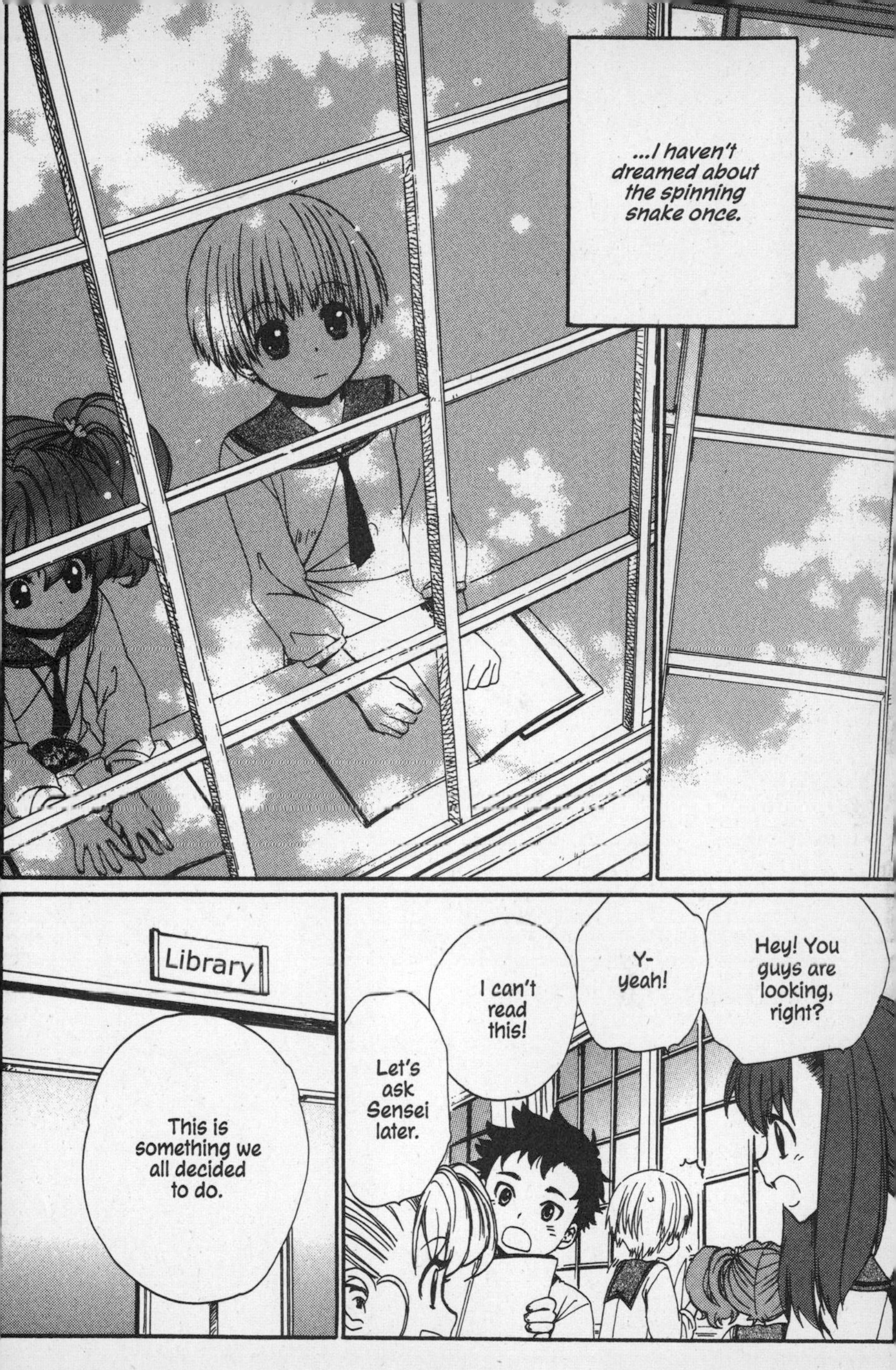
...I haven't dreamed about the spinning snake once.
Hey! You guys are looking, right?
Y-yeah!
I can't read this!
Let's ask Sensei later.
Library
This is something we all decided to do.

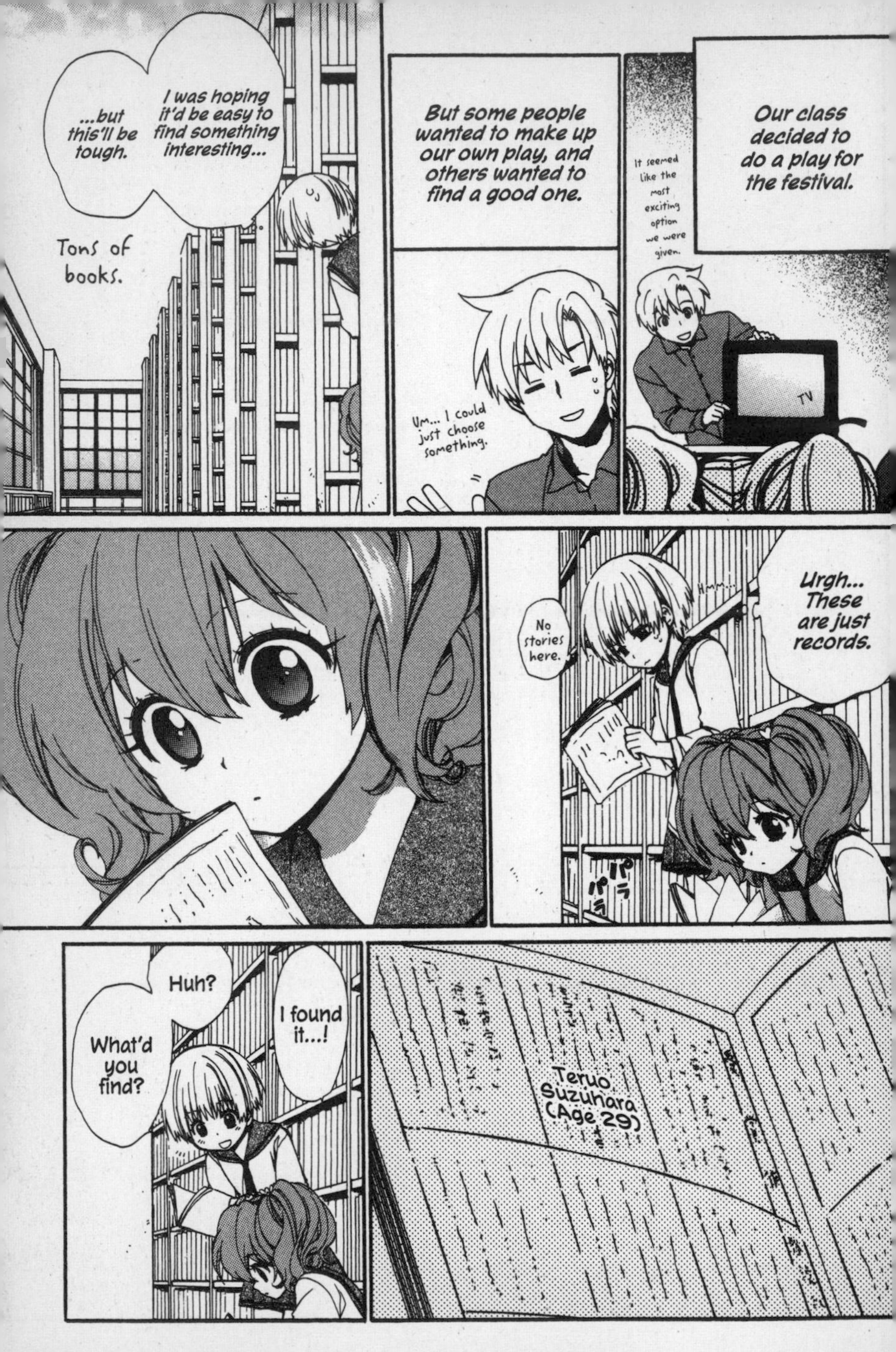
Our class decided to do a play for the festival.
It seemed like the most exciting option we were given.
TV
But some people wanted to make up our own play, and others wanted to find a good one.
Um... I could just choose something.
I was hoping it'd be easy to find something interesting...
...but this'll be tough.
Tons of books.
Urgh... These are just records.
Hmm...
No stories here.
パラ
パラ
Teruo Suzuhara (Age 29)
I found it...!
Huh?
What'd you find?

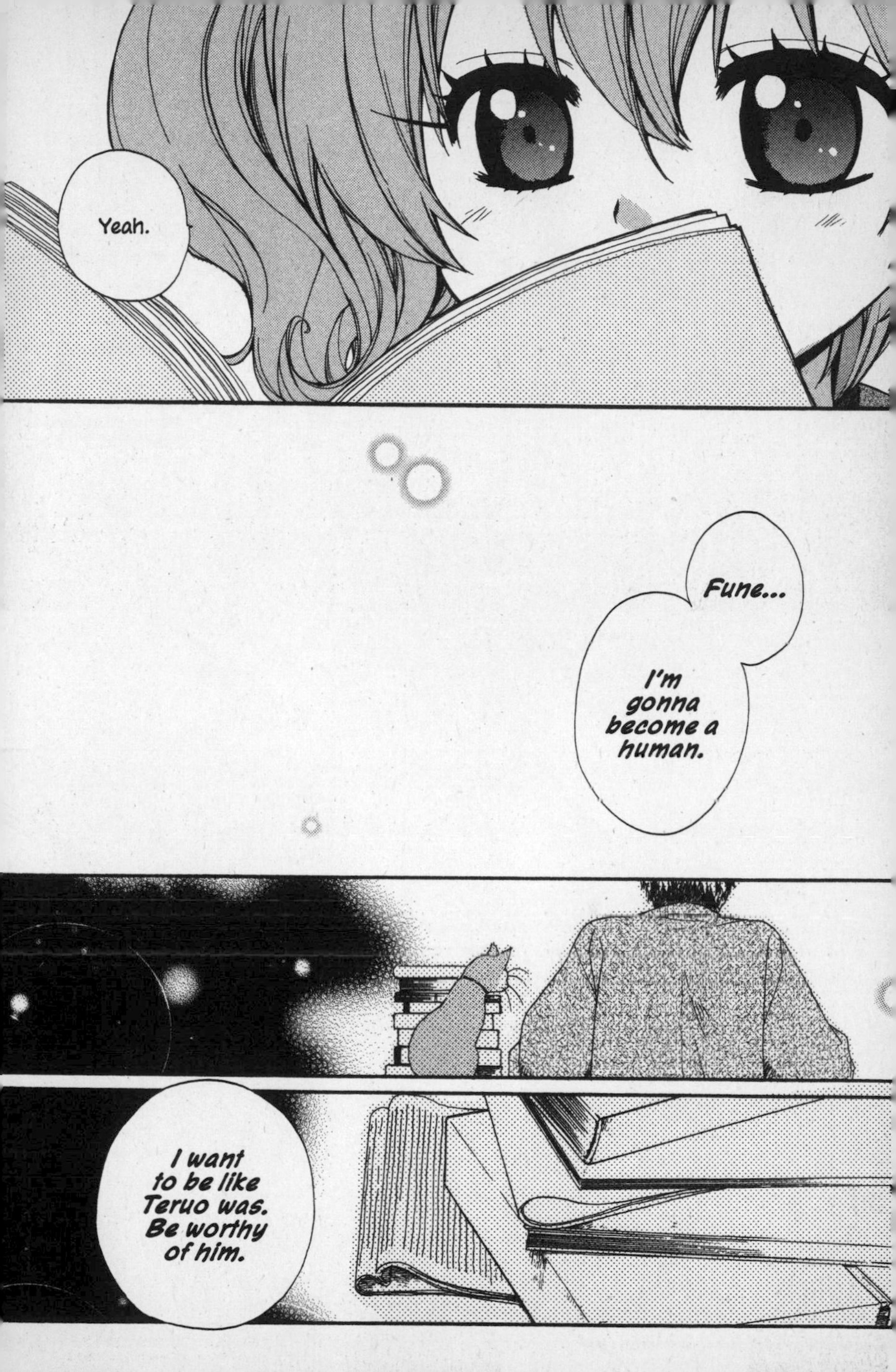
Yeah.
Fune...
I'm gonna become a human.
I want to be like Teruo was. Be worthy of him.

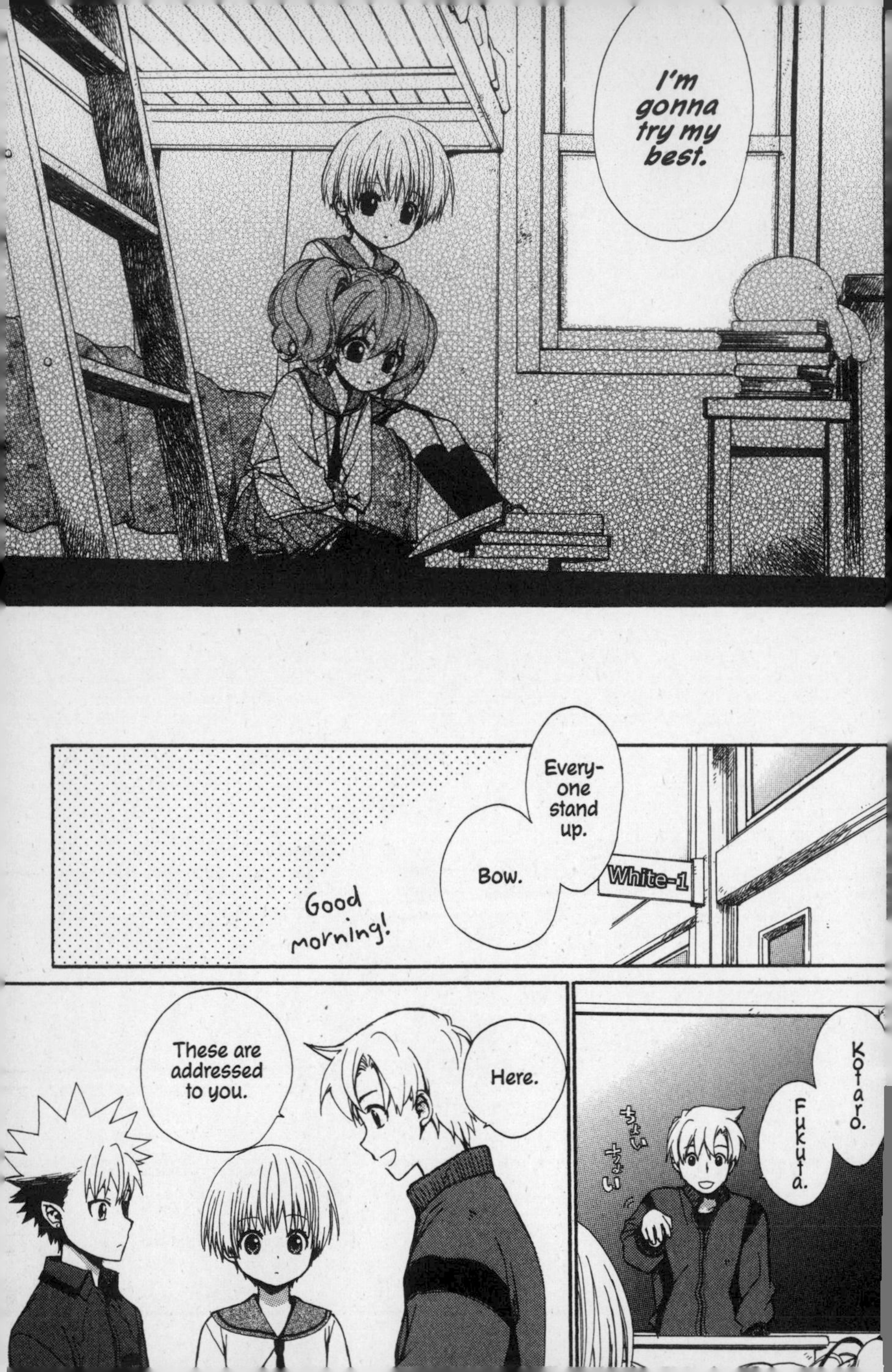
I'm gonna try my best.
Every-one stand up.
White-1
Bow.
Good morning!
Kotaro.
Fukuta.
ちょい ちょい
Here.
These are addressed to you.

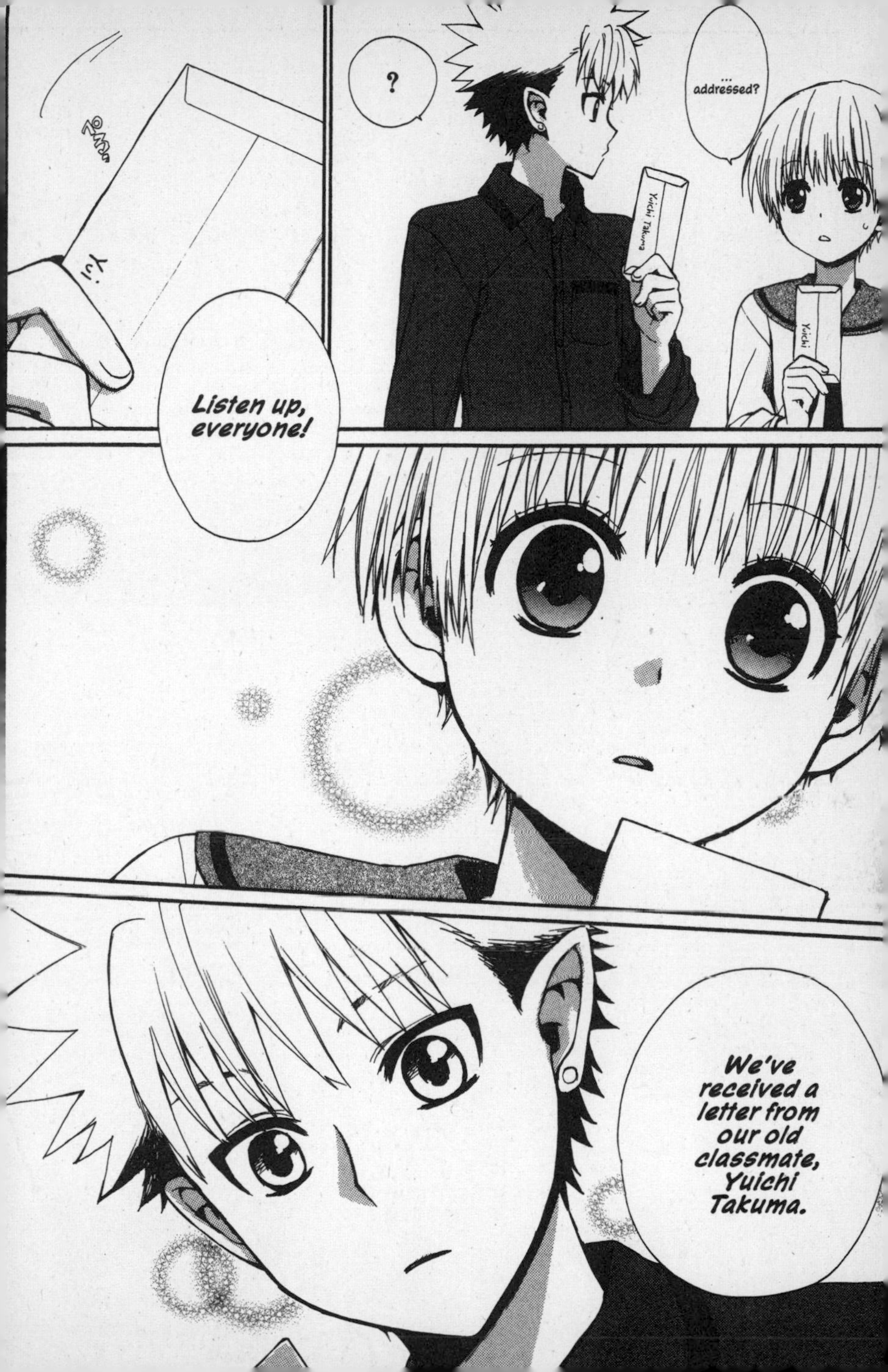
... addressed?
?
Yuichi Takuma
Yuichi
Listen up, everyone!
We've received a letter from our old classmate, Yuichi Takuma.

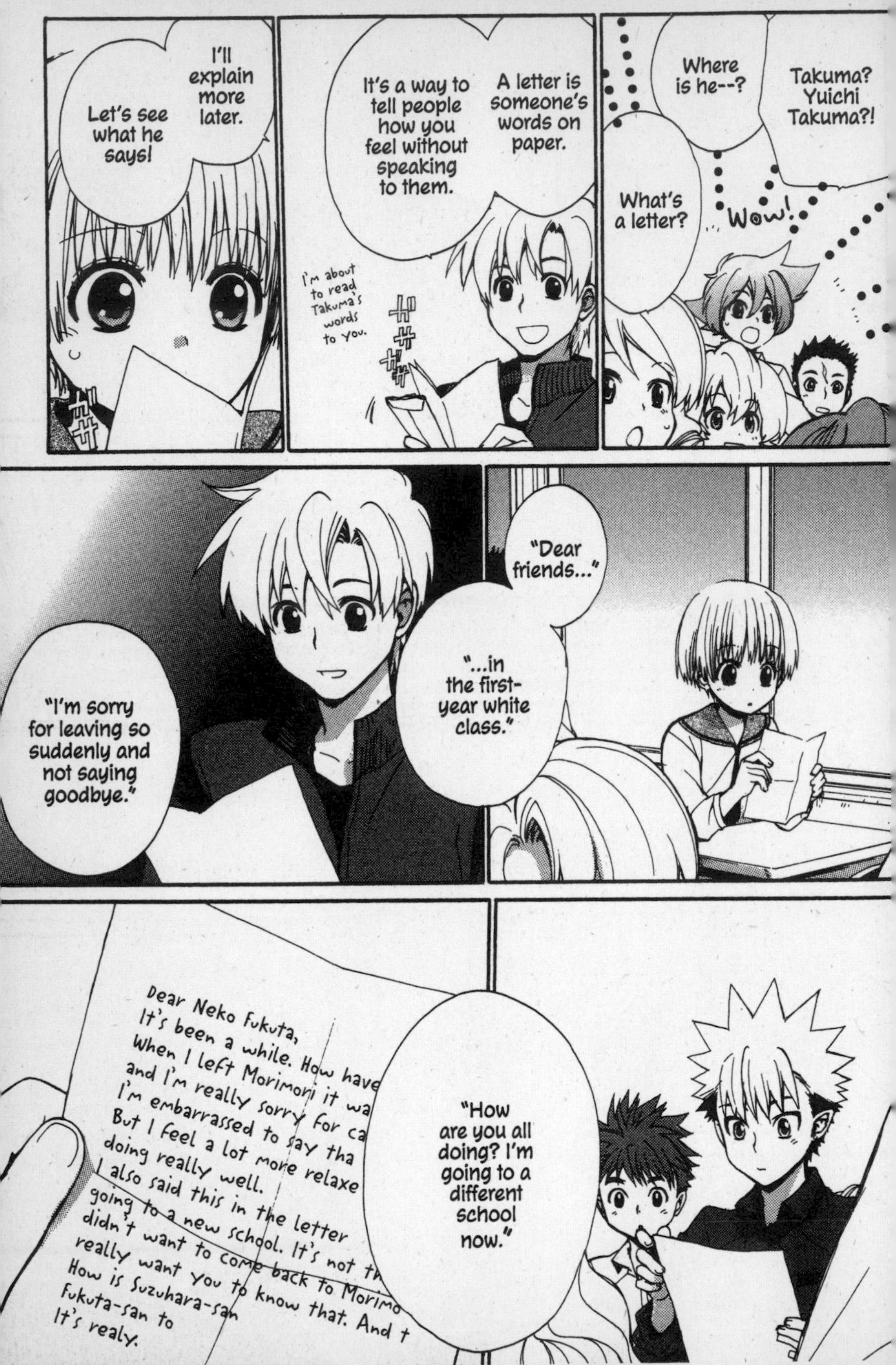
Takuma? Yuichi Takuma?!
Where is he--?
What's a letter?
Wow!
A letter is someone's words on paper.
It's a way to tell people how you feel without speaking to them.
I'm about to read Takuma's words to you.
I'll explain more later.
Let's see what he says!
"Dear friends..."
"...in the first-year white class."
"I'm sorry for leaving so suddenly and not saying goodbye."
"How are you all doing? I'm going to a different school now."
Dear Neko Fukuta,
It's been a while. How have
When I left Morimori it wa
and I'm really sorry for ca
I'm embarrassed to say tha
But I feel a lot more relaxe
doing really well.
I also said this in the letter
going to a new school. It's not th
didn't want to come back to Morimo
really want you to know that. And t
How is Suzuhara-san
Fukuta-san to
It's realy.

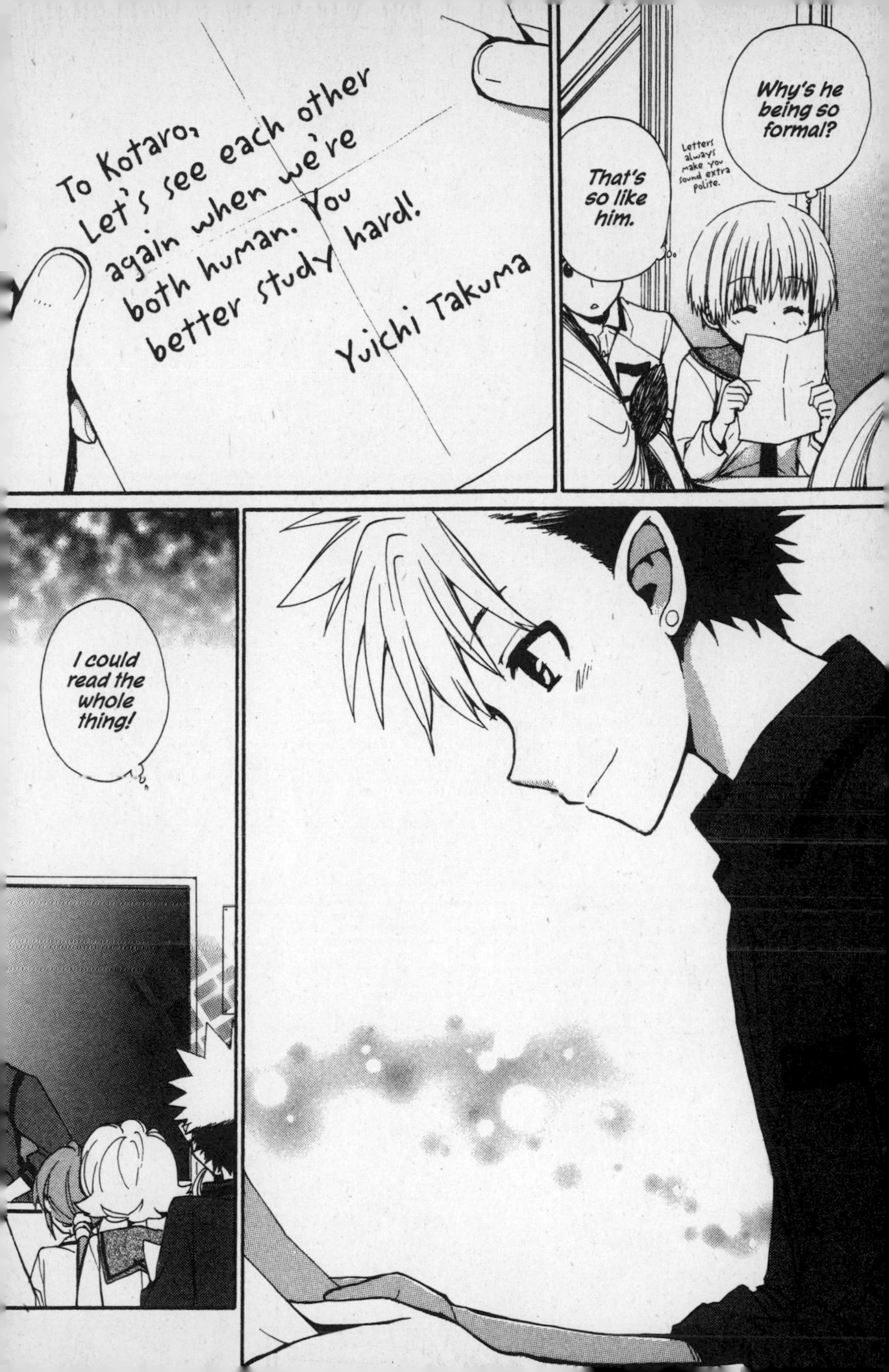
Why's he being so formal?
Letters always make you sound extra polite.
That's so like him.
To Kotaro,
Let's see each other again when we're both human. You better study hard!
Yuichi Takuma
I could read the whole thing!

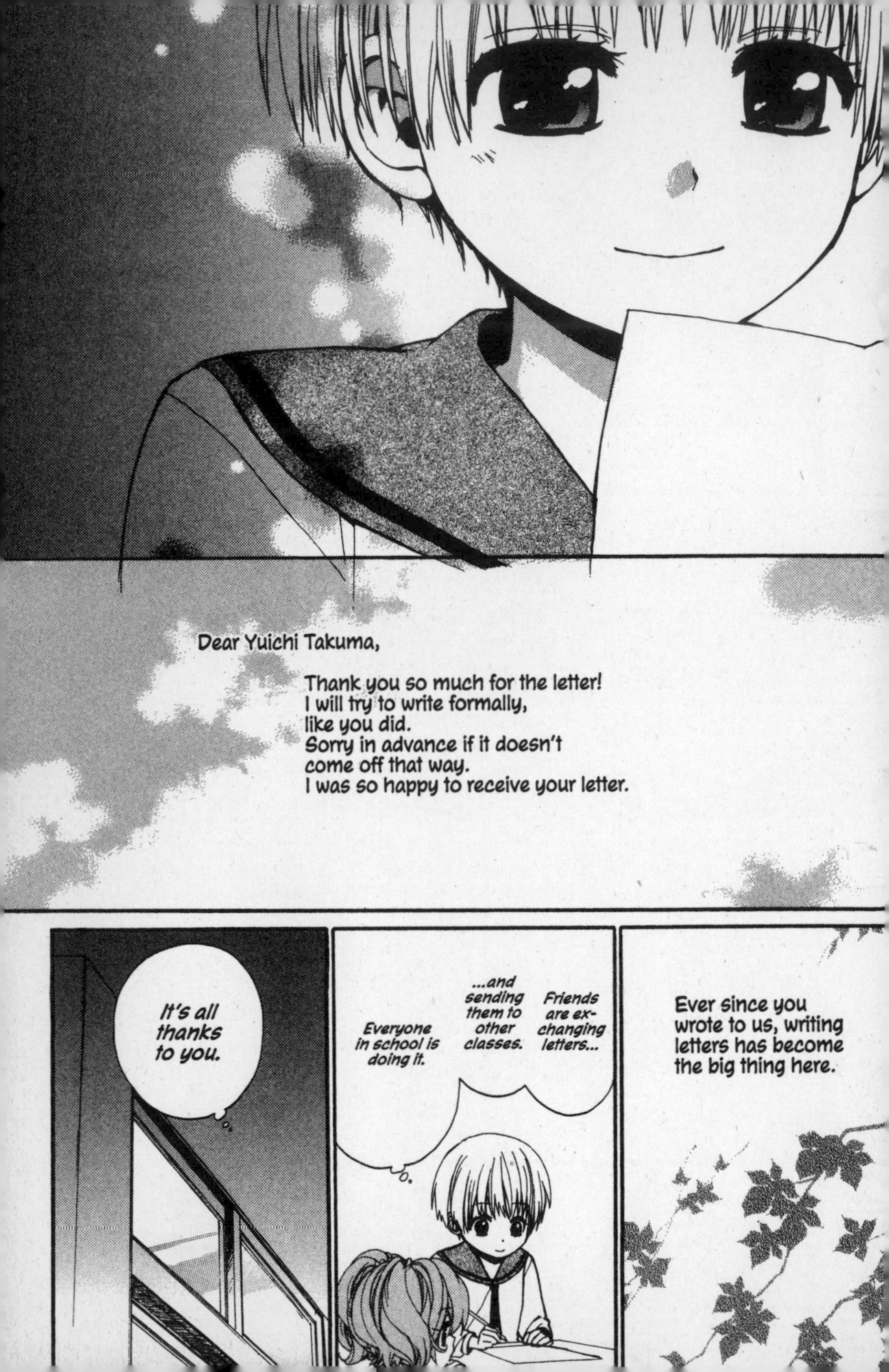
Dear Yuichi Takuma,
Thank you so much for the letter!
I will try to write formally,
like you did.
Sorry in advance if it doesn't
come off that way.
I was so happy to receive your letter.
Ever since you wrote to us, writing letters has become the big thing here.
Friends are ex-changing letters...
...and sending them to other classes.
Everyone in school is doing it.
It's all thanks to you.

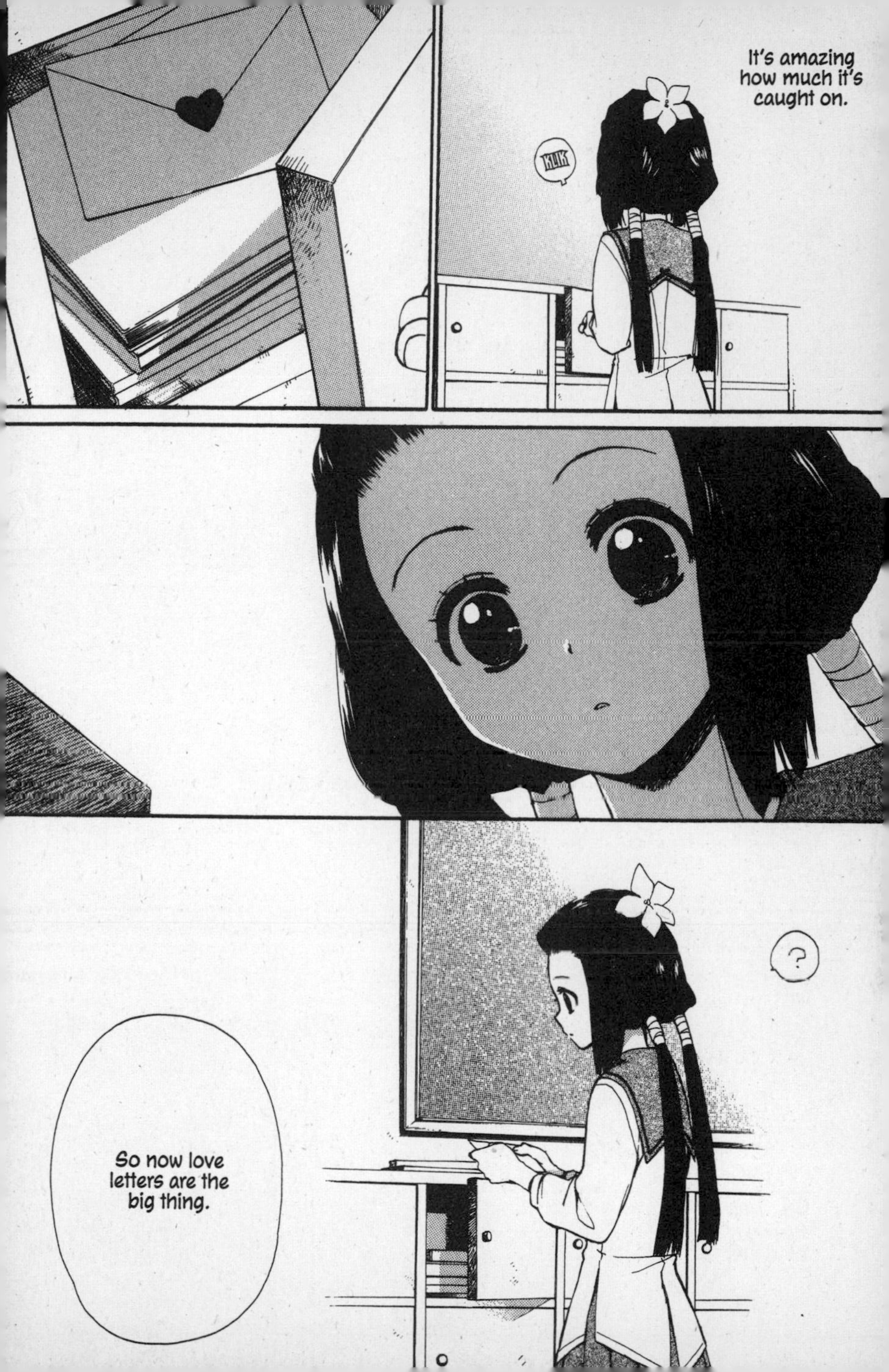
It's amazing how much it's caught on.
KLIK
?
So now love letters are the big thing.

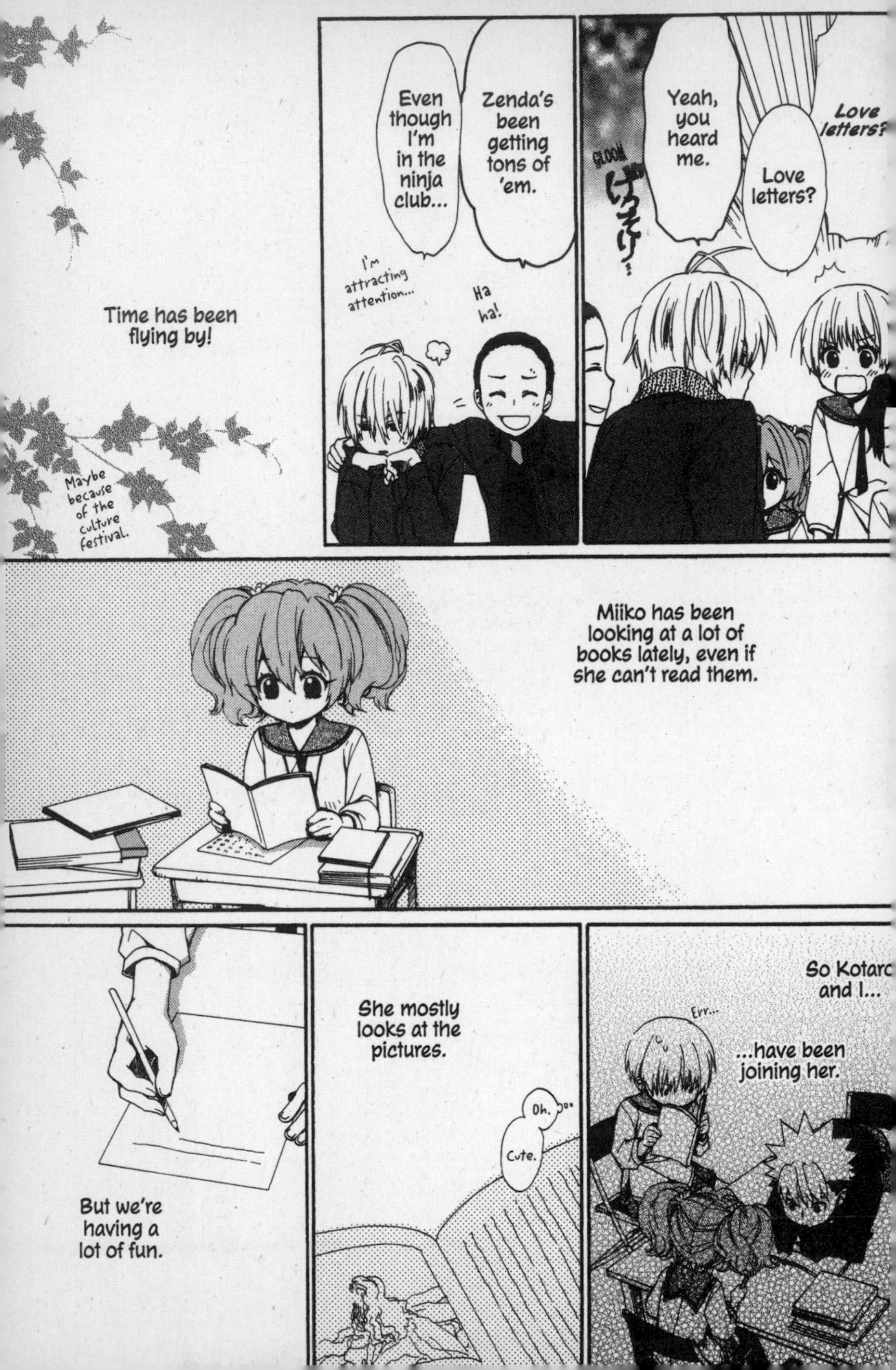
Love letters?
Love letters?
Yeah, you heard me.
GLOOM
げっそり…
Zenda's been getting tons of 'em.
Even though I'm in the ninja club...
I'm attracting attention...
Ha ha!
Time has been flying by!
Maybe because of the culture festival.
Miiko has been looking at a lot of books lately, even if she can't read them.
So Kotar
and I...
...have been joining her.
Err...
She mostly looks at the pictures.
Oh.
Cute.
But we're having a lot of fun.

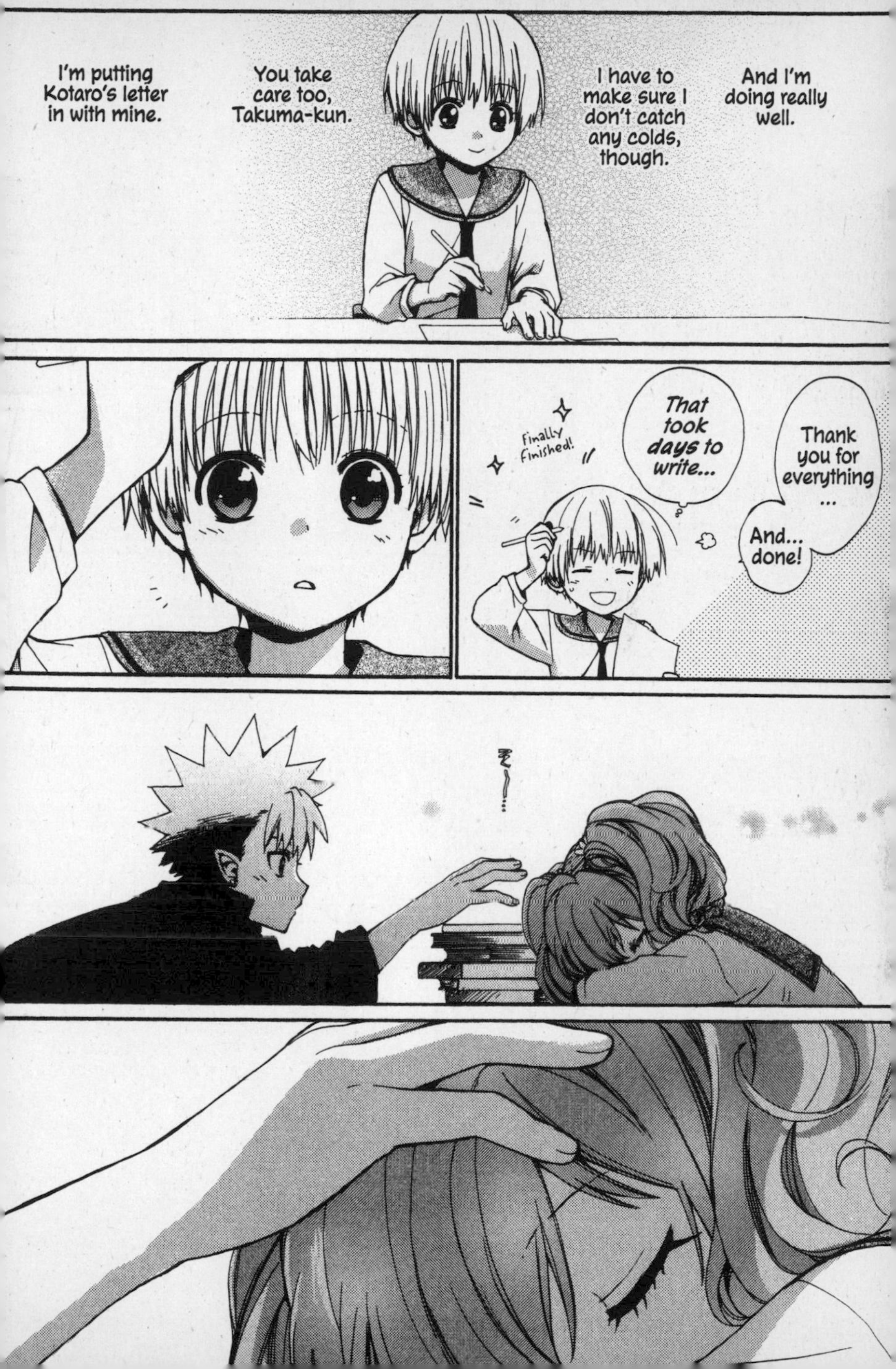
And I'm doing really well.
I have to make sure I don't catch any colds, though.
You take care too, Takuma-kun.
I'm putting Kotaro's letter in with mine.
Thank you for everything ...
And... done!
That took *days* to write...
Finally finished!

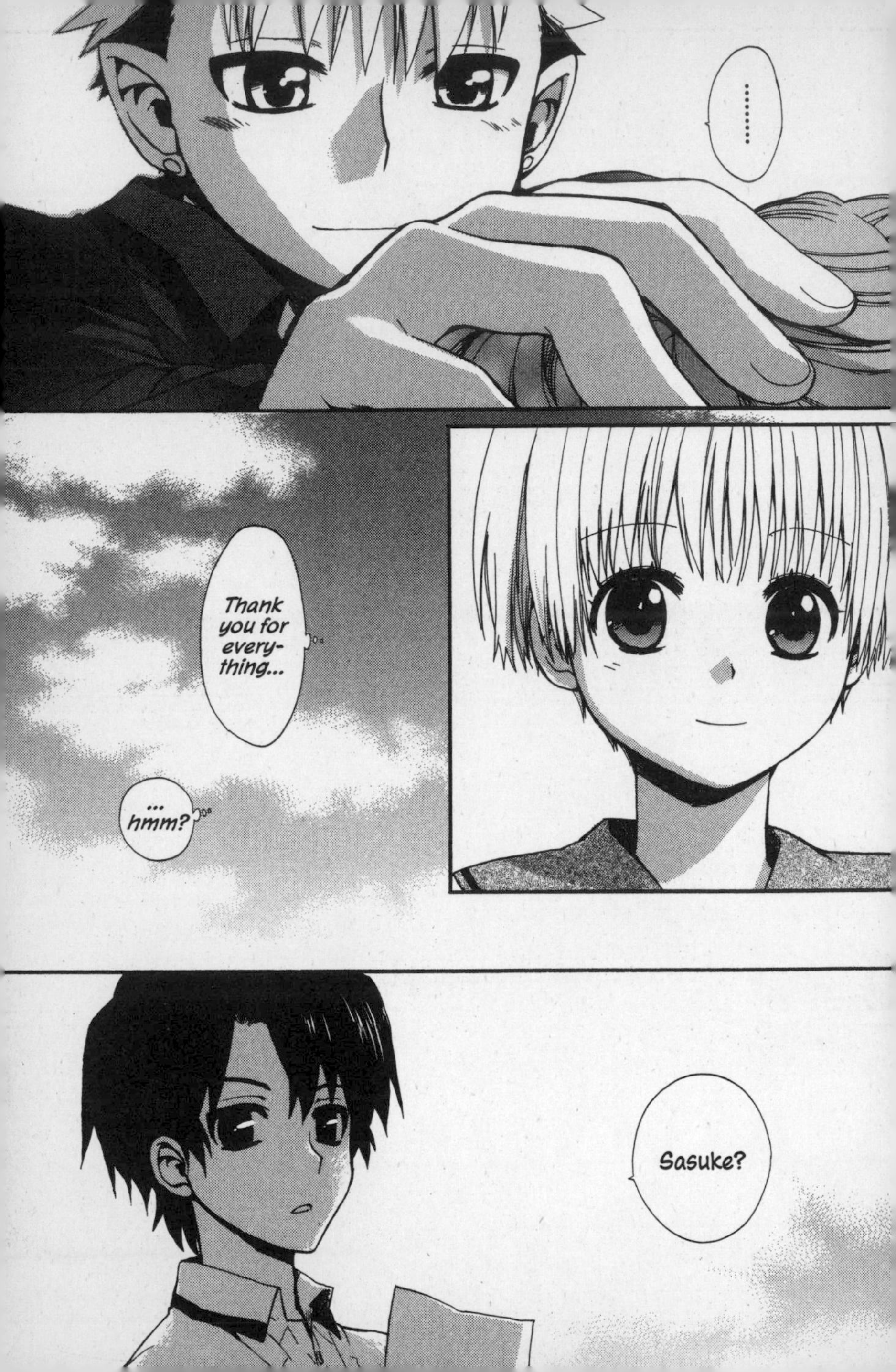
......
Thank you for every-thing...
... hmm?
Sasuke?

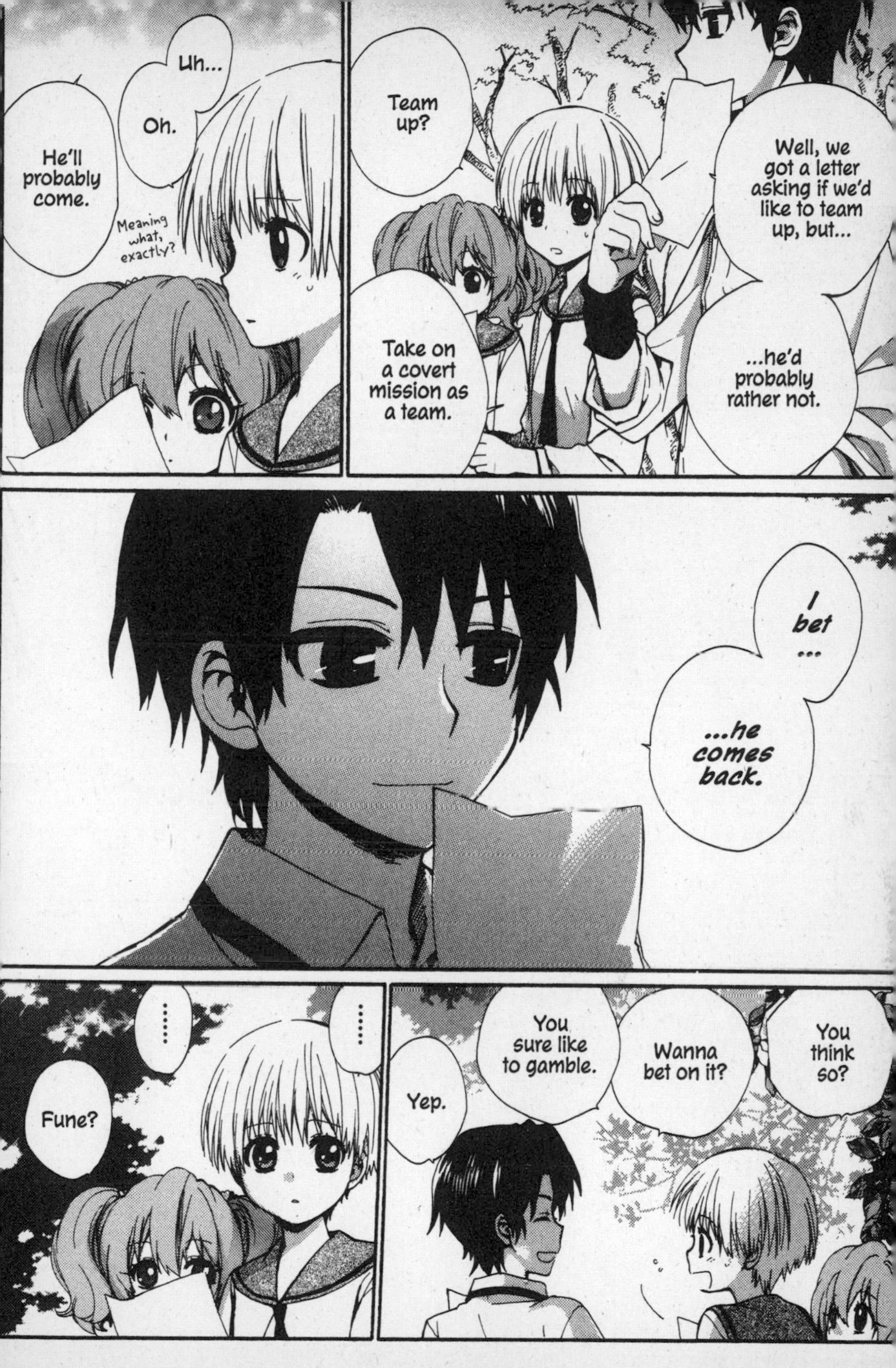
Well, we got a letter asking if we'd like to team up, but...
...he'd probably rather not.
Team up?
Take on a covert mission as a team.
Uh...
Oh.
He'll probably come.
Meaning what, exactly?
I bet...
...he comes back.
You think so?
Wanna bet on it?
You sure like to gamble.
Yep.
......
......
Fune?

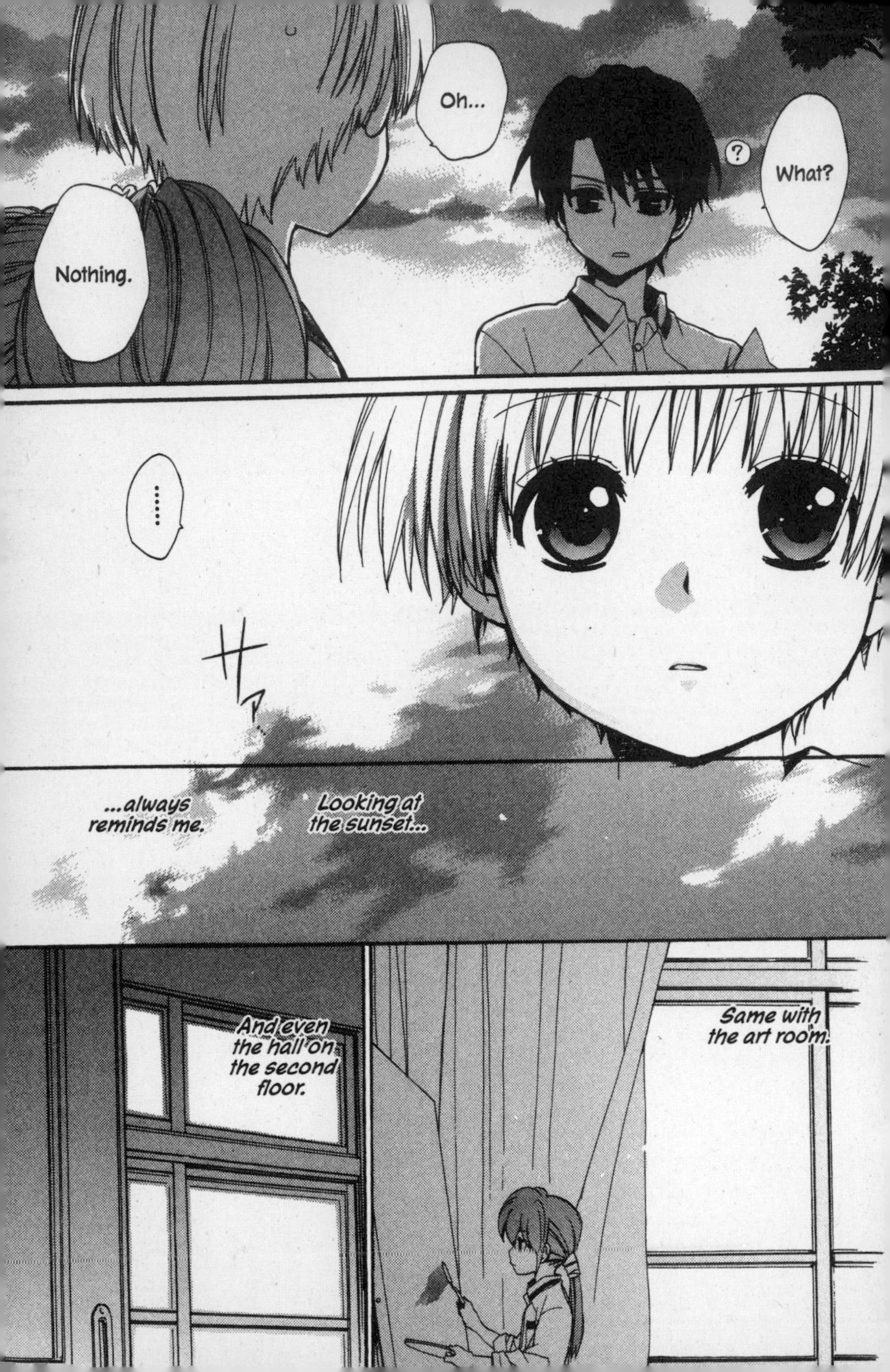
?
What?
Oh...
Nothing.
......
Looking at the sunset...
...always reminds me.
Same with the art room.
And even the hall on the second floor.

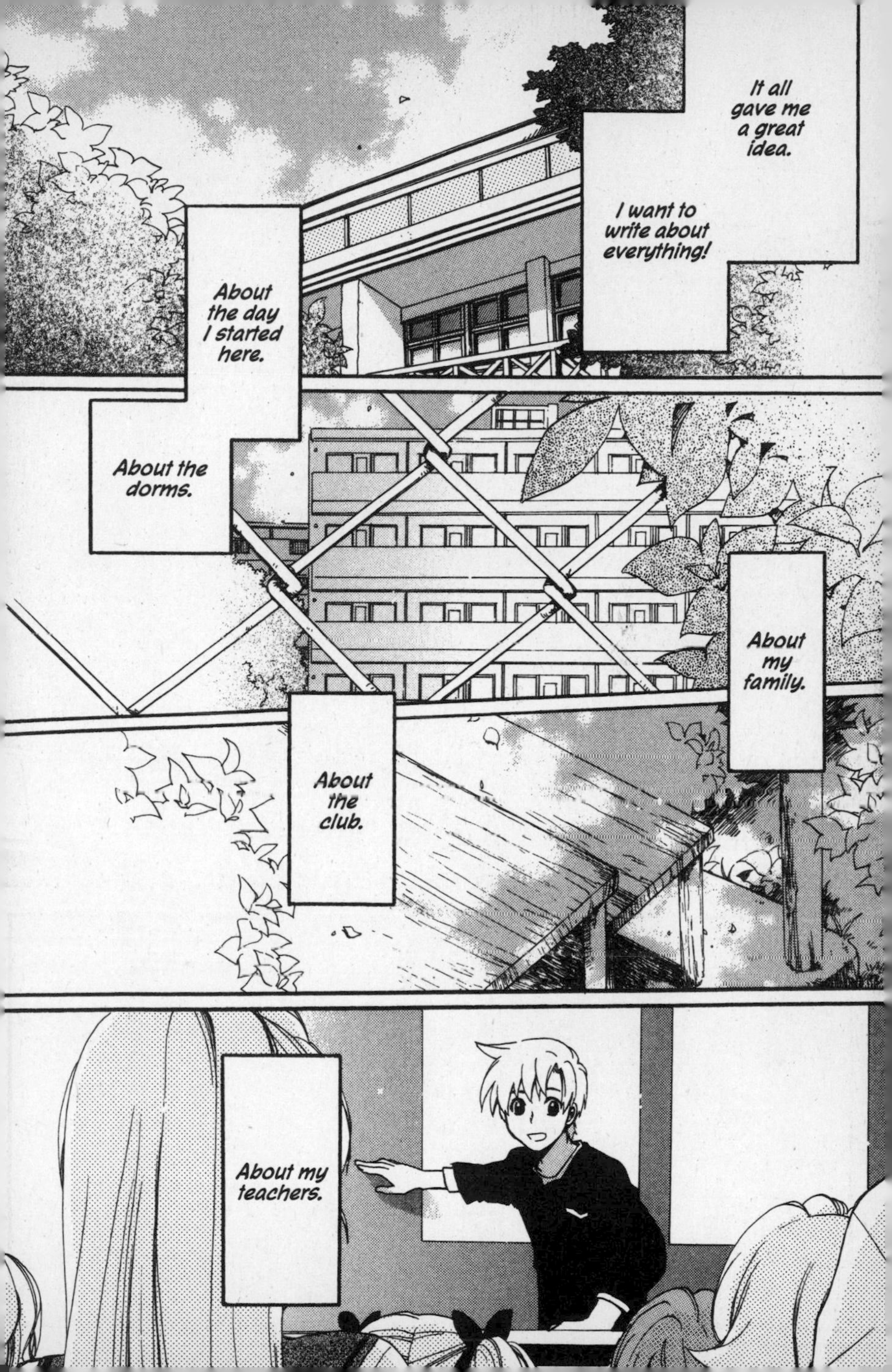
It all gave me a great idea.
I want to write about everything!
About the day I started here.
About the dorms.
About my family.
About the club.
About my teachers.

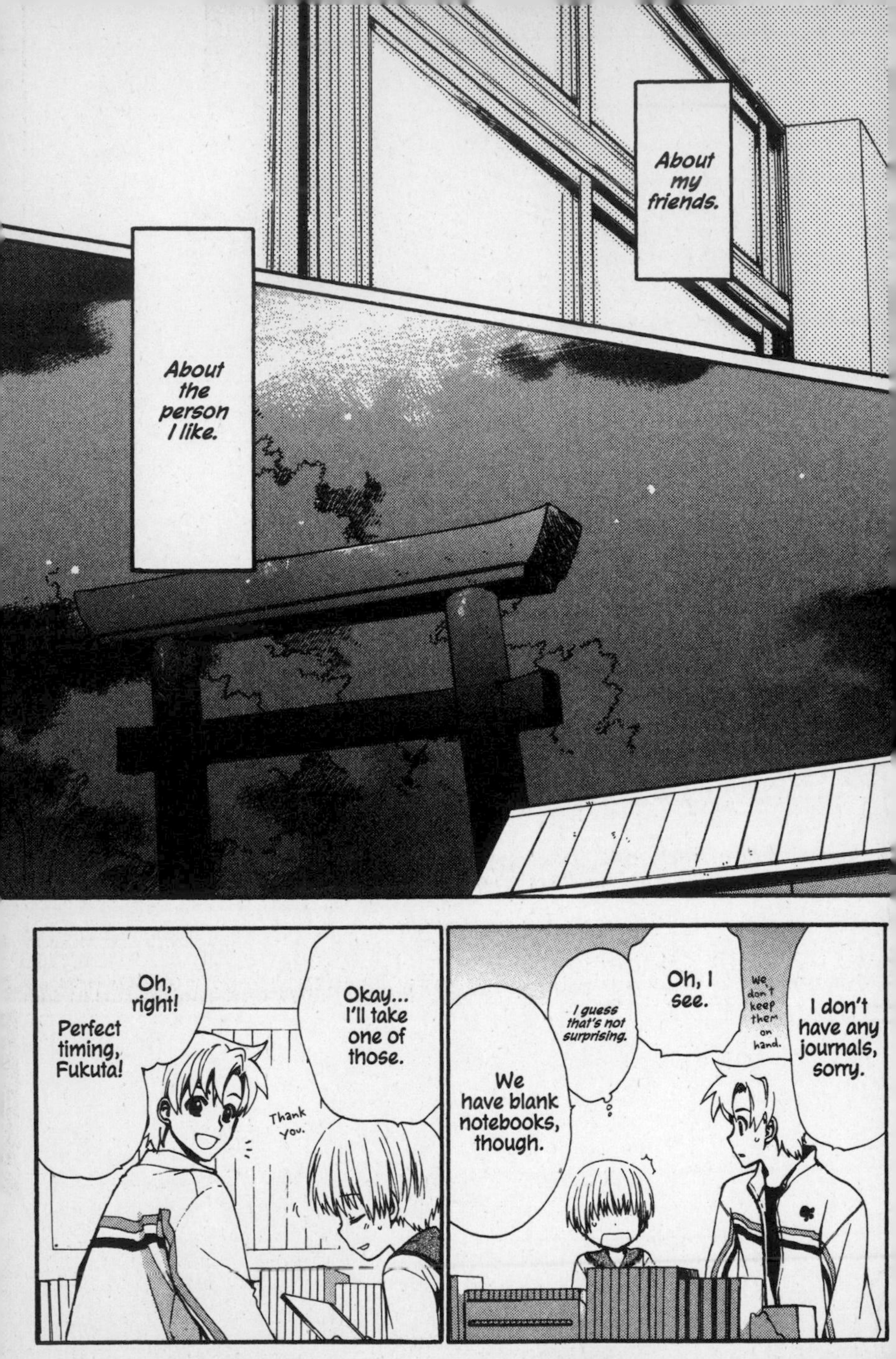
About my friends.
About the person I like.
I don't have any journals, sorry.
We don't keep them on hand.
Oh, I see.
I guess that's not surprising.
We have blank notebooks, though.
Okay... I'll take one of those.
Thank you.
Oh, right!
Perfect timing, Fukuta!

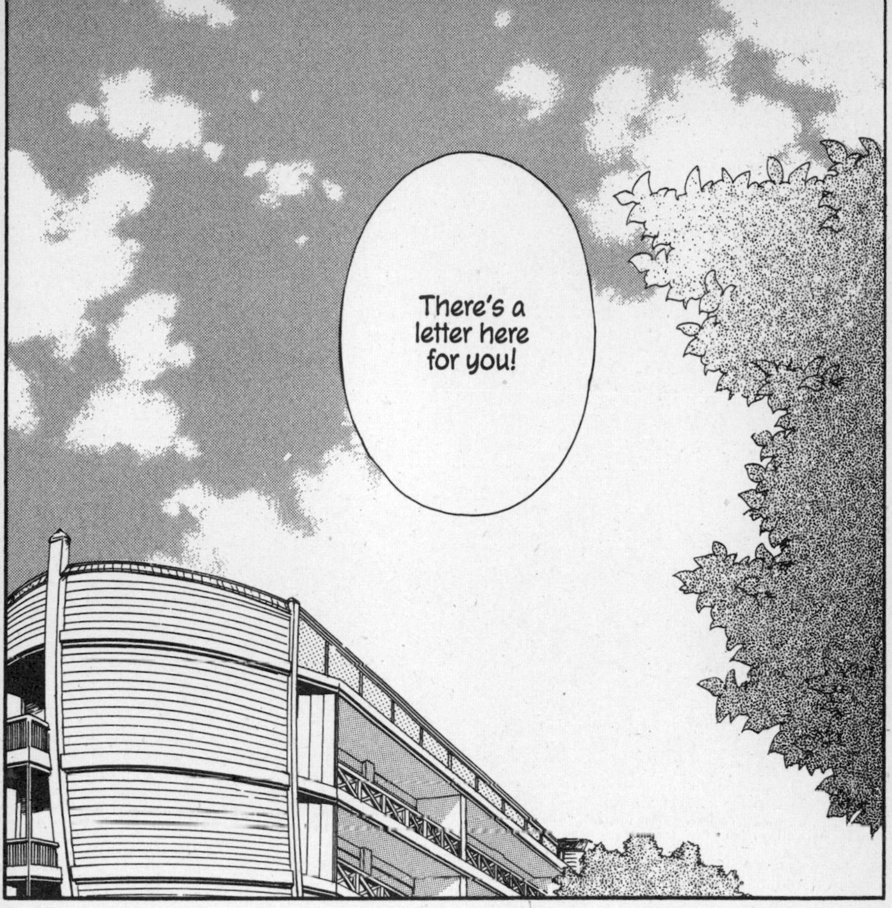
There's a letter here for you!

I'll start by writing...

...about this letter.

Animal Academy / End

Postscript [7]

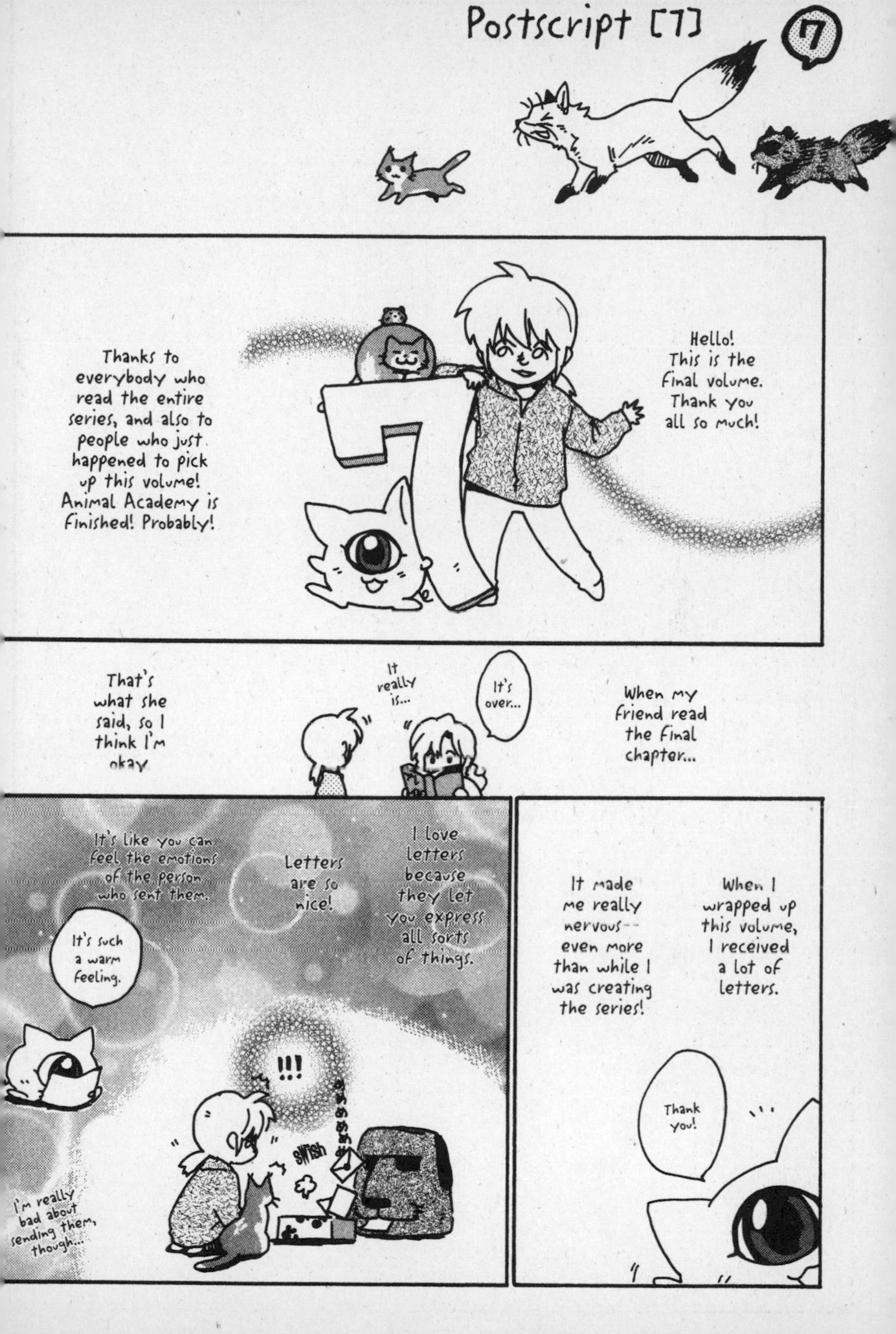
7
Hello! This is the final volume. Thank you all so much!
Thanks to everybody who read the entire series, and also to people who just happened to pick up this volume! Animal Academy is finished! Probably!
When my friend read the final chapter...
It's over...
It really is...
That's what she said, so I think I'm okay.
When I wrapped up this volume, I received a lot of letters.
It made me really nervous-- even more than while I was creating the series!
Thank you!
I love letters because they let you express all sorts of things.
Letters are so nice!
It's like you can feel the emotions of the person who sent them.
It's such a warm feeling.
!!!
SWISH
I'm really bad about sending them, though...

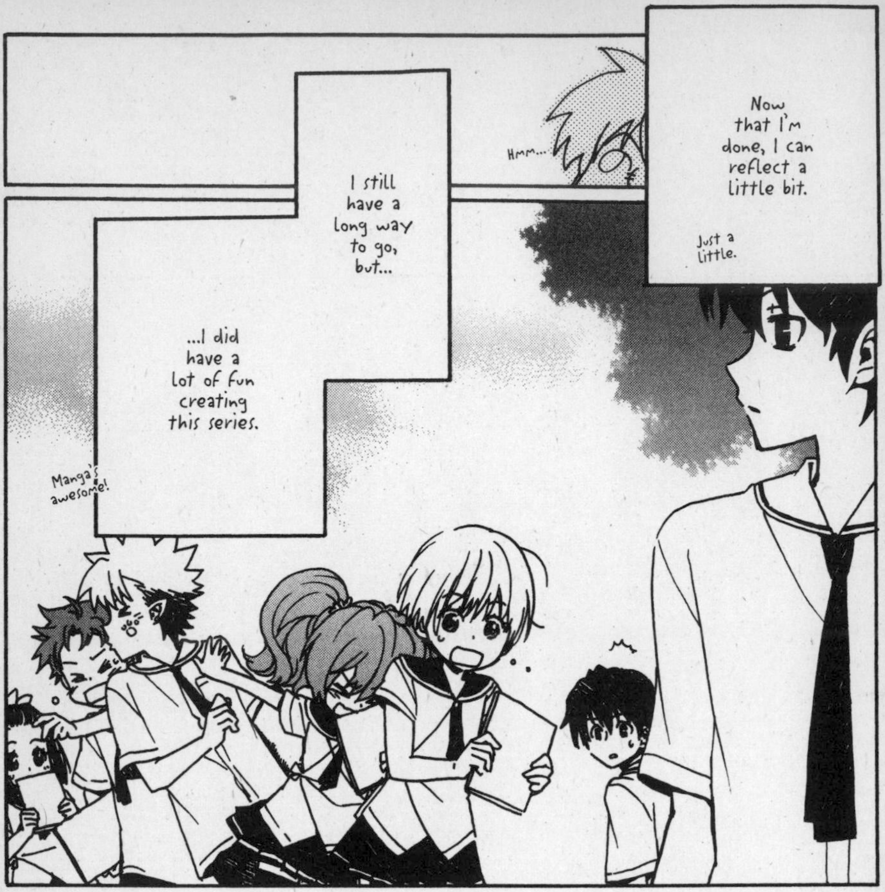
Now that I'm done, I can reflect a little bit.
Just a little.
Hmm...
I still have a long way to go, but...
...I did have a lot of fun creating this series.
Manga's awesome!

So much happened along the way, but I am so thankful to everyone who supported me and helped me: my friends and family, my editor, anyone I made work for and, of course, my fans.

I hope we can see each other again in the future! See ya!

Thank you!

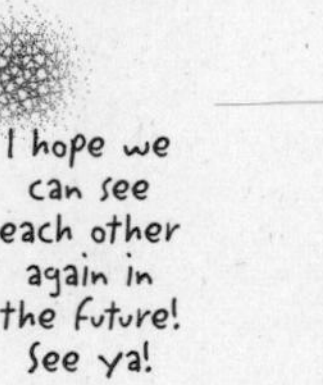

Thank you✿
- I. nami
- O. miwa
- K. miwa
- M. yu-ki
- T. tomoko
- W. satiko
- My editor
  And many more!

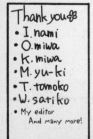

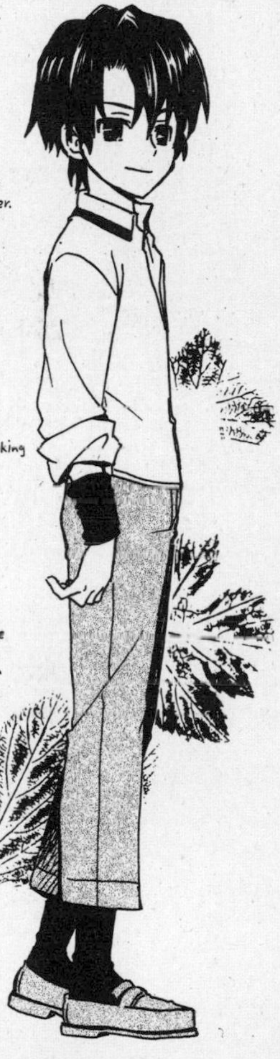

The Sagami Brothers

○ Humans. ○ Believed to be cats.
○ They were raised in the mountains by a strict father who always pitted them against each other. Their mother died of an illness. Kurou and Shirou, the cats who are always with them, are strays the brothers picked up when they were younger. Random fact: their real birthday is January 6.

Yusuke Sagami →

○ Morimori High School 1st year student, Red Class. ○ Class number: 4.
○ He's a ninja placed at the school to pass information to the outside world. He's naturally good at almost everything. He's left-handed. Looking down on Sasuke has become a habit for him.

Sasuke Sagami ←

○ Morimori High School 1st year student, White Class. ○ Class number: 5.
○ The serious, gloomy younger brother who's overwhelmed by regret. His inability to beat Yusuke at anything has given him something of a complex, but he's nearly given up trying. He hates Yusuke on an intellectual level. He also has low self-esteem.

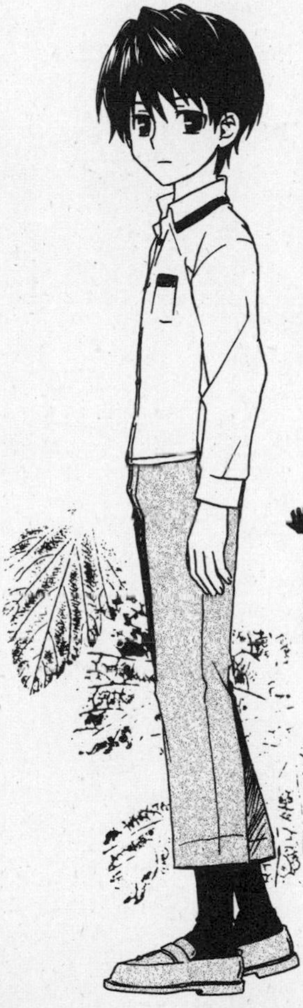

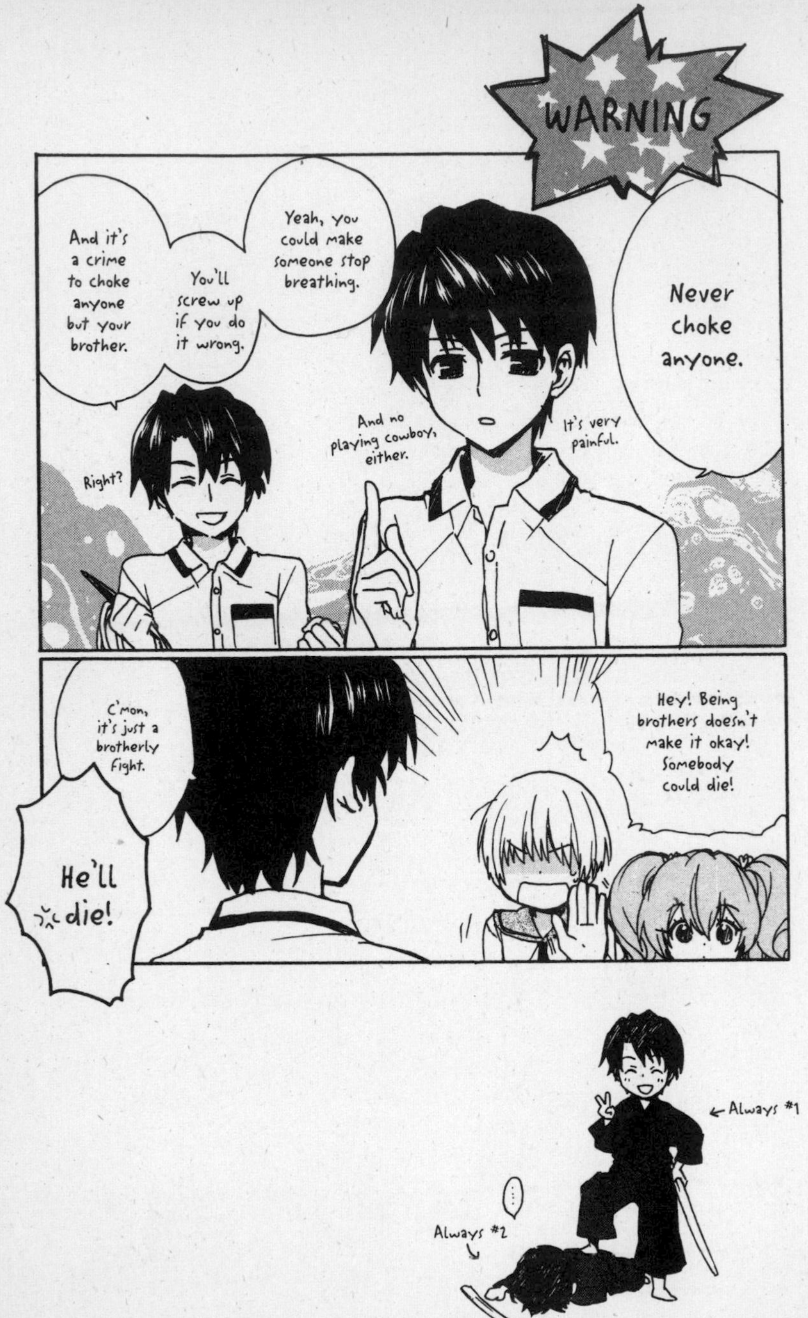
WARNING
Never choke anyone.
It's very painful.
And no playing cowboy, either.
Yeah, you could make someone stop breathing.
You'll screw up if you do it wrong.
And it's a crime to choke anyone but your brother.
Right?
Hey! Being brothers doesn't make it okay! Somebody could die!
C'mon, it's just a brotherly fight.
He'll die!
Always #1
...
Always #2

DOWNLOAD THE REVOLUTION.

Get the free TOKYOPOP app for manga, anytime, anywhere!

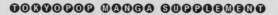

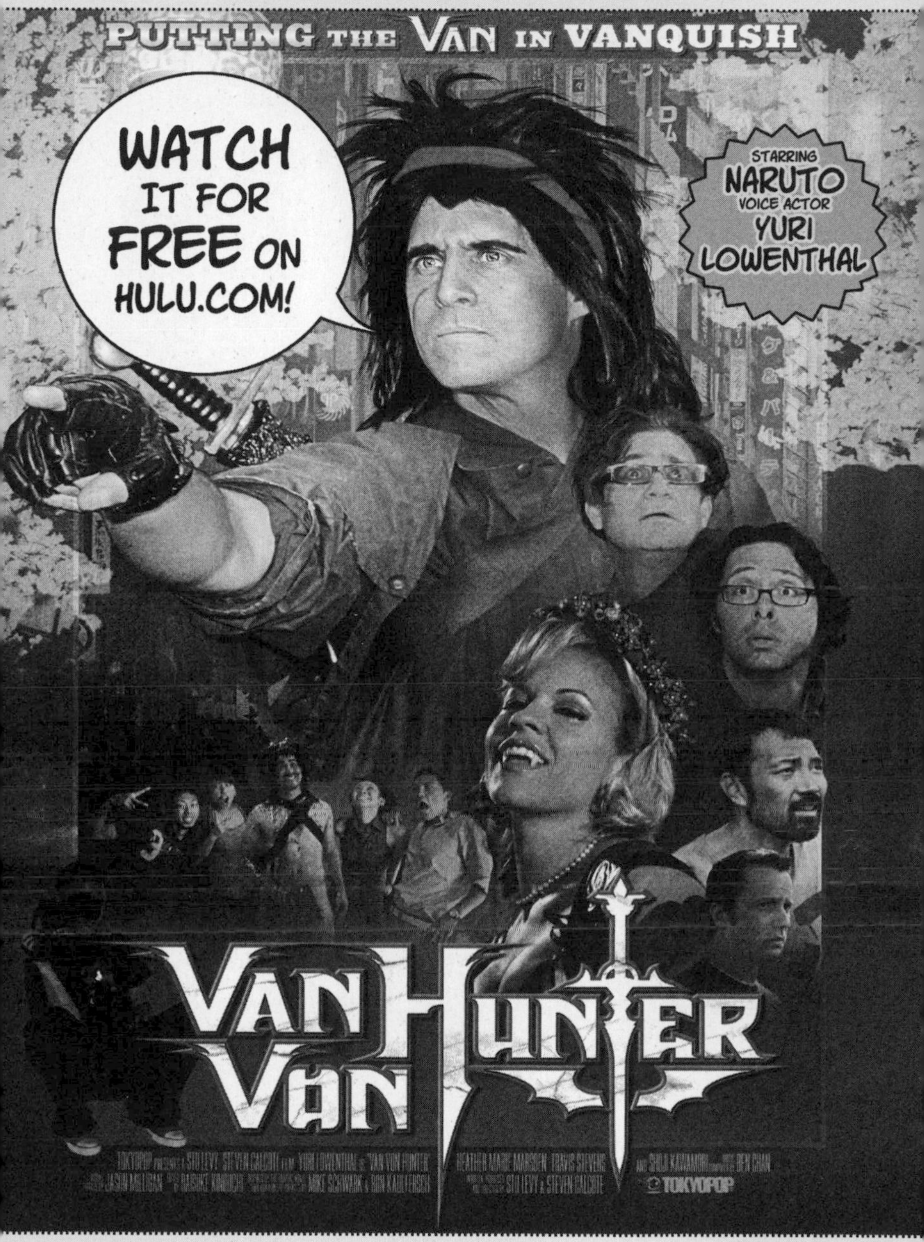
PUTTING THE VAN IN VANQUISH
WATCH IT FOR FREE ON HULU.COM!
STARRING NARUTO VOICE ACTOR YURI LOWENTHAL
VAN VON HUNTER
TOKYOPOP

STOP!

This is the back of the book.
You wouldn't want to spoil a great ending!

This book is printed "manga-style," in the authentic Japanese right-to-left format. Since none of the artwork has been flipped or altered, readers get to experience the story just as the creator intended. You've been asking for it, so TOKYOPOP® delivered: authentic, hot-off-the-press, and far more fun!

1
2
3
4
5
6
7
8
9
10

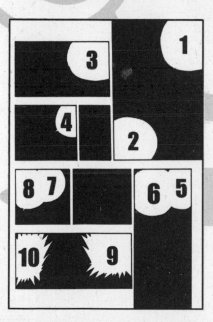

DIRECTIONS

If this is your first time reading manga-style, here's a quick guide to help you understand how it works.

It's easy... just start in the top right panel and follow the numbers. Have fun, and look for more 100% authentic manga from TOKYOPOP®!

THE MANGA REVOLUTION • LEADING
漫画革命

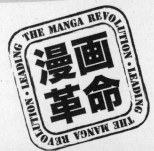